INIGO JONES

AND THE EUROPEAN CLASSICIST TRADITION

INIGO JONES

and the European Classicist Tradition

GILES WORSLEY

Published for

THE PAUL MELLON CENTRE FOR STUDIES IN BRITISH ART

by

YALE UNIVERSITY PRESS

NEW HAVEN AND LONDON

Designed by Gillian Malpass

Printed in Italy

Library of Congress Cataloging-in-Publication Data

Worsley, Giles.
Inigo Jones and the European classicist tradition / Giles Worsley.– 1st ed.
p. cm.
Includes bibliographical references.
ISBN 978-0-300-11729-5 (alk. paper)
1. Jones, Inigo, 1573–1652–Criticism and interpretation.
2. Classicism in architecture–England.
3. Classicism in architecture–Europe. I. Jones, Inigo, 1573–1652. II. Title.
NA997.J7W67 2006
720.92–dc22

2005028851
A catalogue record for this book is available from
The British Library

Frontispiece
Anthony Van Dyck, *Inigo Jones* (detail), c.1635–6, oil on canvas.
State Hermitage Museum, St Petersburg.

Endpapers
Inigo Jones, details from a design for the ceiling of the Marquess of Buckingham's
chapel closet at New Hall, Essex, c.1622–3 (Worcester College, Oxford).

For Joanna

Contents

facing page   Pieter Andreas Rysbrack, portrait bust of Inigo Jones, *c.*1725
(Devonshire Collection, Chatsworth, reproduced by kind permission of the Trustees of the Chatsworth Settlement).

Acknowledgements

THE GENEROSITY OF THOSE INVOLVED IN Jonesian and related studies has made this a particularly pleasurable book to write. Among others, I should like to thank Sir Howard Colvin; Professor Krista de Jonge; Dr Anthony Geraghty; Dr Elske Gerritsen; Michael Hall, who alerted me to the importance of ivories; Richard Hewlings; Professor Lisa Jardine; my former tutor, John Newman, who allowed me to use his transcriptions of Jones's Scamozzi annotations; Dr Frank Salmon; Professor Cinzia Maria Sicca; Dr Christine Stevenson, who provided me with invaluable copies of articles when libraries were inaccessible to me; and Dr Simon Thurley.

Some of the key ideas explored in this book were first thrashed out in London in 2004 at the Georgian Group conference 'Anglo-Netherlandish Architectural Connections in the Seventeenth Century'. I am most grateful to all the speakers and contributors to that conference and especially to Robert Bargery and the Royal Dutch Embassy for their help in organising it.

Most of all, I thank John Harris, the doyen of Jonesian studies and always the most generous of guides and inspirations; Dr Gordon Higgott whose discussions with me on Jones over several years have proved enlightening; and Professor Konrad Ottenheym whose guided tour of Dutch seventeenth-century classicism opened my eyes to that country's riches and who kindly read the draft versions of two chapters of this book.

One of the real pleasures of the research has been the necessity for foreign travel, revisiting buildings not seen for decades and discovering new sites. For their practical support with regard to these trips I thank the Centre for Renaissance Studies at Tours, the University of Utrecht, *Country Life*, the *Daily Telegraph*, *The Times*, the Flemish Tourist Board and the Vicenza Tourist Board.

On a more personal note, I thank the staff of the Royal Marsden Hospital; my daughters, Alice, Emma and Lucy; Ruth Proctor; and, above all, my wife, Joanna, whose strength and love have been fundamental to my life and work. This book is for her.

Giles Worsley
November 2005

facing page Inigo Jones, *Self-portrait* (enlarged detail) (Devonshire Collection, Chatsworth, reproduced by kind permission of the Trustees of the Chatsworth Settlement).

Foreword

With Giles Worsley's untimely death on 17 January 2006, architectural history lost one of its brightest lights. Yale University Press and the Paul Mellon Centre for Studies in British Art had had the good fortune to publish two of Giles's previous books, *Classical Architecture in Britain: The Heroic Age* (1995) and *The British Stable* (2004), both of which received considerable critical acclaim, and it was with great anticipation that we awaited the text of the present work when Giles became ill. A man of strong beliefs and of great integrity, Giles bravely continued work on this book until days before his death and managed to leave it very largely complete. Thanks to the help of his many friends it has been possible to make his text ready for publication, and we are enormously grateful to Sir Howard Colvin, Dr Christine Stevenson, Dr Gordon Higgott and Professor Edward Chaney, all of whom helped with advice in different ways. John Newman deserves a very special thanks for reading and making invaluable suggestions about the text at an advanced stage, although

I am sure that if Giles were still with us he would want to absolve John from responsibility for any minor errors that might remain. At the time of Giles's death much of the picture research for the book had yet to be undertaken, and we are grateful to Emily Wraith who completed this difficult task in the absence of the author.

As Giles Worsley's last completed book, this is a very important addition to the literature on Inigo Jones. Some of the author's main themes, such as the extent to which Palladianism persisted into the seventeenth century in the Veneto and the surrounding area (therefore making Jones's Palladianism a less insular phenomenon) and the idea that Jones was not only the initiator of a grand court architecture in England but also the originator of the astylar country-house style of the late seventeenth century, had been previously tested in periodical articles, but Giles was here able to develop these ideas much more fully as a part of a general reassessment not only of Jones's place in English architectural history but within the context of European architecture as a whole.

Brian Allen
Director of Studies
The Paul Mellon Centre for Studies in British Art
January 2007

Preface

I N THE AUTUMN OF 2004, my late husband, Giles Worsley, began planning this monograph on Inigo Jones. It had started life that summer as a chapter of his forthcoming book *The English Baroque*, but it soon became clear that it was growing too large to be accommodated within that volume and that there were easily enough good, new ideas for it to merit publication as a book in its own right.

Giles had been a fit and healthy non-smoker all his life. When in March 2005 he was diagnosed at the age of forty-three with advanced colon cancer, he responded with extraordinary, but not unexpected courage. A few weeks later, he began intensive chemotherapy treatment as an outpatient at the Royal Marsden Hospital, and the tumours began to shrink. He gradually gathered strength. Every day that he felt up to it, he would sit in our study and lose himself in the world of Inigo Jones, focussing his intellectual energies on these pages. The papers, books, reproductions of drawings and other research materials were there around him. The ideas were all in his head.

Once every three weeks, Giles and I would spend the day at the Royal Marsden Hospital, surrendering ourselves to the ill-defined world of 'hospital time'. Once he had completed his blood tests, doctor's consultation and other medical rituals, he would settle down in the Medical Day Unit, a drip delivering drugs into his bloodstream, and spend the whole afternoon working on his laptop.

After eight months of treatment, the cancer developed a resistance to the drugs and began to grow back aggressively, spreading further into his lungs and liver. The pain returned, but Giles continued working on *Inigo Jones and the European Classicist Tradition*, finalising the text and completing the footnotes and the selection of illustrations. In his final days in hospital, a week before he died, he was sitting up in bed finishing a draft of *The English Baroque*.

When he came home, we still had a few precious days and nights in which to talk. During our conversations, he told me he was satisfied that the Inigo Jones book was complete and that he had done everything he could do on *The English Baroque*. He died peacefully four days later, on 17 January 2006. His work in the year before he died was so brave and so fruitful that its circumstances deserve to be known. For me and for our three daughters, this book represents just one small part of the rich legacy Giles has left us.

Joanna Pitman
April 2006

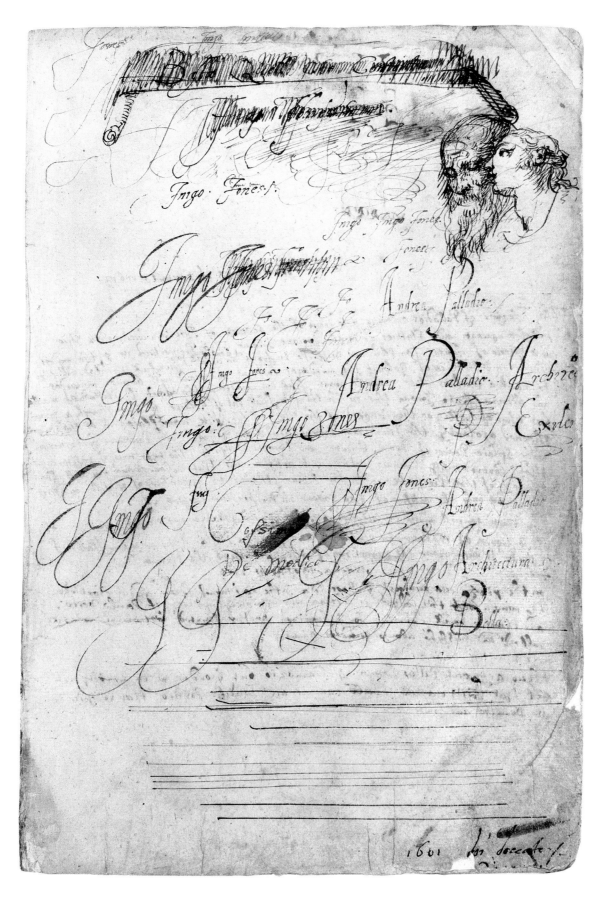

1   Inigo Jones, annotations showing Jones signing his own name and that of Palladio, from Andrea Palladio's *I quattro libri dell'architettura* (1570) (Worcester College, Oxford).

Introduction

I N 1995 IN *Classical Architecture in Britain: The Heroic Age* I set out, among other things, to show that Inigo Jones was not the solitary comet blazing a lonely trail through English early seventeenth-century architecture that he was usually portrayed to be. I argued that Jones's architecture, particularly in its simpler, more astylar version, had a profound contemporary impact and laid the foundations for English architecture in the decades after his death. In my analysis I described Jones as belonging to the Palladian tradition, but made it clear that this meant not simply a narrow adherence to the work of Andrea Palladio but also the belief in a canonical approach to classical architecture based on the primacy of Antiquity, as interpreted principally by Vitruvius, and on the classical orders of architecture as developed by Alberti, Bramante, Raphael and a sequence of other architects including in particular Giulio Romano and Sebastiano Serlio. Though this canonical tradition was epitomised by Palladio, in particular by his *Quattro libri dell'architettura*, to concentrate on Palladio in isolation was to misunderstand the tradition in which he stood.

It is not just within an English context that Jones has traditionally been seen as an isolated figure. This is even truer of his place within European architecture.[1] Jones may be one of England's most celebrated architects but in European terms he tends to be portrayed as a curious throwback, an architect in a remote and disconnected country a generation or two behind, promoting the architectural discourse of the sixteenth century in the seventeenth just as everyone else was moving towards the Baroque.[2] After all, Jones was only seven when Andrea Palladio, the architect whom he revered above all others, died in 1580. Vincenzo Scamozzi, Palladio's pupil and successor, was an old man two years off death when Jones met him in 1614. The impression is of a hapless provincial turning up at the party just as the

guests are all leaving. Alternatively, and here Sir John Summerson could never quite make up his mind, Jones can be seen as a man ahead of his time, heralding the neo-classicism of the middle of the eighteenth century by well over a hundred years, an isolated genius anticipating the issues that would interest future generations but disconnected from his own era.

When a careful examination is made of European architecture in the first half of the seventeenth century, particularly in the years around 1609 to 1614 when Jones made his two most important architectural tours of the continent, a different picture is revealed.[3] Though architectural history that sees Italy, especially Rome, as the prism through which to judge all seventeenth-century building, that considers the Baroque to be the true and only style of that century, might perceive Jones as old-fashioned, that is not how he would have appeared at the time. To northern Italians and many northern Europeans, particularly the Germans, the Dutch and even the French, Jones's work would have seemed part of the mainstream. Had he practised in Parma, Vicenza or Verona his buildings would have passed without comment. Even in Rome, where the Baroque came into its own only after Jones had effectively ceased practising as an architect, he would have found strong support for the ideals he espoused. In northern Europe Jones's campaign to introduce a purer, more classical architecture in England in place of traditional Jacobean forms finds strong parallels with similar movements in southern Germany and the Netherlands. Here his work would have been, and indeed was, seen as innovative and ground-breaking as in all three countries the exuberance of late sixteenth-century architecture was superseded in the first decades of the seventeenth century by a more sober, classically literate language. The first half of this book, after an introductory chapter examining Jones's

2   Inigo Jones, the north front of the Queen's House at Greenwich, 1632–8.

career up to 1613, thus considers what might be called the classicist tendency in contemporary architecture in Italy, southern Germany, France and the Netherlands.

The second half of the book consists of a more nuanced examination of the architectural language Jones used, which moves away from conventional assumptions about Palladianism. In successive chapters Jones's buildings are examined following his own principal of decorum, the fundamental classical belief that different levels of elaboration should be applied to buildings of different status, and chronologically. In looking at Jones's work sequentially in this way the range of Jones's responses to different building types becomes clear, as does the extent to which his architecture developed over time. Relatively humble buildings such as offices and stables are plainly decorated, houses are more elaborate, public buildings yet more so, with royal palaces, particularly Jones's greatest, if unbuilt, work, the Palace of Whitehall, the most elaborate of all. The extent to which Jones relied on different published sources, especially Serlio, Palladio, Scamozzi and Peter Paul Rubens, is examined, with Scamozzi revealed as a far more important and direct source than had previously been appreciated.

In the third section of the book attention turns to the various key motifs used by Jones and to the meanings imbued within them. Traditionally, the Serliana, the pediment and portico and the centrally planned villa have been considered principal markers of Palladianism but they are shown to have a much broader application. They are important elements of Palladian tradition but are not themselves proof of Palladianism. Instead they need to be understood as symbols of sovereignty. This is particularly true of the Serliana, a proper understanding of which requires a detailed examination of its use from the court of Pope Julius II into the seventeenth century. A close analysis of Jones's designs for the Palace of Whitehall shows that the same interpretation can be drawn from the elements out of which it was constructed, such as its fortress-like form, the circular court, the caryatid and the basilican hall. Jones's palace designs are shown to be a synthesis of symbols of sovereignty that directly refer to a long-standing tradition of palace building and to such key buildings as Diocletian's palace at Split, Hadrian's Villa at Tivoli, Charles V's palace at Granada, the Escorial near Madrid, the Louvre in Paris and the Temple of Solomon.

The book concludes with an examination of Jones's legacy, which is seen not only in the work of his pupil John Webb but also in his innovative interest in a more austere architecture that became characteristic of the second half of the seventeenth century, and in his simple domestic exteriors and town planning, which laid the foundations for what has come to be known as Georgian architecture.

This book does not set out to be the definitive monograph on Inigo Jones. That would require a much greater emphasis on Jones's broader cultural position at the Stuart court, in particular the proper integration of his role as a masque designer, which was a major part of his life, with his career as an architect and a broader investigation of the Commission on Building, of which Jones was a critical member. It would demand a more thorough assessment of the different architectural approaches available, even to members of the court, in the first half of the seventeenth century, as has been indicated in the valuable work of Christy Anderson, Elizabeth Chew and Dianne Duggan, among others. A profounder analysis of Jones's architectural library, where concentration on his annotated copy of Palladio means that the numerous annotations in his other architectural and non-architectural books remain relatively unstudied, is needed, as is more work on Jones's relationship with his pupil Webb – in particular, a thorough analysis of Webb's drawings. There is also a surprising amount still to be understood on specific projects by Jones. Can no more be found out about the story behind Lord Maltravers's house in Lothbury, or the sequence of what seem to be hunting-lodge designs from the 1630s and 1640s, for instance? Fortunately, Inigo Jones studies flourish, as can be seen in the work of Christy Anderson, Edward Chaney and Gordon Higgott among others. This book is one contribution among many and its focus is specific, on a close reading of Jones's buildings as they developed over four decades, seen within the principles of decorum, from his simplest projects to his most elaborate, and on placing those buildings in their European context. By taking this approach a different image emerges not only of Jones but also of early seventeenth-century European architecture as a whole.

3 Inigo Jones, *Self-portrait*, c.1615 (Devonshire Collection, Chatsworth, reproduced by kind permission of the Trustees of the Chatsworth Settlement).

Chapter 1

INIGO JONES'S EARLY LIFE

Inigo Jones's life changed dramatically on 18 April 1613 when he set off on a tour of Italy that lasted more than a year and a half and transformed him from a 'picture maker' and masque designer with a growing interest in architecture into England's first great classical architect. The contrast between Jones's clumsy efforts at architectural design before this Italian trip and his designs for the Queen's House at Greenwich made soon after his return reveals the impact of his tour. Yet it would be wrong to think of Jones as a raw youth struck wide-eyed by the wonders of Italy, like the generations of young architects who followed him in the eighteenth century. He was already middle-aged – about to turn forty – an experienced traveller with a distinct interest in architectural theory. He was also well connected at court – he had been responsible for designing the three masques that marked Princess Elizabeth's wedding – and shortly after he left England, on 27 April 1613, was granted the reversion of the post of Surveyor of the King's Works.[1] The tour of Italy in 1613–14 was profoundly influential because Jones was already ripe for transformation.

Jones's early years are frustratingly obscure. The son of Inigo Jones, a London clothworker of Welsh origin, he was baptised in the Church of St Bartholomew-the-Less in Smithfield on 19 July 1573. For the next thirty years the record is silent, although, according to George Vertue, Sir Christopher Wren had information that Jones was apprenticed to a joiner in St Paul's Churchyard, a suggestion that seems plausible given Jones's use in early annotations of English terms for mouldings, translating *ovolo* and *cavetto* as 'boultell' and 'casement'.[2] It is not until 1603 that a firm reference to Jones is to be found, when 'Henygo Jones, a picture maker', occurs in a list of gifts and rewards in the household accounts of the 5th Earl of Rutland.[3]

Some, at least, of the missing years were spent abroad. In *The most notable antiquity of Great Britain vulgarly called Stone-Heng on Salisbury Plain restored by Inigo Jones*, published in 1655 'from some few indigested notes' by Jones, his former pupil John Webb has the architect declare that 'Being naturally inclined in my younger years to study the *Arts of Designe*, I passed into foreign parts to converse with the great masters thereof in *Italy*, where I applied myself to search out the ruins of those ancient *buildings*, which in despite of *time* itself, and violence of *barbarians*, are yet remaining'.[4] Where and when he went is not known, though presumably it was as a painter, not as an architect, that he was studying. The one firm clue is the inscription '1601 doi docato Ven' in his annotated copy of Palladio's *I quattro libri*, suggesting that he bought the book in Venice that year.[5] Certainly by 1605 Jones had developed a sufficient reputation to be described as 'a great traveller' in an anonymous pamphlet describing Jones's part in the festivities marking the visit of James I to Oxford and a thorough knowledge of Italy is implied by the inscription in the flyleaf of the copy of *De rebus gestis a Sixto V Pon: Max.* which Edmund Bolton gave him in 1606, where Bolton hopes that through his friend 'sculpture, modelling, architecture, painting, theatrical design and all that is praiseworthy in the elegant arts of the ancients, may one day find their way across the Alps in our England'.[6] The choice of book was carefully made, for it was a collection of poems by Gianfrancesco Bordino in praise of Pope Sixtus V, who was responsible for many fine new buildings in Rome during his five-year papacy.[7] Jones's thorough knowledge of the Continent is confirmed by a letter written on 9 July 1613, soon after Jones left England for Italy, by Sir Dudley Carleton in Venice: 'I hear my Lord [Arundel] had taken Inigo Jones into his train, who will be of best use to him (by reason of his language and experience) in these parts.'[8]

As independent foreign travel was not easy, it has been suggested that Jones's early travels were in the entourage of Francis Manners, brother of the Earl of Rutland, who left England in 1598 for a tour through France, Germany and Italy (he was in Venice in 1599–1600), and was entertained by both Emperor Mathias and Archduke Ferdinand.[9] The timing fits, since Jones is last recorded in England in April 1597 when he proved his father's will, and a connection with the Manners family is evident in the payment in the Earl of Rutland's accounts on 28 June 1603.[10] Shortly afterwards the earl travelled to Denmark to deliver the Order of the Garter to King Christian IV, and it is believed that Jones travelled in his train, since a 'Mr Johns' is included in the list of guests at an official function on 10 July.[11] This may explain the link with Denmark in Webb's confused claim in *A Vindication of Stone-Heng Restored* of 1665 that Jones's first royal patron was Christian IV of Denmark, who was responsible for 'sending for him out of Italy, where, especially at Venice, he had for many years resided' and that it was in his train that Jones came to England when the king paid his first visit to the English court.[12] As Christian IV's first visit to England was in 1606 and Jones's earliest masque, *The Masque of Blackness*, was performed on 6 January 1605, Webb's account cannot be entirely accurate. It is possible, however, that Jones did spend some time in Christian IV's service.

Certainly it was for Christian's sister, Anne of Denmark, James I's queen, that Jones designed the setting for *The Masque of Blackness*, the first in a sequence of more than fifty masques, plays and court entertainments that occupied much of his time until 1640. More than 450 drawings for scenery and costumes survive, revealing his skill as a draughtsman and his knowledge of contemporary Italian stage designs, particularly those of Alfonso and Giulio Parigi at Florence. In their study of these drawings Stephen Orgel and Sir Roy Strong point to a marked development in Jones's style between 1605 and 1609. The earliest drawings 'belong directly to an existing artistic tradition and betray no knowledge of Italian Renaissance draughtsmanship', whereas by 1609 Jones was drawing in an accomplished Italianate manner.[13] This suggests perhaps another trip to Italy in 1605, as J. A. Gotch argued, but there is no direct evidence for this.[14] Better documented is the trip that Jones made round France with Lord Cranborne in 1609, during which he visited Paris, Bordeaux, Toulouse, Provence and the Loire Valley before returning to England via Paris, and gave him the chance to study the Roman antiquities of Provence (Fig. 4).[15]

On his return Jones was appointed surveyor to Henry, Prince of Wales, in 1610. The post must have assumed an ability to design buildings, though there is no documentary evidence that he designed anything for the prince or that he was responsible for any of the £1,586 spent on St James's Palace. In fact it sounds as if the post was a frustrating one. By 1611 a French garden designer, Salomon de Caus, had been sent over by the French ambassador to design the prince's waterworks at Richmond and that year a Medicean architect from Florence, probably Constantino dei Servi, was summoned to make designs for 'fountains, summer-houses, galleries and other things on a site in which his Highness is most interested', almost certainly Richmond. Thus even before the prince's untimely death in November 1612 Jones seems to have been frozen out by better qualified foreigners. The most important result of his involvement with the prince's court may have been links made with the Earl of Arundel, an intimate of the prince who became one of Jones's key patrons.[16] A connection with the prince's court may also explain Jones's earliest known architectural design, for the monument to Lady Cotton in St Chad's church at Norton-in-Hales, Shropshire (Fig. 5). Rowland Cotton, who was responsible for the commission, was probably attached to Prince Henry's court as Henry is constantly called Cotton's 'master'. Lady Cotton died in 1606 but similarities to the effects in Prince Henry's *Barriers* of January 1610 and the *Masque of Oberon* of January 1611 suggest a date of about 1610–11.[17] Though not without Jacobean elements (particularly the strapwork cartouche of the drawing), the sarcophagus with its winged figures and garlands of fruit is ambitiously classical (Fig. 6). Gordon Higgott draws attention to similarities with Roman sarcophagi found in the necropolis of Aliscamps at Arles, specifically the Leda Sarcophagus, which Jones could have seen on his visit to Provence in 1609.[18]

If involvement with Prince Henry proved frustrating, a more successful relationship was developed with Robert Cecil, Earl of Salisbury, father of Lord Cranborne whom Jones had escorted round France in 1609. Salisbury, Secretary of State from 1596 to 1608 and Lord Treasurer, the king's key minister, from May 1608, was a central figure at the court of James I. He was also a keen builder, as his works at Salisbury House, the New Exchange and Hatfield House demonstrate, and as Lord

4   Inigo Jones, study of the Pont du Gard, near Nîmes, France, *c.*1609 (RIBA Library Drawings Collection, Jones & Webb 102).

Treasurer, controlling the purse strings of the King's Works, highly influential when it came to royal building projects.

Jones's first commission from Salisbury was for the entertainment presented at Theobalds Palace, Hertfordshire, on the visit of Christian IV in July 1606, when £23 was paid 'To Inigo Jones the painter for his Chardges and paines'. In May 1607 and again in May 1608 Jones designed further entertainments for Salisbury, the latter event, at Salisbury House, presumably to celebrate his new post as Lord Treasurer. It is significant for Jones as the first time his masque designs include architecture.[19] It must have been around this time that Jones made his design for a building, for the New Exchange in the Strand in London, which Salisbury had commissioned (Fig. 7). The design must pre-date 10 June 1608 when the first stone was laid. By August the arches of the main

façade were up and on 11 April the following year the building was opened by James I. Jones's design with its arcaded ground floor and grandiloquent centrepiece, where large, fat putti support the coat of arms in a pediment topped by sweeping, oversized scrolls that rise to a tempietto-like cupola, was not followed. Instead, it is assumed that Salisbury relied on the Surveyor of the King's Works, Simon Basil, who was certainly involved in the building, though there is no proof that he was the designer. The result is known from a drawing made by Robert Smythson in 1609, whose florid gables are characteristically Jacobean. However, as Harris and Higgott point out, the purity of the façade below, with its arcade and superimposed Corinthian order, is uncharacteristic of Basil's court style, and it seems probable that Jones revised Basil's design, introducing a decidedly more Italianate feel.[20]

5 Inigo Jones, design for a monument to Lady Cotton in St Chad's Church, Norton-in-Hales, Shropshire, *c.*1610 (RIBA Library Drawings Collection).

The inscription on the monument reads:

FRANCIS ELDEST DAVGHTER TO
SIR ROBERTE NEDHAM OF SHA
VINGTON IN THE COVNTIE OF
SALLOP KNIGHT AND WIFE TO
Sᵣ ROWLAND COTTON OF AL=
KINGTON IN THE COVNTIE
KNIGHT DYED IN CHILD BED BE=
ING DELIVERED OF A DAVGHTER
WHO LIKEWISE DYED ON SON=
DAYE A DAYE OF RESTE BEINGE THE
23ᵈ DAYE OF NOVEMBER ANNO DOMINI
1606

6   Inigo Jones, the Cotton monument in St Chad's church, Norton-in-Hales, Shropshire, *c*.1610, completed after 1634.

7   Inigo Jones, design for the elevation of the New Exchange in the Strand, London, 1608 (Worcester College, Oxford).

In July the same year James I established a commission to repair St Paul's cathedral and its tower. Salisbury was a member of the commission and it was presumably at his bidding that Jones presented a design for a new termination on the central tower to replace the destroyed medieval spire (Fig. 13).[21] Jones suggested not a traditional spire but an eight-sided, ogee-shaped cupola surmounted by a short cone-like spire surrounded by obelisks, with four smaller octagonal turrets at each corner, the whole raised on an arcade of Serliana windows. Harris and Higgott point out that the pinnacles and spire come from Antonio da Sangallo the Younger's design for St Peter's in Rome, engraved by Antonio Labacco (Fig. 10) and that the lunettes on the cupola are like those on Michelangelo's design for the dome of St Peter's, engraved by Etienne du Perac.[22] The inspiration for the Serlian arcade supporting the cupola is presumed to be Palladio's basilica at Vicenza but the direct influence of Sebastiano Serlio should not be discounted, particularly as Jones owned two copies of his works before 1613.[23] Two of the church designs in Serlio's

fifth book have towers that, like St Paul's in Jones's design, are terminated by Serlianas (Fig. 11). A direct precedent for the triple Serlian arcade can be found in Serlio's fourth book. Tellingly, the columns are not placed on pedestals, as in Palladio's basilica, but rise directly from the base level, as in Jones's design (Fig. 12).[24] The form of the two windows in the corner towers may also be derived from Serlio.[25]

Lord Salisbury also involved Jones at his new seat, Hatfield House, Hertfordshire. Here the architect and supervisor was Robert Lemyinge, as several references to his plots and drawings make clear, but advice was also sought from Simon Basil and, apparently, from Jones. Lemyinge produced a design for the south front in October 1609. This had been redesigned by April 1610, which makes it unlikely to be coincidence that Jones rode down to Hatfield on 30 October 1609 and spent two nights there and that on 28 February 1610 the account book of Lord Salisbury's Receiver-General records under the heading 'More money paid about the Buildings there' (i.e., Hatfield), 'To Inigo Jones, as yor ho:

8   The south front of Hatfield House, Hertfordshire, 1610.

reward given him for drawinge of some Architecture'. A further payment of £40 was recorded in the account book of the Receiver-General on 8 November 1610 under the heading 'More moneys paid about the Buildings there'.[26]

Exactly what Jones's role was is uncertain but it may be that he 'improved' the design of the south front, as he seems to have done for the New Exchange, or was perhaps responsible for the tower. The essential treatment of the elevation, with its grid of pilasters, its ground-floor arcade and exuberant central tower, is the same as Jones's New Exchange design, though the detail remains firmly Jacobean (Fig. 8). The payments may also refer to a design for a riding house by Jones, the third surviving architectural drawing made before his 1613 trip to Italy (Fig. 9). The drawing, for the façade of the building, shows a tall and wide central structure under a pediment flanked by lower ranges. Comparison with the section of a similar, later drawing by Jones of about 1620 shows that the flanking ranges were stables. The central space is almost certainly a riding house.[27]

Riding houses, covered spaces for the practice of the equestrian art of *haute école* or schooling the great horse, were a new and fashionable building type among the young men in the circle of Henry, Prince of Wales. The Prince of Wales had two riding houses, at St James's

9   Inigo Jones, design for a riding house, probably at Hatfield House, Hertfordshire, c.1610 (RIBA Library Drawings Collection).

10 Antonio Labacco,
engraving of Antonio da
Sangallo's design for St Peter's,
Rome, 1546. The pinnacles and
spire were a source for Jones's
design for St Paul's cathedral.

11 Sebastiano Serlio, design for a church with Serliana openings
on the towers, from the *Fifth Book of Architecture* (1547) fol. 26v.

12 Sebastiano Serlio, design for an arcade with a Serlian first
floor, from the *Fourth Book of Architecture* (1537) fol. 154r.

13 Inigo Jones, design for a new termination to the tower of St Paul's cathedral, London, 1608 (Worcester College, Oxford).

Palace and at Richmond, and at least two other members of the informal riding academy run at Richmond by M. de St Antoine, Lord Percy and William Cavendish, later built their own riding houses.[28] Lord Cranborne, who returned from six months studying *haute école* in Paris in the spring of 1610, was another member of this circle. The Hatfield accounts record the cost of keeping Lord Cranborne's great horses at Richmond for a month in September 1610 and a payment in March 1612 of £30 to 'Monsieur St Antwaine'.[29] Cranborne's enthusiasm for the sport can be seen in a letter from Lord Salisbury asking Sir Thomas Edmondes, the ambassador in Paris, to find him a French *écuyer* or riding master. Cranborne's accounts the following year duly record payments to M. le Fevre, the rider.[30]

Gordon Higgott dates the design to about 1610. As Jones's principal patron at that time, and father of an enthusiastic horseman who returned from Paris that spring, Salisbury is the most plausible patron for Jones's design. It was presumably intended for Hatfield as it would have been hard, although not impossible, to accommodate a building of this scale at Salisbury's house in the Strand and Lord Cranborne never used the family's secondary seat, Cranborne Manor, Dorset. However, building work at Hatfield in this period is exceptionally well documented and there is no reference to a riding house so it is most unlikely that it was ever built.[31]

The influence of Jones's visit to France with Lord Cranborne the previous year is evident in the design. This is clear from the round-cornered, almost undifferentiated rusticated quoins that recall the stone *chaînes* running up between the windows of the Place Royale in Paris, which had just been completed in 1609. Harris and Higgott show that the design draws heavily on a woodcut of Philibert de l'Orme's house in the Rue de la Cerisaie in Paris, published in his *Le premier tome de l'architecture* in 1567. Prints by de l'Orme also inspired Jones's designs for Oberon's Palace in the masque *Oberon, the Fairy Prince*, prepared late in 1610.[32]

There is also the possibility that Jones was involved in the new stables at Theobalds.[33] The palace was acquired by James I in 1607, from Lord Salisbury, largely because of its excellent hunting. To facilitate this, an impressive quadrangular stable block 122 feet square with slightly projecting wings was built between April 1609 and September 1610. Though no view or elevation is known, its plan was recorded by Robert Smythson and accords with the Parliamentary survey of royal properties made after the Civil War (Fig. 14).[34]

The architect of the Theobalds stables is unknown. As a major royal building it must have been designed by someone in court circles. Simon Basil as Surveyor of the King's Works is one possibility, though the extent to which Basil was involved in design is uncertain.[35] A plausible alternative is Robert Lemyinge who was not only responsible for the design and supervision of Hatfield House in 1607–12 and went on to design Blickling Hall, Norfolk, in 1616–17 but had also been employed as a carpenter on the almshouses at Theobalds in 1607.[36] None the less, the involvement of Inigo Jones should also be considered.

By 1609, when the Theobalds stable was begun, Jones was closely involved in court circles, was showing a strong interest in architecture in his masque designs, such as that for the 'House of Fame' for *The Masque of the Queens* performed that February,[37] and had already produced designs for the New Exchange and the remodelling of the tower of St Paul's cathedral. He shortly made others for Hatfield House and for a riding house, all these being produced for Lord Salisbury who, as noted earlier, was appointed Lord Treasurer in May 1608. Whereupon, as John Harris notes, Salisbury 'began immediately to investigate the Office of Works. From this moment on, Jones as an emergent architect, the British Vitruvius in embryo, began to exert influence towards a reformation of style, even though without any official position'.[38] At the very least it seems highly plausible that Salisbury would have ensured that Jones, his favoured architect, was consulted over the designs of what was the most important new building commissioned by James I before the Queen's House at Greenwich.

If Jones was involved, even in simply giving a more fashionable appearance to Lemyinge's or Basil's design, it is tempting to wonder what form the building took. In particular, were the two projecting wings marked by some form of 'Dutch' gable, as was the case with his contemporary design for the New Exchange? That would then explain the appearance of pairs of 'Dutch' gables shortly afterwards on the stables at Burley-on-the-Hill, Rutland, and on Raynham Hall, Norfolk, as will be discussed below.

Jones's growing interest in architecture is not only evident in his masques and designs for buildings but in his immersion in architectural treatises, through which he taught himself the essence of architectural design. It is to these years that John Newman, in his study of Jones's architectural education before 1614, dates the early annotations Jones made in his architectural books.[39] Jones's earliest notes in his annotated copy of Palladio's

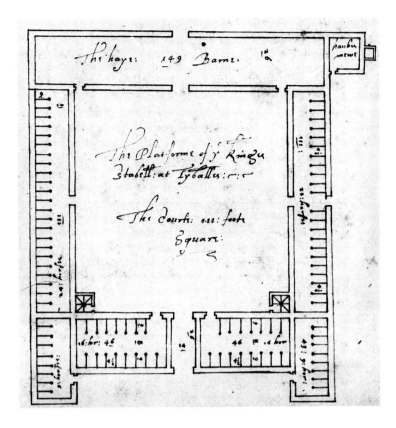

The hay: 149 Barn:

The Platforme of y Kinge's Stable: at Tyballis: r: r

The Court: 112: foote Square:

14 Robert Smythson, survey drawing of the ground-plan of the stables at Theobalds House, Hertfordshire, 1609 (RIBA Library Drawings Collection, Smythson Collection I/4).

I quattro libri are undated but careful study of Jones's evolving handwriting shows that they were certainly made before his 1613 trip. As well as these Newman shows that early annotations pre-dating 1613 survive in Daniele Barbaro's *I dieci libri dell'architettura di M. Vitruvio* (1567); Sebastiano Serlio's *Architettura* of 1560–62 (which included books one to four and part of book five); Serlio's *Tutte l'opere d'architettura et prospetiva di Sebastiano Serlio bolognese* (1601); and Vasari's *Delle vite de' piu eccellenti pittori scultori et architettori* (*Lives of the Artists*, 1568).

The annotations, which are extensive, provide a revealing insight into Jones's self-education as a would-be architect far removed from the inspiration of the buildings themselves. Three topics in particular initially interested him: the practicalities of building techniques and materials; Vitruvius's account of the principles of architecture; and Palladio's exposition of the five orders (Fig. 15). These were soon followed by his study of Vitruvius's description of the various types of antique temples; of the temples illustrated in Palladio's fourth book; and of Serlio's enthusiastic account of the Pantheon. 'Thus', notes Newman, 'the polarities of Jones's architectural interests were established at the outset, practicality and a fascination for the antique.'[40]

In his annotations one sees Jones considering foundations and construction; the design and siting of houses – where Jones found it difficult to reconcile Italian and English practice; staircases; and Palladio's recommendations on the size and proportions of rooms and on the measurements of doors and windows. At the same time as he studied the practicalities of house building Jones also considered the theory of architecture, with Vitruvius as his principal mentor, though he also relied heavily on Barbaro's commentary on that text. The close study of proportion was an important theme. So too were Vitruvius's six principles of architecture – *ordine, dispositione, bel numero, compartimento, decoro, distributione* – and Vitruvius's complex idea that though buildings should be designed in accordance with standards of proportion, the particularities of individual buildings might demand deviations from proportional consistency. As Jones put it, 'no rule to teach this but by sharpness of wit first know the ordering measures and from them take the altering of anything'.[41]

From the beginning Jones compared different authors with one another, often having Palladio's *I quattro libri* and Barbaro's edition of Vitruvius open together. This can be seen with the final group of pre-1613 entries that relate to antique temples, where Palladio's fourth book

15

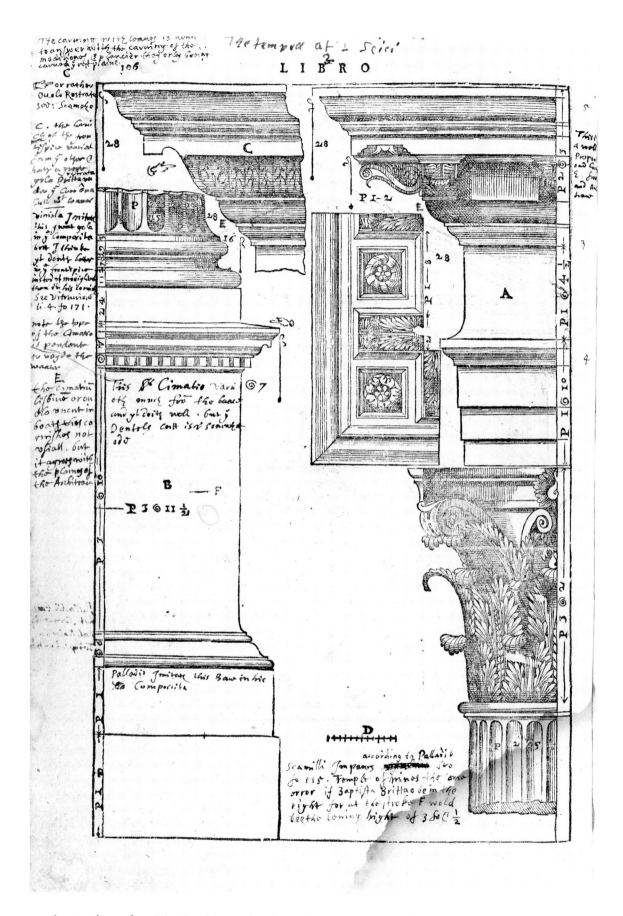

15 Annotated page from Inigo Jones's copy of Andrea Palladio's *I quattro libri dell'architettura* (1609) IV, p. 106 (Worcester College, Oxford).

16 Andrea Palladio, design for the Teatro Olimpico, Vicenza. This is one of the drawings studied by Jones before he went to Italy in 1613 (RIBA Library Drawings Collection XIII/5).

and Vitruvius were the key sources. These demonstrate that Jones was already interested in the details of the orders used in antique buildings and the extent to which they corresponded with the model orders published by Palladio in his first book. Through this Jones learnt two valuable lessons that had an important bearing on his subsequent architecture. He became aware of the richness and diversity of antique architecture and his attention was directed to details, sometimes minute details, the subtle importance of which in imparting character to an entire building he came to appreciate more and more.

By 1613 Jones's architectural understanding had matured considerably. He had already grounded himself in the practicalities of building, in the essentials of the classical orders and in architectural theory. The annotations also show that he had had the chance to study some of Palladio's drawings at first hand, which he compared with the illustrations in the *Quattro libri*. These drawings were probably owned by Sir Henry Wotton, the English ambassador to Venice who was in England in 1612–13. At least two of the six drawings specifically connected

with Wotton passed into Jones's hands, for they are now in the Burlington-Devonshire collection at the Royal Institute of British Architects (RIBA).[42] Wotton was an architectural enthusiast who later published the first book in English on architectural theory, *The Elements of Architecture*, in 1624 after his final return from Venice. Confirmation that Jones had access to drawings by Palladio before the Italian trip of 1613–14 comes from a note in his edition of the *Quattro libri* which states: 'The Theatre of Palladio's ordering the front of the scene of brick covered with stucco full of ornament and statues as in the design I have' (Fig. 16).[43] No doubt Wotton would have conveyed his enthusiasm for Italy and for Palladio to Jones, although by now Jones must have realised that while his theoretical studies were all very well, if he really wanted to practise as an architect he needed to return to Italy and study the original buildings at first hand. He must therefore have jumped at the chance to accompany Lord Arundel. Jones's last annotations before 1613 show that he was systematically examining the plates of Palladio's villas, carefully noting the precise location of each villa, in anticipation.[44]

INIGO·IONES·ARCHITECTOR
MAGNAE·BRITANIAE

F·VILLAMOENA·F

17   Francesco Villamena, *Inigo Jones, Architect of Great Britain*, c.1614, engraving (Devonshire Collection, Chatsworth, reproduced by kind permission of the Trustees of the Chatsworth Settlement).

Chapter 2

JONES AND ITALY

For Inigo Jones, the journey he made to Italy with the Earl and Countess of Arundel in 1613–14 was the most momentous event of his life. The excuse for the trip was that the earl had to accompany James I's newly married eldest daughter, the Princess Elizabeth, and her husband, the Elector Palatine Friedrich V, back to Heidelberg. However, Arundel's clear intention was to resume the tour of Italy that had been curtailed the previous November when he had reached only Padua before being forced to return to England on news of the death of Prince Henry.[1]

Jones is never mentioned in Arundel's correspondence, although it is known from Sir Dudley Carleton, the ambassador in Venice, that he was in his train.[2] Much of the itinerary can be tracked in dated annotations in Jones's copy of Palladio's *I quattro libri*. These generally fit what is known of Arundel's movements from his own letters or letters that mention him, apart from an excursion that Jones made to Venice and Vicenza in late July and August 1614, when Arundel was ill in Genoa. However, it is not certain that Jones was always with Arundel at other times. David Howarth, for instance, suggests, although apparently without documentary evidence, that Jones melted away to pursue his interests elsewhere when Arundel spent six weeks studying quietly outside Siena.[3]

After Heidelberg the party headed down the Rhine to Basel and after crossing the Alps arrived at Milan on 11 July 1613. On 17 July the Venetian resident reported that the earl, his wife and a good number of gentlemen had arrived and that he was said to be planning a visit to the baths of Lucca 'though it is hard to believe this is his only object'. He also noted that the Duke of Savoy had written to Arundel pressing him to visit him in Turin, a reminder of the high status and access enjoyed by the earl.[4] On the 31st he wrote that the earl had left

Milan suddenly, offended at being ignored by the Spanish governor, and had set off for Parma on his way to Padua. Parma would have been a particular attraction to Arundel and Jones thanks to the presence of important paintings by Correggio, whose status at the time was exceedingly high. The road taken after Parma is uncertain but a plausible route to Padua would have been through Mantua and Verona. Jones undoubtedly visited these towns: annotations in his copy of Vasari's *Lives of the Artists* show that he studied the Palazzo Tè outside Mantua and although documentary proof is lacking, it is hard to imagine that Jones, who made great efforts to survey the Roman remains in Provence, would have missed Verona, which had the finest array of Roman remains in northern Italy. He would have known of the Arena, or amphitheatre, second only in fame to the Colosseum in Rome, the Arco dei Leoni, the Arco dei Gavi and the Borsari gate, from descriptions and illustrations in Palladio and Serlio.[5] Arundel later recalled the antiquities of Verona in his remembrances of Italy in 1646.[6]

At Padua the Arundels and Jones almost certainly stayed nearby at the Villa Molin, which Scamozzi had built for Nicolo Molin in 1597 (Figs 18 and 19). According to a letter from Sir Dudley Carleton to Sir Ralph Winwood, they stayed at a villa situated two miles beyond Padua on the way to Cattaio.[7] The Villa Molin is two miles from Padua on the way to Cattaio and it is known from Jones's annotations to book four of Palladio's *I quattro libri* that he studied the building, later, comparing his treatment of the balustrade on the portico of the Queen's House at Greenwich with that at the Villa Molin. Since the balustraded galleries are not illustrated in the view of the villa in Scamozzi's *L'idea della architettura universale*, published in 1615, Jones must have observed them at first hand. The double-height central

18 Vincenzo Scamozzi, entrance front of the Villa Molin, near Padua, 1597.

19 Vincenzo Scamozzi, central hall of the Villa Molin, near Padua, 1597.

hall of the villa with its balustraded balcony is a plausible prototype for that of the Queen's House, as is the combination of a full-height rusticated ground floor and plain first floor.

After resting in Padua, a splendid fortnight was spent in Venice at the beginning of September and then a trip made to Vicenza, where Jones's notes are dated 23 and 24 September, before heading south. They reached Bologna on 30 September and Florence on 3 October. Lord Arundel then broke his journey outside Siena before moving on to Rome, where he arrived around 2 January 1614. An excursion was made to Naples in March and April but by 31 April they were back in Rome. On 19 July 1614 the party was reported to be in Florence before heading for Genoa. Confirmation that Jones was still with the party comes from his annotation made in London in 1615 in his copy of the *Quattro libri*: 'I have observed that some loggias are made without the house and others within . . . most commonly in the midst [but] those two in the corners are much used in Genoa.'[8] Here Lord Arundel fell ill, writing on 2 August to his mother that he planned to return to England with as much speed as the weak state of his body permitted. At this point Jones broke away. He was in Venice from at least 30 July to 10 August and in Vicenza on at least 13 and 14 August. On 15 September the earl and countess were in Turin and in October in Paris. They finally arrived back in London in November. It has been presumed that Jones rejoined the earl and countess and returned through France with them, though there is no documentary evidence to confirm this.[9]

Jones's principal interest was, of course, Roman Antiquity, closely followed by the work of Andrea Palladio. His copy of Palladio's *I quattro libri* contains numerous close observations of the buildings he studied (Fig. 20). Yet, as a keenly observant architect Jones cannot have failed to be aware of the architectural climate of his own time and it is important to appreciate what that climate was in order to place Jones's architectural career in its proper context. Contrary to later assumptions, Italian architecture in 1613–14 was more in tune with Jones's architectural interests than is generally appreciated, though to talk of Italian architecture is perhaps a misnomer, for architecture in Italy early in the seventeenth century was sufficiently mature to support a number of different theoretical approaches as well as demonstrating strong regional and indeed local tendencies.

Milan, where Arundel and Jones spent nearly three weeks, was one of the richest and most prosperous cities

I DISEGNI che feguono fono di vna fabrica in Vicenza del Conte Ottauio de' Thieni, fù del Conte Marc'Antonio: ilqual le diede principio. E' quefta cafa fituata nel mezo della Città, vicino alla piazza, e però mi è parfo nella parte ch'è verfo detta Piazza difponerui alcune botteghe: percioche deue l'Architetto auertire anco all'vtile del fabricatore, potendofi fare commodamente, doue refta fito grande a fufficienza. Ciafcuna bottega ha fopra di fe vn mezato per vfo de' botteghieri; e fopra vi fono le ftanze per il padrone. Quefta cafa è in Ifola, cioè circondata da quattro ftrade. La entrata principale, ò vogliam dire porta maeftra ha vna loggia dauanti, & è fopra la ftrada più frequente della città. Di fopra vi farà la Sala maggiore: laquale vfcirà in fuori al paro della Loggia. Due altre entrate vi fono ne' fianchi, lequali hanno le colonne nel mezo, che vi fono pofte non tanto per ornamento, quanto per rendere il luogo di fopra ficuro, e proportionare la larghezza all'altezza. Da quefte entrate fi entra nel cortile circondato intorno da loggie di pilaftri nel primo ordine ruftichi, e nel fecondo di ordine Compofito. Ne gli angoli vi fono le ftanze ottangule, che riefcono bene, sì per la forma loro, come per diuerfi vfi, a' quali elle fi poffono accommodare. Le ftanze di quefta fabrica c'hora fono finite; fono ftate ornate di belliffimi ftucchi da Meffer Aleffandro Vittoria, & Meffer Bartolomeo Ridolfi; e di pitture da Meffer Anfelmo Canera, & Meffer Bernardino India Veronefi, non fecondi ad alcuno de' noftri tempi. Le Cantine, e luoghi fimili fono fotto terra: perche quefta fabrica è nella più alta parte della Città, oue non è pericolo, che l'acqua dia impaccio.

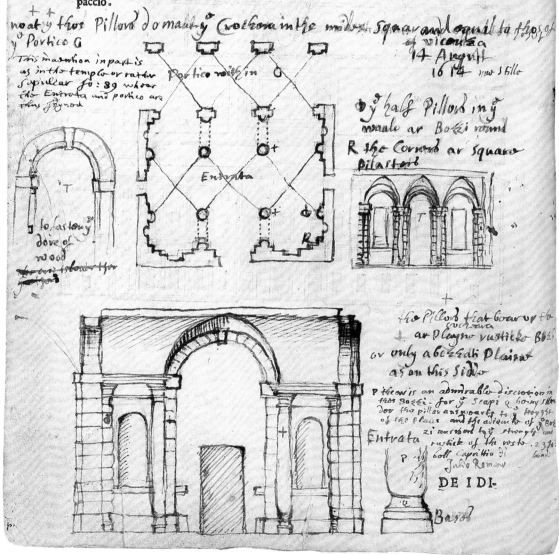

20 Inigo Jones, annotations recording his visit to the Palazzo Thiene, Vicenza, 14 August 1614, from Andrea Palladio's *I quattro libri dell'architettura* (1609) II, p. 12 (Worcester College, Oxford).

21 Aurelio Trezzi and Fabio Mangone, the courtyard of the Seminario Maggiore, Milan, 1613.

in Italy. Nothing is known of what Jones saw or whom he met but Arundel was a prestigious visitor who would have found little difficulty in opening most doors and it must be presumed that Jones spent his time profitably. One figure whom Arundel, a leading Roman Catholic, can be expected to have met was the Archbishop of Milan, Cardinal Federico Borromeo, cousin and successor of the great reformer Cardinal Carlo Borromeo and a major reformer himself. It was under Cardinal Borromeo's direct influence that the two most significant current building projects in Milan were being carried out, the courtyards of the two major seminaries, the Seminario Maggiore, now the Seminario Arcivescovile, and the Collegio Elvetico, now the Palazzo del Senato.

The Collegio Elvetico is perhaps best known today for its curving façade, added by Francesco Maria Ricchino in 1640–45, seen as evidence of the new Baroque movement, just as the public face of the Seminario Maggiore is the elaborately decorative gateway added by Ricchino in 1635. The courtyards, begun two decades earlier to Aurelio Trezzi and Fabio Mangone's designs, reveal a widely different sensibility. The idea of building a colonnade round the courtyard of the Seminario Maggiore was first discussed in 1609, with the decision taken in 1611 and the contract drawn up in 1613. Work on the courtyard of the Collegio Elvetico

was started to Mangone's designs in 1613. Both were based, at Borromeo's instigation, on antique models.[10]

The court of the Seminario Maggiore (Fig. 21) is surrounded by superimposed Doric and Ionic colonnades with paired columns supporting a simple entablature. The Collegio Elvetico follows the same model but with single columns. The immediate model was Vitruvius's description of the Palestra, the Greek place of learning, though Barbaro's and Palladio's reconstructions show only the ground plan of this.[11] The elevations were based on Vitruvius's description of the Greek Forum: 'The Greeks lay out their forums in the form of a square surrounded by very spacious double colonnades, adorn them with columns set rather closely together, and with entablatures of stone or marble, and construct walks above in the upper storey.'[12] Palladio illustrated his own version of the forum,[13] which closely parallels reconstructions of the House of the Ancient Romans as codified by Barbaro and Scamozzi in L'idea della architettura universale.[14] The model finds a precedent at the university of Padua, where a similar colonnaded court had been built to the designs of Andrea Moroni in 1547.[15]

Not everything Jones found in Milan would have seemed as sympathetic to his ideals. He would have had little time for Giovan Battista Crespi Cerano's complicated and fussy façade of S. Paolo Converso of 1611.[16]

Yet it would be fascinating to know whether Jones and Arundel discussed the Seminario Maggiore and the Collegio Elvetico with Borromeo and his architects. If they did Jones would have found his architectural beliefs confirmed in the first Italian city he visited.

The other great city of the Po valley was Bologna, which Arundel and Jones passed through on their way to Rome. Here the principal current building project was Giovanni Ambrogio Magenta's S. Salvatore, conceived in 1605 and built in 1613–22 (Fig. 22). Austere but monumental, with giant fluted Corinthian columns and pilasters lining the nave, the church again looked to Antiquity for its model, not this time to the ideal designs of Vitruvius but to the Basilica of Maxentius and Baths of Diocletian, much as Jones later looked to Roman temples and the Baths of Diocletian for inspiration when he came to design the portico and cladding of St Paul's cathedral.[17]

Arundel and Jones passed only briefly through Bologna but Arundel spent six weeks resting at a convent outside Siena. There is no evidence for Jones's whereabouts during this time but the sojourn would have provided the opportunity to meet the Sienese physician, mathematician and amateur architectural theorist Teofilo Gallaccini (1564–1641). Gallaccini is best known for the two works that he subsequently circulated in manuscript, the *Trattato sopra gli errori degli architetti*, written about 1625, and *De capitelli della colonne*, written about 1631. Neither was published in his lifetime, though the *Trattato* finally appeared in 1767. Gallaccini's vision of Antiquity was particularly austere. Inspired by Palladio's first book, and by Palladio's argument that columns should provide the impression of structural stability, he condemned excesses and errors. He had only a narrow vision of what was permissible, did not know or want to know how often ancient buildings departed from his norms and had no taste for licence, which was encouraged in all sixteenth-century theory.[18] Gallaccini's rigour would no doubt have intrigued Jones and chimed with his own desire to reform English architecture of its Jacobean excesses.

Jones spent two months in Naples where he would also have looked sympathetically on the principal current building project, the massive Viceregal Palace (Fig. 23), begun in 1601 by the royal architect Domenico Fontana and finally completed by Bartolomeo Picchiatti, royal architect from 1627.[19] This sober, immensely long building looked back to the Roman palazzi of the mid-sixteenth century and would not seem out of place among Jones's later designs for Whitehall Palace and Somerset House (see Figs 92–3, 189). Edward Chaney also argues, convincingly, that Fabrizio Grimaldi's great door to the Church of S. Paolo Maggiore, begun in 1583, is the source for Jones's unexecuted design for the great door of the Banqueting House, suggesting that Jones was carefully studying contemporary architecture.[20]

It is, of course, with the Roman Baroque that Jones is most explicitly compared, the apparent academicism of his architecture often being set against the dynamism of the Roman Baroque, the implication being that Jones was backward in his architectural approach. However, when Jones travelled through Italy the three great masters of the Roman Baroque were still in their teens and had yet to design their first buildings. Pietro da Cortona (1596–1669) had probably recently arrived in Rome with the undistinguished Florentine painter

22 Giovanni Ambrogio Magenta, interior of S. Salvatore, Bologna, 1613–22.

23   Domenico Fontana, the Royal Palace, Naples, 1601.

24   Carlo Lambardi, façade of Sta Francesca Romana al Foro, Rome, completed 1615.

Commodi. His first architectural commission, the Villa del Pigneto, came nearly a decade and a half later in 1625. The first architectural commission of Gianlorenzo Bernini (1598–1680), the baldaquin of St Peter's, was not started until 1623. Franceso Borromini (1599–1667) arrived in Rome only in 1619 and did not receive his first great architectural opportunity, S. Carlo alle Quattro Fontane, until 1637. Though Carlo Maderno's façade of Sta Susanna of 1597–1603 had introduced a new sense of movement and dynamism that was later exploited by the architects of the Roman Baroque this was still unusual in 1614.[21]

Instead, Jones would have found a strong classicist tendency evident among artistic circles in Rome, epitomised by the figures of the painters Annibale Carracci, who had arrived in Rome in 1595, Guido Reni and Domenichino and by Giovanni Battista Agucchi (1570–1632). Agucchi, secretary to Pietro Aldobrandini, the powerful *cardinale nepote* and papal secretary to Clement VIII (1592–1605), was, with Carracci's cousin Ludovico, the theorist of this group. His 1611 description of Aldobrandini's villa at Frascati, which was consciously modelled on Roman imperial residences, was laden with references to the antique.[22]

The movement was particularly strong in the second decade of the century and found expression in Carlo Lambardi's restoration of Sta Francesca Romana al Foro, completed in 1615, which experimented with a façade with giant orders of the Palladian type never seen in Rome (Fig. 24).[23] The specifically Roman model was also still powerful, as Jones would have been able to see on the Janiculum Hill where the Acqua Paola, completed in 1612 by Flaminio Ponzio, was based on the model of an antique triumphal arch.[24] An important figure in this Roman classicist movement was Giovanni Ambrogio Magenta (1565–1635), the architect of S. Salvatore in Bologna. Magenta had visited Venice by 1604 and it was probably thanks to him that the bi-axial plan of the 1611–12 design for the Barnabite Church of S. Carlo ai Catinari seems to resemble that of the recently completed, Palladian-inspired Church of Sta Lucia in Venice. Magenta's influence was later particularly strong on Ludovico Ludovisi, *cardinale nepote* to Gregory XV (1621–3), who turned to Magenta to obtain a plan of Palladio's S. Giorgio Maggiore during discussions about the Church of S. Paolo in Piazza Colonna in 1625. Thus if Jones found the time amid his studies of Roman Antiquity to converse with leading architects, artists and theorists in Rome he would have found much to support his architectural views. However, the death of Gregory XV in 1623 put an end to the dominance of this classicist tendency. Under his successor Urban VIII it was Bernini and Borromini who flourished.[25]

It has long been accepted that the cathedral at Livorno in Tuscany, built by Alessandro Pieroni between 1594 and 1606, and its setting the Piazza Grande, influenced Jones's design of Covent Garden. John Evelyn noted that it was Livorno which 'gave the first hint to the building both of the church and the Piazza in Covent Garden'.[26] If it is assumed that Jones was in Turin with Arundel, it would be intriguing to know if he met Alessandro Tesauro, the Sabaudian amateur architect who has been compared to Palladio's patron Daniele Barbaro. He would certainly have found much in common. Tesauro, who had extensive links across northern Italy, was a friend of Cardinal Federico Borromeo and provided the cardinal with a plan for the Ambrosiana in Milan in 1604. He was also consulted over the cathedral in Bologna in 1605, was responsible for the fact that the new mausoleum of the House of Savoy, the Santuario della Madonna at Vicoforte, was laid out on the plan of a centralised antique temple in 1597 and acted as architectural advisor to the Duke of Savoy in the creation of the library and museum in the Grand Gallery at Turin. Tesauro's own villa at Salmour, which he designed in about 1620, has an unusually Scamozzian resonance for Piedmont (Fig. 25).[27]

Above all it was in the Veneto and Emilia that Jones would have found the architectural tradition developed by Bramante, Serlio, Giulio Romano, Palladio, Scamozzi and, in Verona, Michele Sanmicheli, at its strongest. The architecture of this part of Italy has often been marginalised by architectural historians who give primacy to Rome. North Italian architecture frequently developed out of step with that in Rome and, except for the case of Palladio, has tended to be downplayed for that reason. Yet it needs to be examined on its own terms, not simply by comparison with what was happening in Rome. This is particularly true for any study of English architecture, where direct links with the Veneto were usually stronger

25   Alessandro Tesauro, Villa Tesauro, Salmour, *c.*1620.

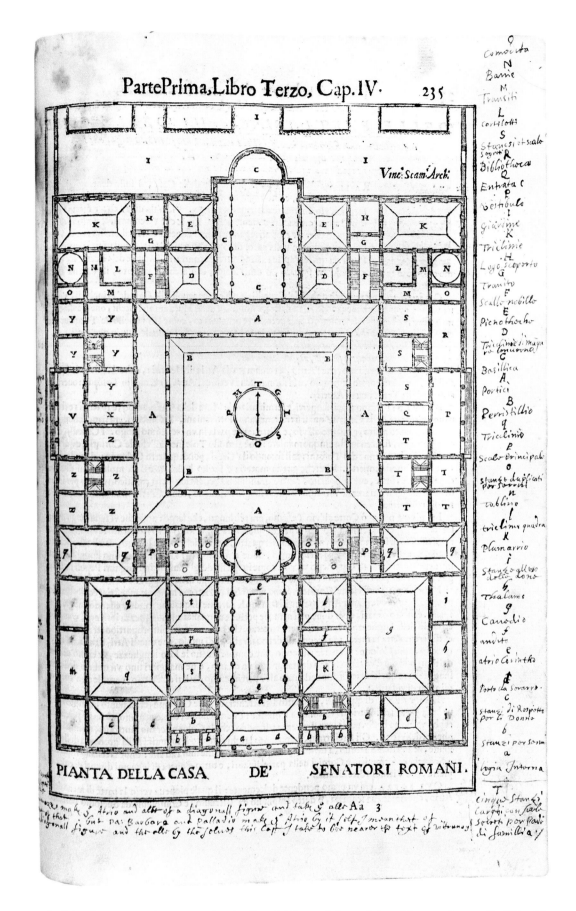

PIANTA DELLA CASA   DE' SENATORI ROMANI.

26   Inigo Jones, annotations concerning the Casa dei Senatori Romani, from Vincenzo Scamozzi's *L'idea della architettura* (1615) II, p. 235 (Worcester College, Oxford).

than those with Rome. That was certainly the case with Jones, who would have found a string of architects still working within the canonical tradition.

The best known of these is Vincenzo Scamozzi (1548–1616), whom Jones sought out in August 1614, not least to discuss his memories of Palladio. Though he criticised Scamozzi in his writings, describing him as 'purblind', this must have been a revelatory moment for Jones. He certainly studied Scamozzi's buildings carefully and often emulated them, as will be seen in chapter 7.[28] Certainly, Scamozzi's rigorously logical, scientific attitude had much in common with Jones's own opinions. Jones stayed at Scamozzi's Villa Molin, as noted, and in Vicenza he was clearly struck by Scamozzi's Palazzo Trissino sul Corso (1588) on its prominent site at the heart of the city. He used the courtyard elevation as the model for Cupid's Palace in one of his masques (see Figs 131 and 132)[29] and the (unbuilt) elevation as the model for his first design for the Prince's Lodging at Newmarket (1618–19; see Figs 125 and 126).[30] Jones brought some of Scamozzi's drawings back to England and was probably responsible for acquiring others for the Earl of Arundel.[31] He also bought a copy of Scamozzi's *L'idea della architettura universale* in 1617, as soon as it was distributed in the north by the Venetian-Flemish bookseller Justus Sadeler. Annotations in the margin show that Jones studied the text seriously (Fig. 26).[32]

By 1614 Scamozzi's best days were behind him. The stream of buildings erected in the 1580s and 1590s had dried up and many of the projects on which he worked in the years immediately before he met Jones had proved abortive.[33] Yet this was not because the classicist tradition was running dry, as can be seen by examining the work of two other leading architects of north-east Italy, Domenico Curtoni and Giovanni Battista Aleotti.

In Verona, as well as the Roman antiquities, Jones might have been interested to examine the work of Michele Sanmicheli (about 1487–1559), second only to Palladio in his importance in developing the classical tradition in that region. Sanmicheli had spent his formative years in Rome from 1500 to 1509, during the time when, in Serlio's phrase, Bramante 'brought back to life . . . the fine architecture which, from the ancients to that time, had lain buried'.[34] He had been profoundly influenced by Bramante and Raphael and had established a sophisticated classical language in Verona that was praised by Serlio in the dedication of his fourth book.[35]

Jones would have found this tradition being maintained and developed by Sanmicheli's nephew Domenico Curtoni (1556–about 1627). His massive Palazzo della Gran Guardia on its dominant position facing the Roman amphitheatre would have struck him particularly forcefully (Fig. 27). Begun in 1610, this was largely complete by 1614 when lack of money brought work to a halt, the whole of the arcade and two-thirds of the upper floors having been finished.[36] With its rusticated, arcaded base, its piano nobile with paired Doric columns and imposing entablature, this was built on a scale that exceeded even the grandest Palladian palazzo. Its inspiration is obviously Sanmicheli, the most immediate source being the Palazzo Pompei in Verona,[37] but Curtoni was not simply following Sanmicheli. The use of paired Doric columns over an arcaded rusticated base suggests that he had also looked back to a key influence on Sanmicheli, Bramante's Palazzo Caprini in Rome. This key early Renaissance building had been drawn by Palladio and though subsequently altered had been illustrated by Antoine Lafrery in *Speculum romanae magnificentiae* (1549).[38]

In the Palazzo della Gran Guardia Jones would have seen a contemporary architect reveal a similar interest to his own in developing the architectural tradition of the High Renaissance, as mediated through architects of the mid-Cinquecento, on the grandest scale. Jones would no doubt have been sympathetic to Curtoni's domestic projects, particularly the robust Palazzo Pellegrini, built by 1610.[39] What would probably have interested him most about Curtoni was the way that he returned directly to Antiquity. Just across from the Palazzo della Gran Guardia he would have been able to see Curtoni's Teatro Filarmonico. Curtoni had won the competition for this in 1604 and by 1613 much of the building was finished, with the Sala Accademia vaulted the following year.[40] Like Palladio's Teatro Olimpico in Vicenza, this was intended as a re-creation of an ancient Roman theatre and, though never completed, what survives is Curtoni's giant, freestanding Ionic portico (Fig. 28). Here, as Jones did later at St Paul's church, Covent Garden, and St Paul's cathedral, Curtoni was pushing beyond his masters in his return to antique sources, in particular through the revival of the use of the portico in civic architecture.

The strongest parallels between Inigo Jones and a contemporary North Italian architect came not with Scamozzi or Curtoni working in the Venetian Republic but with the architect, mathematician, hydraulic engineer and stage designer Giovanni Battista Aleotti (1546–1636), who was appointed architect to Alfonso II d'Este, Duke of Ferrara and Modena in 1575. Aleotti, who worked extensively across the Po valley, referred to

27   Domenico Curtoni, Gran Guardia, Verona, 1610.

28   Domenico Curtoni, Teatro Filarmonico, Verona, 1604–13.

29   Giovanni Battista Aleotti, interior of the Teatro Farnese, Parma, 1618–19.

Vitruvius and Alberti as the *due chiari lumi* (two clear lights) and was profoundly influenced by the writings of Serlio, Vignola and Palladio, which he united in an austere, ordered architecture.[41] The façade of the Oratorio di Sta Croce in Argenta (1610) with its superimposed orders can be read as a miniature version of a Palladian palazzo. The façade of the Church of S. Carlo in Ferrara (1613) looks back to the Roman Arco dei Gavi in Verona and closely parallels Scamozzi's tomb of Doge Nicolo da Ponte (1582) based on the same source.[42]

Like Jones, Aleotti was also a talented creator of complex stage designs and a theatre designer. The most important of his theatres was the Teatro Farnese in Parma, built in 1618–19, the prototype of the modern theatre (Fig. 29). Its auditorium is dominated by a double-height arcade of superimposed Serlianas and seems to owe much to Palladio's basilica at Vicenza.[43] Parallels with Jones are also evident in the small town of Gualtieri, twenty miles north-east of Parma. Here at the end of the sixteenth century Aleotti had laid out a large three-sided arcaded piazza, with a church to one side, in

front of a new palace for the Bentivoglio family. Work on the piazza seems to have been completed by 1610 and the new church was finished in 1613.[44] The parallels with the Piazza at Covent Garden are strong and it would be interesting to know whether Jones was aware of or discussed Gualtieri, which lies on one of two possible routes that he might have taken from Parma to Mantua.[45]

Though Aleotti and Curtoni were at the height of their powers in the years that Jones visited Italy, they were born a generation before him. Baldassare Longhena (1596–1682), the first half of whose career coincided with that of Jones, was born a generation later but was equally influenced by Palladio and Scamozzi. Longhena was said to be Scamozzi's pupil and inherited the favour of his last patrons, the Contarini. His first work, a villa now destroyed, for Pietro Contarini at Mira in 1616, was strongly indebted to Scamozzi.[46] So too was his first palace in Venice, the Palazzo Giustinian-Lolin (1619–23), built for a branch of the Lolin family who had also been patrons of Scamozzi.[47] The magnificent cathedral of Sta Maria at Chioggia, a commission acquired for Longhena in 1624 by Alvise Duodo, the nephew of Scamozzi's principal patron, was a deliberate revival of Palladian models.[48] Longhena was the most sophisticated of the architects brought up in the Palladian tradition, which he later married with a powerful Baroque sensibility, most successfully at Sta Maria della Salute in Venice (1631–87), but his roots remain clear.

There is no doubt that what Jones sought on his extensive travels round Italy were the remains of Roman Antiquity and the works of Palladio, but as a keen observer he must have been sensitive to the architectural climate of the day. It is not known if he mixed with any contemporary architects or theorists, but with Arundel's connections he was in a position to meet anyone he wished. What matters is not whether Jones saw or was influenced by any specific building. In most cases there is no proof that he did or was. What is important is that throughout Italy, but most particularly in the Veneto and Emilia, he would have found himself in an architectural climate sympathetic to the beliefs he had acquired in England. He would here have felt that his work lay within the mainstream of an important European architectural movement, and that it was the obvious, modern way to build.

Chapter 3

JONES AND SOUTHERN GERMANY

In NORTHERN ITALY CLASSICAL ARCHITECTURE had been accepted for generations as the correct way in which to build. This was not the case north of the Alps in Germany. Knowledge of the Italian revival of classicism had spread early from Italy to Germany, as would be expected given the strong trading links between the two countries. This is evident in several early and highly sophisticated classical buildings such as the Fugger Chapel in the Church of St Anna in Augsburg (1509–19), the ordered classical regularity of the Fuggerei, mercantile landlord housing also in Augsburg (1519–43) and the Serlian Residenz at Landshut (1536).[1] Despite these, classicism as a rigorous framework for designing buildings, as opposed to a source of decoration, had never become rooted in Germany in the sixteenth century. In this Germany resembled England. Instead, the prevailing architectural language at the beginning of the seventeenth century was one of richly ornamented façades dominated by elaborate gables applied to buildings whose forms were essentially late medieval, not classical, as in Johannes Schoch's Friedrichsbau of 1601–7 at the Schloss at Heidelberg (Fig. 30).[2]

In the first two decades of the seventeenth century this began to change as a succession of austere, classically correct Italianate buildings were commissioned by some of the leading princes and cities of southern Germany. Most of the architects involved were German but all had spent time in Italy, generally northern Italy. The dominant impression from their buildings is of rows of regularly placed vertical rectangular windows, with architraves and sometimes pediments, set in otherwise bare elevations, perhaps separated by stringcourses, often with quoins at the corners and balustrades along the rooftops.

An early example can be found in Munich, seat of the Wittelsbachs, where the Jesuit College of 1585–97 has a clean, Italianate façade of regularly arranged windows

with correctly detailed architraves and pediments, separated by stringcourses, over a rustic (a reduced ground floor), the upper windows embracing panels with oval *oeil-de-boeuf* windows (Fig. 31).[3] The design would not have looked out of place in one of Serlio's books and clearly influenced Johann Alberthal's Klericalseminar for the Jesuits at Dillingen of 1619–22.[4]

Seventy miles to the east of Munich in Salzburg, where the ruling archbishops were growing rich from the profits of salt extraction and gold mining, Archbishop von Raitenau set about transforming the medieval city into a 'German Rome'. He laid out grand squares and commissioned a new cathedral and archiepiscopal residence from Vincenzo Scamozzi in 1603–4.

30   Johannes Schoch, Friedrichsbau, Schloss Heidelberg, 1601–7.

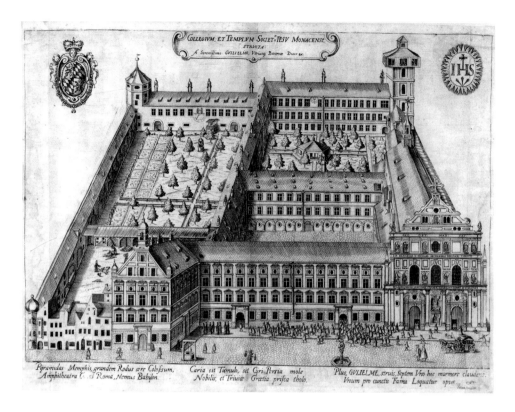

31 Johann Smisek, early seventeenth-century engraving showing Frederik Sustris's Jesuit College, Munich, 1585–97.

Archbishop von Hohenems, who succeeded in 1612, continued von Raitenau's work, calling in the Italian architect Santino Solari (1576–1646) to construct Scamozzi's cathedral to a revised design and to build him a *villa suburbana*, Schloss Hellbrunn, in 1613.[5] This severe building with its grandly classical external staircase was set in an elaborate Italian garden complete with grottoes and a Roman theatre, a miniature exedra dominated by a statue of *Roma*. In 1614 Scamozzi also probably designed the Matthias Gate as part of the restoration of the west wing of the imperial residence on the Hradzin in Prague for Emperor Matthias between 1613 and 1615.[6]

Further west in the Duke of Württemberg's lands on either side of the Rhine the key figure was a German architect, Heinrich Schickhardt (1558–1635). Schickhardt had spent three months in northern Italy studying ancient and modern architecture in the early 1590s and accompanied Duke Frederick I on a Grand Tour to Rome in 1599–1600. His sketchbook suggests that he was particularly impressed by Genoese palaces, Florentine pleasure gardens and Roman villas and churches.[7] The immediate response was the sober, Protestant Church of St Martin at Mompelgard or Montbéliard (now in France) of 1601 whose giant Doric

pilasters support a plain entablature and frame alternately segmental and triangular broken pedimented windows. Schickhardt was also responsible for laying out the new town of Freudenstadt in the Black Forest, founded in 1599, around a large central square.[8]

The idea of an austere Doric pilastered façade was picked up again at the Hofkirche (or court church) at Neuberg-an-der-Donau, designed in 1603 by the painter Joseph Heintz (1564–1609) for the Wittelsbach Philip Ludwig von der Pfalz and built in 1607 (Fig. 32).[9] Heintz had spent many years in Rome and Venice and worked for a time for Emperor Rudolf II. He also built the Rathaus, an austere, astylar building with vertical rectangular windows whose steeply ramped perron or double staircase to the first-floor entrance is a clear reference to the archetype of the modern town hall, Michelangelo's Campidoglio in Rome.[10]

Ten miles to the north of Neuberg-an-der-Donau the ruling prince-bishop of Eichstatt, Johann Konrad von Gemmingen, commissioned Elias Holl (1573–1646) to rebuild the castle of Willibaldsburg in 1609. An almost exact contemporary of Jones, Holl had been appointed Civic Architect of Augsburg in 1602, the year after a trip to northern Italy in which he recorded that he 'had a

32   Joseph Heintz, Hofkirche, Neuberg-an-der-Donau, 1607– 18 (tower, 1624).

33   Elias Holl and Johann Alberthal, Schloss Willibaldsburg, Eichstätt, *c.*1609–12.

was even more remarkable: a giant order of Doric columns was interspersed with round-headed windows, the whole recalling Serlio's illustrations of Roman amphitheatres, though these do not have giant orders.

34   South façade of the Englischer Bau, Schloss Heidelberg, 1612–19.

good look round Venice . . . marvellous things that will surely be useful to me in my building work'.[11] The result was the most austere so far of this series of Italianate buildings, its regularly spaced windows with correct classical architraves set in plain walls that are enlivened only by a stringcourse and quoins at the corners of the towers (Fig. 33).[12]

If any building symbolised the success of the new movement it is the now ruined Englischer Bau at Heidelberg, built in 1612–19 as part of the residence of the Elector Palatine Friedrich V, another Wittelsbach. Its austere architecture is in marked contrast to the castle's richly ornamented Friedrichsbau completed less than a decade earlier.[13] The south façade was a regular, plain twelve-bay, two-storey elevation of two two-bay projections with scrolled gables (Fig. 34). The north elevation

35 Jakob Wolf, Rathaus, Nuremberg, 1616–22.

models, believed to date from 1607–9, survive for a proposed civic loggia to be built on the Perlachplatz opposite the town hall (Fig. 36). Their columns, arcades, Serlianas, pedimented windows, entablatures and balustrades represent the most ambitious classical designs so far suggested for a German building, demonstrating the direct influence of Palladio's basilica in Vicenza and perhaps the Palazzo Contarini in Venice.[15] Both are usually associated with Joseph Heintz but are probably alternatives by different architects for the same competition. By 1607 Heintz had already designed two important façades in Augsburg in a rich, somewhat ill-digested Michelangelesque language, that of the new Zeughaus in 1602–7 and that of the Siegelhaus in 1604–6.

The survival of these two loggia models, together with the rich classical decoration of the Zeughaus and Siegelhaus, demonstrates the determination of the city fathers of Augsburg to introduce a more overtly Italianate architecture to their city. Neither design for the loggia was built but the Neuer Bau, erected on the site in 1611, was equally bold in its classicism, with a tall rustic of blocky Doric pilasters and a piano nobile of pedimented windows set between Ionic pilasters that could have come straight out of Serlio.

The architect of the Neuer Bau was Elias Holl, designer of the Willibaldsburg at Eichstatt. He worked with Heintz on the Zeughaus and the Siegelhaus but his subsequent buildings shook off their somewhat confused Michelangelesque mannerisms. Over the next decade Holl built a series of strikingly classical buildings in Augsburg, many of which bear direct comparison with Jones's work in England. His Kaufhaus of 1611, a seventeen-bay elevation with piano nobile and attic over ground-floor shops, with a modillion cornice and quoins

36 Joseph Heintz (attributed), model of the proposed loggia at Augsburg, 1607 (Augsburg Stadt Kunstsammlungen Maximilianmuseum, Inv. 3454).

Friedrich, whom Lord Arundel and Inigo Jones escorted to Heidelberg in 1613, had close connections with England through his marriage to James I's daughter and he subsequently commissioned an elaborate garden from Salomon de Caus who, as seen, had previously worked for Anne of Denmark and her son Henry, Prince of Wales. These connections have often led to the attribution of the Englischer Bau to Inigo Jones, though without any supporting evidence.

The most imposing of this string of Italianate buildings is the extension to the Rathaus in the imperial city of Nuremberg, forty miles north of Eichstatt, built in 1616–22 (Fig. 35). This was designed by the City Architect Jakob Wolf (1571–1620), who had earlier been sent to Italy by the city council.[14] A long, relatively low building with two rows of closely set windows, the upper level with alternating segmental and pyramidal pediments, set below pagoda-like pavilions in the centre and at the corners, it almost rivals Philip II's great palace of the Escorial in Spain in its austere splendour. This is perhaps not coincidental, as will be discussed below.

If one is looking for parallels to Jones's work the most interesting are those with the rich, proud imperial city of Augsburg, the commercial hub of southern Germany, thirty-five miles to the west of Munich. Two remarkable

37   Elias Holl, St Anna Gymnasium, Augsburg, 1613–15.

at the corners, could be mistaken for a palazzo in Rome. The St Anna Gymnasium of 1612 (Fig. 37) anticipates the compact, astylar hipped-roofed houses, such as that for Sir Peter Killigrew, which Jones introduced to England (see Fig. 85),[16] just as the simple elevation of the Schutzenhauses of 1614 parallels Jones's astylar ranges at Arundel House.[17]

In these buildings Holl developed a voluted and pedimented central gable that breaks decisively with the much more elaborately ornamented gable that was a dominant feature of contemporary German architecture.[18] There are a scattered handful of German precedents for such gables but they were not a common feature of German sixteenth-century architecture and seem to have been an innovation in Augsburg.[19] Though often described as 'Dutch' gables, their use at Augsburg anticipates their appearance in the Netherlands. Palladio provides some precedents, as does Serlio, but in neither case do the gables have volutes.[20] A central voluted gable can be found on Scamozzi's Palazzo Contarini at San Trovaso, which was being reconstructed in 1608, but by then they had already been used in Augsburg.[21]

Holl is best known for the impressively large Augsburg Rathaus, begun in 1615 (Fig. 38). This great palace, a rival to Antwerp's Town Hall and the Doge's Palace in Venice, was a clear statement of Augsburg's pride, rising

eight stories to a central pedimented gable flanked by volutes and twin octagonal towers, relieved only by pedimented windows, stringcourses and quoins.[22]

It is an extraordinary design, though elements recall the Jesuit College in Munich (see Fig. 31), and it is at first sight hard to imagine what could have led Holl to such an unusual scheme. The clue lies in the pedimented gable – its verticality emphasised by lower wings on either side – which soared over the Augsburg rooftops, just as the pedimented gable of the Sanctuary rose above the Temple of Solomon in Jerusalem in the famous reconstruction by the Jesuit Juan Bautista Villalpando (Fig. 39).

Villalpando's elaborate reconstruction of the Temple of Jerusalem, *In Ezechielem Explanationes et Apparatus Urbis ac Templi Hierosolymitani, commentariis et imaginibus illustratus*, was published in Rome in two volumes in 1596 and 1605. In it he set out to prove 'that the entire foundation and design of Roman and Greek architecture, or of any other of the most noble and ancient architectures, was taken from the design of the Temple of Solomon'.[23] To Villalpando the Temple of Solomon was the perfect building because its form and proportions had been inspired by God. Villalpando believed that the temple concurred with Vitruvius and was the primary source of the five orders of architecture, with Jewish

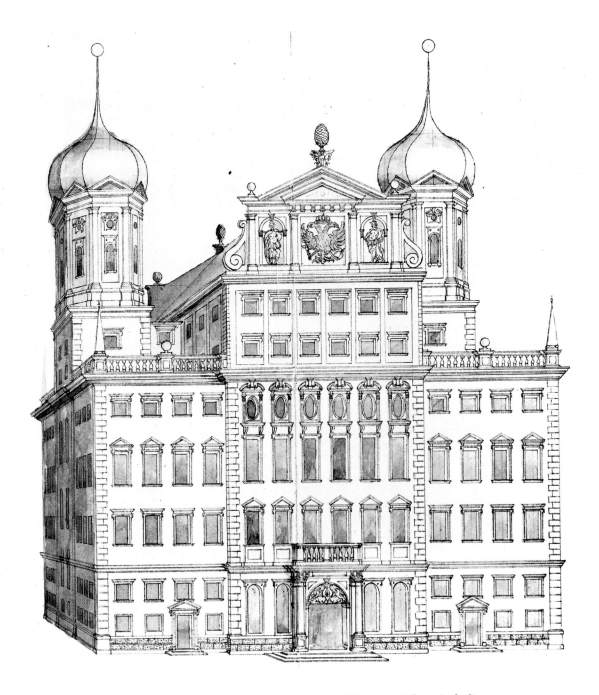

38   After Elias Holl, perspective drawing of the Rathaus, Augsburg, *c.*1615 (Worcester College, Oxford).

architecture seen as part of a continuum with Greek and Roman buildings. To prove this he designed a series of immensely elaborate engravings based on the notoriously obscure description of the temple given in the Bible by the Prophet Ezekiel. Villalpando was not the first theorist to try to reconstruct the Temple of Solomon but his was by far the most elaborate and it proved highly influential, particularly as it was included in numerous Bibles.

Villalpando's version of the temple is set on a massive stone base, supported by curved buttresses. On this sits a long, relatively low, approximately square, building divided into a complex of courtyards and punctuated by a series of taller pavilions each capped by a small, square cupola. In the middle of the complex is the Sanctuary. Like the Augsburg Town Hall, this is a multi-storeyed building divided into a series of distinct vertical units culminating in a pedimented gable that rises high over

VNIVERSI TEMPLI HIEROSOLYMITANI ORTHOGRAPHIA QVAE OSTENDIT ORIENTALEM FACIEM MVRI ATRII EXTERIORIS ET PARTEM MVRI PORTICVS GENTIVM QVAE DEINDE DICTA EST SALOMONIS

39 Juan Bautista Villalpando, reconstruction of the Temple of Solomon from *In Ezechielem Explanationes*, 1604, III, pl. XIV.

the surrounding buildings. Within it is a great hall, as in the Augsburg Town Hall.

The Town Hall at Augsburg is not alone in presenting strong parallels with Villalpando's version of the Temple of Jerusalem. The Town Hall at Nuremberg (Fig. 35) is no less unprecedented in German architecture and when compared with the principal façade of Villalpando's temple the similarities are clear (Fig. 39). Both are long, three-storeyed buildings with an endlessly repetitive sequence of windows (33 on the town hall, 35 on the temple), surmounted by pagoda-like pavilions capped by square cupolas. As will be seen, the Temple of Jerusalem, which had already been an inspiration for the Escorial, the greatest of recent European royal palaces, built in 1563–84 by Juan Battista Herrera for Philip II, was one of the models for Inigo Jones's proposed palace at Whitehall for Charles I of about 1638 and for the Town Hall at Amsterdam, begun in 1648.

At first sight this strongly royal iconography might make the use of the Temple of Solomon as the model for their town halls by a sequence of republican city states surprising. Yet Augsburg, Nuremberg and Amsterdam were proud of their status as imperial free cities that owed no allegiance except, somewhat tenuously, to the emperor, hence the imperial eagle originally boldly displayed in the central panel of the gable of the Town Hall at Augsburg. Where in a monarchy authority rested in the king and was symbolised by his palace, in the imperial free cities it lay with the town council and was symbolised by the town hall. By building these grand town halls, deliberate rivals in scale to the palaces of princes, carefully modelled on the Temple of Solomon, the free cities asserted their own authority and independence.

Thus Holl and Jones as well as being near contemporaries had much in common. Both were introducing rigorous Italianate architecture to cultures that had only had limited exposure to classicism. Both looked directly to Serlio and found inspiration in the Temple of Solomon. Both were prepared to use the full panoply of the classical orders – the Neuer Bau can be compared to the Banqueting House though it is not as confident in its execution – as well as simple, astylar designs. The parallel between the work of the two men is strongest in Jones's design believed to be for Brooke House in London of about 1617 (see Fig. 81).[24] With its giant scrolled, pedimented central gable over an astylar elevation relieved only by stringcourses and window surrounds, this could almost be read as a reduced version of the Augsburg Rathaus.[25] Jones's use of the giant gable is unprecedented in England. Did he develop the idea independently, perhaps having seen Scamozzi's Palazzo Contarini, or did he get it from Holl?

There is no evidence that Jones visited Augsburg and it is unlikely that the Earl of Arundel would have been diverted via Augsburg on his journey from Heidelberg to Basel when a trip down the Rhine would have been much more logical. Jones could have seen Lucas Kilian's engraving of the Rathaus of 1619,[26] though this would have been too late for Sir Fulke Greville's house, which John Smythson recorded the same year.[27] However, Jones could have returned alone to England from Venice via Germany. It is known that he separated from Arundel in August 1614 and although it is assumed that the two subsequently rejoined and returned together through France there is no documentary proof that they did so. If Jones returned directly from Venice the logical route would have been via the Brenner Pass and Augsburg. Had he done so, he would have arrived as Holl was designing the Rathaus.[28]

What makes this possibility particularly intriguing is the presence of two drawings of the Augsburg Rathaus, one a perspective, one a section, in the Jones–Webb

Collection (Fig. 38), together with another of Holl's adjacent Perlachturm.[29] Though it is not known when these drawings joined the collection it is remarkable that they are there at all. It is hard to imagine that they would have made their way independently to England, or that Webb would have had much interest in them after Jones's death. This suggests that they were acquired by Jones, perhaps directly from Holl.

Ultimately, whether Jones knew of or was influenced by Holl and his German contemporaries matters less than the way the architects in both countries were using a restrained classical vocabulary to reform architecture. The contrast at Heidelberg between the Friedrichsbau (1601–7) and the Englischer Bau (1612–19) is as marked as that between Holland House, Kensington (about 1606–7), and Jones's design for the Queen's House at Greenwich (begun in 1616). Jones subsequently developed a much more academic form of classicism than that seen in southern Germany, one based much more closely on Palladio and Scamozzi, but when one looks at his work in the mid-1610s, such as the design for Sir Fulke Greville, and considers his plainer, astylar buildings, the parallels with what was going on in Germany at the same time are clear.

The tragedy for Germany was that this incipient classical movement was cut short by the Thirty Years War, which broke out in 1618. This caused widespread destruction and turmoil, particularly in southern Germany. The Elector Palatine was forced into exile after his defeat in the Battle of the White Mountain in 1620; Heidelberg was sacked and the castle gutted. The population of Augsburg fell from about 48,000 to 16,000.[30] Munich was occupied by the Swedes. Even the inhabitants of Salzburg were forced to retire behind their fortifications. Though the cathedral façade was largely completed in 1628, its towers were not built till 1652–5. One wonders how architects such as Schickhardt, whose scheme for the Gesandtenhaus in Stuttgart for the Duke of Württemberg was abandoned because of the war, might have developed.[31] Would the impact of Scamozzi's *L'idea della architettura universale*, published in 1615, too late to be taken up by the Germans before the outbreak of the Thirty Years War, have been as profound as it was in England and the Dutch Republic? For Holl, who lived on for nearly three more decades but built little after the Rathaus, the situation must have been particularly disappointing. It is as if Jones built nothing after the Banqueting House and had to be judged accordingly.

38

Chapter 4

JONES AND FRANCE

THE LIMITED INFLUENCE OF FRANCE on Inigo Jones's designs has long been accepted.[1] The York House Watergate (1626–7), which may have been designed by Jones, though the attribution has never been firmly established, is believed to have been inspired by the Fontaine Médicis of the Palais du Luxembourg in Paris, attributed to Salomon de Brosse.[2] Even more direct is the influence contemporary French fashion had on Jones's interior designs in the mid-1630s, particularly for Queen Henrietta Maria, sister of Louis XIII. A series of drawings by Jones, principally for chimneypieces for the Queen's residences at Somerset House and the Queen's House at Greenwich, are based closely on French sources. One is derived from a drawing by an unknown French designer still held with Jones's collection of drawings (Figs 40 and 41), others are inspired by Jean Barbet's *Livre d'architecture, d'autels, et de cheminées* and Pierre Collot's *Pièces d'architecture ou sont comprises plusiers sortes de cheminées*, both published in 1633. The survival of another contemporary French drawing for a chimneypiece inscribed 'from ye French ambasator' suggests that the designs may have come directly from the French court.[3]

Parallels between Jones's architecture and that in France lay much deeper, however, than the latest fashionable interior designs. They can be seen in domestic architecture, in urban planning, in a common interest in the use of the portico, in a direct return to antique example for key contemporary buildings and in a growing interest in the classical tradition evident at both the English and the French courts.

Inigo Jones knew France well. In his first documented architectural tour in 1609 he travelled with Lord Cranborne to Paris, down to Bordeaux, by Toulouse to Provence and then back via the Loire Valley. As briefly noted earlier, it was a trip that not only allowed him to study the major French monuments of Roman Antiquity but also took him through all the principal French cities, providing a solid introduction to contemporary French architecture.[4] If he returned to England through France with the Earl of Arundel in 1614 he would have had time to catch up with the latest developments in and around Paris as Arundel spent several weeks in Paris awaiting an audience with the king, leading Thomas Edmondes to complain to Sir Ralph Winwood that the earl and countess had been lodged in his house for nearly three weeks.[5]

French architecture had taken a far different route from English, Dutch and German architecture over the previous half-century. In all four countries there had been a strong early interest in Italian classicism in the early decades of the sixteenth century but in the latter three this proved short-lived. In France the repeated involvement of French troops in Italy meant that knowledge of contemporary Italian architecture was strong and it was promoted by the French monarchs keen to utilise the language of Antiquity to bolster their prestige. Consequently, Italian classicism as an architectural discipline and not just as a source of decorative detail was accepted as the essential foundation for good architecture in France from the 1540s in a way that it was not in Germany, the Netherlands and England. This was reinforced by the return to France of Philibert de l'Orme, probably in 1536 after about eight formative years in Rome, who proved to be the most classically aware of all French sixteenth-century architects, and by the arrival at the French court at Fontainebleau in 1541 of the key Italian architectural theorist Sebastiano Serlio.[6]

Of Serlio, heir of Peruzzi and hence of Raphael and Bramante, de l'Orme later wrote 'C'est luy qui a donne le premier aux Francois, par ses livres et desseings, la cognoissance des edifices antiques' (It is he who by his books

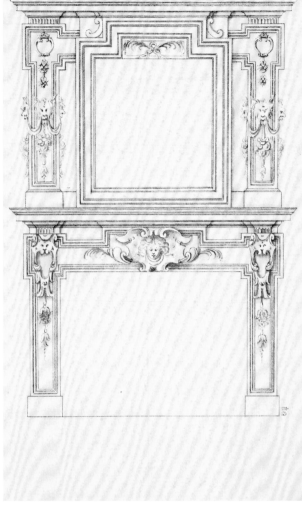

40 Inigo Jones, design for a chimneypiece at Somerset House, London, 1636 (RIBA Library Drawings Collection).

41 French designer, design for a chimneypiece, early 1630s (RIBA Library Drawings Collection).

and designs first gave to the French knowledge of antique buildings).[7] Serlio helped consolidate the essential building blocks of French classical architecture that remained dominant in polite architecture for the next hundred years and influential in French building well into the eighteenth century. Instrumental in this was the publication of the seventh book of his *Tutte l'opere d'architettura et prospetiva* in 1575, long after his death in 1554. Serlio's book was a conscious adaptation of Italian models to French climate and customs. In the introduction to the seventh book he repeatedly refers to different Italian and French customs, commenting for instance that 'nor shall I omit showing several sorts of windows in the Italian manner and also some in the French style for building above roofs yet observing ancient custom'.[8]

The point is made perhaps most clearly in his Twenty-fifth House, 'on a noble site inside the city', which is essentially a Roman palazzo adapted from Bramante's classic Palazzo Caprini, complete with arcaded, rusticated ground floor and a piano nobile with paired columns set between pedimented windows, adjusted to French custom: 'And since dormer windows – the custom here above the last cornice – are of great ornament to buildings, almost like a crown placed on top, I wished to observe the French custom on this habitation . . . in the same way, the covering of this house is to be in the French style so that many habitable places could be built in the attics.'[9]

What Serlio stressed was the Italian custom of regularly spaced, symmetrical elevations determined by the

42　Giuliano da Sangallo, Poggio a Caiano, near Florence, 1485–92.

spacing of vertical rectangular windows under a unified roofline, of which important early examples are Giuliano da Sangallo's Poggio a Caiano near Florence, designed in the early 1480s (Fig. 42), and Luca Fancelli's Nova Domus at the Palazzo Ducale in Mantua of 1480.[10] Poggio a Caiano is best known for its innovative use of the portico but, if this is mentally stripped away, the resulting elevation with vertical rectangular windows symmetrically placed against a plain background round a central axis under a hipped roof became an essential building block of later classical architecture. Palladio used it, for instance, on the rear, less architectural, elevations of his villas, such as the Villa Badoer and the Villa Pisani at Bagnolo, and Serlio crystallised the form in his seventh book, a typical example being in his chapter LXI (Fig. 43). Here Serlio combined a simple Italian elevation with the French (or northern) fashion for steeper roofs with dormer windows.[11] Such regular, symmetrical elevations, generally without an emphatic central accent, with vertical rectangular windows, hipped roofs and dormers, formed the foundation of advanced French domestic architecture from the second half of the sixteenth century. Some of these buildings were decorated with pilasters, most were astylar. They tended to be organised into series of pavilions, each under its own pronounced hipped roof, another way in which the Italian and French traditions merged.[12]

Such buildings remained the fashionable style of the court of Henri IV (1589–1610) and would have been seen by Jones on his visits to France. Good examples on the outskirts of Paris included the now demolished Château de Montceaux-en-Brie, designed by Jacques II Androuet du Cerceau and Salomon de Brosse for Henri IV's mistress in 1596 and ultimately occupied by the queen, Marie de' Medici, and the Château de Rosny built for Maximilien de Béthune, later Duc de Sully, Henri IV's key minister, begun in about 1598 (Fig. 44).[13] This approach remained popular in court circles under

43　Sebastiano Serlio, seventh proposition for off-square sites, from *The Seventh Book of Architecture* (1575), fol. 155.

44 Château de Rosny, Rosny-sur-Seine, Yvelines, begun c.1598.

Henri's son, Louis XIII (1610–43), as can be seen in the Château de Lery, built for Marie de' Medici's Italian banker Zanobi Lioni in 1632.[14] Henri IV's major urban schemes in Paris, the Place Royale (now the Place des Vosges), begun in 1605, and the Place Dauphine of 1607, were built in the same style.[15]

The essential elements of this style, symmetrical elevations with regular vertical windows under a hipped roof with dormers, were among the key innovations introduced by Jones to England in buildings such as the stables of Arundel House of about 1618 (see Fig. 80) or the house for Lord Maltravers of 1638 (see Fig. 82). The central five-bay, two-storey, hipped roof with dormers

45 Château de Breteuil, Yvelines, c.1600.

range of the Château de Breteuil, for instance, built for Thibault Desportes, *grand audiencier* of the Chancellerie de France in about 1600, anticipates Jones's Maltravers design, though following French fashion the roof is much steeper (Fig. 45).[16] In Paris, the façade of the Hôtel de Chalon-Luxembourg of 1623–5, attributed to Jean Thiriot, is essentially a heavily decorated version of the Château de Breteuil and of Jones's Maltravers design.[17] There are also striking parallels between the pair of houses designed by Inigo Jones in about 1630 flanking St Paul's, Covent Garden (see Fig. 86), and the three-bay pavilions with pitched roofs and dormers set round the two squares of the new town of Richelieu, Indre-et-Loire, designed in 1631 by Jacques Lemercier (about 1585–1654).[18]

For Jones the common acceptance of this manner of building in France may have been a powerful stimulus to introduce it to England but (unlike the interiors for Queen Henrietta Maria) Jones was not simply introducing a French fashion to England. Instead of using French precedents Jones turned directly to Serlio for his models, as will be seen in chapter 6. Had Jones been deliberately emulating French architecture he would have introduced the French fashion for taller pitched roofs and for breaking up elevations and roofs into a series of pavilions, as well as the early seventeenth-century French preference for richly ornamented elevations. Though simple French domestic architecture of

46   Jean Androuet du Cerceau, courtyard elevation of the Hôtel de Sully, Paris, 1625.

47   Pierre Le Muet, 'Distribution de la cinquiesme place', *Manière de bien bastir* (1647).

this date could be exceedingly plain, as the pavilions at Richelieu and Pierre Le Muet's *Manière de bien bastir* of 1623 show (Fig. 47), more prestigious projects, like the Hôtel de Sully of 1625, tended to be richly ornamented (Fig. 46).[19] A seven-bay, two-storey house with hipped roof and gables, the essential form of the Hôtel de Sully can be compared to Coleshill House, Berkshire (a nine-bay, two-storey house with hipped roof and gables built in the Jonesian astylar tradition; see Fig. 94). The simplicity of Coleshill's elevation, however, contrasts with the elaborate door surround, richly ornamented pediments over the windows, rusticated window surrounds and wonderfully ornate dormers of the Hôtel de Sully. The bones may be the same but the result is far different.[20]

This was partly the result of Jones's belief in decorum or propriety in architecture. As will be shown in chapter 6, the Serlian manner introduced by Jones was principally used in England on service buildings, simple suburban villas or small country houses for which architectural restraint was appropriate. Yet even when buildings required greater elaboration, Jones and his followers did not emulate the French model's ostentatious use of quoins, window surrounds and contrasting brick and stone, preferring more restrained, Italianate elevations. For Jones the introduction of what might be called the Serlian elevation was not a question of following a French model but of introducing the sound classical

48   François Mansart, Château de Balleroy, Calvados, 1631.

principles laid down by Serlio that had been common in France for decades, while at the same time ignoring the French passion for ornament that had come to overlay them.

In eschewing ornament on Serlian-inspired elevations in the 1610s Jones was anticipating a similar movement in France towards greater simplicity in elevations. This transition is perhaps best traced in the work of François Mansart, whose Château de Balleroy of 1631 was solidly in the traditional manner with heavy quoins, vigorous window surrounds, elaborate dormers and a strong contrast between the brick of the wall and the stone of the dressings (Fig. 48). By contrast the Hôtel de la Bazinière in Paris of 1653 used no more decoration than Jones did at Maltravers House in 1638 (Fig. 49).[21] As already pointed out of Germany, this move towards simpler, more austere elevations was one of the most important developments in seventeenth-century northern European architecture. It is equally evident, though not necessarily contemporaneously, in Germany, France, England and the Dutch Republic.

One of Jones's most important creations was the new urban quarter of Covent Garden, marked not only by its central square but also by its regular façades. In England Covent Garden was unique in its ambition in the first half of the seventeenth century. This was not true of France where urban planning on this scale was a noted feature of the period. Jones would have seen two ambi-

tious new urban quarters in Paris, Henri IV's Place Royale and the Place Dauphine. Of the third of Henri IV's great town planning projects, the Place de France, laid out by Claude Chastillon and Jacques Alleaume in 1610, only a small part was completed.[22] Other model towns or new quarters were being laid out elsewhere in France at the same time. On the north-east border the new town of Charleville was built from 1608 for Charles de Gonzague, Duc de Nevers, by the ducal architect Clément Métezeau.[23] In the same year Henrichemont was laid out, probably by Hugues Cosnier, as a new town at the centre of the principality of Boisbelle by the Duc de Sully. The town was arranged round a central square with houses built according to strict rules of symmetry to designs made by Salomon de Brosse.[24] A similar project could be found in south-west France, at Montauban, where a serious fire in 1616 forced the rebuilding of much of the town by the municipality round a regular central square.[25] Perhaps the closest parallel with Covent Garden was the new town of Richelieu, Indre-et-Loire, designed round two squares just as Jones was designing Covent Garden. Jones's work at Covent Garden was thoroughly in tune with contemporary French urbanism.

There are also parallels to be seen in the approach, though not necessarily the built results, of the leading French architect of the first decades of the seventeenth century, Jones's close contemporary Salomon de Brosse

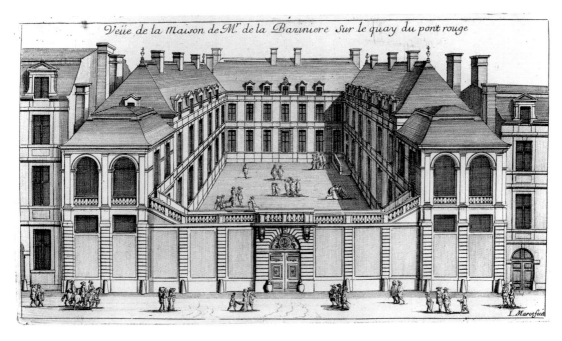

49   Jean Marot, engraving of François Mansart's Hôtel de la Bazinière, Paris, 1653, from *Le Grand Marot* (before 1659),
no plate number (RIBA Library Drawings Collection).

(about 1571–1626). Like Jones, de Brosse can be seen as representing a move away from an architecture in which the classical orders were seen essentially as sources of decoration to one in which they were treated as a rigorous system for controlling architectural design. As Rosalys Coope puts it, 'In [French architecture in] the 1580s and 1590s classical elements were more often than not employed merely decoratively, sometimes in a distorted and frivolous manner which had no true relationship to the building itself. Indeed, the building largely became a two-dimensional background for this "classical" ornament. As he outgrew the influence of this late sixteenth-century mannerist style, de Brosse returned to de l'Orme's conception of classicism in which all the separate elements of a building were considered as an integral part of the whole composition. He eliminated arbitrary and irrelevant details and concentrated on the essentially architectural character of his work, especially developing two aspects of it, the application of the Orders and composition in mass.'[26] The same words could be applied to Jones.[27]

De Brosse also shared Jones's interest in turning directly to antique example, seen in the use of the Vitruvian Tuscan temple as the model for St Paul's church, Covent Garden (1631). The Salle des Pas Perdus in the Palace of Justice in Paris, rebuilt, to a design traditionally and confidently attributed to de Brosse, after the medieval hall was almost completely gutted by fire in

1618, has a monumental spaciousness unknown in French sixteenth-century architecture that reveals a deliberate attempt on de Brosse's part to emulate the grandeur of the ancient Roman basilicas. De Brosse's design was particularly influenced by the antique reconstructions of his grandfather Jacques Androuet du Cerceau. Thirty years later the historian of Paris Henri Sauval specifically compared the Salle des Pas Perdus to the basilicas of the Greeks and Romans and to Palladio's basilica in Vicenza (which he considered their equal).[28]

This approach can also be seen in his last building, the Temple at Charenton of 1623, just outside Paris, where de Brosse turned like Jones to Vitruvius to find a solution to the problem of identifying an appropriate model for a Protestant church (Fig. 51). Although demolished after the Revocation of the Edict of Nantes in 1685, the Temple is well recorded in engravings by Jean Marot. These show a substantial rectangular building with a relatively plain exterior but an impressive interior with a giant Doric colonnade supporting two layers of galleries. De Brosse's model was Vitruvius's description of the basilica at Fano, probably relying on the French translation made by Martin in 1547. As at Fano, there are eight giant columns along the length of the hall and four across its breadth; the ambulatory runs right round the space between the columns and the wall; and the interior columns rise through two storeys, a great innovation in France. The staircases, one in each of the four

45

50 Jacques Lemercier, courtyard elevation and portico of the Chapel of the Sorbonne, Paris, 1635–48.

begun in 1612 by Rosato Rosati, with whom Lemercier may have studied, but what is unique in contemporary French or Italian architecture is the freestanding, ten-columned, pedimented portico on its courtyard elevation (Fig. 50).[31] In adding a fully blown portico or temple front to the chapel of the Sorbonne Lemercier was revealing a classical purity of vision rivalled at the time only by Jones's contemporary porticoes of St Paul's cathedral and St Paul's church, Covent Garden, in London. The foundations for the portico of St Paul's cathedral were laid in 1635, the year that work began on the chapel of the Sorbonne.[32]

Could Jones have known of Lemercier's plans? It is possible that Jones was aware of Jean Marot's engravings of the chapel of the Sorbonne made in about 1634.[33] The exchange of such architectural information between courts is a subject that deserves further examination. As noted earlier, Jones's fashionably up-to-date interior designs for the French-born Queen Henrietta Maria

51 Jean Marot, engraving of Salomon de Brosse's temple at Charenton-le-Pont, Val-de-Marne, 1623, from *Le Grand Marot* (before 1659), no plate number.

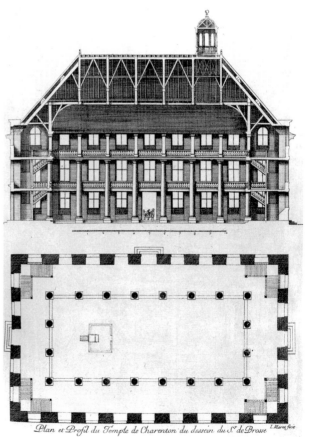

Plan et Profil du Temple de Charenton du dessein du S.ʳ de Brosse I. Marot fecit

corners, and the asymmetrical third doorway in one of the long elevations also follow Vitruvius. Charenton proved a particularly important model for French Protestant temples and later for a sequence of synagogues in the Dutch Republic.[29]

Parallels can also be traced between Jones and Riche-lieu's architect, Jacques Lemercier, who as the King's First Architect was Jones's direct equivalent in France. Lemercier, who studied in Rome from around 1607 to 1612 — therefore probably in Rome at the same time as Jones — was esteemed for his knowledge of antique and current architecture. His contemporary Henri Sauval described him as 'the Vitruvius of our times', a description that Jones probably also enjoyed, if Ben Jonson's parody of 'Colonel Iniquo Vitruvius' in his masque *Love's Welcome at Bolsover* of 1634 can be taken as evidence.[30]

Among Lemercier's most important buildings was the Chapel of the Sorbonne in Paris, which Cardinal Riche-lieu decided to rebuild in 1633. The plan and many of the details owe much to S. Carlo ai Catinari in Rome, were based on drawings that were probably sent directly from the French court via the French ambassador. They were not alone. A little earlier Queen Marie de' Medici had sent the designs of the Luxembourg Palace in Paris, begun in 1614, to courts across Europe. According to Dézallier d'Argenville: 'Il fit plusiers plans. Celui que la reine préféra fut envoyé par ses orders en Italie et dans plusiers autres royaumes d'Europe aux architectes célèbres dont la princesse souhaitait avoir l'avis' (Numerous plans were made. Those that the queen preferred were sent by her orders to Italy and in many other kingdoms of Europe to celebrated architects whose advice the princess sought). England seems to have been among that number, for John Thorpe's book in the Sir John Soane Museum, London, contains a plan inscribed 'Queen mothers howse fabor Sct Jarmins alla Paree'.[34] Later in the century Louis XIV sent copies of designs by J. Hardouin Mansart for the Invalides to Charles II in 1678 and those for the Château de Marly to William III's favourite, the Earl of Portland, Superintendent of the King's Gardens, in 1700.[35]

Architectural historians tend to concentrate on the possible influence of printed sources, specifically books, as this is, within limits, relatively easy to identify. A published book is evidently in the public domain, while evidence from booksellers' catalogues and archives such as accounts, diaries and library catalogues, not to mention surviving copies, is proof that a book was known. Proving the exchange of unpublished information, whether in letters or drawings, is much harder. Letters and drawings are much less likely to survive than books printed in significant numbers. These examples – generally known only through a single chance reference – are likely to be representative of other, now forgotten, interchanges between the French and English courts.[36] It should not be assumed that the English court was ignorant of the latest architectural developments in Paris.

52   Ceremonial trowel used during the first stone-laying of the Oostkerk in Middelburg
and illustrating the intended portico by Pieter Post for the church, 1648 (Zeeuws Museum, Middelburg).

Chapter 5

JONES AND THE NETHERLANDS

THE THIRTY YEARS WAR MAY HAVE cut short the emergent classicism in southern Germany but not in the Dutch Republic. Here a sophisticated architectural movement inspired by Vitruvius, Palladio and Scamozzi developed in the late 1620s, picked up strength in the 1630s and became general in the 1640s. Nowhere else are the parallels with England so strong. Not only was Inigo Jones probably aware of what was going on, he himself seems to have been a significant influence. For this reason I shall examine the Dutch architectural experience in detail, though again what is important is not what Jones might or might not have known but the broader similarities that show the strength of the early seventeenth-century classicist movement in northern Europe.

Early seventeenth-century Dutch architecture showed an impressive fluency in its handling of the classical orders, thanks in part to the depth of artistic talent in the country. Architectural painting, epitomised by Hans Vredeman de Vries, was a well established tradition that was entirely absent in England and the quality of architectural draughtsmanship was much higher.[1] It is no coincidence that those most closely associated with the new classicist movement were artists turned architects.

Innovation and novelty, not the orderly application of an established architectural code as laid down by Vitruvius or Palladio, drew the highest praise in the architecture of the era. This approach flourished during the twelve-year truce between the Dutch Republic and Spain, declared in 1609 after decades of war, which led to a period of intense economic and architectural activity marked by the great westward extension of Amsterdam, laid out in 1610–15.[2] The florid but highly sophisticated quality of contemporary Dutch architecture is revealed in the work of the leading architect of the time, Hendrick de Keyser (1565–1621), who was

responsible for the tomb of William the Silent in Delft (1614–21), together with such buildings as the adjacent Town Hall of 1618–20 and the house he designed in 1617 at Herengracht 170–72 in Amsterdam (Fig. 53).[3]

The end of the truce in 1621 brought renewed warfare that closed this period of prosperity and architectural activity but the impact of the war was widely different from that in contemporary Germany. Secure behind

53   Hendrick de Keyser, Herengracht 170–72, Amsterdam, 1617.

54   Jacob van Campen, Coymanshuis, Keizergracht, Amsterdam, 1625.

their river barriers, the Dutch began to thrive as Amsterdam replaced Antwerp as the commercial centre of northern Europe. The city continued to grow rapidly, as did many smaller towns. There was money to build public buildings, churches, town houses and country houses and it was on the back of this boom that the Dutch classicist movement spread.

A key figure in this new movement was a well connected Haarlem-based painter turned architect, Jacob van Campen (1596–1657). Haarlem painters such as Hendrick Goltzius and Cornelis van Haarlem had long shown a strong interest in classical examples and classical architecture. As early as 1604 Carel van Mander had expressed his disapproval in his *Schilder boek* of the fashion for sculptural invention then dominating contemporary Dutch architecture, complaining that freedom of design was abused so much that 'in the course of time a great heresy has arisen among the masons, with a frenzy of decoration . . . very disgusting to behold'. Van Mander emphasised instead the use of correct proportions as an elementary part in the training of painters and architects.[4] Perhaps it is not surprising that the leading architects of the new classicist movement came from the town.

Van Campen, though a painter like Jones, came from a wealthy background. His parents were members of

prominent Amsterdam ruling families and provided him with financial independence and a network of outstanding connections spanning the twin poles of Dutch life, the aristocratic and the mercantile.[5] Van Campen's earliest essay in architecture was in Amsterdam, on the Keizergracht, where he designed the façade of the Coymanshuis in 1625 for two brothers, Joan and Balthasar Coymans (Fig. 54). This was the first attempt in Holland to use correct, strictly applied classical pilasters and Konrad Ottenheym suggests that the superimposed Ionic and Composite orders, alternating segmental and triangular pediments (since removed) over the first-floor windows and slightly projecting centre mean the Coymanshuis should be read as a paraphrase of Inigo Jones's Banqueting House in Whitehall (1619–22; see Fig. 107). Though the proportions are uncomfortable and the relationship of the grid of pilasters to the windows is not entirely resolved, the contrast with earlier Amsterdam houses, such de Keyser's Herrengracht 170–72 (see Fig. 53) is marked. Superfluous ornament has been stripped away and the emphasis is deliberately on the horizontal, not the vertical, until then a key element in Dutch domestic architecture.[6]

Knowledge of the Banqueting House may have been brought back by the Coymans's brother-in-law, Joan Huydecoper, a young rich merchant with a particular fondness for architecture who had spent six months in London in 1623, the year after the Banqueting House had been completed. Huydecoper became one of Philips Vingboons's earliest clients and among the driving forces behind van Campen's Amsterdam Town Hall.[7] Another conduit for information about the Banqueting House would have been the de Keyser family, whose history reveals the close links between Amsterdam and London. In 1606 Hendrik de Keyser, master mason to the City of Amsterdam, had been sent to London to examine Hendrik van Paesschen's Royal Exchange, which was to be the model for the new Amsterdam Bourse.[8] While there he engaged Nicholas Stone as his apprentice. Stone, who married de Keyser's daughter, returned to London in 1613 and was master mason at the building of the Banqueting House in 1619–22. In 1621 Hendrik de Keyser's son Willem joined him as an apprentice. News of the ambitious Banqueting House project would no doubt have passed swiftly back to the de Keysers in Amsterdam and from them to the city's architectural community.[9]

The Coymanshuis was among the buildings illustrated in *Architectura moderna*, published in 1631 by Salomon de Bray (1597–1664), another Haarlem-based painter turned architect. In his foreword de Bray explained that the illustrations in the book provided the opportunity to compare contemporary architecture in Holland with the architecture of the ancients and to judge and measure the buildings according to the true reason of 'Mathematical Building'. His aim was to demonstrate that architecture was the supreme art because of its antiquity and scientific character, with the hope that 'by continuing in its course, architecture will regain her position on the higher rung'.[10]

De Bray's work as an architect included a plan for the enlargement of Haarlem as well as models and drawings for the Nieuwe Kerk.[11] He was also responsible for an extension to the Stadhuis in 1631, whose slightly clumsy use of segmental and triangular pedimented windows within a tight framework of pilasters has much in common with the Coymanshuis, and a new gallery wing for Castle Loenersloot consisting of an arcade supporting three pavilions of about 1630.[12] De Bray's most ambitious design was for remodelling the Huis te Warmond, a medieval castle near Leiden, in 1629. His work was destroyed in 1777 but is known from a copy of the drawings made by Pieter Saenredam, another artist member of van Campen and de Bray's Haarlem circle (Saenredam's collection of sixteenth-century drawings, including a number of studies of ancient buildings in Rome, would no doubt have interested van Campen and the others[13]). With its superimposed Doric and Ionic pilasters, mezzanine windows, alternating segmental and triangular pediments over the first-floor windows and flat entablatures over ground-floor windows that rest on a stringcourse, together with the use of busts placed within shell surrounds over windows, de Bray's design for the Huis te Warmond is heavily indebted to Palladio's Palazzo Chiericati (Fig. 55).[14]

Similar in its ambitious, but not entirely assured, classicism was the Koningshuis at Rhenen, demolished in 1812 but recorded in a pair of topographical drawings in 1641 by Saenredam.[15] This was built by the States of Utrecht from 1629 for Friedrich V, the Elector Palatine and deposed 'Winter King' of Bohemia, who had been forced into exile in 1620. The designer is believed to be Bartholomeus van Bassen (about 1590–1652), another painter-architect, who issued the commission to build it on the king's behalf.[16] The Koningshuis at Heidelberg, built for Charles I's brother-in-law, whose Englischer Bau (1612–19) (see Fig. 34) had been a key example of the new classicist architecture in Germany, is clearly of interest. Saenredam's drawings show what might be considered a transitional building, E-shaped with a steeply

pitched, two-storey sloping roof and conventional entrance front. The north or garden elevation, which was two storeys high, with superimposed orders, alternating segmental and triangular pediments over the windows and elaborate scrolled gables masking the tall end of the two-bay projecting wings, was more sophisticated. Despite the sharply pitched roof and the scrolled gables the similarity with the Banqueting House in Whitehall is strong. Van Bassen may also have been influenced by Vincenzo Scamozzi, whose L'idea della architettura had been published in 1615. Jan Terwen suggests that the Koningshuis's projecting staircase may have been inspired by that intended for Scamozzi's Villa Verlato and indeed its form is taken from one of the staircases illustrated in L'idea.[17]

Scamozzi proved a key source for the Dutch classicists and is a possible source in the design of Ter Nieuburch, the suburban palace on the outskirts of The Hague of

55 Andrea Palladio, Palazzo Chiericati, from *I quattro libri dell'architettura* (1570) II, p. 7.

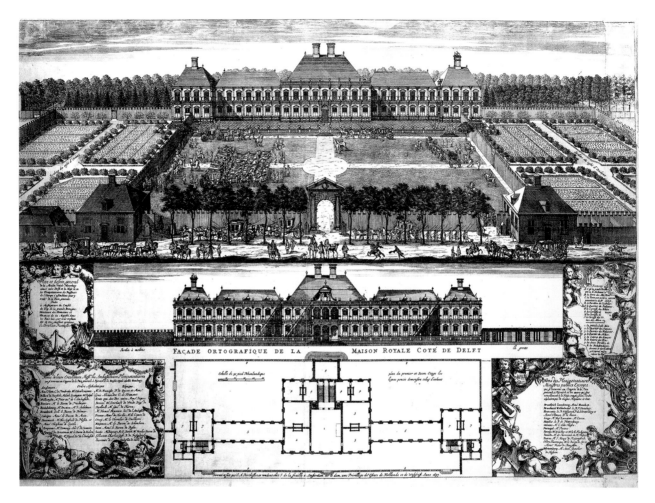

56　J. A. Rietkessler, engraving of 1697 of Ter Nieuburch, The Hague, 1630–4 (Koninklijk Huisarchief, The Hague).

the Dutch Stadholder, Frederik Hendrik, Prince of Orange (Fig. 56). The site was bought in July 1630, the year the title of Stadholder became hereditary, and by 1632 the construction and interior decoration was sufficiently advanced for an official visit by foreign dignitaries, the Gentlemen Deputies of Ireland. By the time Sir William Brereton visited in 1634 work was nearly finished.[18]

Frederik Hendrik, whose mother was French, was strongly influenced by French culture, as was his court.[19] At the age of 14 he had spent a year at the court of his godfather Henri IV in 1610, travelling to France again in 1619.[20] His first major building, the hunting palace Honselaarsdijk, had been rebuilt between 1621 and 1631 in the form of a French château with four corner pavilions connected by wings and a low entrance range round a *cour d'honneur*.[21] The French garden designer André Mollet was employed from 1633 and the French architect Simon de la Vallée, who arrived the same year, was

responsible, with van Campen, for the interior of the palace and especially the monumental stone staircase. De la Vallée, who had trained under his father Marin de la Vallée, chief contractor at the Palais de Luxembourg in Paris, was called the Stadholder's architect from 1634 until he left for Sweden in 1637.[22]

Frederik Hendrik retained the habit of looking to France for advice, asking M. Tassin, *intendant* of the Duc d'Orléans and agent of the Orange family in France, in 1643, to show designs for the annexe buildings, chapel and gardens at Honselaarsdijk to the best French architects and gardeners for their opinion.[23] So it is not surprising that the prince turned to France when he was deciding how to rebuild Ter Nieuburch. A surviving design is closely based on the Palais de Luxembourg which, given that it was set out according to French not Dutch measurements, was probably sent from France, perhaps by Simon de la Vallée.[24] Frederik Hendrik rejected this plan and instead decided to build a palace with a 33-bay façade, divided into a series of pavilions each under its own roof.[25]

Thanks to the pavilions the first impression of Ter Nieuburch is profoundly French, indeed reminiscent of the Tuileries in Paris, much of which had been built by Henri IV and which Frederik Hendrik would have known well from the year he spent in Paris in 1610. The plan of the central pavilion, however, with its tripartite division into entrance hall and flanking ranges of rooms, is not French but characteristic of the Veneto (Fig. 56). It suggests a close examination of Palladio's villa plans, particularly the staircase of Palladio's Villa Ragona and the central hall and side ranges of the Villa Angarano.[26] Similarly, though the details of the elevation of Ter Nieuburch have been read as French because many can be paralleled at the Louvre, Scamozzi's architecture provides an alternative source.

According to Sir William Brereton, who visited in 1634, the palace was meant to have an extra storey but the foundations forced a change in plan.[27] Were the central pavilion of Ter Nieuburch's garden front three stories high there would be a strong similarity to the central section of Scamozzi's design for the Palazzo Cornaro in Venice, illustrated in L'idea (Fig. 57). Like Ter Nieuburch, the Palazzo Cornaro is articulated by pilasters, uses alternating triangular and segmental window pediments and the lower two storeys are Doric and Ionic.[28] Given that van Campen had looked to Scamozzi for the Coymanshuis and the Huis ten Bosch at Maarssen in 1625 and 1628, and Salomon de Bray to Palladio at the Huis te Warmond in 1629, and given the clear influence of Palladio on the plan, there is no reason why Frederik Hendrik's architect should not also have been looking to Scamozzi for the elevations in 1630–34.

The authorship of Ter Nieuburch remains uncertain. Van Bassen, described as 'perspective painter and architect', was paid for making two plans of the house, garden and plantations together with two large drawings of the elevation of the building 'in the state in which it is now and is still projected to be completed' in January 1633. However, it is uncertain whether he was involved in the initial design. Simon de la Vallée has been suggested as the architect but he did not arrive in the Dutch Republic until 1633. Another possibility is van Campen but, though he acted as the general supervisor of the interior decoration from 1632, there is no evidence that he was involved with the exterior.[29]

Despite its ambition, the execution of Ter Nieuburch remains uncertain. This is particularly evident in the way

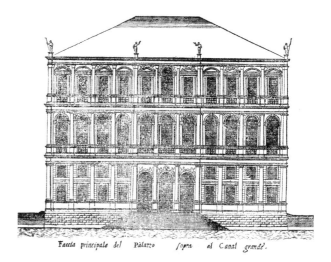

57   Vincenzo Scamozzi, Palazzo Cornaro, Venice, from *L'idea della architettura universale* (1615) I, p. 246.

the pedestals of the pilasters rise above the window frames and in the curious way the first-floor segmental window pediments are placed above triangular pediments on the floor below, not, as would be more conventional, over segmental pediments (and vice versa).[30] As such it has much in common with the Coymanshuis, the Huis te Warmond and the Koninghuis at Rhenen. In this first wave of Dutch classicist buildings there is an ambition to engage with a new classical language articulated with pilasters and pedimented windows, with Palladio and Scamozzi serving as the key sources, but at the same time a lack of rigour.

Whoever was responsible for Ter Nieuburch, Frederik Hendrik took a close interest. A passionate enthusiast for architecture and gardening, he was the instigator of an impressive building campaign that involved the restoration and construction of palaces and gardens throughout the Dutch Republic, and as such he was a crucial figure in the rise of Dutch classicist architecture. Even more closely involved was Constantijn Huygens (1596–1687), Frederik Hendrik's highly cultivated secretary from 1625. Their passion for architecture is evident in their extensive architectural libraries, which included various editions of Vitruvius, Alberti, Vignola, Scamozzi, Serlio, Palladio, Cataneo, Colonna, du Cerceau, de l'Orme and Rubens's *Palazzi di Genova*, a list that compares closely with what is known of Jones's library.[31] It was the partnership of Huygens and van Campen, with Frederik Hendrik in the background, that gave Dutch classicist architecture the authority it had so far lacked.

53

Huygens's connections with England were strong and he was well informed about architectural developments there. In 1614, while still a young man, he had come to know the English ambassador to The Hague, Sir Henry Wotton, often making music in his house. Wotton, who had previously spent eight years as ambassador to Venice (and returned twice more), could have helped inspire an early interest in architecture in Huygens. He was already an enthusiast for Palladio and owned a number of his drawings, which he had discussed with Inigo Jones before the latter's departure for Italy the previous year.[32] Later, Huygens was deeply impressed by Wotton's *Elements of Architecture*, published in 1624, and tried to have it translated into Dutch to use as the introduction to an abortive Dutch edition of Vitruvius.[33] It was with another ambassador to The Hague, Sir Dudley Carleton, whom Jones had met while he was ambassador in Venice in 1613, that Huygens visited England in 1618. This was the first in a sequence of visits between then and 1624 in which Huygens proved an enthusiastic visitor of buildings, among them Greenwich Palace, where he could see Jones's Queen's House under construction.

Thanks to his diplomatic missions, Huygens is the one person in the Netherlands known to have seen both Palladio's and Scamozzi's buildings in the Veneto and Jones's Banqueting House in London.[34] In Italy, which he visited in 1620, Huygens spent time in Verona, where he studied the amphitheatre and other monumental Roman remains; Vicenza, where the embassy was formally received in Palladio's basilica and Huygens visited the Teatro Olympico, which he described as 'bastiment moderne, mais à la verité tel qu'en Europe ne se peut voire chose plus belle' (a modern building, but in truth in Europe one cannot see anything more beautiful); and Padua.[35] Three weeks in Venice then gave him the opportunity to visit the buildings of Sansovino, Sanmichele, Palladio and Scamozzi, leading him later to write in his long poem on his own life:

Fana, fora, statua, veteris praeceptia Vitruvi
Exemplis firmata novis et marmore vivo.

([They show] churches, squares, statues, and the
   classical rules of old Vitruvius
Reconfirmed with new examples and in living
   marble.)[36]

Huygens was impressed to find the same ideals being followed in London. It is known from a letter written from London to his parents in 1621 that he admired Jones's buildings, which he later set as a standard against

which to judge his own works. The following year, as secretary to the Dutch Embassy, he attended the inaugural *Masque of the Augurs* in Jones's Banqueting House on 6 January. Given his interest in architecture and his privileged diplomatic connections it is highly likely that Huygens would have met Jones. Indeed, it is possible that he was stung by barbed comments from Jones about the state of Dutch architecture. In his 1639 treatise *Domus* Huygens explained the importance of the classical rules, that all theory was based on Vitruvius's Ten Books and that modern Italian books on architecture could be used as convenient guidebooks towards understanding Vitruvius's obscure text. He added that he had been forced to strive for the improvement of Dutch architecture because of insults by some people – architects and scholars – from abroad. Konrad Ottenheym suggests that Jones may have been one of these.[37] Jones's opinion of contemporary Dutch architecture is clear from an annotation in his copy of Alberti's *De re aedificatoria*: 'and not as the Flemings breaking of orders to seem full of invention but have no reason of Proportion'.[38] According to *Domus*, this scornful laughter about Dutch architecture made Huygens eager to search for the principles of true architecture and consequently his new house in The Hague was designed entirely in accordance with the rules of Antiquity and modern Italy, not focussed on decorative details and intricate sculptured ornament.[39] To prove that correct architecture could also be found in Holland Huygens made and distributed prints of his design. Inigo Jones was undoubtedly one of the targets he had in mind. As he wrote to a friend in 1637, 'I have built a house, had prints made of it and will send them to you; Inigo Johns [sic] will see that his manner does not differ much from this one . . . Mr Inigo Jones will be able, if he pleases, to learn that the good Vitruvius is not totally excluded from Holland.'[40]

Thus the house that Huygens built, with van Campen's help, in The Hague in 1633–7 (Fig. 58) was intended to be his contribution to the recovery of Vitruvian architecture. In a letter to Rubens in November 1635 Huygens wrote that with it he hoped to revive a little of the ancient architecture, though he feared that it was only a small step thanks to conditions in Holland and his finances.[41] The result was a compact house with a plan that owed much to Ter Nieuburch, though the overall disposition, with a shallow forecourt enclosed by wings and a wall, followed the form of the French *hôtel particulier*.[42] The house, which was nine-bays wide, two-storeys high, with a pitched roof and dormer windows, carefully followed the architectural hierarchy of the clas-

58 Pieter Post, engraving showing the Huygenshuis, the Hague, by Constantijn Huygens and Jacob van Campen, 1633–7.

sical orders, with a garden gate in the Tuscan order, the entrance gate in the Doric order, the front façade articulated by superimposed Ionic and Composite pilasters and the back wall of the entrance hall embellished with a triumphal arch with Corinthian pilasters.[43]

In a later letter written in July 1639, in which Huygens sought Rubens's approval of the house, he talked of the 'regular equality of one part with the other' found in the ancients and among the good Italians of his own time who searched for the same. (The words 'égalité regulière' and 'architecture ancienne et moderne' appear again and again in Huygens's letters and his poetry.[44]) He must have been somewhat deflated when Rubens declared the design insufficiently Vitruvian.[45]

Huygens aspired to spread the Vitruvian message through the publication of a complete edition of Vitruvius in Dutch, enriched by various supplements to explain some complicated aspects of his theories (including Wotton's *Elements of Architecture*). This was never realised, though an edition of Vitruvius, in Latin not Dutch, by Johannes de Laet was published in Amsterdam in 1649.[46] Instead, Huygens was most influential through the practical encouragement he gave to those promoting the new movement, both privately and as a member of the Prince of Orange's Council of Nassau

Domain Land, the authority which managed the palaces owned by the House of Orange.[47]

Jacob van Campen benefited directly from Huygens's patronage. Huygens had turned to him for help with the correct details of the orders on his house. Together they immersed themselves in the study of Vitruvius. 'Mr van Campen has come to see me for this reason and is helping me with Vitruvius in the most perfect manner', wrote Huygens to a friend in 1634.[48] Van Campen had learnt fast after his first, somewhat clumsy, architectural attempt at the Coymanshuis in 1625. Three years later he had produced a much more polished design for Balthasar Coymans's brother-in-law, Pieter Belten, at the Huis ten Bosch at Maarssen (Fig. 59).[49] Here a more convincing temple front with giant Ionic pilasters and pediment was applied to a country house, the first time this had happened in northern Europe and as such a momentous innovation.[50]

Huygens must have been responsible for introducing van Campen to Count Johan Maurits of Nassau-Siegen, for whom he began the Mauritshuis in 1633 (Fig. 60).[51] This, like the Huygenshuis, lay on the Plein, a valuable stretch of land immediately to the east of the Binnenhof or ducal court in The Hague, which had been carefully laid out to enhance the town after Frederik Hendrik

59   Jacob van Campen, Huis ten Bosch at Maarssen, 1628.

60   Jacob van Campen, Mauritshuis, The Hague, 1633.

61 Jacob van Campen, Noordeinde Palace, The Hague, 1639.

prevented the Treasury Advice Committee selling off the land in small plots to make the most profit. The Mauritshuis and the Huygenshuis were intended as embellishments to the town and as models of the new architecture.[52]

At the Mauritshuis, one of the most prestigious architectural commissions of the day, van Campen finally displayed his full mastery of the classical language. Like the Huygenshuis, the Mauritshuis, whose plan also owes much to Ter Nieuburch, takes the form of a compact villa under a hipped roof.[53] As befitted the higher status of its owner, the architectural detail used is a step more elaborate than that of the Huygenshuis: the pedimented windows have brackets and are separated vertically by swags of fruit, the house has a giant order of Ionic pilasters and a more imposing entablature and the lakeside pediment is enriched with a vivid sculptural relief.

It would have been Huygens who involved van Campen in the interior decoration of Honselaarsdijk and Ter Nieuburch, and at Buren Castle, also owned by Prince Frederik Hendrik, in 1636. Huygens must also have gained him the commission for the Noordeinde

Palace in The Hague in 1639, which was remodelled for the prince's son Willem, who was betrothed that year to Charles I's eight-year-old daughter, Princess Mary (Fig. 61). Though this marriage to a royal princess did not actually take place until 1648, its prospect raised the status of the House of Orange, and Noordeinde needs to be seen as a quasi-royal palace. Appropriately, its degree of architectural enrichment is one level up from the Mauritshuis, with which it shares the plan of a French *hôtel particulier*. Instead of a combination of brick and stucco, the palace is entirely built of stone, the entrance is marked by a four-columned, single-storey (pedimentless) portico and, like Ter Nieuburch, the building has a continuous grid of double-height pilasters, Composite over Ionic as recommended by Scamozzi.

Van Campen was not entirely reliant on Huygens. In a reminder of the varied sources of architectural patronage in the Dutch Republic, in particular the twin streams of princely or aristocratic patronage centred on The Hague and bourgeois or mercantile patronage centred on Amsterdam, van Campen also enjoyed a profitable career in Amsterdam. Thanks to the support

62   Jan Jurriaensz. van Baden, *Interior of the Nieuwe Schouwburg, Amsterdam, c.*1653 (built by Jacob van Campen, 1637), Collection of The John and Mabel Ringling Museum of Art, the State Museum of Florida, Sarasota, Museum purchase.

of his cousin Nicolaas van Campen, one of the city officials, he was commissioned to build new ranges for the city orphanage, the Burgerweeshuis, in 1632–5, with a continual order of giant Ionic pilasters. This was followed by the new municipal theatre, the Nieuwe Schouwburg, in 1637 (Fig. 62), which was designed as a roofed ancient theatre and articulated with a continual order of giant Corinthian pilasters and columns. Van Campen was also responsible for a sequence of impressive churches, at Hoge Zwaluwe and Renswoude (1639; see Fig. 72) and the Nieuwe Kerk at Haarlem (1645).[54]

A distinctive feature of van Campen's buildings, including the Huis ten Bosch, the Mauritshuis, the Burgerweeshuis and the handsome entrance gate of the Schouwburg, is the use of angled volutes to the Ionic order, evidence that he was using Scamozzi's version of the order (Fig. 63). This was typical of the Dutch classicist movement, which took Scamozzi, not Palladio,

as its principal guide, as Ottenheym has remarked: 'Scamozzi's austerity and rational order, his emphasis on strict observance of the classical proportions, his warnings against unnecessary expense and excesses and his approval of the golden mean, found willing ears in Holland. Scamozzi's book confirmed prevalent views, providing them with a framework within the classical theory of architecture, which was the key to his success. The focus on Antiquity in erudite circles was as great in the Republic as it was in Venice, and Scamozzi's method of presenting ancient examples as a source of inspiration and as a preface to each building assignment must have appealed to his readers in Holland, where the idea also prevailed that ancient works were the only guideline for the revival of contemporary architecture to the level of a fully fledged, high art form.'[55] What is more, Scamozzi's *L'idea della architettura*, unlike most architectural treatises, included the dignified citizen's house within his theory of architecture, a fact that would undoubtedly have gone down well in the bourgeois-dominated Dutch Republic.

Ready availability of *L'idea della architettura*, first in the expensive original Italian edition among the cognoscenti, then in a series of cheaper Dutch editions, helped Scamozzi's popularity in the Dutch Republic. Justus Sadeler, member of a renowned Antwerp family of engravers and print dealers settled in Venice but with good contacts in the Netherlands, bought the remaining 670 copies of *L'idea* shortly after Scamozzi's death in August 1616. It was soon available in the Netherlands, where Rubens bought a copy in Antwerp on 28 June 1617. As the popularity of the Dutch classicist movement grew so did demand for a more accessible edition and in 1640 a Dutch translation of the sixth book, on the orders, was published. This was followed in 1657 by a concise pocket-sized edition of that book, without any theoretical explanations or philosophical reflections but with an exact description of all the parts of the five orders, produced by Simon Bosboom, city stonemason for Amsterdam Town Hall. In 1655 Dancker Danckertsz bought the original wooden blocks of *L'idea* and three years later published a Dutch edition of the third book, with its illustrations of Scamozzi's buildings, together with an improved reprint of the sixth book and some unpublished plates by Scamozzi. This was followed by a further edition in 1661. Danckertsz explained that his decision was driven by his desire 'to enlighten the Netherlands with Scamozzi's torch and with his excellent ingenuity, so that all the errors in building can be avoided, and in future our Netherlands can share in the glory and splendour of the ancient architects'. A further edition was published in 1661.[56] By contrast, it was only in 1646 that the slim Dutch summary edition of Palladio, a translation of Le Muet's French translation of the first book of the *Quattro libri*, appeared.[57] The first English edition of Scamozzi, of book three, was not published until 2003.

In general, it was the principles established by Scamozzi, and in particular the correct form of the classical orders, that attracted Dutch architects and builders, not the specific forms of his buildings. Apart from symmetry in layout, ground plans based on book three are rare in seventeenth-century Dutch architecture. Two exceptions, along with the Koningshuis at Rhenen, are Pieter Post's Huis ten Bosch (1645–7) and Jacob Roman's Zeist Castle (1677–86). Direct quotations from Scamozzi's elevations are not common in town and country houses, except to the extent that more elaborate houses followed Scamozzi's (and Palladio's) common villa form of a compact house with a central portico, though it is the essence not the detail of specific villas that is followed. Also, whereas Scamozzi, like Palladio before him, had frequently used freestanding porticoes or porticoes-in-antis, the Dutch universally preferred attached porticoes with pilasters. When faced with the challenge of a grand public building it was *L'idea* architects turned to, not the *Quattro libri*. The wings of van Campen's Noordeinde Palace in The Hague are taken from Scamozzi's engraving of the Palazzo Cornaro (see Fig. 57). This must also have been the source for the exterior and interior elevations of the anonymous monogrammist SGL's unsuccessful design for the Amsterdam Town Hall, whose plan was expressly intended as a reinterpretation of Scamozzi's House of the Roman Senators, as were those produced by Philips Vingboons and van Campen.[58]

63   Vincenzo Scamozzi, Ionic order, from *L'idea della architettura universale* (1615) II, p. 101.

64   Arent van 's-Gravesande, St Sebastiaansdoelen, The Hague, 1636.

Van Campen was important not only for his own work but for his encouragement of a younger generation of assistants, Daniel Stalpaert (1615–76), Philips Vingboons (1607–78), Arent van 's-Gravesande (1600–about 1662) and Pieter Post (1608–69), who went on to spread the classicist movement across the Dutch Republic, just as Inigo Jones encouraged Isaac de Caus, Nicholas Stone, Edward Carter, John Webb and Roger Pratt. All began as van Campen's draughtsmen – he was notorious for providing only sketches of his designs – before pursuing their own careers. With their emergence van Campen's architectural activity declined, except when a monumental task like the Amsterdam Town Hall was on offer.[59]

Stalpaert was van Campen's assistant on the Amsterdam Town Hall. As city architect of Amsterdam from

65   Pieter Post, Vredenburg, Beemster-Polden, 1642–7, engraving.

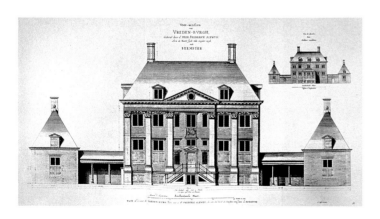

1648 he held a key post in the richest city in Northern Europe and was responsible for a significant number of public buildings, including the Nieuwezijds Huiszitten-weduwenhof (1650), the impressive 's Lands zeemagazijn (1655) and the Oosterkerk (1669).[60] Vingboons had a prosperous career building numerous town and country houses for Amsterdam's regents and trade magnates. These included Keizergracht 319 in Amsterdam (1639), which showed how the traditional tall, narrow, gabled Dutch townhouse could be reworked in classical form, and Klonviersburgwal 95 in Amsterdam (1642), which applied the pilastered temple front to a town house. His work was extensive enough to merit publication in two volumes, *Afbeelsels der voornaemste gebouwen*, in 1648 and 1674.[61] Van 's-Gravesande designed the St Sebastiaansdoelen, next to the Mauritshuis (1636; Fig. 64), probably the first example of a two-storey building with a central, three-bay pediment with four giant pilasters and similarly scaled, astylar flanking ranges, an elevation that became common across northern Europe. He subsequently became city architect of Leiden where he built the Lakenhal in 1639–40 along similar lines to the Huygenshuis and the Marekerk, an octagonal church, whose design was modified by van Campen.

Post, who like van Campen and de Bray began his career as a painter in Haarlem, helped van Campen at the Mauritshuis and Noordeinde Palace before going on to enjoy an extensive career that encompassed private houses, public buildings and churches and numerous public positions. As well as court architect he was permanent architect to such bodies as the States of Holland, the States General, the Rhineland Dike Board and various cities such as Leiden, Delft and Maastricht.[62] Post's buildings range from Vredenburg, a self-conscious villa in the Veneto manner for Frederick Alewijn, though the result is indisputably Dutch (1642–7; Fig. 65), to the octagonal Oostkerk in Middelburg of 1647 (which would have been much more impressive had the planned giant portico been built; see Fig. 146) to the Stadhuis at Maastricht (1659–64). In these Post showed himself a master of the carefully calibrated ornament. The portico of the Oostkerk at Middelburg would have pronounced the supreme authority of God. The Stadhuis at Maastricht is as richly decorated as Noordeinde Palace, a physical reminder that real power in the Dutch Republic lay with the cities, not the aristocracy. The pediment and giant pilasters of Vredenburg announced the wealth, sophistication and status of its owner.

This careful application of classical ornament to measured effect is particularly evident in Post's work for

Prince Frederik Hendrik, to whom he was appointed Court Architect in 1646. Unlike hereditary monarchs such as Charles I with their assured status, Prince Frederik Hendrik's position was delicate. He was Prince of Orange and hereditary Stadholder but was not sovereign in the Dutch Republic, though the dominant city merchant class suspected he wanted to be. Thus for Frederik Hendrik architecture was a subtle game of asserting and enhancing princely status without directly challenging the delicate balance of power between Stadholder and Republic by making too obvious a statement of sovereignty. At Noordeinde and his two last major architectural projects, the Huis ten Bosch (1645–50) and the remodelling of Honselaarsdijk (1646–52), both the work of Post, Frederik Hendrik subtly employed the new classicist language to stress the status of the House of Orange by using symbols associated with sovereignty but without making them too ostentatious.

The most powerful symbol of sovereignty (as will be seen in chapter 8) was the freestanding portico like that proposed by Inigo Jones in his design for the Palace of Whitehall (about 1638). Such a portico would have been too bold a statement for Frederik Hendrik but he did mark the entrances to the remodelled Honselaarsdijk with a prominent pediment and single-storey portico with a flat balustrade (not pediment). This could be read as no more than a balcony but could also be interpreted as diminutive versions of Inigo Jones's recently completed portico of St Paul's cathedral (see Fig. 153), an imposing declaration of royal authority by a monarch into whose family Frederik Hendrik planned to marry his son.

The other distinctive architectural motif at Honselaarsdijk, placed prominently on the end pavilions, is the single-bay pedimented aedicule supported by pairs of superimposed pilasters. This was almost certainly another subtle insinuation of princely status as the same motif was used to mark the entrance and garden pavilions on François Mansart's Château de Blois, built for Louis XIII's brother and heir apparent, Gaston d'Orléans in 1635–8 (Fig. 66).[63] Since M. Tassin, the Duc d'Orleans's *intendant*, was the Orange family's agent in France, and given Frederik Hendrik's link with French architects and gardeners, there can be little doubt that the prince would have known of Mansart's work at Blois.[64]

Post's remodelling of Honselaarsdijk demonstrates the twin architectural currents that influenced Frederik Hendrik. The division into separate pavilions, the pilastered aedicules, steeply sloped roofs and roof-top balustrades seem to come straight from France. Yet the use of a dominant pediment in the centre of the building and segmental and triangular window pediments is not found in contemporary French architecture. These are specifically Italianate motifs. There is thus a Janus-like quality, looking both to France and to Italy, to princely architecture in the Dutch Republic, unlike contemporary England where under Inigo Jones French influence was restricted to interior decoration.

The Huis ten Bosch, begun in 1645 on the outskirts of The Hague, was a more modest structure, as befitted its status as a villa for Frederik Hendrik's wife, Amalia (Fig. 67). However, those literate in the new classicist language would have placed it in the tradition of the compact, centrally planned, suburban princely residence, a type that can be traced back to Francesco di Giorgio and which received its fullest treatment in Serlio's unpublished sixth book. This association is emphasised by the octagonal cupola that rises prominently over the Huis ten Bosch. The octagonal central hall was one of the symbols of sovereignty used repeatedly by Serlio in his designs for the suburban princely residence.[65]

The new classicist movement was not just a matter of pediments, pilasters and rich architectural ornament. As in Jones's work, it was an all-encompassing approach to architectural design that began with the essential structure of the building and then applied increasing levels of ornament depending on its function and status. It ranged from simple office buildings and houses, articulated through no more than symmetry, the regular grid of windows, a hipped roof and dormers, like the pair of lodges at Ter Nieuburch (see Fig. 56), through to the expressive richness of Noordeinde Palace (see Fig. 61) and the Maastricht Stadhuis.

66 François Mansart, design for the garden front of the Château de Blois, Loire-et-Cher, France 1635–8 (Bibliothèque Nationale de France, Département des Estampes Va407, de Cotte 958).

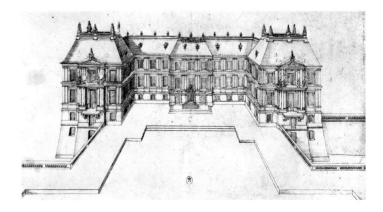

67 Jan van Call, drawing of c.1690 of the Huis ten Bosch, The Hague, by Pieter Post, 1645 (Municipal Archives, The Hague).

The closest parallels between contemporary Dutch architecture and the work of Inigo Jones are to be found at the more austere end of the spectrum. At Hofwijck (Fig. 68), the country house designed for Huygens by Post in 1639, the new classicist language was reduced to its simplest elements: upright vertical windows set symmetrically in a plain brick façade under a pitched roof with dormers. Exactly the same formula could be found at Chevening House, Kent, designed by Jones more than a decade earlier (see Fig. 84).[66] The differences lie in dimensions: Hofwijck is only three bays as opposed to seven bays wide, and three rather than four storeys tall and in decoration Chevening has quoins, architraves over the windows and a more elaborate cornice.

The standard design for a modest Dutch country house applied the same formula across a three-, five- or sometimes seven-bay elevation. A good early example, dating from about 1639, is Akerendam. Sometimes the name of the architect is known. Vingboons designed a particularly fine example, Gansenhof, in Utrecht (1655). Usually, however, as at Veebeek, Brabant (1640s) and Oolde, Gelderland (1663), the houses are anonymous. Across the Channel exactly the same formula can be found in Jones's design for Lord Maltravers of 1638 (see Fig. 82).[67] This building type remained commonplace in the Dutch Republic throughout the seventeenth and eighteenth centuries and became equally popular in England.[68]

As can be seen in both countries, the essential pattern could be expanded as necessary. Post's new range for the States of Holland at the Binnenhof in The Hague (1651; Fig. 69) extended the façade to seven bays and added a half-height third floor, while Vingboons's Herengracht 364–70 in Amsterdam is spread across thirteen bays, linking together the rear elevations of three separate houses.[69] Both, and in particular the Binnenhof range, bear close comparison with Jones's elevation believed to be for a warehouse or for tenements for Lord Maltravers (1638; see Fig. 83). Again, the difference lies solely in the limited extra decoration applied by Jones.

Vingboons was also responsible for the first Dutch version of a remarkably direct example of English influence, the mews or stables placed at the rear of a town house and approached by a separate service lane. The mews was an English, and above all London, response to the problem of housing horses and coaches in dense

68   Pieter Post, Hofwijck, Voorburg, 1639.

69   Pieter Post, range for the States of Holland at the Binnen-hof, The Hague, 1651.

urban developments. It appeared first at Covent Garden, laid out by Inigo Jones, and then at Great Queen Street in the 1630s.[70] Shortly afterwards it appeared in Amsterdam. Vingboons's *Afbeelsels der voornaemste gebouwen* includes a house, Singel 548, built for Joan Huydecoper in 1639, with its own mews building. Vingboons's second volume, published in 1674, has two more Amsterdam houses with mews, one built for Gillis Marcelis at Singel 460 in 1661, the other for Joseph Deutz at Herengracht 450 in 1669–71.[71]

Since the plots between the canals were narrow and no service street ran behind these houses, both these later mews opened onto principal, not service, streets (Keizergracht and Herengracht). This was an extravagant use of prime frontage. It was presumably to overcome this problem that a service street suitable for use as a mews was included in the second phase of the expansion of

Amsterdam, begun in 1662. The expansion, intended to provide sites for Amsterdam's rich merchants, continued the two principal streets of Keizergracht and Prinsengracht laid out in 1610. In that first phase houses between the two streets lay back to back, separated only by gardens. In the second phase, a smaller street, Kerkstraat, was insinuated between them. At least some of the buildings on Kerkstraat served as mews for houses on Keizergracht. This can be seen in Jacob Bosch's 1660 map of Amsterdam where about eleven houses in two blocks in Keizergracht between Leydsegracht and Spiegelstraat are shown in common ownership with low buildings without gables, apparently mews, in Kerkstraat.[72]

During the 1640s the Dutch classicist movement spread beyond the country's aristocratic elite to its richer citizens and then became standard among ordinary burghers' houses. The pilastered temple front was applied

70 Jacob van Campen, Amsterdam Town Hall, 1648.

to a town house by Vingboons at Klonviersburgwal 95 in Amsterdam of 1642, in the same year that Post applied it to the villa at Vredenburg (see Fig. 65). In cities such as Amsterdam, however, the belief that architectural ornament should be governed by the rules of propriety, and in particular by social status—evident in The Hague in the carefully graduated ornamentation of the Huygenshuis, the Mauritshuis and the Noordeinde Palace—had little appeal. Where status was based on wealth not birth, clients sought the maximum impact they could afford with their buildings, which explains why pilasters and pediments proved popular and widespread. The most extreme expression of this was the Trippenhuis at Kloveniersburgwal 29 in Amsterdam, built for the immensely rich Tripp brothers by Justus Vingboons in 1660. Despite being the wealthiest merchants in Amsterdam, the brothers, considered to be *nouveaux riches* from Dordrecht, were not allowed to take part in city government. The house, built of stone with a lavish seven-bay, four-storey façade with giant Corinthian pilasters and elaborately ornamented frieze—it was even originally intended to have a cupola—was their response, almost a rival town hall.

By 1648 the new classicist architecture was so firmly established in the Dutch Republic that Philips Vingboons could proudly declare that 'the love of architecture following the proportions and rules of Antiquity has so increased here that it is miraculous that so many excellent works have been constructed in such a short time'.[73] The final seal of approval for the new style came the same year when the city of Amsterdam commissioned a new town hall from van Campen to commemorate the Treaty of Westphalia, which brought an end to the Eighty Years War with Spain and guaranteed the independence of the Netherlands (Fig. 70).[74] It was conceived on a scale to rival the town halls of Antwerp, Nuremberg and Augsburg, or indeed a royal palace, and, appropriately, the pediment supports the figure of Peace.

The town hall brought together all the different functions of the municipality in one giant structure, a concept that answers Vitruvius's description of the Roman forum in which the senate, court-house, mint,

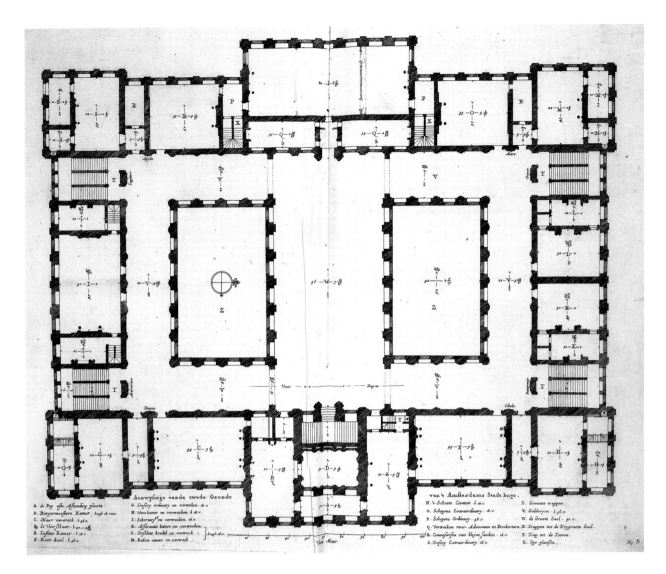

71   Jacob Vennekool, engraving of 1661 of the plan of the principal floor of Amsterdam Town Hall by Jacob van Campen, 1648, pl. B (British Library).

prison and other administrative bodies were housed on a single square.[75] Like at least two of the unsuccessful designs, its plan owed much to Scamozzi's House of the Roman Senators, from which van Campen took the basic form of a large central hall flanked by two court-yards, the dimensions of the hall following Vitruvius's prescription for the ideal basilica (Fig. 71 and see Fig. 26). This was a palace of the people, a reminder of where power really lay in the Dutch Republic. The overtly Roman derivation was particularly appropriate in a city that wished to present itself as a new Rome, where the mayors were referred to as 'consuls' and city councillors as 'senators'. There is also a deeper, religious symbolism to the town hall.

The building is crowned by a dominant, arcaded cupola with Corinthian columns, a motif taken from the iconographer Ripa for whom it symbolised Faith. Here it declares the City of Amsterdam to be the podium for the True Religion. The same motif can be found in the murals celebrating the life of Prince Frederik Hendrik at the Huis ten Bosch.[76] Beside it, barely visible behind the outstretched arm of Mercury, appears the Temple of Solomon in a guise that differs from the town hall only in the number of bays and the addition of corner turrets. It has been suggested that the town hall, like those of Nuremberg and Augsburg, should also be read as an interpretation of the Temple of Solomon. Support for this belief comes from the fact that early prints show that

65

72   Jacob van Campen, Renswoude church, 1639.

the superimposed pilasters on the façade were initially intended to be Corinthian (as the proportions of the lower order confirm), not Composite and Corinthian as executed.[77] The superimposed Corinthian order is a key feature of Villalpando's reconstruction of the Temple of Solomon.[78] The form of the imposing central hall with its round-headed clerestory windows may be inspired by François Vatable's reconstruction of the temple.[79] Other references to Solomon occur throughout the building. The virgin representing Amsterdam in the tympanum on the main façade is shown sitting on two lions, a reference to Solomon's throne placed on two lions; a representation of the Judgement of Solomon dominates the Tribunal, the symbolic heart of the building where the death penalty was pronounced; and a painting of Solomon praying for Wisdom looks down over the council chamber. The reference to the Temple of Solomon also probably explains why the town hall is placed east–west, ignoring the street pattern, and why, though still unfinished, the town hall was inaugurated after seven years – the Temple of Solomon took seven years to build.

Fascination with the form and symbolism of the Temple of Solomon was widespread in seventeenth-century Amsterdam. Juan Bautista Villalpando's influential reconstruction, *In Ezechielem Explanationes et Apparatus Urbis ac Templi Hierosolymitani, commentariis et imaginibus illustratus*, published in 1596 and 1605, was well known and van Campen had already used Villalpando's base with its curving buttresses as the model for the churches he built at Renswoude and Hoge Zwaluwe in 1639 (Fig. 72 and see Fig. 39).[80] The same feature was repeated at Daniel Stalpaert's Oosterkerk in Amsterdam in 1669 and, particularly appropriately, at the Portuguese Synagogue in Amsterdam, built by Elias Bouman in 1675.[81]

The economic prosperity of the Dutch Republic in the middle decades of the seventeenth century thus led to a burst of architectural activity across every building type, from royal palaces and town halls, through churches and public buildings to town houses, suburban villas and country houses. It was this that allowed the new classicist movement to spread so quickly. Conditions were far different in the Southern Netherlands. Here Rubens and others had hoped that a definitive peace settlement in the Netherlands would lead to the re-opening of the River Scheldt and the revived prosperity of his native Antwerp, formerly the great commercial centre of northern Europe. It was in anticipation of this that he had brought together illustrations of the palaces of Genoa as models for the improvement of Antwerp's town houses. However, the publication of the *Palazzi di Genova* came in 1622, the year the Twelve Year Truce of 1609–21 ended. Despite Rubens's attempts as a diplomat working for the Archduchess Isabella to extend the truce, war broke out and continued for another twenty-seven years. Antwerp, cut off from the sea, never recovered its prosperity and the revival of private building activity Rubens had anticipated never happened.[82] The same was true across the Southern Netherlands, where relative economic and demographic recession meant there was little demand for civic and commercial buildings or country houses. By contrast, the ecclesiastical reforms of the Counter-Reformation stimulated the renovation and building of countless new churches, largely driven by architects and clergymen who were more interested in the latest developments in Rome.[83] Thus the Southern and Northern Netherlands moved in different architectural directions.

Not all of these churches looked to Rome. In Antwerp, a city whose close commercial links with London were reinforced by the strong cultural connections with

73   W. von Ehrenburg, interior of S. Carlo Borromeo, Antwerp, by François d'Aguilon and Pierre Huyssens, 1615–21 (Musée des Beaux-Arts, Brussels).

the court of Charles I through Rubens and Anthony van Dyck, a different approach was taken at the Church of S. Carlo Borromeo. This was a church with which Rubens was closely connected and, though often perceived as the epitome of the Baroque painter, he should not be thought to have seen his work as antithetical to the pre-eminence of Antiquity.[84] He had left Antwerp for Italy in 1600 'in order to study at close quarters the works of the ancient and modern masters and to improve himself by their example in painting'.[85] Several years were spent in Rome where he studied antique remains closely, often subsequently incorporating them into his paintings.[86] Rubens's reverence for the antique is also clear from his preface to the *Palazzi di Genova*. 'We see that style of architecture called barbaric or Gothic is gradually waning and disappearing in these parts; and that a few admirable minds are introducing *the true sym-*

metry of that other style which follows the rules of the ancient Greeks and Romans [my italics], to the great splendour and adornment of our country; as may be seen in the famous temples recently erected by the venerable Society of Jesus in the cities of Brussels and Antwerp.'[87] The Jesuit church in Antwerp is that of S. Carlo Borromeo (Fig. 73).[88] Though at first sight it could hardly be more different, it has interesting parallels with Jones's St Paul's, Covent Garden.

Antwerp had been the centre of Vitruvian studies in the Netherlands ever since publications by Pieter Coecke van Aelst in 1539 and Hans Vredeman de Vries in 1577. Wenzel Coebergher (about 1561–1634), the architect to the archducal court in Brussels, had spent more than twenty years in Rome and had studied Vitruvius and the Italian theoreticians thoroughly. At the beginning of the seventeenth century he was preparing a manuscript with corrections of the treatises by Palladio, Serlio and Vignola in accordance with Vitruvius's directions.[89] It is not surprising that one of the most convincing attempts at Vitruvian reconstruction should have occurred in Antwerp.

Preliminary designs for the Church of S. Carlo Borromeo were drawn up in 1613, work started in 1615 and the building was completed in 1621. The intellectual concept behind the design was probably the work of the Jesuit rector of the college, François d'Aguilon (1566–1617), a distinguished mathematician and physicist, whose 1613 treatise on optics was illustrated with engravings by Rubens. He was also an authority on the scientific approach to architecture set out by Vitruvius and his followers. [90]

D'Aguilon was assisted by another Jesuit, Pierre Huyssens (1577–1637), who had already designed a church for the order at Maastricht but, as none of his other buildings repeats the idiosyncratic programme found at S. Carlo Borromeo, he should probably be seen as the executant architect brought in to make d'Aguilon's scheme practical. D'Aguilon certainly produced a series of ideas before Huyssens became involved. If this is the case then his essentially amateur status helps explain the originality of S. Carlo Borromeo when compared with other contemporary churches in the Southern Netherlands.[91]

S. Carlo Borromeo is astonishingly opulent. The façade, of two different stones, is richly ornamented with elaborate window surrounds, numerous pilasters and columns, full Doric, Ionic and Composite entablatures and elaborate sculptural decoration culminating in a relief of the Virgin in the tympanum. The interior was no less lavish (it was rebuilt after a fire in 1718) with marble colonnades supporting high colonnaded galleries, sumptuous plasterwork and a gilt-coffered barrel-vaulted and part-coffered roof. The whole was set off by the elaborate altar and numerous paintings by Rubens. The expense was enormous and the Antwerp Jesuits found themselves severely censured by their superiors. Huyssens was even forbidden to continue with the practice of architecture.[92]

It is perhaps the richness of S. Carlo Borromeo's decoration that causes it to be conventionally described as Baroque but what stood out to contemporaries was its respect for Antiquity. In words that echoed those of Rubens, Godfrey Henschen noted that 'The Society of Jesus has at Antwerp . . . a magnificent temple constructed of Ligurian marble. The form of this temple was designed according to the rules of Vitruvius (in contrast

to what is commonly done in this country where Gothic structures are preferred).'[93]

The reference to Vitruvius is probably specific. What sets S. Carlo Borromeo apart from contemporary or earlier churches is its distinctive use of galleries. Such galleries are one of the most distinctive features of Vitruvius's description of his basilica at Fano and it is as a reconstruction of this that S. Carlo Borromeo should probably be seen.

Intriguingly, the S. Carlo Borromeo church (1615–21) and the Augsburg Rathaus (1615–20) are almost exact contemporaries and reveal strong parallels, in particular the use of a pedimented, voluted giant gable flanked by set-back octagonal staircase towers. Such towers (which are clearly distinct from the west-front towers of churches such as the cathedral at Salzburg) are extremely uncommon. As there seems to be no obvious precedent in either German or Netherlandish architecture it is tempting to associate them with the octagonal Temple of the Winds at Athens, which was described by Vitruvius and illustrated by Fra Giacondo and Cesariano.[94]

S. Carlo Borromeo should thus be read as a fundamentally neo-classical building but one heavily laden with ornament for reasons of propriety. The mistake easily made at S. Carlo Borromeo is to take the agenda of later neo-classicists and assume that only austere, severely restrained art and architecture could be inspired by Antiquity. S. Carlo Borromeo, intended as a triumphant Counter-Reformation statement in a city that had once been a hotbed of Protestantism, was a building that merited – in d'Aguilon's mind at least – the most elaborate treatment money could buy. That was in no way seen as contrary to the spirit of Antiquity.

Despite the deliberate reference to the basilica at Fano, d'Aguilon was not simply motivated by a desire to reconstruct an ancient Roman basilica. He would certainly have been aware of Roman Catholic thinking about the Early Christian church, including Cardinal Borromeo's writings, and his church should be seen as an attempt to recapture the spirit of the churches of the early Christians. It is perhaps no coincidence that S. Carlo Borromeo bears marked similarities to the early Christian Church of S. Agnese in Rome.[95] For architects and churchmen in the sixteenth and seventeenth centuries there was nothing inherently pagan about classical architecture, as can be seen from the way the Temple of Solomon was presented as the origins of classicism. They must also have been aware that the ancient basilicas in Rome presented the best explanation of what Early Christian churches had been like.

Inigo Jones certainly knew of S. Carlo Borromeo, which was much celebrated. When the Countess of Arundel, wife of one of his principal patrons, visited Antwerp in the summer of 1620 she sent word that she had seen the church and found it a 'marvellous thing'.[96] No doubt she described it to Jones on her return. Given his involvement with Rubens, who spent eight months at the court of Charles I in 1629–30, just as he was designing St Paul's church, Covent Garden, Jones would almost certainly have been aware of the Vitruvian thinking that lay behind S. Carlo Borromeo. The results may look different but the thinking behind the two churches, both attempts to find an appropriate manner in which to build a contemporary church, one Roman Catholic, one Protestant, grounded in Antiquity and the Early Church, is surprisingly similar.

74   Inigo Jones, *Self-portrait*, c.1620 (RIBA Library Drawings Collection).

Chapter 6

JONES, SERLIO AND THE ASTYLAR MANNER

INIGO JONES'S VISIT TO ITALY LEFT HIM in the perfect position to succeed Simon Basil as Surveyor of the King's Works on Basil's death in September 1615. Thereafter he remained at the heart of English architecture until the outbreak of the Civil War in 1642, and continued to design until shortly before his death in 1652. However, tracing the course of his architectural career is frustrating because much of his work has been lost, generally unrecorded. Only six buildings by him or commonly attributed to him survive: the Banqueting House at Whitehall; the Queen's Chapel at St James's Palace; Chevening House, Kent (much altered); the pavilions at Stoke Park, Northamptonshire; St Paul's church, Covent Garden (rebuilt closely following Jones's designs after a fire in 1795); and the Queen's House at Greenwich.[1] For much of his work only the records of the Office of Works and a selection, inevitably random, of his and John Webb's drawings survive. Nothing of substance remains of his extensive work at Newmarket, including the Prince's Lodging, his first important completed building, and the hunting lodges at Bagshot Park and Hyde Park have disappeared without known visual record. His great portico at St Paul's cathedral did not long outlive him. Of the numerous gates he designed only that for Lord Cranfield at Beaufort House, subsequently moved to Chiswick House, survives (Fig. 75). Interiors formed a substantial part of Jones's career and one might have a different impression of him had more survived: his work for Queen Henrietta Maria at Somerset House, Oatlands Palace and Wimbledon House has all gone, as have interiors such as those of the House of Lords and the Sculpture Gallery at St James's Palace and work for the Duke of Buckingham at Whitehall Palace and New Hall, Essex. Except for views of the House of Lords (Fig. 76) and a handful of drawings, mainly for chimneypieces, little is known of what they were like.

Given this pattern of partial survival, it is not surprising that analysis of Inigo Jones's architectural language has tended to focus on his grander and better documented buildings, the Banqueting House, the Queen's House at Greenwich, the Queen's Chapel, St Paul's, Covent Garden, St Paul's cathedral and the unexecuted designs for Whitehall Palace and Somerset House. However, the focus placed on them has distorted understanding of Jones's work (and thus his place in both English and European architecture), presenting it as more exclusive than it really was. A full appreciation of Jones's architectural language needs to start from the understanding that it traverses the spectrum of building types, from simple office buildings to the grandest palace and that each had its place in the hierarchy of design.

75   Inigo Jones, the Beaufort House gate, now at Chiswick House, London, 1621.

76 Peter Tillemans, *Queen Anne in the House of Lords* (*c*.1708–14), showing Inigo Jones's coffered ceiling of 1623–4.

Jones's architecture was not based simply on the use of the orders but on the graduated application of classical ornament to buildings whose essential design is based on symmetry and order. The degree of ornament was dependent on the particular purpose of the specific building, that is, on the fundamental classical belief in propriety or decorum.[2] As Jones wrote on 20 January 1614, soon after his return from Italy: 'In all inventions of capricious ornaments, one must first design the ground, of the thing plain, as it is for use, and on that vary it, adorn it, compose it with decorum according to the use and the order it is of.'[3] Or as Henry Wotton put it in *The Elements of Architecture* in 1624: 'Decor is the keeping of a due Respect betweene the Inhabitant, and the Habitation.'[4]

Thus domestic buildings and service buildings such as stables and offices required little if any decoration. For the private suburban retreat or a parish church, like the Queen's House at Greenwich and St Paul's, Covent Garden, the orders are evident but their use restrained

or the simpler orders chosen. For grand public buildings, a royal palace or a great cathedral, the full panoply of the orders was appropriate. All these buildings lie in a consistent aesthetic framework.

Failure to appreciate this, and the consequent narrow interpretation of Jones, is part of the reason why he has traditionally been presented as such an isolated figure in English and European architecture. It also explains much of the confusion over his role as a 'Palladian' architect for, in focussing on only one aspect of Jones's work, the sources on which he drew have been made to appear narrower than they were in reality. The role of Serlio in Jones's architecture, for instance, has been consistently downplayed in favour of an assumed overwhelming reliance on Palladio. This confusion has led to such constructs as Sir John Summerson's 'Artisan Mannerism' – essentially a rag-bag of everything classical in the early Stuart period other than Jones's grander buildings – and 'Puritan Minimalism', the belief that the astylar architecture that emerged in the middle years of the seventeenth century should be read as a deliberate, politically inspired, reaction to Jones's elaborate, court-based, classicism, instead of being an integral part of Jones's own architecture from his earliest years as Surveyor. Concentration on the 'Palladian' aspect of Jones's work has also led to unnecessary agonising over whether a building as apparently 'un-Palladian' as Chevening House, Kent, could be by Jones.[5]

The belief in propriety or decorum, the idea that architecture was essentially hierarchic and that buildings should reflect the appropriate place in the social hierarchy of their owner, or the significance of their function, through their degree of elaboration both in form and ornament, was a fundamental part of the High Renaissance classical tradition. In this the Vitruvian notion of decorum, which argued that the different orders represented a range of human characteristics, from masculine Doric to maidenly Corinthian, and that different orders on temples were thus appropriate to represent different gods, was a key influence. In his fourth book, which sets out the general rules of architecture, Serlio starts his account by observing how the ancients exercised decorum by matching the orders of the temples with the natures of the gods to whom they were dedicated: robust Doric work for Jupiter, Mars and Hercules; Ionic, mixed delicate and robust, for Diana, Apollo and Bacchus; Corinthian for the goddess of virgins, Vesta. He suggests a comparable approach for the architecture of his own day: 'in these modern times it seems to me that the procedure should be different, but not too far

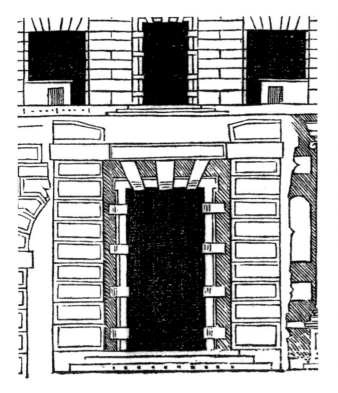

from the ancients. What I mean is that, following our Christian customs, I would (as far as I could) dedicate sacred buildings, according to their types, to God and to His Saints, and I would give secular buildings, both public and private, to men according to their rank and professions.'[6]

It is known that Jones studied Serlio carefully. He owned at least three editions of Serlio's work – the 1560–62 edition with books one to four and part of book five, now at Queen's College, Oxford; the 1601 edition with seven books, now owned by the Canadian Center for Architecture in Montreal; and the 1619 edition, with seven books, now in the RIBA, London. The first two, bought before 1613, were extensively annotated by Jones, the third by John Webb who subsequently owned it.[7] Serlio was a major source for Jones's designs for masques, gateways and window details – one surviving Jones drawing dated April 1618 is for a window adapted from Serlio's seventh book (Figs 77 and 78) – and, certainly in the case of Maltravers House, for whole buildings.[8]

77 (*above*)　Sebastiano Serlio, detail of an entrance to a palace, from *Tutte l'opere d'architettura et prospetiva* (1619) VII, p. 63.

78 (*below*)　Inigo Jones, study of a voussoired window after Serlio, 1618 (RIBA Library Drawings Collection).

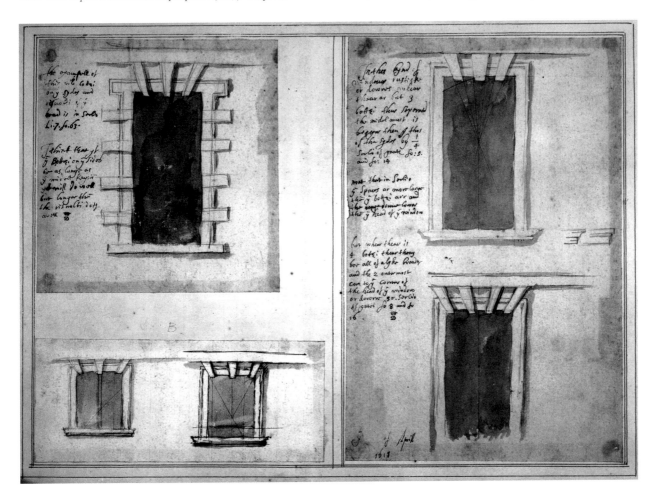

79   Inigo Jones, design for a riding house, possibly for Syon House, Middlesex, early 1620s (Worcester College, Oxford).

Equally important was Aristotle, whose *Nicomachean Ethics* had discussed the required exhibition of 'magnificence' by the rich and powerful, providing a moral basis for architectural display. This argument was perhaps most succinctly set out in text and images by Serlio in his sixth book of architecture, 'On Habitations'. 'In the beginning men made their habitations for their commodity without any decorum whatsoever. . . . gradually with more experience and greater skill they began to augment their habitations, giving them a degree of ornamentation. And, depending on the region, they made use of the material which they found most suitable, with the result that with the passing of the years men of better judgement began to harmonise commodity with decorum, particularly in more civilised places. I intend to discuss this unification of decorum and commodity in this my sixth book, beginning with the meanest hovel of a poor peasant, rising step by step up to the house of a Prince.'[9] This he duly does, first in the countryside and then in the city: from the 'habitations of the poorest men in cities . . . far from the piazzas and noble places', to the 'craftsmen who are comfortably wealthy', the 'merchants' houses', the 'rich citizen's house', the 'noble gentleman's house', the 'condotierro's house', the 'palace of the Praetor', the 'palace of the governor' and finally to the 'palace of the exceedingly illustrious prince'.[10] At each stage the building becomes more elaborate and more richly ornamented.

For Serlio this was the essence of good architecture: 'as regards the laying-out of a well-conceived and proportioned building with the commodity in harmony with the decorum, all those who have not studied worthy architecture over many years and who are unable to draw, that is to design, should give way to those who can provide a good account of these matters. But O God in heaven, how many there are who put on the mantle of this beautiful and noble art but who in this respect are blinder than moles!'[11] Though Serlio's sixth book was never published the ideas in it pervade his other books and proved influential on other architects. Pierre Le Muet, whose *Manière de bien bastir* of 1623 follows a similar pattern of growing elaboration based on decorum, may have consulted the sixth book in manuscript, which seems to have served as his inspiration.[12]

To appreciate the practical implications of Jones's belief in decorum it is necessary to examine not just Jones's grandest buildings but also his simpler buildings, offices, stables and houses, where growing elaboration can be identified as their status rises, an elaboration that culminated in Jones's palace designs.

One of Jones's earliest recorded buildings was the Clerk of Works Office at Newmarket, built in 1619–20. Though since demolished, its appearance was recorded in a drawing by John Webb.[13] This was a building of the utmost simplicity, only two bays wide and two storeys high, but its simplicity belies its significance. It was care-

Adam A Bierling delin: Wenslar fecit, 1646

80   Wenceslaus Hollar, *The Courtyard of Arundel House, London*, showing the stables probably built by Inigo Jones, *c.*1618 (British Museum).

fully designed to be symmetrical round a central door and dormer window, with a discreet note of distinction evident in the eared architraves of the door and ground-floor windows and in the use of a platband (or string-course) dividing ground and first floors. This was, after all, the Newmarket base of the King's Works.

The significance of this building lies in the fact that it represents an approach to design that, as already seen in chapters 2 and 4, had been commonplace in Italy since late in the fifteenth century and in France since the mid-sixteenth century but had yet to establish itself in England: the plain, symmetrically designed building, with evenly spaced vertical rectangular windows, the door commonly placed in the centre, and the gable of the roof running parallel to the street, often expressed as a hipped roof, and not, as had been traditional, with the gable facing the street elevation. This shortly became the fundamental building block of English architecture for more than two centuries, forming the basis of a style of architecture that has come to be known as Georgian but whose origins in England lie in the second decade of the seventeenth century.

The Clerk of Works Office is particularly significant because it is the sort of structure that (unlike grander buildings) is seldom recorded and unlikely to survive. To it can be added at least one, probably two, stables by Jones. Equestrian buildings played a large part in Jones's early career because seventeenth-century stables were

often buildings of display, the setting for one of the elite's most prestigious possessions, the horse, to whose design considerable architectural energy was devoted.[14] As well as the possibility, discussed in chapter 1, that Jones was involved in the stables at Theobalds of 1609 and designed a riding house and stables for Lord Cranborne in 1612, he built stables and a riding house for James I at New-market in 1615–17, together with more stables in the same town for Sir Thomas Compton and Mr Dupper, and designed a stable for camels at Theobalds in 1622–3.[15] Apart from the Cranborne design, and a similar design for another riding house and stable dated by Gordon Higgott to about 1620, which may have been intended for Lord Percy at Syon House, Middlesex (Fig. 79),[16] no visual record of these buildings survives but they probably took a similar form to the Clerk of Works building. This was certainly the case with the stables at Arundel House on the Strand in London.

Two evocative engravings by Wenceslaus Hollar show the outer court of Arundel House, the London home of Jones's key early patron the Earl of Arundel (Fig. 80).[17] The yard, busy with people, horses and coaches, is com-posed of timber-framed buildings, except along its east side. In marked contrast is a six-bay brick or stone range that stands out for its up-to-date architectural language: ordered, astylar, two storeys with platband, vertical rec-tangular windows, a modillion cornice, a roofline paral-lel to the front elevation and dormer windows. This is

the same language as the Clerk of Works building at Newmarket. That it was the stable is shown by the large gaggle of horses gathered before it and the coach houses beside it. Both engravings show that the range was unfinished, suggesting that it was only the first stage in an intended complete rebuilding of the entrance court-yard.

There is no reason to believe that these stables were not part of Jones's remodelling of Arundel House around 1618 in which he also designed an 'Italian' gate, built that year (see Fig. 110) and is generally credited with work on the gallery wing known from Cornelius Bol's *View of the Thames with Arundel House* (about 1640) and Hollar's bird's-eye view of London.[18] Comparison with the Clerk

of Works's building at Newmarket shows that a date of about 1618 is plausible for the stables. If so, they are the first accurately recorded examples of the new astylar classical language in its context.

A second stable can plausibly be attributed to Jones. This was for another major early patron, George Villiers, favourite of James I and Charles I and created first Marquess in 1618 and then Duke in 1623 of Buckingham. Buckingham, a keen horseman, employed Jones on his lodgings at Whitehall in 1619–20 and at New Hall, Essex in 1622–3.[19] Subsequently he used Sir Balthazar Gerbier at both York House and New Hall in 1624–5. (Jones is sometimes cited as the architect of the Watergate at York House in 1626 but the attribution is uncertain and it could well have been the work of Nicholas Stone.[20])

In 1621 Buckingham bought Burley-on-the-Hill, Rutland, which he used principally during the hunting season, entertaining the king there that year. Nothing is known of the house, which he much improved, as it was destroyed by fire during the Civil War but what survives, though altered after another fire in 1705, is the impressive stable range. Thomas Fuller, writing in his *History of the Worthies of England* of 1662, described these as one of Buckingham's particular achievements and as superior to any other stable in the country: 'where the horses (if their pabulum so plenty as their stabulum stately) were the best accommodated in England'.[21] No documentary evidence survives to date the stables, which a survey by parliamentary commissioners shows held forty horses, but they must have been built before Buckingham's murder in 1628. Given that Burley-on-the-Hill func-tioned essentially as a grand hunting lodge, they were probably built immediately after Buckingham acquired the property in 1621.[22]

The original appearance of the stables is known from a copy of a survey of the park, perhaps made in 1689 or 1690. This shows a two-storey astylar building with ver-tical rectangular windows, platband, unbroken roofline and curved 'Dutch' gables (probably removed after the fire) over slightly projecting wings.[23] Though the windows are deeper it is in essence an extended version of the Clerk of Works building at Newmarket, with added gables. These can be compared to that on Inigo Jones's design believed to be for Brooke House in London of about 1617 (Fig. 81)[24] and to those on Palla-dio's Villa Barbaro at Maser, where they are also used to emphasise the ends of single-storey office ranges. Similar gables could be found on Sir Roger Townshend's Raynham Hall, Norfolk, a composite of fashionable con-temporary stylistic motifs, designed in about 1622.[25]

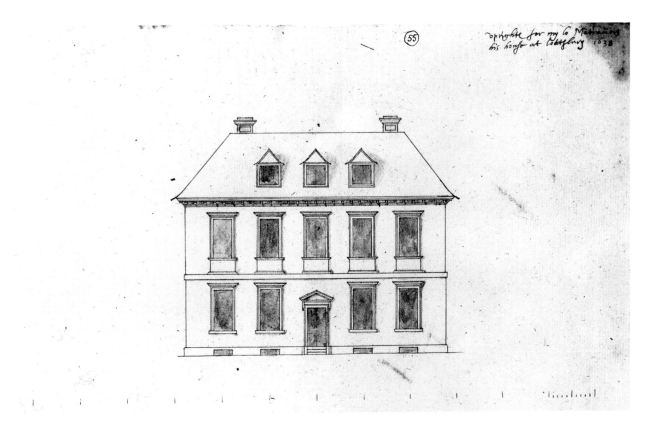

82   Inigo Jones, design for Maltravers House, Lothbury, London, 1638 (Worcester College).

83   Inigo Jones, design, perhaps for tenements, believed to be for Maltravers House, Lothbury, London, c.1638 (Worcester College, Oxford).

There is no documentation for the stables at Burley-on-the-Hill but the innovative quality of the design, the specific reference to Palladio, the parallels with the Clerk of Works Office and the Brooke House drawing, coupled with Buckingham's position as royal favourite known to have employed Jones in 1619–23, make Jones the most obvious candidate for its design.

No subsequent designs by Jones for stables are known but a number of designs for houses developed the same essential idea of an astylar building with vertical rectangular windows, platband, roofline parallel to the façade and dormer windows. The best documented of such designs by Jones is his drawing for a house for Lord Maltravers at Lothbury, London, which is not only in his hand but dated, 1638 (Fig. 82). This remains a somewhat mysterious design, particularly given the traditional association with it of a drawing made to the same scale on identical paper and to a similar design. This is for a 152ft-long, thirteen-bay building whose limited number of doors has led to suggestions that it could have had a commercial use, although tenements are perhaps a more plausible suggestion (Fig. 83).[26] Since Lothbury House was destroyed in the Great Fire of London in 1666 and no further visual or written documentation survives, there is no evidence to show whether Jones's designs were built.

As at the Arundel House stables, Jones uses a simpler modillion cornice, though the greater dignity of a house over a stable is expressed in the use of aprons below the first-floor windows and the pediment over the doorcase. Yet, though the Maltravers design has the advantage of being dated and definitely by Jones, there is no evidence that it was built and as it comes relatively late in the 1630s it is of little value in demonstrating Jones's influence on the spread of astylar architecture during that decade. Three other houses by Jones make the point more clearly.

Chevening House, Kent, is one of those attributions to Jones that, though longstanding, has always been found problematic, principally because the house does not fit preconceptions of what a 'Palladian' architect like Inigo Jones should have designed. Documentary evidence for Jones's authorship is loose as the first attribution comes from Colen Campbell in the second volume of *Vitruvius Britannicus* of 1717 where the building 'is said to be designed by *Inigo Jones*'.[27] A family history written by Thomas, seventeenth Lord Dacre (1717–1786), noted that 'Richard [thirteenth] Lord Dacre . . . rebuilt his house at Chevening Upon a plan of Inigo Jones, as 'tis said; and it really seems to be so, being Built in a good

Taste; see a View of it in Campbell's *Vitruvius Britanicus*'. Lord Dacre cannot be relied on for the attribution to Jones because he may have taken it from Campbell, but his statement that the house was built by the thirteenth lord is particularly valuable. As Avray Tipping noted, the only alternative builder is the Earl of Sussex (grandson of the thirteenth baron, inherited 1662) who can be discounted by the fact that his daughter, mother of the compiler of the family history, was still alive when he was writing and would no doubt have corrected him had he been wrong.[28]

Attributions to Jones by Campbell have to be taken sceptically as Campbell was keen to boost the stock of buildings believed to be by him. Other buildings that he attributes to Jones in volume two of *Vitruvius Britannicus*, the Whitehall Palace designs and the design for the York Watergate, as well as the Loggio, grotto, stables and Great Gates at Wilton, are now known or, in the case of the Watergate, generally believed, not to be by Jones. On the other hand, Chevening is neither a prominent building nor does it have a particularly Jonesian look about it—unlike the other misattributions in volume two—so the attribution to Jones is not one that Campbell would automatically make. Campbell's note of doubt—'is said to be designed by *Inigo Jones*'—could well have arisen from the fact that Chevening did not fit his preconceptions of a Jonesian building (as was later the case with many twentieth-century scholars). If so, that perhaps makes its inclusion more plausible. A possible connection to Jones comes through Lord Dacre's brother-in-law, Thomas Wotton (later second Lord Wotton of Marley), whose uncle was the keen architectural enthusiast Sir Henry Wotton who knew Jones well and was probably the source of some of his drawings by Palladio. Sir Henry, who as noted earlier was ambassador to Venice, was in England in 1615–16 and 1619–21 and finally returned from Italy in 1624.[29]

Lord Dacre (1596–1630), the builder of Chevening, succeeded to the estate in 1616. The house must have been built by his death in 1630 but it is not certain when it was begun. The most probable date is relatively soon after Dacre succeeded. He came of age and married in 1617, a plausible stimulus for a new house, while the general paucity of building work during the economically difficult years of the Franco-Spanish war from 1624 to 1630 makes it unlikely that construction would have been begun in those years.

Chevening was engraved by Campbell but, like many of his engravings, the result was 'improved' to fit his eighteenth-century sensibilities.[30] The best source for the

84 Detail of an estate map of 1679 showing Chevening House, Kent, by Inigo Jones, before 1630 (*Country Life*).

appearance of the house is an estate map of 1679 (Fig. 84), whose detail has been helpfully appended by Andor Gomme to Campbell's engraving to give a more accurate rendition of what the house would have looked like.[31] The house was seven bays wide and two and a half storeys high over a raised basement. It was astylar, with quoins, platbands between each floor, a pedimented front door, vertical rectangular windows, a block cornice, hipped roof, dormer windows and balustraded viewing platform on the roof. Despite the addition of the basement, the pedimented front door, the quoins, the extra attic floor and the slightly grander cornice, the result is clearly of the same family as the Clerk of Works building, the Arundel House stables and the Burley-on-the-Hill stables but taken up perhaps two degrees in scale and decoration as befitted the seat of a peer.

In his article on Chevening, Gomme, drawing partly on Gordon Higgott, notes the various elements that point to Jones as the architect. Jones used a similar cornice, which appears to be a reworking of that on the Colosseum, on the Queen's Chapel at St James's (1623–5), the Somerset House Chapel (1630–35) and St Paul's cathedral (1634–42). He particularly notes the value of such cornices, which appear to be unique to Jones before 1630, when 'far off the eye'. Lugged window architraves are distinctive in Jones (for instance, at the Queen's House) and the door surround appears to show what Jones called *pilastrelli*, fillets duplicating the verticals of the architrave, as in the penultimate design for the

Banqueting House and the elevation of the west front of St Paul's cathedral. The great stair was of stone, which fits Jones's practice but was otherwise unusual in the 1620s. Finally, the plan of the house can be seen as Palladian in inspiration.[32]

If confirmation is needed that Chevening is a plausible attribution to Jones then it comes from Killigrew House in Blackfriars, City of London. This is recorded in two drawings by John Webb, a plan and an elevation, the elevation inscribed 'Sr Peter Killigrew in ye Blackfryers Mr Surveyors Desygne' (Fig. 85).[33] Killigrew House can be read as a condensed version of Chevening. Both houses are compact, palazzo-like blocks, with vertical rectangular windows on the first floor, half-height attic windows, hipped roof, quoins and platbands. The principal difference between the two is that at Killigrew House the raised basement has been eliminated and the full-height ground floor replaced by a rustic, making the house a slightly curious mix of villa and palazzo. The details of Killigrew House are slightly more elaborate: the keystoned window surrounds of the rustic and the round-headed, rusticated front door, a second platband below the first-floor window, a more emphatic, almost cornice-like platband below the second-floor windows and the coved entablature supporting the roof.

Except for Webb's two drawings nothing is known of Killigrew House, which would have been a large and

85 John Webb (?1640s) after Inigo Jones, design for Sir Peter Killigrew's house, Blackfriars, London, *c*.1630 (Worcester College, Oxford).

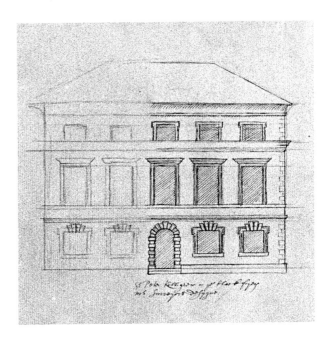

86 Unknown French painter, *Covent Garden, London, c.*1640 (private collection).

innovative design for the City of London. It is not even certain that it was built or, if it was built, when. Sir Peter Killigrew (about 1593–1667) was a loyal royalist who accompanied Charles I on his unsuccessful trip to Spain to woo the Infanta in 1623.[34] One possible date for the house would be about 1633, when Killigrew succeeded his brother to the family estates. However, Jones is unlikely to have taken on such a small commission in the year he turned down the Earl of Pembroke's much more tempting offer to rebuild Wilton House.[35] A more plausible date is the mid-1620s after Killigrew's return from Spain in 1623. Summerson suggested that the stimulus was the knighthood and pension he received soon after Charles I's accession in 1625.[36] An early date would fit Jones's design for what is believed to be Brooke House, which has been dated to about 1617 (see Fig. 81).[37] When the dominant scrolled gable is removed, the essential design is that of Killigrew House: five bays, two and a half storeys with the attic floor over a prominent cornice. The differences lie in relatively minor details such as the length of the ground-floor windows, the treatment of the door and central first-floor window and the addition of aprons.

The difficulty with Brooke House, Maltravers House and Killigrew House is that the first two were probably never more than designs and there is no proof that the third was ever built. The pair of houses of about 1631

flanking St Paul's, Covent Garden, known from Hollar's engraving and an anonymous painting of about 1640 by a French artist, are on firmer ground (Fig. 86).[38] The west elevation of the Piazza at Covent Garden is such a careful composition, with the church flanked by a pair of elaborate, rusticated, clearly Jonesian, gateways and then by the pair of houses, that it must in its entirety be by Jones. Two and a half storeys high, three bays wide, with vertical rectangular windows, a hipped roof and dormers, their essential articulation follows Killigrew House and Brooke House with a relatively low ground floor, prominent piano nobile, emphasised by aprons under the windows, balustrade and architraves over the windows, and relatively small attic windows above. They thus fit a recognisable pattern of Jones's domestic architecture stretching from the Arundel House stables and the Clerk of Works office at Newmarket of about 1618–19 through to Maltravers House of 1638. The other two sides of the Piazza take up the essential form of the two houses, repeating the form of the piano nobile, attic, hipped roof and windows, but with the low ground floor replaced by a tall rusticated arcade and the upper windows framed by Tuscan pilaster strips.

Up to the very end of the 1620s this regular, astylar, hipped-roof manner seems to be associated exclusively with Jones. Thereafter a significant number of examples can be found in the years preceding the Civil War. Some

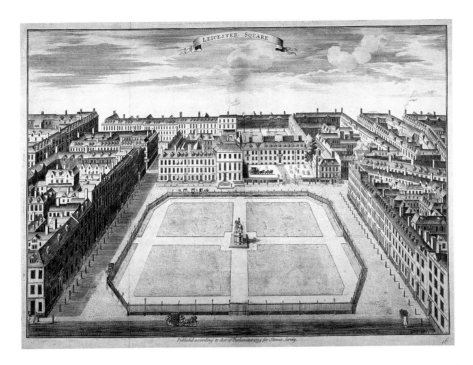

87   Sutton Nichols, engraving of Leicester House, London, 1631, from John Stow, *Survey of London* (1754).

of these are anonymous, like Forty Hall in Enfield, the first firmly dated house known to have been built in the new manner and not associated with Jones. The house, which survives and is dated 1629, was built for Sir Nicholas Raynton, a wealthy haberdasher who was Lord Mayor of London in 1632. Two and a half storeys high, with vertical rectangular windows, modillion cornice and hipped roof, it reads like an ill-digested version of Chevening.[39] Similarly anonymous is Leicester House in Leicester Square, London, for which Robert Sidney, second Earl of Leicester, was granted a licence to build in 1631 – though, given Leicester's status and connections at court (he was employed on embassies to Denmark in 1632 and France in 1636–41), the architect is likely to have been someone associated with Jones. It cost the impressive sum of about £8,000. The first representation is in Sutton Nichols's view of Leicester Square of 1727 but there is no reason to believe this does not show the house of 1631, the pergola over the front door being particularly characteristic of the years before the Civil War (Fig. 87).[40] The house was ten bays wide, with a three-bay wing, two storeys high over a raised basement, with vertical rectangular windows, a hipped roof and dormers. George Vertue's drawing of 1748 provides the useful extra detail that the house had a modillion cornice similar to that in Jones's Maltravers House design.[41]

Where architects are known or plausible attributions can be made, they came from a circle closely connected with Jones. Edward Carter, son of the Chief Clerk of the Office of Works, was the Earl of Bedford's surveyor at Covent Garden. He signed the account for Jones's church there, built in 1631–2, and was Jones's deputy in the great repair of St Paul's cathedral from 1633. A drawing in the Berkshire Record Office by him is inscribed 'Plot for the new building of East Hampstead Lodge, By Mr. Edward Carter' (Fig. 88). It must date from between 1628 when William Trumbull acquired the estate and his death in 1635, though there is no evidence that it was executed.[42] The drawing shows a nine-bay house with symmetrically arranged vertical rectangular windows, architraves over the lower windows, a platband, carefully detailed entablature, hipped roof and dormers. It is slightly crude compared with Jones's work (the junction of the hipped roof and entablature is mishandled) but the overall form and detail is Jonesian in inspiration. Given his involvement with the Earl of Bedford, Carter may also have been responsible for the Evidence House at Bedford House, known from the French view of Covent Garden of about 1640 (see Fig. 86).[43] This shows half of a three-bay, two-storey building with vertical rectangular windows, a balcony for the central first-floor window, the whole elevation capped by a three-bay pediment.

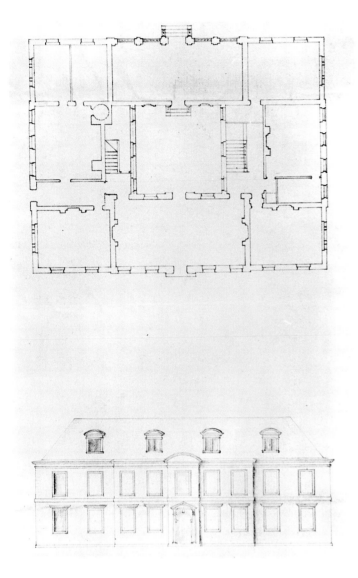

88 (*above*) Edward Carter, 'Plot for the new building of East Hampstead Lodge' (Berkshire Record Office D/ED/P5).

In 1633 St Clere in Kent was completed for Sir John Sedley. This lies only five miles from Chevening and should probably be read as a conscious imitation.[44] The date of 1635 is inscribed on West Woodhay in Berkshire, built for Sir Benjamin Rudyerd. This lies very much within Jones's Maltravers model: two storeys high, with vertical rectangular windows, platband, quoins and hipped roof with windows (Fig. 89).[45] Frustatingly, no architect is known. Nor is any architect known for Aldermaston Court, Berkshire, which was rebuilt in 1843 but is known from an earlier engraving. The house, for Sir Humphrey Forster, a rich, ardent royalist, was apparently built in 1636. It can be read as an extended version of West Woodhay, with a seven-bay centre flanked by two-bay projecting wings, the principal difference being the addition of a modillion cornice.[46] Less expected is the use of Salomonic twisting columns supporting pediments over the two front doors, as used in 1637 by John Jackson in the porch of St Mary's church, Oxford. Though there is no documentary evidence to support such an attribution, the unusual use of the Salomonic order would make Jackson a plausible candidate for the designer of Aldermaston House. Jackson was also responsible for the original entrance front of Welford House, Berkshire, built for Richard Jhones 'to such drafte model manner or forme and direction as John Jackson of the Cittie of Oxon gent has drawn described or set forth', in about 1652. This follows Aldermaston Court in having projecting two-bay wings with modillion cornice, hipped roof and dormers.[47] Welford and Aldermaston lie six and twelve miles respectively from West Woodhay.

At first sight Wilton House, Wiltshire, the great seat of the Earls of Pembroke, might seem out of place in this list of relatively small, restrained houses (Fig. 90). With its imposing central Serlian window, corner towers and balustrade, the house as it survives today seems far different from Chevening, West Woodhay or Aldermaston. None the less, close analysis of the building and the complicated story of its design shows how Wilton sits in the context of Jones's smaller domestic architecture, while at the same time providing a bridge between these buildings and his great royal works.[48]

Charles I, wrote John Aubrey,

did love Wilton above all places, and came thither every summer. It was he that did put Philip . . . Earle of Pembroke upon making this magnificent garden

89 (*left*) West Woodhay, Berkshire, 1635 (reduced to its original proportions by Claude Phillimore, 1950–51).

90   Inigo Jones, Isaac de Caus and John Webb, Wilton House (south front), Wiltshire, 1636–49.

and grotto, and to new build that side of the house that fronts the garden, with two stately pavilions at each end, all *al Italiano*. His Majesty intended to have it all designed by his own architect, Mr Inigo Jones, who being at that time, about 1633, engaged in his Majesties buildings at Greenwich, could not attend to it; but he recommended it to an ingeniouse architect Monsieur Salomon de Caus, a Gascoigne, who performed it very well; but not without the advice and approbation of Mr Jones.

Aubrey has clearly made a slip of the pen in referring to Solomon de Caus (who had died in the 1620s), and he presumably meant Salomon's relative Isaac, who in March 1636 was ordered 'to take downe . . . that side of Wilton house which is towards the Garden & such other parts as shall bee necessary & rebuild it anew wth additions according to ye Plott which is agreed'. De Caus, who had constructed the grotto in the Banqueting House at Whitehall in 1623–4 and another grotto in the garden at Somerset House in 1630–33, was closely involved in the Jonesian circle. Though primarily a designer of gardens and waterworks, he described himself as 'ingenyeur and architecte', was joint-surveyor with Edward Carter at Covent Garden and appears to have acted as executant architect on the houses in Covent Garden designed by Jones.[49] In 1638 he provided designs for Stalbridge Park, Dorset, for the first Earl of Cork and he was probably responsible for a series of impressive courtiers' stables, certainly those at Wilton and probably those at Bedford House, London (built for the

Earl of Bedford after 1627), Fonthill House, Wiltshire (built after 1631 for Lord Cottington, Chancellor of the Exchequer), and Holland House, built for £4,000 by Henry Rich, first Earl of Holland, in 1638–40.[50]

The original scheme for Wilton, which is known from a drawing prepared (but in the end not used) for an engraving to accompany de Caus's *Wilton Gardens*, was for a 330ft-long elevation with a central, six-columned attached portico flanked by eight-bay ranges broken by Serlian windows (Fig. 91). Some of the details, particularly of the portico, are not as clear as they could be, but the building would have had a rustic piano nobile and attic under a hipped roof, the first-floor windows would have had aprons and entablatures and the end windows would have been emphasised by swept architraves, pediments and slightly projecting balconies or pergolas.

With its matching king's and queen's apartments, this was in effect a quasi-palace for the annual royal visit. It was certainly grander than anything Charles I ever built for himself. In the event, the death of the earl's newly married son Charles in January 1636, and the forced return of the colossal £25,000 marriage portion paid by the bride's father, the Duke of Buckingham, meant that this scheme was too ambitious. Instead the decision was made to build just half the elevation. The initial suggestion, known from a unique engraving intended for *Wilton Gardens*, was a faithful reduction of the grand design, the only significant alteration being the proposed addition of an aedicule over the central Serlian window for emphasis. An alternative drawing proposed the addi-

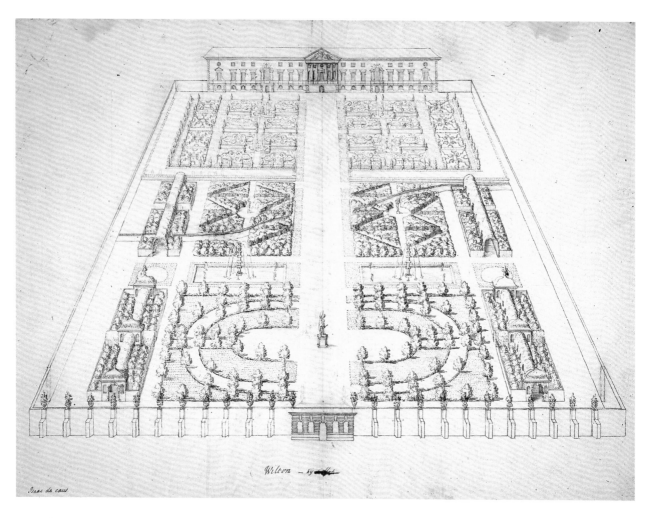

91 After Inigo Jones, great design for Wilton House, Wiltshire, c.1631 (Worcester College, Oxford).

tion of a balustrade, presumably inspired by the innovative balustrade of the Queen's House at Greenwich, which was being completed in 1635. The final scheme included the balustrade, though the original sharply pitched roof was still evident, together with a tower at each end of the elevation.[51]

Exactly who was responsible for what at Wilton has been much debated by architectural historians but it is possible to argue that the grand design is entirely the work of Inigo Jones, with de Caus responsible for the amended designs, 'not without the advice and approbation of Mr Jones'. Every feature of the grand design can be paralleled in Jones's other work. The bays flanking the Serlian window can be closely compared with Killigrew House: both have a rustic with prominent keystones in the window surrounds (though the windows at Wilton are segmental), a piano nobile with a double platband, entablatures over the windows, an attic floor and a

hipped roof. Jones used aprons under the first-floor windows on the designs for Brook House and Maltravers House and at Covent Garden and modillion cornices were a consistent feature of his work from the Arundel House stables to Maltravers House. Yet though much of the detail of the grand design sits comfortably within the pattern of Jones's domestic work, the overall concept is best seen in the context of his palace designs, specifically those for Somerset House.

Two designs survive for Somerset House, the London palace of Queen Henrietta Maria, an undated first design (Fig. 92) and what is termed the 'second designe', which is dated 1638 (Fig. 93). This second design is in effect a reduced version of the first, with the mezzanine stories removed and the architectural detail simplified. The Somerset House and Wilton designs both follow the same essential pattern, with a porticoed centrepiece flanked by long ranges of full-height and mezzanine

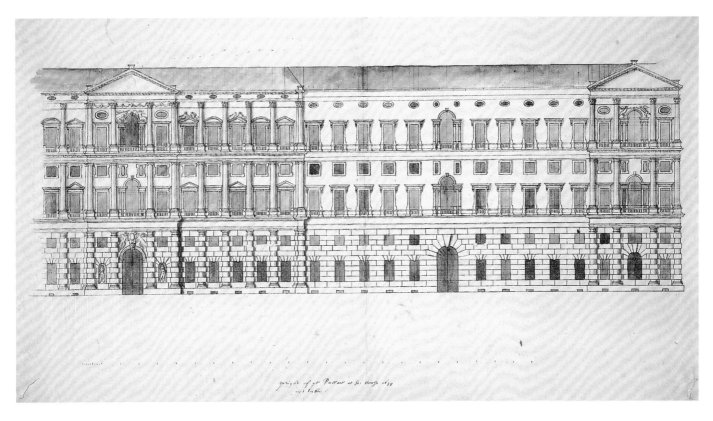

92   John Webb, after Inigo Jones, first design for the Strand elevation of Somerset House, London, 1638 (Worcester College, Oxford).

93   John Webb, after Inigo Jones, second design for the Strand elevation of Somerset House, London, 1638 (Worcester College, Oxford).

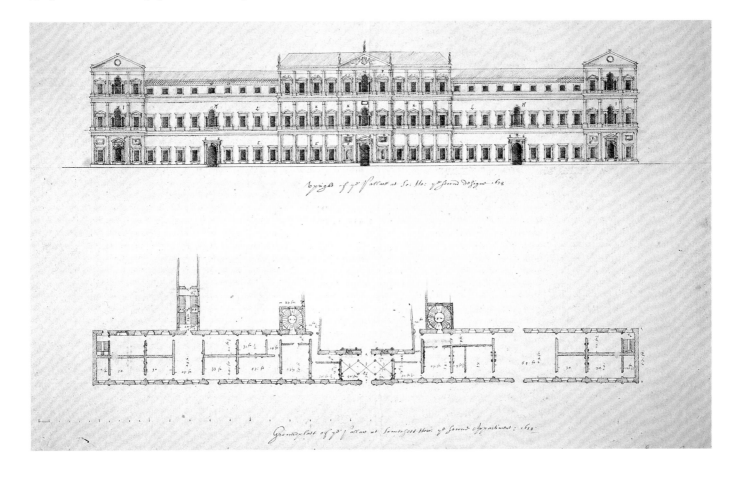

94 Sir Roger Pratt, Coleshill House, Berkshire, *c.*1649–*c.*1662.

95 Sebastiano Serlio, fifth proposition for off-square sites, from *The Seventh Book of Architecture* (1575) p. 147.

windows broken by Serlian windows under a hipped roof. Indeed, the upper two floors of Wilton can be read as a slightly shortened version of the intermediate storey at Somerset House. The parallels also extend to the details used. As Howard Colvin points out, the swept architraves on the end bays at Wilton are also found on the Somerset House design, as are seated figures over the Serliana windows, a feature of the Wilton Serliana and *oeil-de-boeuf* windows. Though the first Somerset House design has balustrades under the piano nobile windows, the second uses aprons, as at Wilton.

There is thus nothing stylistically about the grand design for Wilton that is inconsistent with Jones's thinking. It also shows that the ideas he was working on for palace architecture at the end of the decade must have been of interest to him throughout the 1630s

because the grand design for Wilton probably dates from the very beginning of the decade. The fourth Earl of Pembroke succeeded his brother in 1630 and may well have turned to Jones shortly afterwards.

It is known from the Receiver-General's accounts that work on the garden at Wilton was under way, to de Caus's designs, in 1632 or 33 and that work on the house did not begin until 1636 but this is not to say that preliminary plans for the house had not been drawn up at the same time or before the garden. It is likely that this was done by 1631. This preliminary design was by Jones but when the time came to adapt preliminary designs in about 1633, as Aubrey records, Jones was too busy to take them further himself. The project was therefore handed over to de Caus but with Jones exercising a supervisory brief. Wilton, and particularly the grand design, remains firmly within Jones's ambit.

One final house inspired by Jones's astylar manner needs examination: Coleshill House, Berkshire, built for Sir George Pratt (Fig. 94). The building history of Coleshill is complicated, the story not being made simpler by the fact that the house replaced an adjacent half-constructed house, that drawings survive by John Webb including a chimneypiece inscribed 'for Sir George Pratt at Coleshill neere Faringdon in Barkshyre' and that construction was not completed until about 1662.[52]

The suggestion that Jones was involved in the design of Coleshill has been current since the eighteenth century and the story remains confused. John Bold suggests that Jones was consulted about the first house by the royalist Sir Henry Pratt, that Webb produced designs for fitting up its interior before it was burnt down in or soon after 1647 and that the house as built was designed by Sir Roger Pratt for his cousin Sir George Pratt later in the 1650s. Mowl and Earnshaw enthusiastically argue for Jones's direct involvement. They cite in particular the note in the commonplace book of Sir Henry Pratt (who inherited in 1728 and died in 1768) that

> Sir G. Pratt began a seat in ye prest Cucumber Garden and raised it one storey when Pratt and Jones caused it to be pulled down & rebuilt where it now stands. Pratt and Jones were frequently here and Jones was also consulted abt ye ceilings. John Buffin [a joiner at Coleshill] who often saw them frequently declared this to Wm Pepal who came to Coleshill in 1700.

However, two things stand against this eighteenth-century testimony. The first is that Sir George Pratt was an enthusiastic republican, not someone to whom Jones would be naturally sympathetic. Moreover, Sir George succeeded in 1649, by when Jones would have been 76. Three years earlier in March 1646 Jones had been described as 'a very aged, infirm man, scarce able to walk abroad' when he appeared before the Committee for Compounding.[53] When Wilton was badly damaged by fire the following year the Earl of Pembroke is recorded as having 're-edifyed it, by the advice of Inigo Jones' but Jones, 'being then very old, could not be there in person, but left it to Mr Webb'.[54] This hardly suggests that Jones would have been 'frequently' at Coleshill.

Nevertheless, Coleshill is strongly Jonesian in feel. Its plan is indebted to the Queen's House in its double-height entrance hall flanked by apartments formed by reception rooms and closets. Again, the design was rooted in Serlio. There are strong parallels with Serlio's fifth proposition for off-square sites (Fig. 95).[55] Coleshill reads almost as if Jones's Serlio-inspired design for Maltravers House has been stretched over a nine-bay elevation. The diminutive basement of Maltravers House is raised to form a semi-rustic finished with channelled rustication, a sweeping staircase added, along with quoins, dramatic chimneys, a rooftop balustrade and cupola. Otherwise the house varies hardly at all from Maltravers House: Coleshill has a pedimented, bracketed front door, vertical rectangular windows with architraves, the first-floor windows sitting on aprons supported by a platband, a modillion cornice and hipped roof and dormers. The most likely solution is that Jones provided advice and guidance to the young Roger Pratt.

Contemporary with these astylar houses is a series of buildings in London and the country that follows the same model of the symmetrical house with vertical rectangular windows, hipped roof and dormers but with the addition of pilasters. The earliest known example of this is Balmes House in Hackney, built after 1634 by the former lord mayor Sir George Whitmore, which had paired Doric pilasters and a steeply pitched hipped roof with two floors of dormer windows.[56] In London this was followed by fourteen large houses on the south side of Great Queen Street for which one William Newton obtained a licence in 1636. Some at least of these were built the following year, perhaps to the designs of Peter Mills, a tiler and bricklayer who subsequently became Bricklayer to the City of London. In 1638 Newton followed this with a further licence to build thirty-two houses on the west side of Lincoln's Inn Fields, most of which were built by 1641. The only surviving example is Lindsey House, which may have been designed by Nicholas Stone, though others survived long enough to be photographed (Fig. 96).[57] To their number can be added the giant pilastered elevation of Lees Court, Kent, of about 1640.[58]

What is particularly significant in a London context is the way these houses abandoned the traditional preference for presenting the gable end to the street and replaced it with a roofline parallel to the street, with a continuous cornice and dormers. The novelty of this approach is shown from Wenceslaus Hollar's 1658 aerial view of the area bounded by Lincoln's Inn, Holborn and St Martin's Lane, which underwent major expansion

96   Nicholas Stone (attributed), Lindsey House, Lincoln's Inn Fields, London, c.1640.

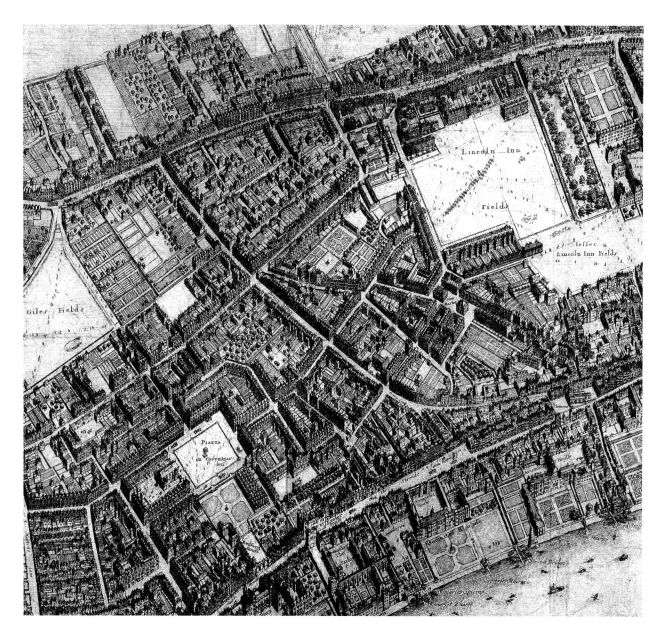

97   Wenceslaus Hollar, aerial view of the area from Lincoln's Inn to Holborn and St Martin's Lane, London, 1658 (British Library).

during the 1630s, with Covent Garden as its core (Fig. 97). Hollar's view, which is confirmed by contemporary views of houses around Covent Garden, shows that most of the new housing built during these years still expressed the gable to the street. This was even true of the houses built as part of the Covent Garden development outside the Piazza, as in Bow Street, King Street, Henrietta Street and Hart Street, as is confirmed by two views of Covent Garden made in about 1640 (see Fig. 86).[59] At least some of these houses have architecturally ambitious gables recalling contemporary Amsterdam and the Dutch House at Kew of about 1631.[60]

It would be interesting to know to what extent Jones encouraged the move away from the gabled front through his work on the Commission for Building, of which he was a member from at least 1618. This had been set up in 1615 to examine and regulate construction in the capital and Jones certainly had a hand in drafting new proclamations that imposed specific rules on new buildings about uniform frontages, minimum thickness for walls and the prevention of overhangs, bay windows and thatched roofs. In 1618 Jones was also appointed to a separate commission specifically charged with controlling building on and around Lincoln's Inn Fields, the area where most of this innovative building could be found.[61] The power Jones could exercise through his position on the Commission for Building can be seen in the way he interfered in the rebuilding of Goldsmiths' Hall in 1634. Having noticed work afoot 'upon some occasion of passing by', he forced the company to rebuild its hall larger and to a regular design to further the embellishment of the City. He also managed to insinuate his own man as architect, Nicholas Stone, recently appointed Master Mason to the Crown, and provided direct assistance to him. When Stone presented the full design to the company in February 1635 the minutes record: 'And he gave this Court to understand that in the doing thereof Mr Jones his Majesty's surveyor took special care and did advise and direct before the perfecting and finishing of each piece according to the several draughts now showed.' The design was closely inspired by Serlio.[62] Four years later Jones intervened again in a similar way, this time with the backing of the Privy Council, over the rebuilding of St Michael-le-Querne, again in the City. The parish had already received a 'modell' for the new church from Anthony Jerman and Mr Holmes when the Privy Council tried to impose a new design on it by Jones. Jones and the parishioners in the end faced each other in front of the king and Privy Council over the issue. The final outcome is uncertain.[63]

Houses such as those in Great Queen Street lack the refinement found in Jones's work and have a tendency to add decorative details that Jones would have found redundant in his own designs but they show how the architectural ideals he espoused were spreading down the social and architectural scale. They also show that, as in the Dutch Republic, the careful control of architectural ornament he favoured, in which pilasters were reserved for the grandest buildings such as the Banqueting House at Whitehall, broke down in the face of the bourgeois desire for embellishment.

There seems little reason to doubt that what might be called the Serlian manner emerged from Jones's circle, inspired by his work since the stables at Arundel House in 1618. In his work on such buildings Jones was neither particularly innovative in a strict sense nor alone. In France, as seen in chapter 4, the Serlian manner had been accepted since the 1540s. In Germany it can be found as early as the sixteenth century at the Fuggerei in Augsburg. In England the street elevations of Hendrik van Paesschen's Royal Exchange, built in 1564–8 (Fig. 98), anticipate Jones by half a century with their regular grid of vertical rectangular windows beneath a hipped roof

98 Wenceslaus Hollar, 'Winter' from the *Four Seasons*, detail showing the street elevation of Hendrik van Paesschen's Royal Exchange, 1564–8 (British Museum).

and dormers.[64] So too do the elevations of Gresham House in the City of London, built in 1561–6, and, if Glover's illustration is to be trusted, Osterley Park, Middlesex, built about 1567.[65] Yet these buildings, like the Fuggerei, had no stylistic progeny and it was not until the next century that the approach they foretold entered the architectural mainstream in both countries.

The direct and indirect influence of Serlio on Jones and his circle is considerable. It is implicit in the French buildings that Jones must have seen on his visits to France but what is clear about the work of Jones and his circle is that though the French example came from a similar source, the English turned directly to Serlio for their model. This is not surprising, for Serlio was one of the few architectural authorities who provided Jones and his contemporaries with practical guidance in designing relatively small, relatively architecturally unpretentious houses, for which the ambitious models of Palladio and Scamozzi were of little use. Serlio had the advantage of having been translated into English by Robert Peake in

99   Isaac de Caus, the stables at Wilton House, Wiltshire, 1630s.

1611, though Peake's translation did not include the most influential of Serlio's books, book seven, 'On Situations', which had been published in Germany in 1575 and which Jones owned in the 1601 and 1619 editions. This was of particular value as it concentrated on domestic work and on the practical problems, or 'situations', that an architect was likely to encounter.[66] Serlio was also particularly valuable, especially in books three, four and seven, in providing details of all sorts of architectural elements from window surrounds to doorcases to brackets to cornices that could be copied by an architect far more easily than anything in Palladio.

100   Sebastiano Serlio, the Fifteenth House, from *The Seventh Book of Architecture* (1575) p. 37.

It would be fair to say that Jones and his circle plundered Serlio's seventh book for inspiration. This can clearly be seen in Jones's design for Maltravers House (see Fig. 82), which is a slightly refined version of one of Serlio's smaller house designs in his seventh book. It is particularly evident in the treatment of the window surrounds, the platband and the aprons below the first-floor windows (see Fig. 43).[67] Slightly grander in its architectural treatment is Serlio's fourth proposition, where the elevation is ornamented with a sequence of giant half-columns, a model that provides the precedent for the Lincoln's Inn Fields and Queen's House façades.[68] The elevations belonging to the Ninth Plan provide a model for the combination of vertical rectangular windows and *oeil-de-boeuf* windows found on the stables at Fonthill House and Bedford House.[69] The Seventeenth House provides a possible source for the paired pilasters of Balmes House.[70] The elevation and plan of the Fifteenth House was used by Isaac de Caus as the basis for the stables at Wilton House (Figs 99 and 100).[71] The influence of Serlio's seventh book on Nicholas Stone's Goldsmiths' Hall in the City of London of 1635, where Jones's advice was sought, is also obvious.[72] One source for the rusticated arcade of Covent Garden is the Twenty-fifth Habitation in the City.[73] The third proposition on columns is a probable model for Lees Court and the fifth proposition for off-square sites for Coleshill.[74] Elements of the Fourth House can be traced in Killigrew House, particularly the treatment of the rusticated doorcase but also in the division of the elevation into three distinct units by the emphatic use of platbands and cornices.[75] It is also possible that Jones's design for the entrance bay of an unidentified house of about 1616 may owe something to Serlio's Twenty-Fifth House in the City.[79]

Simple and restrained though they are, Jones's designs for stables, offices and smaller houses, together with those designed by his circle, had a profound influence on the course of English architecture. As the simplest building blocks of Jones's architectural language, it is impossible to understand him as an architect without them.

Chapter 7

JONES, PALLADIO, SCAMOZZI AND RUBENS

Inigo Jones has been associated with Andrea Palladio by commentators ever since Colen Campbell stated that '*It is then with the renowned* Palladio *we enter the Lists, to whom we oppose the Famous Inigo Jones*', in his introduction to *Vitruvius Britannicus* in 1715.[1] The pairing is visibly expressed at Chiswick House where statues by Michael Rysbrack of Palladio and Jones, which once guarded the entrance to Lord Burlington's original drawing office in the Bagnio, flank the steps up to the front door. It is a pairing that Jones himself was happy to promote on the flyleaf of his copy of the *Quattro libri*, which he repeatedly signed 'Andrea Palladio' and 'Inigo Jones' (Fig. 102).[2]

The association of Jones and Palladio was particularly strong in the twentieth century, especially in the second half, when the concept of Palladianism was one of the dominant forces in architectural history, driven by a strong Palladio industry in Vicenza and by an equally powerful concern with Palladianism in Britain that was crystallised by Sir John Summerson's *Architecture in Britain 1530–1830*, first published in 1953, and by Rudolf Wittkower, whose *Palladio and English Palladianism*, published in 1974, brought together a collection of influential essays on the subject originally published in the 1940s and 50s. Palladio has thus been the prism through which Jones has tended to be studied, with research on Jones focussed overwhelmingly on his connections with Palladio. His annotated edition of Palladio's *Quattro libri* was transcribed and published in 1970, and subsequently became a major source of research into Jones's ideas, but his annotated editions of Vitruvius, Alberti, Serlio, Vignola and Scamozzi remain unpublished and relatively little studied.[3] Jones's ownership of Palladio's drawings is always cited as critical to understanding his development as an architect but the fact that he also owned at least

102   Inigo Jones, annotations showing Jones signing his own name and that of Palladio, from Andrea Palladio's *I quattro libri dell'architettura* (1570) (Worcester College, Oxford).

some drawings by Scamozzi and had access to many others is largely passed over in silence.[4] Moreover, a commonly accepted image of what a Palladian building

101 (*facing page*)   Adriaen van Stalbemt and Jan van Belcamp, *A View of Greenwich*, c.1632 (Royal Collection), detail showing, in the foreground, King Charles I and Queen Henrietta Maria at the centre of the group of figures, and, in the background, the palace and, in front of the wall, the unfinished Queen's House.

should be like has tended to dominate analysis of Jones's work. Buildings which fit that image, such as the Banqueting House, have been intensively studied but those which do not, such as his design for Maltravers House, have received relatively little attention or been found problematic, as is the case with Chevening House and the pavilions at Stoke Park, Northamptonshire.[5]

Palladio certainly exerted a powerful influence on Jones, as can be seen from the detailed analysis of Palladio's buildings and writings in his annotated copy of the *Quattro libri* and the extremely large number of Palladio's drawings that he acquired, by far the largest part of his collection of drawings.[6] As seen in the previous chapter, Jones used the *Quattro libri* to educate himself about architecture in the years that preceded his 1613–14 trip to Italy, providing a fundamental grounding in the practicalities of building, the orders, ornament and architectural theory. During that visit the book served as his notebook as he studied Palladio's buildings and Roman remains in detail, often noting down how the published version differed from what had actually been built. After his return to England, Jones continued to make annotations in the *Quattro libri* into the 1630s.

This repeated return to the *Quattro libri* over three decades allowed Gordon Higgott in an important article to explain how Jones developed his theory of design through his study of Palladio and of Barbaro's edition of Vitruvius. In particular Higgott was able to show that Jones was not, as Wittkower and others had suggested, the simple Platonist for whom architecture embodied perfect geometrical numerical forms to reflect the harmonious structure of the cosmos. According to this theory, Jones's design method was strictly rational and mathematical, with plans and elevations generated on a modular system to incorporate harmonic ratios. Instead, Higgott was able to show that Jones evolved a theory of architecture that reconciled the demands of classical precept and proportion with the visual requirements that the parts of a building should correspond harmoniously and appear correctly proportioned to the eye.[7]

The Italian tour confirmed Jones's enthusiasm for the richness and the variety of Roman architectural forms and helped him acquire a feeling for how the parts of a classical building should correspond in plan and elevation. In the first few months after his return Jones's notes in the *Quattro libri* and his Roman sketchbook show him seeking principles for the design and use of architectural ornament based on his experience in Italy and his knowledge of Roman architecture from published

sources. He praises Palladio's imitation of the best of antique basement mouldings but cautions against the slavish imitation of precedent by noting that the architect remains free to compose his own ornaments 'with reason'. Architects should look to the antique for the best models but be free to vary these models provided they did so in a reasoned way. The notes show that Jones was aware that parts of a classical building could be designed to express visual characteristics like strength or slenderness and that a key regulating factor in the composition of architectural features was the size and status of the relevant building. In perhaps his most famous comment, Jones contrasted 'solid' exteriors where fanciful ornaments were to be avoided and enriched interiors where all ornaments were permitted, a well ordered building being like a wise man who outwardly 'carrieth a gravity in Publicke Places . . . and yt inwardly hath his Immaginacy set free'. Jones's mature conviction was that variety governed by reason was fundamental to good design and that this involved both the functional and the decorative aspects of architecture.[8]

By contrast, Jones found little guidance on theoretical principles in the text of the *Quattro libri*. He made no notes in Book Two about the proportional ratios in Palladio's villa plans. Instead, Jones's ideas on proportion in architecture can be traced to Vitruvius and to passages of commentary by Barbaro which give emphasis to the scope in Vitruvius's system for varying proportions within limits to allow for the optical factor. The idea that ancient architects proportioned their buildings in a flexible manner, adjusting measures within certain limits according to the needs of the site, informed many of Jones's annotations about Roman ornament in book four of the *Quattro libri*. Central to Jones's thinking on proportional harmony was the Vitruvian concept of symmetry or commensurability between members. Just as ornaments had to agree in character, so proportions had to answer one another in corresponding ratios.[9]

A study of his surviving drawings and buildings suggests that at the initial, setting out, stage of a plan or elevation Jones was guided by the precepts in Vitruvius and Palladio on room proportions and ceiling heights. He favoured square and double square proportions for room plans and the same ratios frequently appear in larger divisions of elevations. Hence the double square proportion of the plan of the Banqueting House, the cube of the hall at the Queen's House and the double cube of the main internal space of Somerset House chapel, while the sketch elevation of Temple Bar is for a square of sixty feet, with the attic equal in height to the columns of the main order and two-thirds the height of the whole lower order. Square and double square are also common on Jones's gateway elevations. Yet other elevations – such as the Banqueting House façade and the second of Jones's schemes for Newmarket – do not yield squares or any obvious set of ratios. Interestingly, the first, but not the second, Newmarket scheme was contained almost exactly in a double square, indicating that at the more advanced stage in the design process Jones readily abandoned geometrical formulae when additional practical and visual considerations came into play.[10]

Jones was also less constrained by precedent and proportional formulae at a more detailed level of design. Pragmatism and a quest for visual coherence led him to modify his larger ratios and mould the proportions and ornaments of his orders to suit the purpose of the design or the distance that parts of the buildings would be from the eye. Success depended on Jones's judgement in adjusting proportions and ornaments to achieve the unified effect. Jones continued to be convinced by Barbaro's argument that there were no hard and fast rules in Vitruvius, only limits within which the judicious architect could vary with reason, and he therefore castigated Scamozzi's pedantic insistence on rules and formulae.[11]

Palladio was also a major source for Jones's use of direct quotations from ancient Roman buildings, which is evident from as early as 1617 when he made a design for the Star Chamber whose plan relied directly on Palladio's plans of the 'Temple of Jupiter the Thunderer' (the Temple of Vespasian) and the 'Temple of the Sun and the Moon' (the Temple of Venus and Rome).[12] This approach proved a consistent element in Jones's work throughout his career. The ceiling of the Marquess of Buckingham's chapel closet at New Hall, Essex (about 1622–3; Fig. 104), is modelled on Palladio's illustration of the 'Temple of Neptune' (Fig. 103), as the ceiling of the Queen's Chapel at St James's Palace of 1623–5 is derived from that of the 'Temple of the Sun and the Moon'.[13] In the mid-1630s the west front of St Paul's cathedral (see Fig. 152) was based on the 'Temple of the Sun and Moon' (see Fig. 153) with details from the Temple of Antoninus and Faustina and Hieronymus Cock's illustrations of the Baths of Diocletian, and the plan of the Council Chamber in the proposed Palace of Whitehall was also based on the 'Temple of the Sun and Moon'.[14] Palladio was not Jones's only source for Roman buildings, however, as the use of Cock's engraving reveals. The choir screen at Winchester cathedral of 1637–8 is based on Serlio's illustration of the Arco dei Gavi at

Verona (see Figs 185 and 186), although the design also incorporates elements from Serlio's designs in his seventh book.[15] In turning directly to classical exemplars for detail and as a model for specific buildings (as opposed to attempting to reconstruct the ideal buildings described by Vitruvius in which, as seen above, St Paul's church, Covent Garden, had been anticipated by Salomon de Brosse's Temple at Charenton and by François d'Aguilon's S. Carlo Borromeo in Antwerp) Jones seems to have been unusual among his contemporaries.

Palladio's own buildings were also a source for Jones but the Banqueting House at Whitehall of 1619–22 is perhaps the only one of Jones's buildings whose overall design, rather than details, may be directly derived from Palladio (Fig. 107). The rustic basement, the equal height of the two principal storeys articulated by superimposed pilasters and attached columns, separated by an emphatic entablature and the slight but emphatic projection of the three central bays, and the use of alternate segmental and triangular pediments over the windows, can all probably be traced to a preliminary design by Palladio for the Palazzo Chiericati owned by Jones (Fig. 105).[16] The treatment of the upper floor, with a channelled, rusticated wall, pairs of smooth Composite pilasters at the end and swags alternating with figurative masques, looks to Palladio's Palazzo Thiene (Fig. 106) but this is unusual.

For all the importance of Palladio to Jones, specific references to Palladio's buildings in Jones's work are surprisingly uncommon when compared, for instance, with the overt borrowings in Poussin's paintings from Colen Campbell in *Vitruvius Britannicus* or by Frederick the Great's architects at Potsdam.[17] In making this comment it should be appreciated that, as will be seen in chapters 8, 9 and 10, many of the architectural elements traditionally considered as evidence of 'Palladian' architecture – specifically the portico, the Serliana and the centrally planned villa – are better understood in the context of a much broader tradition as symbols of sovereignty, not as evidence of a specifically 'Palladian' aesthetic.

While Palladio's *Quattro libri* was probably the most important book in Jones's library, he had access to many others. It is fortunate that more than forty of Jones's books survive at Worcester College, Oxford. The architectural books include Leon Battista Alberti's *L'architettura* (1565), Pietro Cataneo's *L'architettura* (1567), Philibert de l'Orme's *Le premier tome de l'architecture* (1569), Giovanni Antonio Rusconi's *Della architettura* (1590), Giacomo Barozzi da Vignola's *Regole delli cinque ordini d'architettura* (1607), Vincenzo Scamozzi's *L'idea della architettura universale* (1615) and Gioseffe Viola Zanini's *Delle architettura* (1629), of which Alberti, Rusconi, Vignola, Scamozzi and Zanini are all annotated. Annotations can also be found in Palladio's *L'antichità di Roma di M. Andrea Palladio* (1588) and Giorgio Vasari's *Delle vite de' piu eccellenti pittori, scultori, et architettori* (1568).[18] As well as the books at Worcester College, copies of Serlio annotated by Jones can be found at the Queen's College, Oxford, and the Canadian Center for Architecture, Montreal. Jones's annotated copy of Daniele Barbaro's edition of Vitruvius of 1567 is at Chatsworth and his annotated copy of Gian Paolo Lomazzo's *Trattato dell' arte, della pittura, scoltura et architettura* (Milan, 1584) is in a private collection.[19] He almost certainly owned other architectural books that have disappeared. He must, for instance, have had a copy of Antonio Labacco's *Architettura* because he refers to it many times, on one occasion with the words 'as I have noted in his booke', but its present whereabouts are unknown.[20] Many of these books, particularly those by Vitruvius, Lomazzo, Serlio and Scamozzi, had a profound influence on Jones.

Jones was also willing to quote from the buildings of a wide range of different architects. As well as Serlio, to whom as noted in chapter 6 he turned repeatedly, Edward Chaney has suggested Fabrizio Grimaldi's west door of the Church of S. Paolo Maggiore (1583) as the source for Jones's unexecuted design for the great door of the Banqueting House (1619), and Gordon Higgott argues that the 'Italian' gate at Arundel House (1618) was based on Galeazzo Alessi's Porta del Molo, Genoa (1553; Fig. 108), with the addition of an elaborate, scrolled broken pediment and central panel taken from Michelangelo's Porta Pia in Rome (1561).[21] Higgott also suggests that the essential massing, particularly the projecting attic, of the 'Italian' gate at Hatton House of 1622–3 (Fig. 110) was likewise derived from the Porta Pia.[22] As will be seen below, Michelangelo's Palazzo dei Conservatori may have been one source for the pavilions at Stoke Park, which can be confidently attributed to Jones. Domenico Fontana was the source for the enframement of the windows of the chapel at Somerset House of 1623 (Figs 111 and 112) and the north and south nave doors of St Paul's cathedral of 1637. Other quotations can be found from the Flemish and French architects Jacques Francart, Jean Barbet and Pierre Collot, principally in work for Queen Henrietta Maria in the 1630s (see Figs 40 and 41).[23] Most of these quotations are to be found in designs for gates and for interiors, where Jones allowed himself more licence, not as the essential framework

103 Andrea Palladio, ceiling detail from the 'Temple of Neptune', from *I quattro libri dell'architettura* (1580) IV, p. 133.

for buildings. Here the buildings of Scamozzi emerge as the single most important source in Jones's architectural language.

Much has been made of Jones's negative comments about Scamozzi, whom he described as 'purblind' for not recognising that decorative elements such as friezes and medallions need to be enlarged if they are being placed high on a building, otherwise nobody will see them: 'this secret Scamozzi being purblind understood not'. With a decided air of superiority Jones notes in his copy of Vitruvius's *I dieci libri*, 'Most writers of architecture do leave over those parts which they understand not, as Scamozzi, Sir Henry Wotton.' Scamozzi is also criticised for not following Vitruvius in the placing of the kitchen

FIDEI   COTICVLA   CRVX

104   Inigo Jones, design for the ceiling of the Marquess of Buckingham's chapel closet at New Hall, Essex, *c.*1622–3 (Worcester College, Oxford).

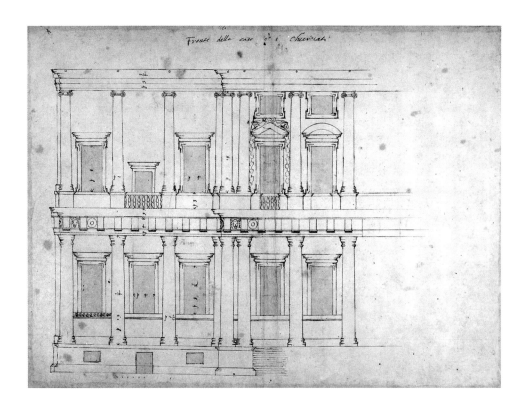

105 (*above*)   Andrea Palladio,
design for the Palazzo
Chiericati, Vicenza, late 1560s
(RIBA Library Drawings
Collection, Palladio XVII/5r).

106 (*right*)   Andrea Palladio,
Palazzo Thiene, Vicenza, from
I quattro libri dell'architettura
(1580) II, p. 14.

107 Inigo Jones, the Banqueting House at Whitehall, 1619–22.

in the House of the Ancients and because the external and internal orders of his Palazzo Trissino sul Corso did not agree. 'In this as in most things Scamozzi errs', Jones declares when Scamozzi attacks Palladio for making the upper order shorter than the lower, 'all of which shows the ignorance and malice of Scamozzi against Palladio'. 'Scamozzi for Jones', as Howard Burns has declared, 'is his anti-hero, his architectural Volpone, whose defects of character and taste acquire in his eyes an almost commanding stature – though in the end they serve above all to confirm, by comparison, Palladio's superiority.' Perhaps the key to understanding Jones's comments on Scamozzi comes in that reference to 'the ignorance and malice of Scamozzi against Palladio'. Jones revered Palladio – 'I spoke with Scamozzi on this matter . . . but Palladio sets down what is most proper' – a reverence that Scamozzi, perhaps struggling to escape

the shadow of the great architect, may not have found congenial.[24]

These intemperate notes, none the less, should not blind one to how much Jones had in common with Scamozzi. Konrad Ottenheym notes how Scamozzi's rigorously logical, scientific attitude tied in with Jones's own opinions and suggests that this approach to the arts had a common starting point in Lomazzo's *Trattato dell'arte* of 1584. For Jones, Lomazzo's work, the only theoretical treatise translated into English, in 1598, was a major influence. Jones annotated his copy of Lomazzo during his tour of Italy in 1613–14 and retained a strong interest in him in later years.[25] The bulk of the surviving notebook-sketchbook at Chatsworth, which dates from the 1630s, relates to his reading of the author.[26] Both Scamozzi and Jones abhorred fanciful inventions in architecture, with Jones's attack on 'composed orna-

ments the which proceed out the abundance of designs' fitting exactly Scamozzi's warnings against broken pediments and 'unreasonable' ornaments in the conclusion of book six.[27]

Jones may have criticised Scamozzi at times but his annotations of *L'idea* reveal an exhaustive analysis of his thinking and designs.[28] There are only two dated references in the annotations, on the titlepage, inscribed with his name and 'March 25 1617', presumably showing when he bought the book, and in his comments on the plan of the house of the Roman senator, which is inscribed in the left margin 'Ha: Court [Hampton

108   Galeazzo Alessi, Porta del Molo, Genoa, 1553.

109   Michelangelo, Porta Pia, Rome, 1561, from Giacomo Vignola, *Regola delli cinque ordini d'architettura* (1607).

110   Inigo Jones, design for the Italian gate at Hatton House, London, 1622–3 (RIBA Library Drawings Collection).

Court] 28 Septe 1625'. However, Higgott points out that evidence from the handwriting shows that Jones revisited the text a number of times, some of the inscriptions dating from early in his career, others from the 1630s. Unfortunately, the annotations shed no light on which of Scamozzi's buildings Jones had seen. There is not even any specific comment about the Villa Molin, where he probably stayed, or the palazzi he must have seen in Vicenza, the Palazzo Trissino sul Corso (which he criticised in his copy of the *Quattro libri*) and the Palazzo Trissino al Duomo.[29]

111 Domenico Fontana, design for a Doric doorway, from *Della trasportatione dell'obelisco vaticano et delle fabriche di nostro signore Papa Sisto V . . . libro primo* (1590) p. 18.

112 Inigo Jones, enframement of the windows of the chapel at Somerset House, London, 1623 (RIBA Library Drawings Collection).

One can tell what Jones found of particular interest in Scamozzi from what he underlined and what he noted in the margins. He also made plans easier to read by writing the uses of the different rooms alongside. Some subjects were analysed in detail, others ignored. He constantly compares what he reads with the works of other authors, particularly Vitruvius and Palladio, noting, for instance, how Scamozzi differed from Vitruvius and Palladio in his reconstruction of the Roman atrium.[30] He also points out those points at which Scamozzi has picked up an idea from someone else (especially if due credit is not given) and where he differs in his interpretation. For example, he notes that the plan of the Villa 'Il Paradiso' at Castelfranco was based on Palladio's Villa Godi, that the niches in the plate of the Composite order are taken from Palladio's Corinthian room and that those of the Corinthian order from Palladio's design for a bridge, and he chides Scamozzi for claiming credit for an invention that he later admits was taken from Vitruvius. Scamozzi is particularly criticised

for passing off a plan of fortifications as his own.[31] Jones also shows his awareness of Scamozzi's dislike of Genoese architecture.[32]

Sometimes what interests Jones are broad principles. From chapter fourteen of book one, 'Come si deono fare le inventioni e disegni, e le maniere piu risolute per disegnare', he picks out 'experience serves art more than invention'; 'easy and simple inventions the best and imitate nature in the body of a man'; 'what is commendable in invention is the beautiful union of parts, of site and of form'; 'how designs ought to be made unaffected'; 'answering of doors commended'.[33] 'A man judged by his house' sees Jones picking up a reference to his perennial interest in decorum.[34] 'All that we have in building of good and fair is by tradition from the Ancients' echoes another repeated belief of Jones's.[35] Elsewhere it is practical solutions to problems he seeks: the use of squared-up paper when dealing with irregular sites; how to design stairs; how doors might be panelled; notes on foundations and the thickness of walls.[36]

The chapters on the different orders are pored over in particular detail, showing how important Jones felt it was to get these right, with comments such as 'diminution of columns well observed by Scamozzi and to be imitated'; 'the ancients used not to put any members under the modillion being double and square as being far from the eye'; 'many members in the mouldings make the thing seem bigger as in the fluting of the columns'; 'tender mouldings give gravity and beauty, as the too solid and swelling make it deformed'; and 'to follow the mouldings of the ancients, which are tender, strong and have a certain grace'. [37] Jones is particularly interested in the specific temples from which Scamozzi derived his orders (generally citing the illustrations in Palladio's *Quattro libri*, though noting that one detail is taken from Serlio's illustration of the Arch of Benevento) and constantly compares his solutions with Vitruvius. [38] At times he is not afraid to criticise specific details whether by Scamozzi, describing the 'cassment and fillete' of the base of the Corinthian order as 'too petti in my opinion . . . it doth not well', or taken from Antiquity, as in the Corinthian capital: 'me thinkes this Tundino between the smaller members doth not well but it is an Imitation of the Antiche: Tempell of Napels cf. 104 Palla'. [39]

Scamozzi's writings on the suburban villa are also of interest: 'villas made by the Romans for health and pleasure'; 'Augustus delighted much in villa'; 'a villa suburbana should not be far off from the city'; 'villa delights more than the city and why'; 'liberty of the villa'; 'healthful air in villa'. Almost all Scamozzi's account of the form of the suburban villa and virtually all the description of his villa at Lonigo are underlined and extensively annotated. [40]

On the other hand, certain issues in Scamozzi seem not to have interested Jones. There are no notes against the chapters dealing with geometry, a general lack of interest in the proportions of Scamozzi's palace designs (though he carefully writes down the dimensions of some) and no notes on the proportion of ornaments above the column or Scamozzi's proportioning of pediments and pedestals. [41] What cannot be denied, though, is that, for all his quibbles and complaints, Jones studied Scamozzi's *L'idea* in great detail and that it profoundly influenced his architectural thinking.

A careful analysis also reveals how much Jones owed Scamozzi in the specific designs of his buildings. This is first evident in Jones's preliminary designs for the Queen's House at Greenwich for Queen Anne of Denmark and in two other contemporary designs for villas often associated with it. [42] For the Queen's House

Jones, appointed Surveyor of the King's Works almost exactly a year earlier, received payments for two designs for the new building by 8 October 1616: £10 for one, £16 for the second, executed, design. [43]

Since Jones acquired his copy of Scamozzi's *L'idea* (published in 1615) only on 25 March 1617 (the date inscribed on the flyleaf), it has been assumed that Scamozzi could not have influenced the early designs for the Queen's House. [44] Only three years earlier Jones had stayed with Lord Arundel in the Villa Molin. It is known that Jones met Scamozzi on 1 August 1614 in Venice and discussed some of the issues to be dealt with in his book, which was coming close to publication. [45] Jones certainly found what Scamozzi had to say of value because soon after he had bought *L'idea* he annotated the chapters on villa design. What is more, five sheets of Scamozzi's preparatory drawings for *L'idea* survive with Jones's collection of drawings at Chatsworth and it is probable, as Burns suggests, that they were acquired by him (see Fig. 120). [46] This is certainly the opinion of Professor Cinzia Sicca, who is cataloguing the collection of John Talman, through whose hands these drawings subsequently passed. [47] These early working drawings for *L'idea* were presumably no longer needed by Scamozzi in the latter half of 1614 when he met Jones, which may explain why he would have been happy to sell them to him. [48] Another drawing by Scamozzi survives among Palladio's drawings at the RIBA. [49] Nor was it only drawings that Jones acquired from Scamozzi. His copy of Strabo's *Geografia* was previously owned by Scamozzi and seems to have annotations in his hand as well as in Jones's. [50] Harder to gauge is the influence of two chests of Scamozzi's drawings which no longer survive but which were recorded in an inventory of Lord Arundel's possessions drawn up in 1655. Given Arundel's importance to Jones as an early patron, Jones would probably have been shown these, [51] giving him not only extensive direct knowledge of Scamozzi and his work but also access to his drawings (including one for the Rocca Pisani (see Fig. 120)) in 1616, before his purchase of *L'idea*. [52]

For what is generally agreed to be a preliminary design for the Queen's House at Greenwich Jones turned to the Scamozzian villa he knew best, the Villa Molin at La Mandria, where he had stayed with Arundel in 1613. Two drawings by Jones survive for this, together with a record drawing of the groundplan by John Webb that is believed to correspond (Figs 113 and 114). [53] The first clue comes in the treatment of the balustrade between the columns of the portico. It has already been noted by others that this detail in the Queen's House as

113 (*above*) Inigo Jones, elevation of the preliminary design for the Queen's House at Greenwich, 1616 (RIBA Library Drawings Collection).

114 (*right*) Inigo Jones, elevation of the east or west side of the preliminary design for the Queen's House, Greenwich, 1616 (Worcester College).

115 (*below right*) Vincenzo Scamozzi, side elevation of the Villa Molin, near Padua, Italy, 1597.

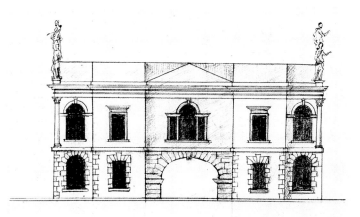

built is based on the example of the Villa Molin. Jones commented on it in his annotated version of the *Quattro libri*.[54] What has not been noted is that this is also true of this third preliminary design. If the treatment of the balusters in the Queen's House as built is reliant on the Villa Molin, then the same must be true of the preliminary design.

The fairly close adaptation of the Villa Molin (see Fig. 18) in the design for the Queen's House is apparent in the principal elevation. Both buildings have a central projecting first-floor, six-columned portico over a solid base flanked by single windows with a false balustrade. Both have a full-height rusticated ground floor and a plain upper floor. There are differences. In the Queen's House design the attic windows and projecting clerestory have been eliminated, the order has been upgraded to Corinthian, the treatments of the window surrounds and the doorcase have been changed and the portico

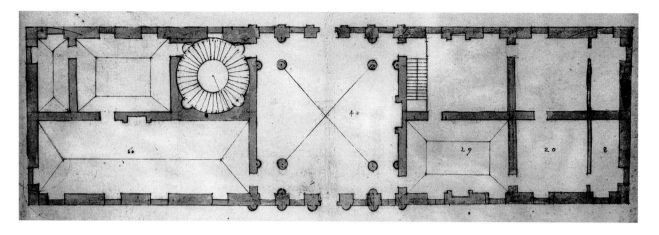

116   Inigo Jones, design for the ground plan of a villa, *c.1616* (RIBA Library Drawings Collection).

columns rearranged. Instead of equally spaced columns the end columns are grouped in pairs. It has been suggested that the model for this may be Palladio's Villa Pisani at Bagnolo and Villa Trissino at Meledo but a precedent can also be found for this in Scamozzi's Rocca Pisani at Lonigo (see Fig. 120).[55] It is particularly noticeable in this design that the ground and first floors are comparable, though not equal, in height. By contrast, most of Palladio's villas have a low rustic and dominant piano nobile.[56] However, it is possible that the rusticated, round-headed doorway and the emphatic keystones over the windows derive from a drawing by Palladio in his collection for a project for the lower level of the façade of the Palazzo Iseppo Porto.[57] Other parallels between the Villa Molin and the Queen's House design emerge in studying the plan.[58] In both cases a projecting portico led by way of a narrow room to a dominant central hall, double height at the Villa Molin, single height at the Queen's House. The side elevation also follows the Villa Molin, with the solid side walls of the porticoes pierced by a round-headed opening, and the centre of the elevation is marked by a Serlian window (Figs 114 and 115).

A second design, often associated with the Queen's House and contemporary with it according to Harris and Higgott, also reveals a debt to Scamozzi (Fig. 116). Known only from a ground plan, this is far different from the preliminary design in that it is long and thin instead of essentially square. It has been associated with the Queen's House because like the Queen's House as built it has a forty-foot entrance hall and circular staircase.[59] However, the scheme does not allow for the road that the Queen's House was built to cross and so may be for a different site, perhaps Newmarket.

None of Palladio's villas or palazzi matches the long, thin dimensions of this unusual groundplan but Scamozzi had built a closely similar house at the Villa Verlato at Villaverla, sixteen kilometres north of Vicenza, in 1574. This was thirteen bays wide with a six-bay attached portico, a central hall and smaller rooms on either side divided by a spine wall (Fig. 117).[60] There are, of course, differences. The Villa Verlato was to have had a grand external staircase to the garden, instead of Jones's spiral stairs, and its hall is neither vaulted nor quite square.[61] There is no comparable vaulted hall in Scamozzi's *L'idea* and the probable source is the hall of Palladio's Palazzo Iseppo Porto in Vicenza, where the columns are similarly grouped in the corners of the hall, supporting a cross vault.[62]

However, the spiral staircase comes from Scamozzi not Palladio. Although Palladio illustrates four different models for spiral stairs in his first book and although circular stairs are included in the plans of the Palazzo Chiericati, the Villa Cornaro and his reconstruction of the private house of the Greeks, the form of spiral stairs in Jones's villa design, with four semi-circular niches, is found not in Palladio but in Scamozzi's chapter on staircases.[63] Here he writes at length about the origins in Antiquity and current use of the spiral staircase, asserting that 'It seems no temple, spa or other building was without such a staircase' and noting that he included one in the Palazzo Trissino sul Corso in Vicenza. This is illustrated in *L'idea* though without niches.[64] No elevation survives for this first preliminary design but, as will be argued below, in chapter 11, it is possible that John Webb's later design for the smaller version of Durham House, which derives from the Villa Verlato, may be based on it (see Fig. 209).[65]

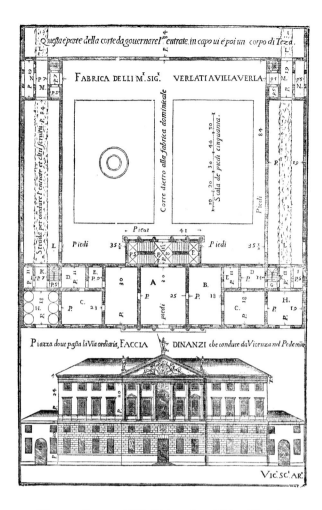

117 Vincenzo Scamozzi, Villa Verlato, from *L'idea della architettura universale* (1615) I, p. 287.

Scamozzi was certainly the source for a third contemporary villa design, also known only from plan (Fig. 118).[66] Though this is often associated with the Queen's House, most recently by Howard Burns, the orientation on the drawing argues against this as the house is set north–south, not north-east–south-west as is the case with the Queen's House.[67] The projecting portico is similar to that of the Villa Molin but in this case the sloping stairs on either side show that it is derived from Scamozzi's design for a villa on the Brenta between Stra and Dolo (Fig. 119).[68] However, the plan of the villa, the central, circular niched hall and the portico-in-antis, is taken from Scamozzi's Rocca Pisani at Lonigo and the Villa Bardelini at Monfumo (Fig. 120).[69] Jones also shows curving colonnades that would presumably have linked pavilions. This is not a feature found in Scamozzi's *L'idea* but is taken from Palladio's illustration of the Villa Trissino at Meledo.[70] Given the

long-standing association of centrally planned villas and porticoes with royalty, discussed in chapters 5 and 8, it is not surprising that Jones should have considered this model for Queen Anne of Denmark.

Jones's chosen design for the Queen's House is unknown because only the rustic had been completed when the death of Queen Anne in March 1619 led to the abandonment of the project, though it clearly differed from all the preliminary schemes.[71] However, Jones was probably responsible for adding a classical frontispiece for Queen Anne to Byfleet House, Surrey, in 1617 (Fig. 122). A sixteenth-century house used by the queen as a hunting lodge, Byfleet House was demolished in 1686 and is known only from a rough sketch by John Aubrey. In 1617 a warrant was issued to pay the queen £250 towards the cost of repairs and Aubrey's sketch shows that she added a three-bay pilastered centrepiece with an arcaded ground floor with Ionic pilasters, segmental and triangular pediments over the windows on the first floor and what appears to be a scrolled gable.[72] The sophisticated classicism of the scheme and the fact that the queen had long employed Jones to design masques and was then using him at the Queen's House at Greenwich make him the obvious architect.

The sketch is too rough to be certain but a possible source for the arcaded ground floor is Scamozzi's Palazzo Cornaro, which as already seen in chapter 5 was particularly influential in the Dutch Republic (see Fig. 57). Alternatively, Jones may have been inspired by Palladio's Villa Thiene, where he had sketched a similar arcaded and pilastered elevation (which Palladio had not illustrated) on 13 August 1614 (Fig. 121).[73] The Villa Thiene portico may also have been the source for the arcaded portico at Houghton Conquest, Bedfordshire, which bears strong similarities to that at Byfleet and has also been attributed to Jones (Fig. 123).[74] This was built for Mary, Dowager Countess of Pembroke, who bought Houghton Conquest in 1615 and died in 1621. She was a close friend of Jones's important current patrons, the Earl and Countess of Arundel, and mother of the third and fourth Earls of Pembroke for whom Jones later worked at Wilton House. The strong similarity with the work at Byfleet, the link with Jones's Villa Thiene sketch and the concurrence of patronage makes the portico at Houghton Conquest a plausible attribution to Jones.[75]

Jones's interest in Scamozzi is equally evident in his designs for the Prince's Lodging at Newmarket made for the Prince of Wales shortly after those of the Queen's House, in 1618–19 (Figs 124 and 125). It has long been accepted that the first design is derived from Scamozzi's

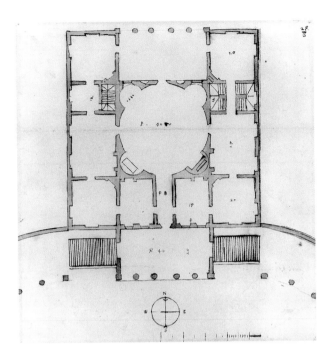

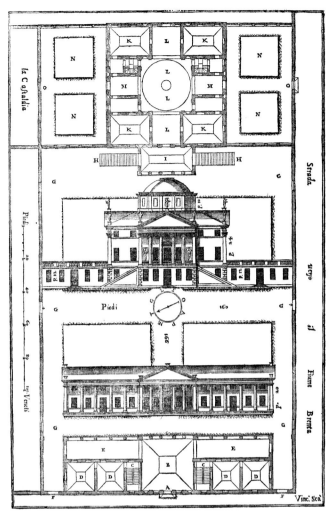

118   Inigo Jones, design for the ground plan of a villa, *c.*1616 (RIBA Library Drawings Collection).

119 (*right*)   Vincenzo Scamozzi, design for a villa on the Brenta between Stra and Dolo, from *L'idea della architettura universale* (1615) I, p. 277.

120 (*below*)   Vincenzo Scamozzi, preparatory drawing with mirror writing for the engraving of the Rocca Pisani (Devonshire Collection, Chatsworth, reproduced by kind permission of the Trustees of the Chatsworth Settlement).

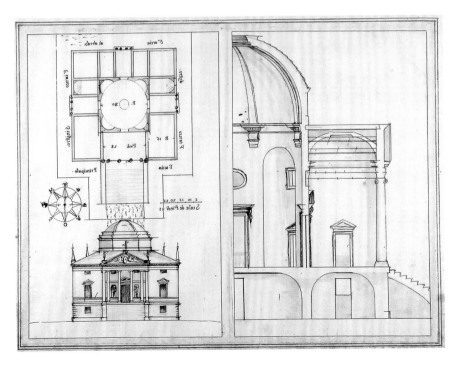

elevation of the Palazzo Trissino sul Corso in Vicenza (Fig. 126) and that the second is a reduced version of the same stripped of its orders (with the addition of a hipped roof and dormers from Serlio).[76] Jones appears to have re-used the central element of the second Newmarket design on the west elevation of the Queen's Chapel at St James's Palace in 1623–5 (Fig. 127). However, it may be that he was also referring here to another antique building in Rome, the Curia in the Forum, which he would certainly have studied during his time in Rome. Though not illustrated by Serlio or Palladio, a good representation can be found in Etienne du Perac's *Vestigi di Roma* of 1575 (Fig. 128). This shows a building of identical dimensions to the Queen's Chapel with a similar central round-headed window flanked by two rectangular windows and, most tellingly, a modillion cornice identical to that used by Jones at the Queen's Chapel.

Scamozzi's hand can also be found at Jones's Banqueting House at Whitehall of 1619–22 (see Fig. 107). Here Jones adopted Scamozzi's characteristic hierarchy of the orders, Composite superimposed over Ionic, something found repeatedly in Scamozzi's palazzi (see Fig. 126) but not in those of Palladio.[77] Jones also uses Scamozzi's Ionic order with its angled volutes, not Palladio's (see Fig. 63). The differences between Palladio's and Scamozzi's versions of the Composite capital – or Romano as Scamozzi described it – are too slight to be significant but the base of the order used by Jones at the Banqueting House follows Scamozzi (with some of the detail removed), not Palladio.[78] Jones also derives the cornice, brackets and surrounds to the windows from Scamozzi's Composite door surround, with minor alterations taken from the Corinthian door surround. Those of the lower windows are a simplified version of the same. This is particularly evident in the detail of the narrow panels running down each side of the windows – a detail that flummoxed Jones when he came to adapt Scamozzi's design for the upper windows as these do not rest on a solid base, leaving the panels floating uncomfortably just below the windows.[79]

During the expensive war with France and Spain from 1624 to 1630 Jones's busy career designing buildings for the Crown dried up for lack of money. Yet this left him time to design buildings for others, such as the pair of pavilions at Stoke Park, Northamptonshire. These are all that survive of an ambitious new house for Sir Francis Crane, work on the body of the house being incomplete when Crane died of gangrene after an operation in April 1636.[80]

The Stoke Park pavilions have floated in and out of attributions to Inigo Jones ever since Colen Campbell declared in the third volume of *Vitruvius Britannicus* in 1725 that 'This Building was begun by Inigo Jones; the Wings, and Collonades, and all the Foundations, were made by him; but the Front of the House was designed by another Architect, the Civil Wars having also interrupted this Work.'[81] John Bridges, who died in 1724, stated in his *History of Northamptonshire* that Crane 'brought the design from Italy, and in the execution of it received the assistance of Inigo Jones'.[82] Oliver Hill and John Cornforth had no difficulty with the attribution, declaring, without further analysis, that the attribution is convincing because of 'the appearance of the colonnades and pavilions'.[83] Sir John Summerson and Sir Howard Colvin were more circumspect: Summerson did not find the attribution satisfactory and Colvin placed Stoke Park under doubtful or inadequately documented works.[84]

The south elevations of the two pavilions, which can be read as condensed versions of the Prince's Lodging at Newmarket with similar window surrounds to the piano nobile, a rustic and a small attic windows with a similar entablature over the side window, and an attic, present no problems (Fig. 129 and see Fig. 125). The quadrant colonnades look back to Palladio's Villa Trissino at Meledo, a plausible source for Jones. The problem with Stoke Park is that the inner elevations of the pavilions do not tie in with the commonly held notions of Jones's or Palladio's work either in their proportions or in the contrast between the solid of the first floor and the void of the ground floor over which it sits, a spatial relationship made even more uncomfortable by the size of the first-floor round-headed window.

The element that seems hardest to fit the accepted view of Palladio and Jones is the contrast between the solid mass of the pavilions at first floor and the void of the colonnade below. The combination of ground-floor void and first-floor solid and the combination of a giant and lesser order can be traced back to Michelangelo's Palazzo dei Conservatori in Rome of 1563–84 (Fig. 130). This spatial dynamic was explored by Palladio in the Palazzo Chiericati and repeatedly by Scamozzi, at the Palazzo Trissino sul Corso (Fig. 131), both in the courtyard and on the façade along the Corso at the Villa Ferramosca a Barbaro and at the courtyard of the Palazzo Strozzi (see Fig. 134).[85] As is typical with Jones, version of the Ionic order used is Scamozzi's not Palladio's . The round-headed first-floor window that dominates the internal elevations is found only at the Villa Maser in

I DISEGNI che feguono,fono della fabrica del Conte Ottauio Thiene a Quinto fua Villa.
Fù cominciata dalla felice memoria del Conte Marc'Antonio fuo padre, e dal Conte Adriano fuo
Zio : il fito è molto bello per hauer da vna parte la Tefina , e dall'altra vn ramo di detto fiume affai
grande:Ha quefto palagio vna loggia dauanti la porta di ordine Dorico: per quefta fi paffa in vn'al
tra loggia,e di quella in vn cortile ; ilquale ha ne i fianchi due loggie, dall'vna, e l'altra tefta di que
fte loggie fono gli appartamenti delle ftanze, dellequali alcune fono ftate ornate di pitture da Mef
fer Giouanni Indemio Vicentino,huomo di belliffimo ingegno . Rincontro all'entrata fi troua vna
loggia fimile à quella dell'entrata , dallaquale fi entra in vn'Atrio di quattro colonne , e da quello
nel cortile,ilquale ha i portici di ordine Dorico,e ferue per l'vfo di Villa. Nõ vi è alcuna fcala prin
cipale corrifpondente a tutta la fabrica:percioche la parte di fopra non hà da feruire, fe non per fal
uarobba,& per luoghi da feruitori.

121   Inigo Jones, annotations recording his visit to the Villa Thiene at Quinto on 13 August 1614, from Andrea Palladio's *I quattro libri dell'architettura* (1609) II, p. 64 (Worcester College, Oxford).

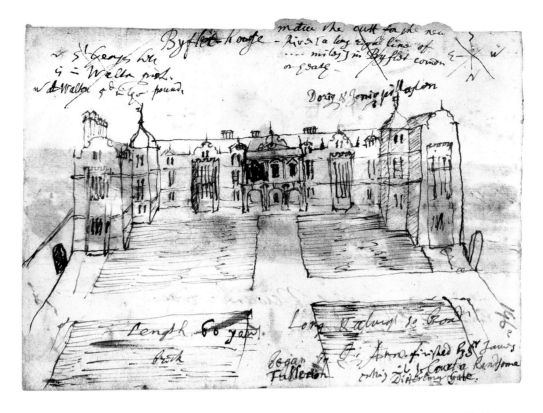

122   John Aubrey, sketch of Byfleet House, Surrey, showing the classical centrepiece probably added by Inigo Jones in 1617 (Bodleian Library, Oxford, Aubrey MS 4).

123   W. Kimpton, drawing of 1785 of the north front of Houghton Conquest, Bedfordshire. The central portico is attributed to Inigo Jones, c.1615 (Trustees of the Bedford Settled Estates).

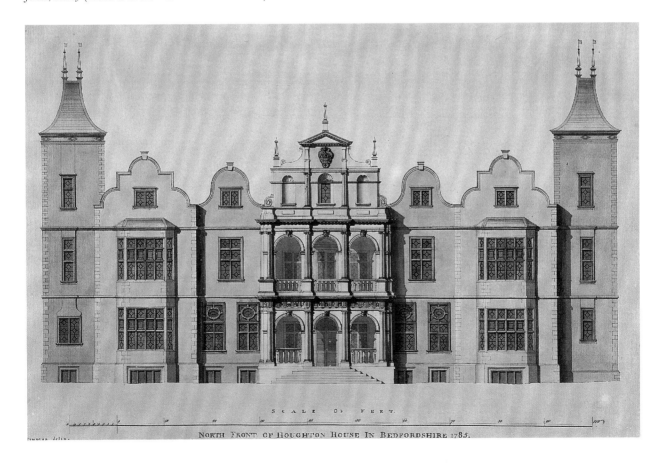

SCALE OF FEET.

NORTH FRONT OF HOUGHTON HOUSE IN BEDFORDSHIRE 1785.

124   Inigo Jones, first design for the Prince's Lodging, Newmarket, 1618–19 (RIBA Library Drawings Collection).

125   Inigo Jones, second design for the Prince's Lodging, Newmarket, 1618–19 (RIBA Library Drawings Collection).

Palladio but is a repeated feature of Scamozzi's buildings, appearing in five of his designs in *L'idea*.[86] As already seen, Jones followed this in his first design for the Prince's Lodging at Newmarket (Fig. 124) where the form of the round-headed window with a keystone and paired blocks supporting the arch is exactly the same as at Stoke Park.

That Jones was interested in this combination of solid over void is evident in his scenery design for 'Cupid's

127 (*above*)   Inigo Jones, west elevation of the Queen's Chapel at St James's Palace, London, 1623–5.

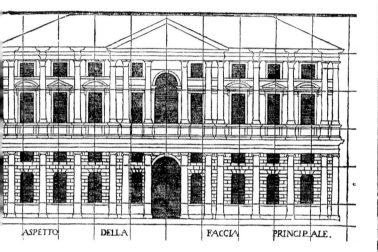

126   Vincenzo Scamozzi, elevation of the Palazzo Trissino sul Corso, Vicenza, from *L'idea della architettura universale* (1615) I, p. 260.

Palace' for an unknown masque (Fig. 132). Though Orgel and Strong link this to the lost masques of 1619 and 1621, Harris and Higgott state that on the grounds of drawing technique the design might be a decade later, which would place it exactly contemporaneously with the Stoke Park pavilions.[87] The design is probably derived from the courtyard of Scamozzi's Palazzo Trissino sul Corso though, interestingly, this elevation is not illustrated in *L'idea*, suggesting that either Jones had a strong visual memory of the elevation or that he had access to an unpublished drawing of it by Scamozzi.[88]

So did Jones design the pavilions at Stoke Park? Sir Francis Crane was an intimate of Charles I. He had been appointed his auditor-general in 1617, the same year he was made a baronet, a member of the Prince of Wales's council in 1623 and in 1626 was made Lay Chancellor

128 (*right*)   Etienne du Pérac, the Arch of Septimius Severus in the Forum, Rome, detail from *I vestigi delle antichità di Roma* (1575) fol. 3.

129　Inigo Jones, the east pavilion at Stoke Park, Northamptonshire, *c.*1629.

of the Order of the Garter, a body close to the king's heart. Crane set up the Mortlake tapestry works in 1619, backed by Prince Charles, who bought the Raphael Cartoons in 1623 to be used as a model for tapestries and settled an annuity of £2,000 on Crane in 1625 to clear debts and encourage manufacturing. Crane was also

130　Michelangelo, Palazzo dei Conservatori, Rome, 1563–84.

closely connected with the Stuarts, Dukes of Lennox and Richmond, and the Howards, Earls of Arundel, important patrons of Jones. He joined first Frances, Duchess of Lennox and Richmond (in 1625) and then (in 1636) Lord Maltravers, son of the Earl of Arundel, in monopolies for making farthing tokens and was helped by Maltravers to buy the extensive estates of Sir Thomas Southwell in Suffolk.[89]

Given this circle of connections it would have been logical for Crane to turn to Jones for a design. None the less, would the architect, who refused the much more prestigious project of rebuilding Wilton House for the Earl of Pembroke because he was too busy, have had the time to take on such a relatively small private commission? Here timing is critical. Information about Jones's rejection of the Wilton commission comes from Aubrey and, as revealed in the previous chapter, he is specific about the timing: 'His Majesty intended to have had it all designed by his own architect, Mr Inigo Jones, who being at that time, about 1633, engaged in his Majesties buildings at Greenwich, could not attend it; but he recommended it to an ingenious architect, Mr

131 Vincenzo Scamozzi, courtyard of the Palazzo Trissino sul Corso, Vicenza, 1588.

132 Inigo Jones, design for 'Cupid's Palace' for an unknown masque *c*.1632 (Devonshire Collection, Chatsworth, reproduced by kind permission of the Trustees of the Chatsworth Settlement).

Solomon de Caus, a Gascoigne, who performed it very well; but not without the advice and approbation of Mr Jones.'[90] This fits what is known from the accounts of the Office of Works, which show that work resumed in earnest on the Queen's House in 1632.[91]

Crane acquired Stoke Park and its park of four hundred acres in 1629. At this point, England was still at war with France and Spain. For several years Jones's architectural career had been on hold, with no significant new projects except the conversion in 1629 of the Cockpit at Whitehall Palace into a theatre. In 1629 negotiations were in hand to develop the urban quarter of Covent Garden to Jones's designs and build a new church there (though building work did not begin before the early 1630s).[92] In 1631 there followed a new lodge for the king at Bagshot Park, Surrey, and the launch of the commission to repair St Paul's cathedral, to which Jones was appointed Surveyor in February 1633, as noted before.[93] On top of this Jones was commissioned in 1632 to catalogue the king's collection of antique coins.[94] When all this is combined with his

extensive duties as a masque designer and work at the Queen's House it is no wonder that Jones was too busy to take up the Wilton commission in 1633. In 1629 or 1630, however, when Crane probably started work on his pavilions, Jones would have had the time to indulge him. Campbell's and Bridges's attributions to Jones deserve to be accepted.

Strong Scamozzian influence is still apparent in the late 1630s in Jones's palace designs for Somerset House and Whitehall Palace. As John Harris has pointed out, the essential form of the central block of Jones's first design for Somerset House of 1638 (see Fig. 92) is derived from Palladio's drawing for rebuilding the Doge's Palace in Venice (Fig. 133).[95] This provided the idea for a three-storey block, richly decorated with columns and pedimented window surrounds, with a pedimented frontispiece flanked by ranges of five bays. But though the bones of the design come from Palladio, the detail is drawn from Scamozzi, specifically from the Palazzo Strozzi and Villa Verlato.[96] From the Palazzo Strozzi (Fig. 134) comes the treatment of the three successive storeys

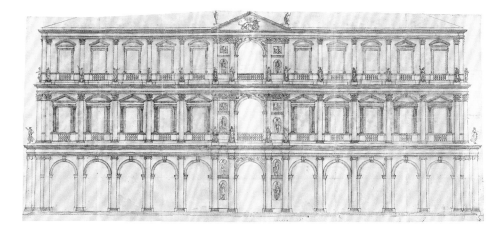

133 Andrea Palladio, design for rebuilding the Doge's Palace, Venice, c. 1577 (Devonshire Collection, Chatsworth, reproduced by kind permission of the Trustees of the Chatsworth Settlement).

with mezzanines on the ground and first storey and an attic lit by oval windows in the frieze; the triangular pedimented windows repeated every second bay on the second storey and the alternating pedimented and segmental windows of the third storey, some with reclining

figures; and the treatment of the central bay.[97] From the Villa Verlato (see Fig. 117) comes the organisation of the windows of the ground floor; the contrast of the rusticated surface of the ground floor and the plain storey above; and the organisation of the first-floor windows in the flanking ranges. The only detail that does not derive from Scamozzi is the use of blocky rusticated Doric columns on the ground floor of the central block and pavilions. These may have been taken from Palladio's Palazzo Thiene (see Fig. 106).

The second design for Somerset House is a reduced version of the first (see Fig. 93).[98] The mezzanine floors have been removed and the architectural detail such as rustication simplified so that the Scamozzian derivation is not as immediate, but the pair of niched spiral stairs shows Jones returning to a Scamozzian feature examined in the first preliminary design for the Queen's House more than two decades earlier.

Elements from Scamozzi can also be found in Jones's contemporary designs for Whitehall Palace. As will be explained in chapter 10, this is a much more complex scheme than that for Somerset House but the end pavilions of the river front in the drawing known as P9 (Fig. 135) owe much to the three centre bays of Scamozzi's design for the Palazzo Cornaro, even down to the putti-like figures in the spandrels of the arches (see Fig. 57).[99] The contrast between a rusticated lower storey with mezzanine and plain upper storey of another river elevation, P8, is a classic Scamozzian motif, as is the

134 Vincenzo Scamozzi, Palazzo Strozzi, from *L'idea della architettura universale* (1615) I, p. 249.

114

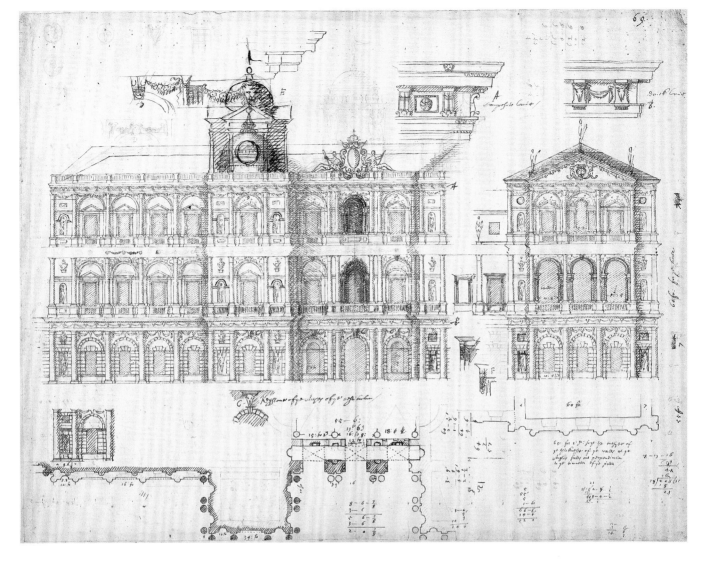

135   John Webb, after Inigo Jones, design for the river front of Whitehall Palace, c.1638, Whinney P9 (Devonshire Collection, Chatsworth, reproduced by kind permission of the Trustees of the Chatsworth Settlement).

positioning of naked figures over the Serlianas and on the pediments over windows (although this feature is also found in Palladio).[100]

By this time Jones had returned to the Queen's House at Greenwich where work had been abandoned in 1619.[101] It was not until 1632 that construction resumed in earnest for Queen Henrietta Maria. By 1635 building work was almost complete, the total cost by 1638 coming to at least £7,500.[102] The result was far different from the Scamozzian composition proposed two decades earlier (Figs 2 and 136). Instead of the classically upright villa-like form of the third preliminary design with its dominant central portico and hipped roof that would have looked at home in the Veneto, the building has a

distinctly cubic feel emphasised by the projecting terrace that forms the approach, the absence of a central pediment, the continuous balustrade disguising the roof and an altered relationship between window and wall in which the windows now appear as isolated elements in a dominant wall surface. On the park front the portico-in-antis is not emphasised by a pediment and with its long, low dimensions presents the impression of a slot cut in the volume of the building, a loggia (see Fig. 143).

Certain important elements remained indebted to Scamozzi, particularly to the Villa Molin: the nearly equal ground and first-floor storeys and their treatment as rusticated and plain surfaces respectively; the round-headed window over the front door; the false balusters

115

136   Inigo Jones, the north front of the Queen's House at Greenwich, 1632–8.

under the first-floor windows; the treatment of the balusters between the columns of the loggia; and above all the double-height hall with its balustraded balcony (Figs 136 and 138). For all that, the Queen's House as built is no longer a Scamozzian building. Indeed it is a building for which it is hard to find direct parallels.

To understand the change in form of the Queen's House it is necessary to look away from the architectural traditions of the Veneto, of Palladio and Scamozzi, to the different traditions of Central Italy. The sense of the Queen's House as a long, low, essentially cubic white building of two storeys of equal height, in which windows were placed in wide expanses of wall, has many parallels with the Medici villas around Florence. Where Palladio's and Scamozzi's buildings give the impression of an architecture based on the articulation of the orders, in Tuscany the prevailing tradition was of an architecture based on mass, where walls were punctured by windows, with articulation added where appropriate in the form of rustication, elements from the orders or elaborate and beautifully detailed window and door surrounds. This approach is clear in Giuliano da Sangallo's Villa Medici at Poggio a Caiano of 1485–92 (see Fig. 42) and remained powerful throughout the sixteenth and seventeenth centuries. It is particularly evident in the villas and other buildings of Bernardo Buontalenti (1531–1608), the lead-

ing architect at the Medici court in the second half of the sixteenth century, as seen at the Villa di Pratolino (1569), the Casino Mediceo di San Marco in Florence (1575), the Villa di Poggiofrancoli (1575), the Villa della Petraia (1588–93) and the Villa Medici at Castello (1588).[103]

To what extent was Jones consciously emulating this Central Italian approach at the Queen's House? He would have been fully conscious of it. English relations with the Medici court at Florence were strong and he would have had plenty of time to explore Florentine architecture during the six weeks the Earl of Arundel spent outside Siena in 1613. There is even the tradition that he designed the church in the Piazza at Leghorn (built in 1581–5 and actually the work of Alessandro Pieroni), which has led some to suggest that he spent time in Tuscany in the earlier, largely undocumented years of his life.[104]

An unusual detail at the Queen's House may be derived from Buontalenti: the terrace and horseshoe steps that form its approach (see Fig. 2). The Villa di Pratolino, built for Grand Duke Francesco I, has been demolished but its appearance is known from a painting in the Museo Firenze com'erà in Florence (Fig. 139). This shows that the villa was approached up a pair of curved, horseshoe steps and across a projecting

116

137 Inigo Jones, the hall of the Queen's House at Greenwich, 1632–8.

138 Vincenzo Scamozzi, the hall of the Villa Molin, near Padua, 1597.

terrace.[105] John Bold points out that this similarity is more marked now than it was when the Queen's House was built because the steps there have been altered. Originally they curved round to face each other but, probably in 1713, they were cut back so that they are now set at an angle. For this reason Bold argues that the source of the steps is Vignola's Villa Farnese at Caprarola.[106] Jones may have been influenced by the detail of the Caprarola steps but what is significant about the Queen's House is not just the precise form of the horseshoe staircases but also its combination with the rectangular projecting, balustraded terrace. This highly unusual feature could also be found at Pratolino.

Other than this, direct quotation from Tuscan sources is hard to identify in Jones's work. Though Jones's love of rusticated doorways may owe something to the Tuscan tradition, he did not follow the Tuscan tradition for beautifully detailed doorways and window surrounds that is one of the joys of Buontalenti's work.[107] The window details of the Queen's House remain in the Palladian and Scamozzian tradition, as does the contrast between the rusticated ground floor and plain first floor. Jones must have been conscious of the Tuscan tradition of an architecture of solid mass penetrated by windows but at the Queen's House he was not deliberately trying

to emulate it. This is clear above all in the use of the balustrade, something not found in Tuscan villas, which all tend to have deep overhanging eaves.

The use of a balustrade to disguise the slope of the roof behind became such a feature of later English and continental architecture that it is easy to overlook how unusual Jones's use of it was at the Queen's House. It is a marked feature of most Cinquecento Italian architecture that entablatures are not capped by balustrades as,

139 Bernardo Buontalenti, *Villa di Pratolino* (detail), 1569 (Museo Firenze com'erà, Florence).

117

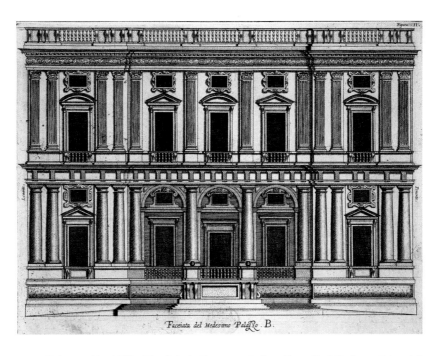

140   Galeazzo Alessi, Villa Giustiniani, Genoa, 1548, from Peter Paul Rubens, *Palazzi di Genova* (1622) I, p. 11.

for instance, in Palladio's and Scamozzi's palazzi and villas. Balustrades tend to be reserved for the grandest public buildings such Sansovino's Libreria Marciana in Venice (1537; see Fig. 175), Michelangelo's Palazzo dei Conservatori in Rome (1544; see Fig. 130) and Palladio's basilica in Vicenza (1549; see Fig. 174). However, there were a number of other examples that Jones would have known about. In Jacques Lemercier's 1607 engraving of Vignola's Villa Farnese at Caprarola (1557) the roofline is shown capped by a balustrade, though this was not executed.[108] More pertinent is the example of the Genoese-based architect Galeazzo Alessi (1512–72).

Alessi, who settled in Genoa in 1548 after training in Rome, where he was much influenced by Michelangelo, is one architect who has suffered, at least within an English context, from the intense attention paid to Palladio. His architecture is no less skilful than Palladio's, and he shows an equally strong interest in Antiquity, evident in particular in the façade of the rebuilt Church of S. Vittore al Corpo in Milan, which is as reverently antique as anything by Palladio. As already seen, Jones apparently borrowed from Alessi in the design of the 'Italian' gate at Arundel House in 1618, which is derived from Alessi's Porta del Molo in Genoa (see Fig. 108).

It may have been with Michelangelo's Capitoline Palace in mind that Alessi disguised the roofline of the Villa Giustiniani of 1548 with a balustrade to create a

building with a sharply horizontal roofline (Fig. 140).[109] Alessi went on to use balustrades on a number of buildings, including the impressive Palazzo Marino in Milan (1558) and in Genoa the Villa Sauli (about 1560) and Villa Grimaldi (1561–8).[110] All three Genoese villas were illustrated in Rubens's *Palazzi di Genova* in 1622–6, which reveals that the use of balustrades in one form or another became relatively commonplace in Genoa, though in the cases of the Villa Sauli and Grimaldi the engraving shows the steep pitch of the roof behind.[111] Jones would have known these examples both through the *Palazzi di Genova* and through his own studies of buildings in the city in 1614.[112]

Here the parallels between the Queen's House and Alessi's Villa Giustiniani are particularly significant. Both buildings are villas, albeit extremely grand villas, suburban retreats, not public buildings like the Capitoline Palace or the Basilica in Vicenza. In both cases there is a conscious attempt to create something out of the ordinary, the idea of an essentially cubic building in which the roofline is masked by the horizontal line of the balustrade. Further, both buildings were designed by architects thoroughly engaged in the study of Antiquity and its use in contemporary architecture.

Alessi may be the source for Jones's introduction of the balustraded roof but he cannot explain the shift in the balance of the building that allows the solid of the wall to predominate. If this was not directly inspired by a desire to emulate Tuscan architecture then something else must help explain this major shift in Jones's approach to design between the preliminary designs of 1616 and the resumption of work in 1632. One possible explanation is the publication in 1626 of the second volume of Rubens's *Palazzi di Genova* and Rubens's subsequent eight-month stay at the Stuart court in 1629–30.

Architectural historians have frequently sought to make a connection between the *Palazzi di Genova* and contemporary English architecture, generally without much success,[113] but its influence on Jones may have been profound.[114] No individual in northern Europe was held in greater cultural esteem than Rubens and this, his sole architectural publication, would have been received with great respect. The book was Rubens's private publication, an expensive gesture given the number and quality of the engravings. Though Rubens was not responsible for making the drawings of the different buildings, which are based on architectural drawings acquired on site, he carefully oversaw the way these were transformed into the published images, annotating them with corrections and crossings out.[115] This was a book with which he was intimately involved.

Rubens's immediate intention was to provide architectural models for his native city of Antwerp[116] but he had a broader ambition. A desire to reform architecture is clear from the foreword in which he declared that 'We see that style of architecture called barbaric or Gothic is gradually waning and disappearing in these parts; and that a few admirable minds are introducing the true symmetry of that other style which follows the rules of the ancient Greeks and Romans, to the great splendour and adornment of our country.'[117]

'True symmetry of that other style which follows the rules of the ancient Greeks and Romans': these are words that could well have been written by Inigo Jones. They might seem strange coming from someone seen as the embodiment of the Flemish Baroque but, as discussed in chapter 5, in his time Rubens was regarded as an authority on true architecture, was closely involved in the Vitruvian basilica of S. Carlo Borromeo in Antwerp (1615–21) and was held in such regard by Huygens, a pioneer of correct architecture in Holland, that he sought his approval for his new 'Vitruvian' house in The Hague.[118]

Thus when Rubens spent eight months from June 1629 to March 1630 at the court of Charles I negotiating the peace treaty between England and Spain, it would not only have been as a great painter but equally as an expert in true architecture that he would have met Jones. It was during this visit that he was commissioned to paint the ceiling of Jones's Banqueting House in Whitehall.[119] The presence of such an authoritative figure at the Stuart court, the only one who could rival his own knowledge, must have had an impact on Jones. The new direction that the Queen's House subsequently took may in part be the result.

While Rubens's commitment 'to the rules of the ancient Greeks and Romans' is clear from his introduction to the *Palazzi di Genova*, the stylistic message he meant to put across is enigmatic as the widely different individual palazzi are published without comment. However, there is one group of buildings that stands out, a sequence of seven designs grouped, presumably deliberately, at the front of the second volume. These are buildings of extreme austerity. In each case the ratio of window to wall is low and in six out of the seven the windows are punched directly into the wall surface, with no decorative mouldings. This is in direct contrast to palazzi illustrated in the first volume, and to many of the palazzi placed later in the second volume, whose façades are much more elaborate. Some of these palaces, the Palazzo Doria, the Palazzo Gambaro and the Palazzo Franzoni, date from the mid-1560s. The others, the Palazzo Balbi-Senarega, the Palazzo Casareto, the Palazzo Cattaneo and the Palazzo Durazzo-Pallavinci, date from the first two decades of the seventeenth century and may have been under construction when Jones visited Genoa in 1614.[120] Could these designs, their significance explained to Jones by Rubens, have influenced the rethinking of the Queen's House? The parallel is perhaps clearest in a comparison with the Palazzo Doria (Fig. 141). Though the Queen's House cannot be said to be derived from the Palazzo Doria in the same way that Jones took many of the details of his other buildings from Scamozzi, the underlying design approach has much in common. Jones was not prepared to go as far as the *Palazzi di Genova* designs in eliminating window surrounds but there is the same sense of windows punched into a dominant wall surface.

Rubens's engravings did not appear in a vacuum. As Ottenheym writes of their influence on subsequent Dutch architecture, 'this form of austere classicism was not based on Rubens's models alone. At issue is the reduction of the ornamental, in favour of the persuasiveness of the basic form, cubage and rhythm of the window openings and door openings in the façade. Anyone who had studied the principles of classicist theory profoundly, would have arrived at the same conclusion. It was Alberti who maintained that the true

141 Bernadino Cantone, Palazzo Doria, Genoa, 1563, from Peter Paul Rubens, *Palazzi di Genova* (1626) II, p. 3.

beauty of architecture lies in the measurement of the walls. All ornaments, including columns and pilasters are a second, added beauty, enhancing the clarity of the mathematical proportions. In Holland well-read patrons of architecture were also familiar with these principles. The Genoese models will have been regarded as a welcome visualisation of this doctrine.'[121]

It is possible that Jones received confirmation that such cubic austerity reflected the architecture of the ancients from what he considered the greatest surviving monument of Roman Antiquity in Britain, Stonehenge. In 1620 James I had commissioned him to examine Stonehenge and commanded him to 'produce out of

142 Inigo Jones, reconstruction of Stonehenge, from John Webb, *A Vindication of Stone-Heng Restored* (1665) p. 42.

mine own practice in Architecture and experience in Antiquities abroad, what possibly I could discover concerning this of Stoneheng'. Jones's deliberations were not published in his lifetime, but in 1655 John Webb published *The Most Notable Antiquity of Great Britain, Vulgarly called Stone-Heng*, in which he explained that Jones had concluded that Stonehenge was a Roman temple of the Tuscan order, open to the sky and dedicated to the god Coelus, the Heaven. His reconstruction shows a circular temple of extreme austerity topped by a continous flat entablature (Fig. 142).[122]

The final element of the Queen's House that needs to be addressed is the loggia on the south front (Fig. 143). The sense that this reads as a narrow slot carved into the volume of the building is far different from those in Palladio's and Scamozzi's porticoes-in-antis. A closely similar feel can be found in two of the Medici villas, that at Poggio a Caiano (see Fig. 42) and the Villa Medici at Artimino, built between 1594 and 1600 by Buontalenti. In Rome the same effect can be found at Pirro Ligorio's Palazzetto di Pio IV of 1561, where a first-floor loggia is punched into what is otherwise an austere elevation (Fig. 144). Ligorio used similar loggias on the Casino of Pius IV and its adjacent Loggetta, completed in 1562, though in these cases the loggias are on the ground floor not the first.[123] Ligorio (about 1510–1583) was another architect with a profound interest in Antiquity who has been overshadowed by Palladio, though he was certainly valued by Jones who, as is known from Wren, owned a book, now lost, of capitals, cornices and friezes drawn by Ligorio from Roman originals.[124] Ligorio acted as a guide to Palladio and Barbaro when they visited Rome in 1554 and Jones would have been aware of Barbaro's praise for his guide in his edition of *Vitruvius*: 'Regarding these antiquities the most diligent messer Pirro Ligorio is as learned as anyone who can be found, to whom is owed infinite and immortal thanks for the study of which he has made regarding antique objects for the benefit of the world.'[125] Presumably, Ligorio saw such loggias as a specifically antique feature and it may well be that Jones took a similar view of the Queen's House loggia.

When it came to the final design for the Queen's House Jones broke the shackles of both Palladio and Scamozzi to design a building that he no doubt thought represented 'the true symmetry of that other style which follows the rules of the ancient Greeks and Romans'. However, in what is likely was the very last building he designed, the buttery probably intended for Cobham Hall, Kent (which will be discussed in the next chapter),

143 Inigo Jones, south front of the Queen's House at Greenwich, 1633–8.

Jones returned yet again to Scamozzi, this time to his Tuscan order (see Figs 150 and 151).[126]

Careful study of Jones's buildings conducted without the blinkers of Palladian presupposition thus reveals that Palladio's influence on Jones is real but, except in a couple of cases, direct borrowings are surprisingly limited. Palladio was a fundamental guide to Jones in the principles and practice of architecture and an important source of details but it is to Scamozzi that Jones returned time and again for the overall framework of a design, for details and for the orders. This is not surprising. As already seen, the school of van Campen, whose work bears much resemblance to that of Jones, was showing no less an interest in Scamozzi at exactly the same time in the Dutch Republic.

144 Pirro Ligorio, Palazzetto di Pio IV, Rome, 1561.

121

G.BRIT.FRAN.ET HIBER.REX F.D. TEMPLUM *SANCTI PAULI* VETUSTATE CONSUMPTUM RESTITUIT

Chapter 8

THE ARCHITECTURE OF SOVEREIGNTY I: THE PORTICO

In many ways Dutch classicist architecture of the middle of the seventeenth century seems remarkably similar to that of Inigo Jones and his circle. There is the same drive to create a rational architecture based on proportion and the careful application of ornament, the same reverence for Vitruvius and Antiquity, the same respect for the modern masters who had tried to revive the best practices of Antiquity, particularly Andrea Palladio and Vincenzo Scamozzi. Some of Jones's works could be swapped with those by Pieter Post or Philips Vingboons and no one would be any the wiser. Yet there are also differences that need to be highlighted because they tell us much about the thinking that lay behind the new classicist architecture. They concern two elements that now seem so ubiquitous in what has come to be known as Palladian architecture that it takes a moment to notice their absence, the pediment and the Serlian window.

Of all architectural elements it is the pediment, whether expressed on a freestanding portico, on an attached portico supported by columns or pilasters or on its own, that today seems to epitomise what is meant by Palladian architecture. While pediments appeared regularly in the work of Palladio and Scamozzi and in the Dutch Republic, they were rarely found in England under James I and Charles I. Conversely, the Serlian, or Venetian window, which became a trademark of eighteenth-century Palladianism, is entirely absent from contemporary Dutch architecture, though it played a large part in Jones's work. The case of the Serlian window will be addressed in the next chapter; that of the pediment and portico in this.

As seen above, in chapter 5, the pediment was an essential element in Dutch architecture from Jacob van Campen's Huis ten Bosch in Maarssen of 1628 (see Fig. 59) and Salomon de Bray's Huis te Warmond of 1629 onwards. A string of pedimented buildings emerged from van Campen's circle in the 1630s: van Campen's Mauritshuis (see Fig. 60) and Constantijn Huygens and van Campen's Huygenshuis (see Fig. 58), both begun in The Hague in 1633; Arent van 's-Gravesande's St Sebastiaansdoelen in The Hague of 1636 (see Fig. 64); Vingboons's Westwijck at Purmer of 1637;[1] his Singel 282–6 in Amsterdam of 1639;[2] van 's-Gravesande's Lakenhall in Leiden of 1639; and Jacob van Campen and Post's Noordeinde Palace in The Hague of 1639 (see Fig. 61).

What stands out from this list is the widespread use of the pediment in the Dutch Republic during the 1630s. Following two private houses in the country (the Huis ten Bosch and the Huis te Warmond), it appeared on a royal palace (the Noordeinde Palace), a nobleman's residence (the Mauritshuis), the house of a cultured courtier (the Huygenshuis), two public buildings (St Sebastiaansdoelen and the Lakenhall), a country villa (Westwijck) and a group of town houses (Singel 282–6). In the 1640s the pediment spread among town houses in Amsterdam (Vingboons's Klonviersburgwal 95 of 1642); country houses (Post's Vredenberg of 1642; see Fig. 65); and in other towns (the anonymous Janskerhof 13, Utrecht, of 1648). By the 1650s the pediment was commonplace in Dutch architecture.

In contrast, no freestanding porticoes were built in the Dutch Republic during these years. Only two were planned, both for churches – van 's-Gravesande's Marekerk in Leiden of 1639–49 and Post's Oostkerk in Middelburg of 1648 (Fig. 146) – but neither was executed, for reasons of cost.[3] The closest the Dutch came to a portico on a domestic building was the single-storey, flat-balu-

145 (*facing page*) Inigo Jones, west portico of St Paul's cathedral, 1633–42, detail of Fig. 153.

146 Ceremonial trowel used during the first stone-laying of the Oostkerk in Middelburg and illustrating the intended portico by Pieter Post for the church, 1648 (Zeeuws Museum, Middelburg).

straded portico at Prince Frederik Hendrik's palace of Honselaarsdijk.[4]

The situation in England before the Civil War was different. Despite the strong interest in classicist architecture in the years leading up to the Civil War, pediments are notable by their absence in domestic architecture. This was not for lack of opportunity. Leicester House in London, built for the Earl of Leicester in 1631, Cornbury Park, Oxfordshire, a substantial country house remodelled for the Earl of Danby in 1631, and Lindsey House in Lincoln's Inn Fields, London, built around 1640, were all fashionably up-to-date houses that in the Dutch Republic would probably have been given pediments.[5] None was.

Instead, pediments are almost exclusively to be found in Jones's designs for royal buildings. There is what may be one of Jones's designs for the Queen's House at Greenwich (1616; see Fig. 118); his design for the Star

Chamber (1617; see Fig. 205); the designs for the Prince's Lodging at Newmarket (1618; see Figs 124 and 125); the preliminary design for the Banqueting House (1619; Fig. 147); designs for Somerset House (1638; see Figs 92 and 93); and designs for Whitehall Palace (about 1638; see Fig. 189).[6] In all these, bar one of the designs for the Prince's Lodging, which is astylar, the pediment is supported by attached columns, not pilasters.

Freestanding porticoes were similarly reserved in England for royal buildings or for churches in which the king took a particular interest. There are the two preliminary plans for the Queen's House (1616); the proposed portico of the grand design for Wilton House, Wiltshire (about 1630; see Fig. 91); the portico of St Paul's church, Covent Garden (1631; see Fig. 157); the west portico of St Paul's cathedral (designed in 1634; see Fig. 153); and the proposed giant portico that would have dominated the central court of Jones's Whitehall Palace (1638; see Fig. 190).[7]

To these can be added a scheme by Jones for a building with a hexastyle portico and balconied roof platform for which a drawing survives from the mid-1630s (Fig. 148). This was probably intended as a lodge in a royal park. The portico associates it with royalty, the rooftop walkway would have been ideal for watching the chase and the building included a good-sized room for feasting after the chase, a key feature of a hunting lodge. It is tempting to associate the design with the hunting lodges Jones built at Bagshot Park, Surrey, in 1631–2 and at Hyde Park, London, in 1634–5.[8] The parallels are closest with the 'New Lodge' in Hyde Park, which was also of two storeys, with a coved eaves cornice and dormers, and had six columns with Composite capitals. However, as the New Lodge probably did not have a pediment the drawing must at best be a preliminary design. A similar function probably lay behind Webb's drawing, presumably after Jones, for a smaller porticoed lodge (Fig. 149).[9] The portico is balustraded and clearly intended as a platform, presumably from which to watch the hunt.

Jones did not discuss the issue in any of his architectural notes but the built and unbuilt evidence shows that he considered porticoes, whether fully expressed with a projecting portico and columns, implied through pilasters and a pediment or simply expressed through a pediment on its own, to be symbols of authority and as such reserved for important religious and royal buildings.

The one apparent exception to this, Wilton House, the only aristocratic house to be considered for a portico, in fact fits the pattern. Wilton was so closely asso-

147 Inigo Jones, preliminary design for the Banqueting House, London, 1619 (Devonshire Collection, Chatsworth, reproduced by kind permission of the Trustees of the Chatsworth Settlement).

ciated with Charles I – as noted earlier, according to Aubrey, 'King Charles the first did love Wilton above all places and came thither every summer' – that it can be considered a quasi-palace.[10] With its matching king's and queen's apartments laid out in a single enfilade it was planned on a royal scale. Royal connections also explain the extensive use of pediments on Webb's unexecuted design for Cobham Hall, Kent, of 1648. This would have had pediments round three sides of the central court and on the end elevations of the two wings. Cobham Hall was the seat of the king's close cousin, James Stuart, third Duke of Richmond and Lennox. Tellingly, the drawing is inscribed 'ye Dukes Pallace at Cobham'.[11]

It is also probable that the design for a porticoed, villa-like building once thought to be a drawing by Jones for a brewhouse at Newmarket Palace or Hassenbrook

House, but which Howard Burns suggests was probably a buttery meant for entertainment, was also intended for Cobham Hall (Fig. 150). As with many of Jones's designs, Scamozzi is the source, in this case his design for a Tuscan portico (Fig. 151). According to Gordon Higgott the drawing is in the hand of Webb, authorised by the elderly Jones's signature, and was drawn in the late 1640s.[12] Given the date, the client is likely to be one of Jones's long-established contacts, as it is hard to believe that the architect, then in his mid-seventies, would have been taking on new clients. The Earl of Pembroke, whom Jones helped rebuild Wilton House after the fire of 1647, would be a plausible candidate but, as Higgott points out, the coronet on the coat of arms is not that of an earl but could be that of a duke. In that case the most plausible client is the Duke of Richmond and Lennox,

148   Inigo Jones, design for a royal hunting lodge, perhaps for New Lodge, Hyde Park, mid-1630s (Worcester College, Oxford).

for whose father Jones had produced two grand designs for gateways at Hatton House in 1622–3,[13] and it is also plausible that the drawing is contemporary with Webb's scheme to rebuild Cobham Hall as a classical palace in 1648.[14] It is possible that Lennox would have preferred Jones to design the house but that the old man passed it to his protégé and that the buttery, his last design, was the one direct contribution he made to the scheme.[15]

There appear to be only two exceptions to the rule that the pediment was restricted to royal situations under the early Stuarts. Palatial (or maybe ducal) aspirations may have lain behind the pediment in the grand screen at Castle Ashby, Northamptonshire, built by the second Earl of Northampton in 1631 but what is remarkable is how exceptional it is.[16] Sir Roger Townshend's attached

portico at Raynham Hall, Norfolk, built between 1622 and 1639, is best understood as a typical novelty of an amateur architect.[17] Amateurs are notoriously independent-minded in their interpretation of architectural conventions.[18]

It was not until the republican Commonwealth that pediments and freestanding porticoes were proposed in significant numbers for buildings in England that were neither royal nor religious. Indeed, the first known examples are Webb's designs for Durham House in London for the Earl of Pembroke, who had sided with Parliament against the Crown, one of which is dated 1649, the year of Charles I's execution (see Fig. 208).[19] Webb went on to design a series of buildings with freestanding or attached porticoes in the 1650s. He added

58.H

149　John Webb, probably after Inigo Jones, design for a royal hunting lodge, mid-1630s (Worcester College, Oxford).

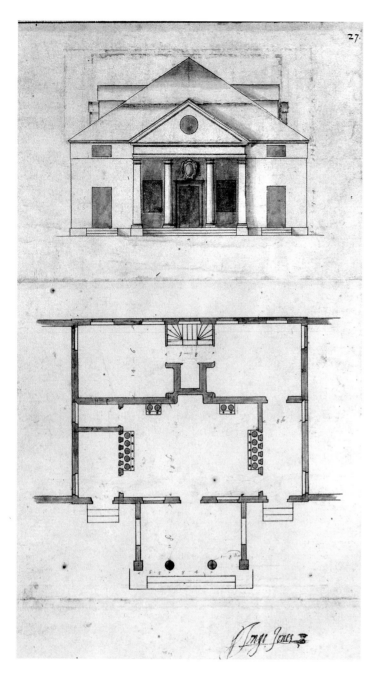

151 Vincenzo Scamozzi, Tuscan order, from *L'idea della architettura universale* (1615) II, p. 58.

150 Inigo Jones, buttery design, drawn by John Webb, probably for Cobham Hall, Kent, *c.*1648 (RIBA Library Drawings Collection).

one to the Vyne, Hampshire (1654), for Chaloner Chute, Speaker of the House of Commons, and included them in his designs for Gunnersbury House, Middlesex (about 1658), and Amesbury Abbey, Wiltshire (about 1659), both of which were built, and Belvoir Castle, Leicestershire (1655), which was not (see Fig. 207).[20] Webb would have been aware that in this more promiscuous use of the portico he was following the example of Palladio and

Scamozzi in the Venetian republic. With England then a republic, the royal exclusivity of the portico had been broken.

The Dutch were also a republic, so it was appropriate that the pediment was widely used not only by the princely house but by nobles, burghers and civic institutions. Even here propriety initially governed the use of the pediment. Initially, when the new classicist architecture was still in the hands of the courtly circle of Prince Frederik Hendrik and Huygens, it was exclusively reserved to royal, aristocratic and public use. In aristocratic circles, where status was graded by rank, the application of classical ornament to houses and, in particular, the use of the pediment was carefully measured to suit. None the less, this careful respect for decorum soon broke down because outside The Hague, and especially in Amsterdam, the Dutch Republic was a bourgeois society dominated by wealth, not rank. In these circles there was none of the reserve felt in aristocratic circles about the application of classical ornament: status was expressed through visible display. Yet even in bourgeois Holland no one dared to add a giant, freestanding portico to his house, not even the princely, ruling family. The single-storey, flat-topped porticoes at Honselaarsdijk and Noordeinde were as far as Frederik Hendrik dared push his assertion of authority. A giant, freestanding portico would have been too overt a claim to be risked. The only place such porticoes were possible in the Dutch Republic was on a church, the house of God.

The portico is so strongly associated today with the country house, and specifically with Palladio's villas, that it is easy to forget that, outside the Veneto, it was principally associated with religious buildings until late in the seventeenth century. This may seem strange given that the portico is generally seen as a symbol of the pagan ancient Romans but that was not the view of many sixteenth- and seventeenth-century religious reformers.

From Giuliano da Sangallo, who suggested a twenty-four-columned portico, onwards, many of the projects for St Peter's in Rome featured a giant, freestanding portico. They included schemes by Raphael (illustrated by Serlio) and Giuliano da Sangallo, with other architects suggesting attached porticoes.[21] These schemes culminated in Michelangelo's plans for a giant portico ten columns wide, stretching the width of the west end, with the central four columns projecting forward under a pediment. His scheme was never built but the designs were published in a series of engravings by Etienne du Pérac in 1569.[22] They were reprinted several times, including in an edition of about 1607, du Pérac's *Ichnographia templi divi Petri Romae in Vaticano ex esemplari Michaelis Angeli Bonaroti Florentini*, published just before Jones visited Rome.[23] Michelangelo's grandiose ideas remained unexecuted, but the west front of St Peter's as begun by Carlo Maderno in 1612 retains the essence of his scheme in its four-bay temple front under a pediment flanked by attached columns and pilasters.[24]

An abortive sequence of church porticoes can be traced across the sixteenth and seventeenth centuries. Palladio in particular was keen to add porticoes to his churches. Ambitious schemes by him survive from the late 1570s to complete S. Petronio in Bologna with a giant freestanding portico, along with designs for churches with porticoes in Venice. Yet the only time that he was able to put these ideas into practice was at the little chapel at Maser (1579).[25] Palladio was not alone in this ambition. An eight-columned portico for the Church of S. Giovanni dei Fiorentini in Rome was suggested by an anonymous sixteenth-century architect and

more examples can be found in Milan.[26] When the ancient Basilica of S. Vittore al Corpo in that city was rebuilt in the 1560s one proposal, probably by Galeazzo Alessi, suggested a ten-columned portico, again reduced to a pilastered screen, presumably for reasons of cost.[27] A project by F. M. Ricchini of about 1616 for the Church of Sta Maria de Loreto suggested an eight-columned freestanding portico.[28] Another scheme, attributed to Aurelio Trezzi, survives for adding a freestanding, six-columned portico to the Early Christian Church of S. Lorenzo, also Milan, in about 1623.[29] To this list of unexecuted porticoes can be added the two already discussed in the Dutch Republic, van 's-Gravesande's Marekerk in Leiden of 1639–49 and Post's Oostkerk in Middelburg of 1648 (see Fig. 146).[30]

Apart from Palladio at Maser, only Lemercier in Paris and Jones in London seem to have been successful in carrying through this long-anticipated ambition, Lemercier at the Chapel of the Sorbonne (1635; see Fig. 50), Jones at St Paul's, Covent Garden (1631; see Fig. 157), and St Paul's cathedral (1635; see Fig. 153).[31] These were the first of a sequence of churches with freestanding porticoes that in the second half of the century included a failed attempt by Gianlorenzo Bernini in 1659 to add a portico of four columns in front of Maderno's façade of St Peter's in Rome; the successful addition by his former assistant at St Peter's, Carlo Fontana, of four-columned porticoes to Carlo Rainaldi's churches of Sta Maria di Monte Santo and Sta Maria de' Miracoli on the Piazza del Popolo in Rome (1662); and the six-columned portico of the Church of the Assumption in Paris built in 1670–76 to designs sent from Rome by Charles Errard.[32] It was a movement that reached its highpoint in the first decades of the eighteenth century when built and unbuilt examples range from S. Nicolo da Tolentino (1706) and S. Simeone Piccolo (1713–19) in Venice, to the proposed cathedral in Berlin (1712), the royal burial church in Stockholm (1713), the Karlskirche in Vienna (1716), Superga outside Turin (1717) and three examples from the Fifty New Churches in London: St George, Bloomsbury (1716), St George, Hanover Square (1721) and St Martin-in-the Fields (1722).

That porticoes, and even implied porticoes, were specifically associated with monarchy or the church in early Stuart England is not surprising. Charles I had a highly elevated sense of monarchy. As Foulke Robarts put it in his *God's house and service according to the primitive and most Christian forme thereof* in 1639, the King was 'Defender of the Faith . . . next and immediately under God, supreme governor over all persons and causes as

152   Inigo Jones, proposed elevation for the west front of St Paul's cathedral, London, *c.*1631 (RIBA Library Drawings Collection).

well ecclesiastical as temporal in his majesty's realms and dominions.'[33] In the Book of Common Prayer it was a liturgical requirement that the congregation pray for the monarch as head of state, godly ruler and God's minister. This weekly liturgical transaction asserted and confirmed the congregation as subjects and figured the king primarily as a godly minister within the established Church.[34] Charles I saw his role as quasi-sacerdotal. Architecture expressed his vision of Church and Crown. The portico, a temple front, was the highest expression

of the classical language; it was right that it should be reserved for God and the monarch. The royal and religious associations of the portico for Charles I were most clearly united in the siting of a chapel with a giant six-columned portico at the heart of Jones's 'preliminary' design for Whitehall Palace (see Fig. 189).

That portico was never built but Charles was directly responsible for Jones's massive west portico of St Paul's cathedral of 1635–42, the most ambitious freestanding portico built since Antiquity (Fig. 153). From 1631 the

CAROLVS D:G:MAG:BRIT.FRAN.ET HIBER:REX F:D:TEMPLVM SANCTI PAVLI VETVSTATE CONSVMPTVM RESTITVIT ET PORTICVM FECIT.

I: Iones Architectus.   H. Flitcroft Delin: H. Huſsbergh Sculp:

153 Inigo Jones, west portico of St Paul's cathedral, 1633–42, shown in an engraved drawing from William Kent's *Designs of Inigo Jones* (1727) II, p. 56.

fabric of the cathedral was effectively in the hands of the king, his councillors and officers rather than the dean and chapter, the architect of the restoration in the broadest sense being William Laud, Bishop of London from 1628 and Archbishop of Canterbury from 1633.[35] Jones's portico design represented a dramatic change from his initial design for the west front, which Higgott dates in terms of drawing style to the early 1630s and perhaps as early as 1631 when planning for the restoration began (Fig. 152). This design had no portico and instead relied on paired, superimposed columns for the nave and pilasters for the towers. Harris and Higgott draw a comparison between the design and the engraving of the Jesuit church of S. Ambrogio in Genoa, illustrated in Rubens's *Palazzi di Genova*.[36] In the light of Jones's contact with Rubens during the latter's stay at the English court in 1629–30, this is a plausible source. However, it was soon abandoned in favour of the porticoed version, probably in 1634 when Charles announced that he intended to pay for the whole

154 Andrea Palladio, the 'Temple of the Sun and the Moon',
from *I quattro libri dell'architettura* (1570) IV, p. 37.

restoration of the west front. In his name £10,661 was
given of which £8,000, produced between 1634 and
1637, came from his own funds, the remainder from
ecclesiastical fines in the Court of High Commission.[37]
The portico of St Paul's was thus Charles I's most substantial architectural gesture, which presumably explains
why the initial design was abandoned for the more
imposing portico design, for its stronger royal associations.

Beyond the fact that the portico was the most prestigious feature in classical architecture, what explains this
persistent desire, seen from St Peter's onwards, to add
what was traditionally associated with pagan temples to
some of the grandest churches in Christendom? Why in
particular should Jones want to add a portico to St Paul's
cathedral, which could never hope to disguise the height
and proportions of its medieval form? The desire to

outdo St Peter's must have been one driving force at
St Paul's. Jones would have known of Michelangelo's
scheme and it is unlikely to be coincidence that his
portico was also ten columns wide. That at St Paul's must
be read in the context of the Anglican challenge to the
Church of Rome. The particular satisfaction felt by the
English in achieving the portico that the Romans had
failed to build at St Peter's is evident in Webb's comment
in 1665 that Jones, 'by adding that magnificent Portico
there, hath contracted the Envy of all *Christendom* upon
our Nation, for a Piece of Architecture, not to be paral-
lell'd in the last Ages of the World'.[38]

The portico is partly based on Palladio's reconstruction of the 'Temple of Sun and Moon'. Jones observed
in his copy of the *Quattro libri* that this temple had been
'dedicated and built by T. Tatio King of the Romans',
making a particularly appropriate connection with the
aims of Charles as King of the Britons. The specifically
royal associations of the portico are emphasised by the
statues of kings that graced it.[39]

Does the precedent of Palladio's reconstruction of the
'Temple of the Sun and Moon' and, equally importantly,
his reconstruction of the 'Temple of Jupiter the Thunderer', explain why Jones's portico was topped by a flat
balustrade where Michelangelo's design for St Peter's and
Palladio's for S. Petronio (which Jones owned) had conventional porticoes with a pediment? Given Jones's
knowledge and love of Antiquity this preference for a
pedimentless portico at first sight seems strange, until it
is realised that such porticoes, known as a narthex, were
a standard feature of Early Christian churches in Rome.
The finest example, and that most directly comparable
to St Paul's, is that of S. Lorenzo Fuori le Mura, which
has a six-columned Ionic colonnade terminated by
square piers (Fig. 155). Though S. Lorenzo's narthex was
built in 1217, the tradition dates back to the earliest
Christian churches. S. Croce in Gerusalemme, built by
the Empress Dowager Helena, mother of the Emperor
Constantine, in 326–8 had a comparable narthex.[40] Of
the seven principal churches of Rome illustrated in an
engraving of 1565 by A. Lafréry, only the Lateran does
not have a narthex (Fig. 156). Sta Maria Maggiore, S.
Lorenzo, Sta Croce and S. Sebastiano all have colonnaded
narthexes without pediments.[41] St Peter's and S. Paolo
Fuori le Mura have arcaded narthexes which had originally been four-sided atria. Jones would have been able
to see these and other examples such as that of S. Giorgio
in Velabro during the months he spent in Rome.

The study of the Early Christian churches as a model
for contemporary religious practice had become partic-

132

ularly important with the Reformation, as a means of distinging between what was the correct way to build and worship and what was later-imposed superstition. Both Anglicans and Roman Catholics sought guidance from the Early Christian church. In Italy, as Andrew Hopkins notes, there was a particular interest in Early Christianity in the second half of the sixteenth century, culminating in the period leading up to the jubilee of 1600 celebrated by Clement VIII. Filippo Neri founded the Oratorians in 1575 with the aim of returning to the simplicity of the Early Christian church. He sponsored Cesare Baronio's *Annales Ecclesiastici*, published in 1588–1607, and Neri, Baronio, Antonio Gallonio and other Oratorians promoted the Early Christian revival at their Church of S. Girolamo della Carità in Rome. Baronio, who restored his own Church of SS. Nereo and Achilleo in 1596–7, was instrumental in the revival, along

155 The narthex of S. Lorenzo Fuori le Mura, Rome, *c.*1217.

156 A. Lafréry, engraving of the seven principal churches of Rome, 1565.

133

with Cardinal Benedetto Giustiniani, who had Carlo Lambardi restore the Church of Sta Prisca on the Aventine Hill in 1600.[42]

Meanwhile Cardinal Carlo Borromeo, appointed Archbishop of Milan in 1560, showed a particular interest in improving the churches in his diocese and formulated his ideas in his *Instructions for ecclesiastical buildings and furnishings* in 1577, which was strongly influenced by Early Christian example. Under his direction in 1569 Pellegrino Tibaldi formed the extraordinary circular crypt of Milan cathedral, with its ring of columns and surrounding ambulatory based on the Early Christian mausoleum in Rome later dedicated as a church to Sta Costanza.[43] It was also during Borromeo's period as archbishop that Martino Bassi faithfully rebuilt the Early Christian Church of S. Lorenzo in Milan with its remarkable, primitive baseless Doric columns, after the dome collapsed in 1573.

One of the elements Borromeo, following Early Christian example, encouraged in his churches was the porch or narthex. This explains why Alessi proposed adding a ten-columned narthex when the ancient Basilica of S. Vittore al Corpo in Milan was rebuilt in the 1560s, a scheme that intriguingly anticipates Jones's design for the portico of St Paul's.[44] It also explains Trezzi's proposal to add a portico to S. Lorenzo in about 1623.[45] Palladio was certainly aware of Cardinal Borromeo's writings on the subject and they probably influenced him in his proposed church porticoes.[46] Narthexes remained exceptional on new churches, though one can be found at the remarkably austere Basilica of Sta Barbara at Mantua, built in 1561–72 by Giovan Battista Bertrani for Guglielmo Gonzaga.[47] This follows the triple division recommended by authorities on ancient churches: narthex, nave and chancel. The extraordinary, stripped nature of the classical orders in Sta Barbara has a powerfully primitive feel, which was presumably Bertani's intention.

Study of the Early Christian church was particularly important in early Stuart England, where conflict over the correct form of worship and of churches was fundamental to the future shape of the Church of England. This interest is specifically stated in a letter James I wrote concerning the Prince of Wales and others on their abortive trip to Spain: 'I have fully instructed them so as all their behaviour and service shall, I hope, prove decent and *agreeable to the purity of the primitive church* [my italics] and yet as near the Roman form as can lawfully be done, for it hath ever been my way to go with the Church of Rome *usque ad aras*' ['even unto the altars'], as far as is

allowable.[48] It was a formula repeated in his lengthy *Premonition*, signed 'James by the Grace of God, King of Great Britain, France, and Ireland; Professour, Maintainer, and Defender of the Trew, Christian, Catholique and Apostolique Faith, Professed by the ancient and Primitive church'.[49]

The years before the Civil War saw considerable debate about the Early Christian church in England.[50] John Pocklington published *Altare Christianum* in 1637, which was followed in successive years by *De Templis: A Treatise of Temples: wherein is discovered the ancient manner of building, consecrating and adorning of churches* by 'R.T.' (described as a Laudian tract[51]) and Foulke Robarts's *God's house and service according to the primitive and most Christian forme thereof*. Robarts summed up the intention when talking about how churches should be divided into a number of discrete elements: 'Distinctiveness of several places in the house of God are not any conceit crept in with Popery: but such as have been constituted and put in use, very early in the Primitive church.' When describing recent improvements to churches he declares that 'The house and service of God shineth among us in the primitive splendour, to the liking of all sober Christians.'[52] Of the two, R.T.'s is the more considered examination, in which he proves that recent continental scholarship on the subject was familiar in England. He frequently quotes continental scholars, particularly Cardinal Bellarmine as well as Lelio Bisciola, Philippus Lonicerus, Petrus Gregorius Tolozanus and Cesare Baronio.

Both writers emphasised the close association of church and monarch. As Foulke Robarts put it: 'We find churches anciently styled basilicae . . . The word basilica therefore is, if one should say an house for a King. For so the church is the house of the great King, viz. Almighty God, or else because Church is such and so far a model of building as becometh no less a man than a King. The Hebrews by the word [?] do express both a Temple and a Palace.'[53] R.T. says much the same: 'King's palaces of old were called Basilica, from Basileus, a King, and the sacred Temples, dedicated to the King of Kings, may be so called.'[54]

Like Cardinal Borromeo, R.T. stressed the importance of the narthex: citing a succession of authorities, he makes it clear that that 'place before the temple, which we call the porch' was one of the three key elements of the church, along with nave and chancel.[55] It is in this light that the portico of St Paul's cathedral should be read, not as a piece of pure classicism, an attempt to graft pagan form onto a Christian building out of excessive

157   Inigo Jones, portico of St Paul's Church, Covent Garden, 1631.

respect for Antiquity, but as a narthex, part of an attempt to restore the church to its primitive state. As such it was a deliberate counterpoint to St Peter's, a statement of the fundamental Anglican belief that the Church of England represented the true Christian Church, based on the Early Christian Church, uncorrupted by subsequent superstition (as it was believed had happened to the papacy).

It may be relevant that Nicholas Stone was paid £30 for a 'porch' of Portland stone at St John the Evangelist, Great Stanmore, Middlesex, which was consecrated in 1632 by Laud as Bishop of London.[56] This may have been intended as a narthex, again copying the manner of the primitive Christians, and this is how one should read the portico of St Paul's, Covent Garden (Fig. 157). This was probably added at the insistence of Charles I, part of the extra expense he forced on the Earl of Bedford in building the church.[57] It is perhaps no coincidence that Jones chose for his church the most primitive of the orders, Tuscan. Jones's model was Vitruvius's description of the Roman Tuscan temple but, again, this should not be read as a simple exercise in neo-classicism. The relationship of pagan temples to Christianity and

their validity as a model for contemporary Christian churches is something R.T. explores in some detail. He notes that the very first Christians did not call their churches temples and that their earliest places of worship were simple but that this changed. 'The word Temple was not used except for temples of the Heathen till the time of Constantine by whose munificent piety stately and beauteous temples were everywhere erected.'[58] R.T. accepted that Early Christian churches took the form of pagan basilicas: 'These basilicas were by a happy metamorphosis changed into Christian churches and still retained their old name.'[59] Nor was it only basilicas that became churches. 'Many of the temples of the heathen, in the apostles' times, and in the time of Constantine the Great, were converted to the worship of the true God, yet retained their old figure and shape.' Indeed, R.T. noted a letter from St Gregory to St Augustine, who converted the southern English to Christianity, stating that though he should destroy the idols in England he should suffer their temples to stand and re-use them.[60] In this context Jones's use of the Tuscan temple for St Paul's, Covent Garden, like the portico of St Paul's cathedral, is not as surprising as it might seem.

135

158   Anthony Van Dyck, *Inigo Jones*, *c*.1640 (Devonshire Collection, Chatsworth, reproduced by kind permission of the Trustees of the Chatsworth Settlement).

Chapter 9

THE ARCHITECTURE OF SOVEREIGNTY II: THE SERLIANA

O F ALL THE ARCHITECTURAL ELEMENTS found in Inigo Jones's buildings, none is more firmly associated with Palladio and Palladianism than the Serliana, a three-part opening, commonly but not exclusively a window, with a central arch separated by columns from flat-headed openings. In England the Serliana is sometimes known as the Venetian or Palladian window. Elsewhere it is often described as the 'Palladian motif'.[1] So strong is its association with Palladianism that the mere appearance of a Serliana is enough for some to assume that the building it appears on can be fitted into the Palladian canon.[2] However, to read the Serliana at this date as simply a stylistic motif, or specifically as a Palladian motif, is a grave misunderstanding, as a study of contemporary English and Dutch classicist architecture shows. The Serliana was clearly important to Jones but not because of its associations with Palladio. There is no precedent in Palladio for the Serlian east window at the Queen's Chapel at St James's Palace, nor for the nineteen Serlian windows on the river front of his design for Whitehall Palace. By contrast, the Dutch, who might have been expected to embrace the Serliana with fervour given its prevalence in Scamozzi's *L'idea della architettura universale* (1615), made no use of it at all during the seventeenth century. To understand Jones's use of the Serliana it is necessary to study its origins in some detail and to realise that its significance lay not in any association with Palladio but in the meaning with which it was imbued as one of the most powerful symbols of sovereignty.

Palladio was only one, and neither the first nor the most active, among many sixteenth-century Italian architects who used the Serliana. Apart from the basilica in Vicenza the Serliana appears on only a couple of villas in his *Quattro libri dell'architettura*.[3] It is the ubiquity of the Serliana in eighteenth-century English neo-Palladian

architecture that has caused it to be associated with Palladio, not the work or writings of the architect himself, as Wittkower realised long ago.[4] As yet there is no comprehensive account of the Serliana.[5] Its symbolic implications have been usefully examined in two specific cases: Charles V's palace at Granada by E. E. Rosenthal and the Uffizi in Florence by Roger J. Crum and Leon Satkowski.[6] Though these authors did not develop the implications of their arguments for other buildings it is possible to construct a similar and consistent account of the Serliana from the court of Pope Julius II in Rome early in the sixteenth century to early in the eighteenth century that treats it principally as a sign of sovereignty.

This is a complex issue because architectural motifs by their nature are mute. It is observers who draw out

159   Etienne du Pérac, engraving showing the coronation of Cosimo de' Medici as Grand Duke of Tuscany in the Sala Regia, Vatican Palace, Rome, on 18 February 1570.

the meanings they embody and those meanings depend on what is commonly agreed at the time, which may differ with different generations or in different localities. An architect may use a motif because of the meaning she or he sees imbued in it, only for a later architect to copy it, unaware of the motif's original meaning, out of homage to the architect or the building.[7] With the Serliana this is particularly complicated because of the variety of ways in which it can be applied. The classic use is the single Serlian window or opening but sometimes a sequence of Serlianas may be used to form a loggia or be linked to form an arcade, most typically round a courtyard. Different uses have different resonances but what is remarkable is how quickly and consistently the single Serliana emerged as a symbol of sovereignty.

The Serliana form was not uncommon in Antiquity, one of the early examples being at the Temple of Dushara at Si' in Syria, which probably dates from late first century BC. The most significant surviving examples are at Diocletian's Palace at Split, begun in AD 295, where a sequence of Serliana windows punctuated the entrance elevation and a Serlian arch formed a screen at the end of the courtyard leading to the imperial apartments.[8] The origins of its revived use in a consistent fashion in Renaissance Italy are uncertain but they probably lie in Milan, a city with important Late Roman remains.[9] Serlian windows are used in the cross-plan arms of Sta Maria della Passione, begun by 1486 to the designs of Giovanni di Domenico Battagio.[10] Though the church was subsequently completed to a different plan, there is no reason to believe that these windows are not orginal. Other pre-sixteenth-century Serlian windows appear above the choir of the nearby Certosa of Pavia[11] and in the 1490s in the cloisters of S. Ambrogio in Milan, designed by Donato Bramante, one of Milan's leading architects.[12] The most impressive of these early uses of Serlianas is at S. Maurizio, whose foundation stone was laid in 1503, where they form a first-floor gallery round the church. The authorship of S. Maurizio is uncertain though it is often attributed to Gian Giacomo Dolcebuono, a pupil of Bramante.[13]

These Milanese Serlianas remained isolated examples and seem not to have led to a consistent pattern of use. That is to be found in Rome but probably following the Milanese lead because the key examples appear in the

160 Raphael, *Fire in the Borgo*, 1514, Vatican Palace, Rome, detail showing the Benediction Window.

circle of Bramante, who fled to Rome following the fall of the Sforzas in 1499. In 1505 Bramante placed a pair of Serlian windows high on the side elevations of the choir of Sta Maria del Popolo in Rome, which he designed for Julius II.[14] The choir's interior was redolent of ancient Rome, with a shell apse and a vault decorated by Pinturicchio in the manner of a vault in Hadrian's Villa at Tivoli. Similar windows were placed in S. Eligio degli Orefici in Rome in about 1509, which was probably designed by Bramante though Raphael's name is often associated with it.[15] A Serliana can be found in a similar architectural position in Raphael's preliminary design of 1510–11 for *The Expulsion of Heliodorus* in the pope's private rooms in the Vatican, although not in the executed version.[16]

The most prominent in this sequence of Serlianas was in the Sala Regia, the papal throne room in the Vatican, where Bramante installed a large Serlian window above the papal throne in 1507 (Fig. 159). This was commissioned by Julius II, whose identification with the window was so keen that its interior and exterior are both inscribed with his name.[17] Julius II, elected in 1503, was the most imperial of all Renaissance popes, determined to re-establish the glories of the papacy by regaining control of the Papal States by force and to boost the papacy's prestige by wrapping himself in the aura of the Roman emperors, whose heirs the popes considered themselves as the physical inheritors of Rome. The pope's formal title of Pontifex Maximus, a title formerly held by the Roman emperors, was a clear and repeated statement of this papal belief.[18] Julius II was keenly aware of the importance of architecture in creating a suitable setting for the papacy, as was evident in his rebuilding of St Peter's and remodelling of the Vatican Palace.[19]

Julius II's successor, Giovanni de' Medici, elected Pope Leo X in 1513, made equally symbolic use of the Serliana. In Raphael's *Fire in the Borgo* of 1514, in the pope's private rooms, Leo IV, bearing the visage of his later namesake, appears on a Serlian balcony issuing the blessing that halted the fire threatening the Vatican in 847 (Fig. 160).[20] A large Serlian window was the central element in Raphael's unexecuted design of 1515–16 for Leo X for the west front of the Medicean Church of S. Lorenzo in Florence.[21] Raphael's final project of about 1518–21 for Cardinal Giulio de' Medici's villa surburbana outside Rome, the Villa Madama, included large

161 Giulio Romano, *Leo X on a Balcony*, 1524–5, Vatican Palace, Rome, detail showing a Serlian balcony in a window embrasure of the Sala di Costantino.

162 Missorium of Theodosius, *c*.388 (Royal Historical Academy, Madrid).

'Ever since antiquity', notes Satkowski, 'architectural enframement in the form of a baldachin or serliana was employed in depictions of enthroned rulers to suggest by the temple-like fastigium the divine nature of their temporal powers.'[25] Such a Serliana might have appeared at the end of a hall or courtyard, where the emperor, raised up several steps, would have been seen in state framed by the central arch, as at Diocletian's Palace at Split, and its use in practice is illustrated by the large silver plate known as the Missorium of Theodosius (Fig. 162).[26] In the seventh-century Cyprus Plates now in NewYork, Saul is shown similarly enframed when David is presented to him, the Serliana form being repeated in three of the other plates.[27] 'Elevated above the floor of the forecourt, [the Serliana] marks with emphatic clarity the edge between the public realm and the *palatium sacrum* and establishes the correct *mise-en-scène* in which the god-emperor might choose to emerge before the eyes of a bedazzled and adoring audience.'[28] Serliana-like 'windows of appearances', as Rosenthal describes them, were also important imperial symbols.[29] Diocletian's Palace originally had at least three such windows on its long façade (Fig. 163). Another surviving example of a 'window of appearance' is the early fifth-century ivory Venatio Panel now in Brescia, in which a figure of

163 Detail of Diocletian's Palace, Split, Croatia, seen in an engraving from Robert Adam, *Ruins of the Palace of the Emperor Diocletian at Spalato* (1764) pl. VII (British Library, London).

Serlianas for the elevation and at the top of the great flight of stairs that formed the entrance.[22] The figure of Leo X, identified by the Medici arms, appears within another Serlian balcony in a window embrasure painted by Raphael's pupil Giulio Romano in the Sala di Constantino in the Vatican Palace in 1524–5, where all the painted scenes were characterised by a desire to create authentically Constantinian or Roman settings and details (Fig. 161).[23] Raphael also placed a Serlian window above Christ and the twelve apostles in his depiction of *The Last Supper* of about 1514, engraved by Mario Dente and Marcantonio Raimondi (see Fig. 183).[24]

The successive use of Serlianas in buildings intimately associated with the papacy was not accidental. In the Sala Regia, Julius II and Leo X would have appeared in state below the Serliana. In the *Fire in the Borgo* and in the Sala di Constantino Leo X displays himself at Serlian balconies. Had the Villa Madama been completed, visitors would have passed through large Serliana openings before meeting the pope. A large Serlian window would have announced the papal connections of S. Lorenzo in Florence, just as at Sta Maria del Popolo, S. Eligio degli Orefici and S. Lorenzo Serlian windows were used as badges of papal involvement and as symbols of the papacy's imperial authority.

164 The Venatio Panel, early fifth century (Museo Civico dell'Età Cristiana, Brescia).

165 Detail of a reconstruction of a Roman circus building from Onofrio Panvinio, *De ludis circensibus* (1600) p. 62 (British Library, London).

authority clutching a sceptre sits, perhaps in the Colosseum, within a Serliana-like opening watching a chariot race (Fig. 164).[30] Though it is now known that the figure was a *quaestor* (a senior official) and not the emperor, it must have been images such as these that made Julius II and Leo X and their architects appreciate the hierarchical significance of the Serliana and consciously revive it to bolster the identification of the papacy with the Roman emperors. The Sala Regia recalled the use of the Serliana in imperial halls or forecourts; the Benediction Window in the *Fire in the Borgo* and the Serliana balcony in the painted window embrasure of the Sala di Constantino confirm its use as a 'window of appearance'.

The accepted association of the Serliana with Roman emperors in the sixteenth century is evident in Pirro Ligorio's map of Rome of 1561, where a Serliana appears over the entrance and 'podium' or imperial seat of the Circus of Nero, on the site of the Vatican. A similar reconstruction of a Roman circus building with Serlian window and terms on the 'podium' was published in Onofrio Panvinio's *De ludis circensibus* in 1600 (Fig. 165).[31]

A single Serlian window or balcony remained closely associated with the papacy in Rome in subsequent cen-

166　Bartolomeo Ammannati, belvedere of the Villa Giulia, Rome, 1551, built for Pope Julius III.

167　Giacomo della Porta, Villa Aldobrandini, Frascati, Italy, 1598–1603, built for Cardinal Pietro Aldobrandini.

168　Pedro Machuca, palace of Charles V, Granada, Spain, 1526.

turies, being used only occasionally, principally in buildings with strong papal connections. The giant Serliana of Bartolomeo Ammannati's belvedere dominates the Villa Giulia of 1551, built for Pope Julius III (Fig. 166). Giacomo della Porta's Villa Aldobrandini, Frascati, built in 1598–1603 for Cardinal Pietro Aldobrandini, *cardinal nepote* of Pope Clement VIII and papal secretary, has a

dominant Serliana in the centre of the garden elevation (Fig. 167).[32] In the seventeenth century Borromini suggested placing a giant Serlian belvedere on the roof of the Palazzo Pamphilj in the Piazza Navona, built in the 1650s for Pope Innocent X. This was never executed but a pair of Serlian windows were included in the palazzo, one on either side of Borromini's adjacent Church of S. Agnese in Agone.[33] A few years later Alexander VIII commissioned Pietro da Cortona to add a prominent Serliana balcony when he remodelled Sta Maria in Via Lata in 1658–62. He was also responsible for Gianlorenzo Bernini's Scala Regia at the Vatican of 1663–5, a staircase framed within a long succession of Serliana openings that formed the ceremonial approach to the papal palace.[34]

169   Giulio Romano, garden façade of the Palazzo del Tè, Mantua, begun 1526.

It was not only the popes who saw themselves as heirs of the Roman emperors. Their direct rivals were the Holy Roman Emperors, of whom Charles V, emperor from 1519 to 1557, was the one who most closely emulated the universal empire of the Romans.[35] Charles V's imperial status was deliberately emphasised in the imagery with which he was surrounded. The architect of this strategy was Mercurio de Gattinara, grand chancellor from 1518 to 1530, whose *Pro divo Carlo* repeatedly referred to Charles's status as the heir to the Emperor Justinian. In this image-making process, Charles V was shown as having been placed on earth by God to fulfil the work begun in the ninth century by Charlemagne.[36] It is thus not surprising that Charles V also sought to benefit from the imperial symbolism of the Serliana.

The only new palace built for Charles V was in Granada in southern Spain, though the shell alone was completed.[37] This was designed in 1526 by the Spanish painter Pedro Machuca but is strongly imbued with the architectural ideals of Bramante and Raphael, which Machuca must have picked up during his time in Rome. Charles V liked to assert himself as the new Augustus and, as Rosenthal has shown, the palace bears a strong imperial iconographic message, including a Serlian balcony in the centre of the south façade (Fig. 168.[38] As John Headley put it: 'In the unfinished palace of Charles V at Granada a political statement of imperial commitment resounds.'[39] Soon afterwards Perino del Vaga's triumphal arch for the entry of Charles V into Genoa of 1529 took the form of a Serliana with columns, as did the triumphal arch into Rome designed by Antonio da Sangallo for Charles V in 1536.[40]

As the example of the Villa Aldobrandini shows, Serlianas could be used on buildings intimately associated with the pope, announcing the power and close connections of the builder. This pattern was also to be found in the circle of Charles V. A positive surfeit of Serlianas appears on the east front of Giulio Romano's Palazzo del Tè in Mantua, begun in 1526 for the captain of the imperial troops in Italy, Federico Gonzaga, created Duke of Mantua by Charles V in 1530 (Fig. 169). As Amedeo Belluzzi and Kurt Forster explain, the iconography of the palazzo is explained by its use to receive the emperor in 1530 and 1532: 'the physical presence of the emperor . . . transformed the Palazzo Tè into an Imperial palace, comparable with the most illustrious archetypes of palaces of the Caesars'.[41] G. B. Bertrani surrounded the forecourt of the Palazzo Ducale in Mantua, the Prato di Castello, with an arcade of repeated Serlianas in 1549, an alternative antique use of the Serliana clearly seen to have similar imperial overtones, perhaps because of its use at the Canopus of Hadrian's Villa at Tivoli. It appears fittingly as a backdrop to the formal entrance of Philip II into Mantua as painted by Tintoretto, now in the Alte Pinakothek in Munich.[42]

A similar use of the Serliana could be found in the northern dominions of Charles V at the Kasteel at Breda, rebuilt in 1536 by Tomaso Vincidor for the emperor's deputy in the Northern Netherlands, Count Hendrik III of Nassau-Breda. Here the courtyard of the castle was dominated by an ambitious staircase that led to a first-floor Serliana balcony (Fig. 170). Vincidor, who had been sent to the Netherlands in 1520 by Leo X to supervise the weaving of the Raphael tapestries for the Sistine Chapel, would have been well aware of the imperial symbolism of the Serliana.[43] Its appearance at the Kasteel can be read as the physical manifestation of the imperial presence.

It was not only the pope and the Holy Roman Emperor who asserted imperial status and symbols. Late medieval and early modern rulers made increasingly fre-

170 Detail from an engraving showing Tomaso Vincidor's Kasteel at Breda, 1536, built for Count Hendrick III of Nassau-Breda.

quent claims to independent *imperium*. Such claims did not seek to compete with the emperor or pope for supremacy but asserted independence from external interference and ascendancy over internal competitors.

171 Juan Bautista da Toledo and Juan de Herrera, detail from a longitudinal section through the Escorial showing the Serlian royal pew in the choir of the basilica, from 1562, engraved by Pedro Perret after a drawing by Herrera or assistants and published as the Fifth Design of Herrera's *Las estampas de la fabrica de San Lorenzo et Real de El Escorial* (1589).

In 1077 Alfonso VI of Castile asserted himself to be 'By the Grace of God Emperor of all Spain'.[44] French lawyers had claimed that the king of France was *imperator in regno suo* from the fourteenth century.[45] It is in this context that the spread of the Serliana from those who considered themselves the direct heirs of the Roman emperors—the pope and the Holy Roman Emperor—to those who saw themselves as independent sovereigns must be understood. This can be seen in the three principal monarchies of western Europe, Spain, France and England, and in those rulers who were struggling to assert their independence.

Charles V's son Philip II did not become Holy Roman Emperor in 1557 but did succeed to his Spanish, Italian and Netherlandish lands. As king of Spain he was entitled to use symbols of sovereignty such as the closed crown. The Serliana was another such symbol. Philip II's principal physical statement of his sovereignty was the Escorial, the palace-monastery he built to the designs of Juan Bautista de Toledo and Juan de Herrera from 1562. At the heart of the palace was the chapel whose gable end was expressed by a pediment interrupted by an arched aperture. Though not a conventional Serliana in that there are no columns or side openings, the way the arched opening intrudes into the pediment recalls the Serliana on the mausoleum of Diocletian's palace at Split, a building with close parallels to the Escorial, and the Missorium of Theodosius (see Fig. 162).[46] The Serlian implications of the arched aperture penetrating the pediment (which is repeated on the north and south gables of the church) are made clear in the choir of the Escorial chapel, where the royal pew, subsequently converted to the organ loft, was expressed as a pedimented Serlian balcony (Fig. 171).[47] When Philip II entered Brussels in 1574 he was welcomed by a triumphal arch in the form of a Serliana supported by caryatids.[48]

The king of France was another independent sovereign but Henri II (1547–59) aspired to greater dignity and hoped to succeed Charles V as Holy Roman Emperor, an elective post. As Volker Hoffmann has shown, Henri II's reign was underpinned by the principles that the king of France knew no emperor; that Henri II was to inherit the imperial throne; and that his mission was to affirm his omnipotence and become the universal monarch. Even as Dauphin in the 1540s Henri was in discussion with the Lutheran princes of Germany to support his candidacy at the next imperial election and the prize seemed within his grasp when they promised that support at the Treaty of Lochau in 1551. It was thus as the putative next Holy Roman Emperor that

Henri II commissioned Pierre Lescot to rebuild the Louvre in Paris as an imperial palace in 1546.

Hoffmann traces these imperial statements in Lescot's decoration of the new façade of the Louvre but the most graphic use by Henri II of imperial Roman iconography came in the principal new room created, the Grande Salle, which was illustrated by Androuet du Cerceau in *Les plus excellents monuments de France* in 1576–9. The entrance to this impressive room was under a balcony supported by four caryatids, commissioned in 1550. At the far end was the 'tribunal', an elaborate version of the Serliana, approached up five steps, with a central arched, vaulted space that framed the royal arms. The Grande Salle was Henri II's version of an imperial Roman basilica and the 'tribunal' was clearly intended as a particularly grand and lavish version of the Serliana, in which the king would have appeared framed like the Emperor Diocletian before the Serliana of his palace at Split.[49] The obvious comparison is with the Sala Regia in the Vatican, which would undoubtedly have been known to the French king from his diplomats, a model which his Grande Salle comfortably eclipsed.[50] Despite this bold imperial statement, Henri II's imperial ambitions were dashed when the Lutheran princes went back on their promise on making peace with the Emperor Charles V in 1552.

Lescot's rival for the Louvre commission was Sebastiano Serlio, and it is Serlio who was responsible for the most considered statement of the symbolism of the Serliana. His designs for the Louvre are probably those published in his sixth book, which was two-thirds finished in 1545. This set out a sequence of designs for buildings ranging from simple houses to a grand royal palace that clearly demonstrates the status associated with the Serliana. Though never published and surviving only in two manuscript versions, Serlio's sixth book, which was written by about 1547, had a profound influence on designs for royal buildings into the eighteenth century.[51]

As Vaughan Hart and Peter Hicks explain in the introduction to their translation of Serlio's complete books on architecture, 'Throughout his various house models in Book VI Serlio used ornament–and the varying degree of ornament offered by the different Orders in particular–to express social status, ranging from the decorative poverty of the simple hut to the ornamental magnificence of the palace façade.'[52] Building for the prince was the ultimate expression of architecture. As Serlio put it, 'The palace of the king should, above all others, be the most magnificent and most opulent in its ornaments.'[53] Consequently, he produced ten different

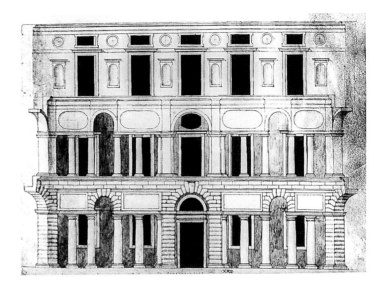

172 Sebastiano Serlio, Serliana-arcaded circular courtyard in the palace of the king, from *The Sixth Book of Architecture*, fol. 71r.

173 Sebastiano Serlio, Palace of the Governor, from *The Sixth Book of Architecture*, fol. 63r.

designs for the prince of which only one does not use Serlianas. Examples range from a Serlian dormer on the king's loggiamento outside the city to a Serliana-arcaded circular courtyard in the palace in the city (Fig. 172).[54] The Palace of the Governor, the prince's representative, has a Serliana porch over the entrance (Fig. 173), an example that makes a particularly telling comparison with the Kasteel of Breda of 1536 (see Fig. 170).[55]

In only one case in book six is the individual Serliana not associated with the prince. That is the 'noble Gentleman's House within the City', which Serlio

174 Andrea Palladio, the basilica, Vicenza, 1548–59.

explains was 'the house of a noble gentleman to be built in the city of Venice'.[56] While in monarchies the Serliana was reserved to the prince, the situation was somewhat different in the Republic of Venice. The three principal exceptions to the rule that the Serliana was used mainly by sovereigns, those aspiring to sovereign status and to their key supporters, are the Republics of Venice, Genoa and Lucca. In Lucca, the Palazzo Pubblico, seat of the Governo and the Consiglio Generale, was rebuilt by Bartolomeo Ammannati in 1578 with three Serlian windows to the Cortile degli Svizzeri and one on the main façade, symbols of sovereignty in a republic no less than a monarchy.[57]

The use of the Serliana in Venice is so frequent that it has often been known as the Venetian window.[58] Venice had its own architectural tradition that set it apart from the rest of Italy and made it particularly receptive to the idea of the Serliana.[59] Three-light windows in the centre of the façade can be seen in medieval Venetian villas and palazzi, such as the Quattrocento Palazzo de Mula at Murano and Villa dal Verme at Aguliano, and these were adapted easily to the Serliana. Serlio, who arrived in Venice in 1527 and published his fourth book of architecture in 1537, acknowledged this: 'In Venice, the noblest of cities, building practice is very different from that of other cities in Italy . . . With this in mind, I would say that these façades could be built with even more open-

ings, respecting the ancient way of building, in the manner shown here.'[60] He published two palazzo designs with superimposed Serlianas, commenting that both were in the 'Venetian fashion'.[61]

Serlio, who at this point had yet to work for a monarch, may have seen the Serliana as an ideal way to improve Venetian architecture, taking the old window form and modernising it to correct classical standards. His example was followed by Michele Sanmicheli, who included superimposed Serlianas in the manner of Serlio's fourth book in his design for the Palazzo Corner, S. Polo, of about 1545, probably the first major Venetian palazzo to use Serlianas. The family's appropriation of the Serliana was particularly appropriate as the Corner were among the oldest and grandest in Venice and the new palace was built for one of the five sons of Zorzi Corner, brother of Queen Caterina of Cyprus, through whom Venice claimed the crown of Cyprus. With the precedent set by the Corner, the use of the Serliana became commonplace on Venetian palazzi.[62]

It is in the context of Venice's republican status that Palladio's handful of individual Serlianas on his villas can be understood. The same is probably true of their use on individual houses in Genoa.[63] Palladio's most famous use of the Serliana is in the superimposed arcades of the basilica at Vicenza, designed in 1548 (Fig. 174). There were distinct structural advantages to the Serliana when

175   Jacopo Sansovino, Biblioteca Marciana, Venice, 1537.

adapting old buildings such as the basilica, as Giulio Romano demonstrated in 1539 at S. Benedetto di Polirone, a building closely associated with the Gonzagas of Mantua. Here Romano was able to manipulate the Serliana to accommodate the existing structure while creating an apparently modern interior.[64] This was a point emphasised by Serlio in his fourth book.[65]

Structural sleight of hand partly explains Palladio's use of the Serliana on the basilica at Vicenza but it is clear that the authority of the city was also being expressed in the use of the Serliana arcade. A precedent can be seen in Sansovino's Biblioteca Marciana in Venice of 1537, a building deliberately conceived as a statement of Venetian authority, where the arcade of the first floor takes the form of Serlianas, though the tight space between the flanking columns means the Serliana is not fully expressed (Fig. 175). The Serlian arcade also appears on Vincenzo Seregni's Palazzo dei Giureconsulti in Milan of 1560–64 and Joseph Heintz's Augsburg Loggia of 1607, both of which are symbols of a the authority of a great city.[66]

Thus by the middle of the sixteenth century the Serliana had become a powerful and widely accepted symbol of sovereignty. It is hardly surprising that it was appropriated not only by those whose sovereignty was assured but also by those who aspired to sovereign status, such as the Medicis in Florence, the House of Savoy in Turin, the Wittelsbachs of Bavaria and the exiled 'Winter King' of Bohemia, Friedrich V of the Palatinate.

In Florence the Medicis were keen to put the city's republican past behind them and assert their own rule, with the long-term ambition of achieving royal status and independence from their position as vassals of the Holy Roman Emperor.[67] Cosimo I de' Medici, who succeeded as Duke of Florence in 1537, was active in pushing this policy, abandoning the family palazzo on Via Larga in 1540 for the Palazzo della Signoria, which he renamed the Palazzo Ducale. During the 1540s Baccio Bandinelli transformed this building into a suitably ducal setting, his key work being the remodelling of the republican Salone dei Cinquecento into an ostensible throne room for Cosimo. At the far end of the hall was the *udienza* or reception platform, approached by way of steps and ornamented with three Serlianas, the outer two of which were windows. The central Serliana would have framed the duke as he conducted ceremonial business.

The parallels with the Sala Regia in the Vatican and Lescot's Grande Salle in the Louvre, created less than a decade later, are striking. In each case, pope, king or duke would have stood or sat on a raised dais to receive supplicants, underneath or framed by a Serliana. Vasari records that Bandinelli also began remodelling *all'antica* the exterior façade behind the Udienza. One Serlian window survives from this project, perhaps intended for

147

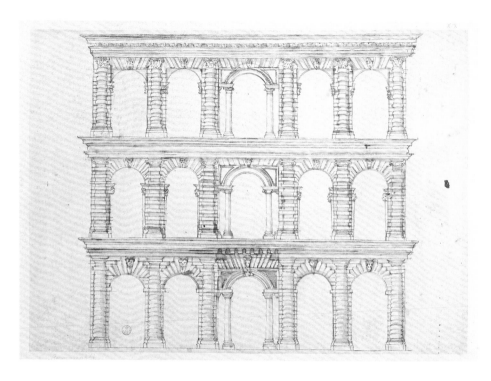

176 Bartolomeo Ammannati, design for the courtyard of the Palazzo Pitti, Florence, 1568–70 (Gabinetto dei Disegni e delle Stampe, Gallerie degli Uffizi, Florence, 2679A).

Cosimo to make public appearances, as Leo IV had been depicted in the Benediction Window by Raphael in the *Fire in the Borgo* or as Charles V could have appeared at his palace at Granada. Serlian openings were also placed at the centre of the ground, first and second floors of the courtyard of the Palazzo Pitti in 1568–70, which Ammannati transformed into Cosimo's official residence (Fig. 176).[68] It was in this window that Florence's ruler would have appeared at public spectacles such as the Naumachia, or nautical extravaganza, held in the courtyard in 1589.

Cosimo tried but failed to persuade Philip II to create him a king in the 1560s but in 1570 he was crowned Grand Duke of Tuscany by the pope, in the Sala Regia in the Vatican under Bramante's Serlian window. Though still a vassal of the emperor, this gave Cosimo a status superior to all his rivals in northern Italy and could be seen as a stepping stone on the road to kingship.[69] 'As shown in Dupérac's engraving of the Coronation scene in the Sala Regia', explains Satkowski, 'Cosimo could now be represented as the universal sovereign seeking to rule with the legal power of Augustus and the moral force of Jesus Christ.'[70]

The identification of Cosimo with Augustus was at its most powerful in the Uffizi, which was begun by Giorgio Vasari in 1560 but was completed after his death in 1574 by Ammannati (Fig. 177). Domenico Poggini's foundation medal of 1561 shows that the ensemble was originally conceived as two separate, facing ranges of buildings but, as completed, these two arms were linked by a short cross arm with a giant Serlian opening at ground level facing the courtyard and the River Arno. Like the Serliana of the Tribunal in the Grande Salle in the Louvre, the central space was vaulted, pairs of columns separated it from the flanking elements and the royal arms were prominently displayed. A further, smaller Serlian opening was placed at first-floor level facing the courtyard. In this upper opening originally sat a statue of the Grand Duke in the guise of Augustus. Where Leo X had himself painted in the guise of Leo IV standing at an imperial Serlian window (see Fig. 160), Cosimo stood in stone at a real Serlian window (Fig. 178). As Crum puts it, 'in the Uffizi façade, the duke's pretensions to Augustan grandeur received their most monumental, public, and daring exposition'.[71] It was presumably the symbolism carried by the Serliana that led Bernardo Buontalenti to consider incorporating Serlianas in the drum of the dome of the ducal mausoleum, the Capella dei Principi, for Ferdinando I in 1602.[72]

177   Giorgio Vasari and Bartolomeo Ammannati, the Uffizi, 1560–c.1574.

A Serliana could also be found on the first floor of the two principal street fronts of the Palazzo Grifoni, remodelled, perhaps by Ammannati, in 1561–74 for Ugolino Grifoni, secretary to Cosimo I. The palazzo can be read as a miniature statement of Medicean ambitions, bearing not only the Serlian windows but the ducal emblems in the cornice, which give the duke an ideal imperial genealogy from Augustus to Charles V.[73] Similar grand-ducal references explain Ammannati's inclusion of a Serlian window above the door to the Palazzo Firenze in Rome in 1572. This was built for Ferdinando, Cosimo's second son, who was created cardinal in 1566.[74] In 1576 the cardinal acquired a new villa on the Pincio, which Ammannati remodelled for him in 1579–87 as the Villa Medici. The garden elevation was dominated by a giant Serlian opening recalling the Uffizi (Fig. 179). As Michael Kiene notes, 'The modifications carried out by Ferdinando de' Medici underlined his status as a "national" cardinal descended from a grand Florentine dynasty.'[75]

The Medici's chief rival in the race for kingship in northern Italy was the House of Savoy. Where the Medici were keen to put Florence's republican past behind them, the House of Savoy had to overcome the ignominy of the collapse of Savoyard sovereignty in

178   Giorgio Vasari and Bartolomeo Ammannati, the Uffizi, 1560–c.1574, detail of the river-front loggia with statue of Cosimo I by Giambologna framed by a Serlian window.

179 Bartolomeo Ammannati, Villa Medici, Rome, 1579–87.

clerestory and a further Serlian window on the façade.[77] Ascanio Vitozzi took this approach still further at the Church of the Madonna del Mondovi at Vico in 1597. This was to be Carlo Emanuele's mausoleum and was designed to have Serlian windows over each of the lateral entrances, Serlian screens separating the four chapels from the central body of the church and Serlian niches within them to hold Savoyard tombs, including that of Carlo Emanuele.[78]

Vitozzi was responsible also for the most prominent use of the Serliana in Turin, on the Castello, the original ducal residence, later known as the Palazzo Madama. Little change was made to the late medieval exterior of the Castello except for Vitozzi's insertion in 1607–8 of a Serlian window and balcony on the main façade, on axis with the principal street into the city. The duke would appear framed by the Serliana at moments of ceremony such as the display of the Holy Shroud, recorded in Antonio Tempesta's engraving of 1613 (Fig. 180).[79] The symbolic importance of the Serliana for Carlo Emanuele (who succeeded in 1580) is also evident in the engraved view of his suburban hunting palace at Viboccone, just north of Turin, in Jan Blaeu's *Theatrum*

180 Antonio Tempestà, *View of the Piazza del Castello, Turin, during the Ostension of the Holy Shroud, 1613*. Detail showing the Castello as remodelled by Ascanio Vitozzi with a Serlian balcony in 1607–8 (Biblioteca Reale, Turin, BRT Inv. IV.23).

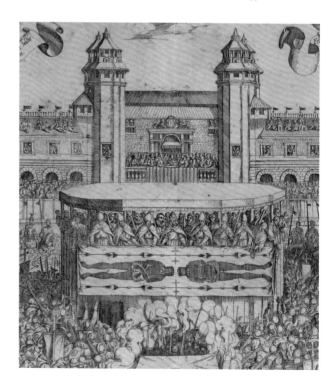

the 1530s. Emanuele Filiberto, another faithful servant of Charles V (he served as Governor-General of the Netherlands), was finally restored to his lands at the Treaty of Cateau-Cambrésis in 1559. Three years later he moved his capital from Chambery in Savoy, which had proved too exposed to the French, to Turin in Piedmont, which like Tuscany was part of the Holy Roman Empire.

Over the next century and a half, as Robert Oresko has shown, the House of Savoy was driven by the desire to achieve royal status and it is in this light that the remarkably varied and inventive use of the Serliana in and around Turin became a leitmotif of Sabaudian royal aspirations.[76]

Emanuele Filiberto built little, concentrating his resources on a massive citadel in Turin, but the family was well connected architecturally. Palladio dedicated his third book of architecture to him in 1570. His wife Marguerite of France was the daughter of Serlio's patron François I and sister of Henri II, who rebuilt the Louvre as an imperial palace. Later, Scamozzi dedicated the second book of his *L'idea della architettura* in 1615 to Emanuele Filiberto's son, Carlo Emanuele.

One of the few buildings for which Emanuele Filiberto was responsible was the Jesuit Church of Santi Martiri in Turin, intended by him as a spiritual citadel to match the military citadel he had built. The church, whose foundation stone was laid in his presence in 1577, was designed round the Serliana, with four Serlianas articulating the interior, Serliana windows lighting the

Sabaudiae in 1682. This shows the palace designed by Vitozzi in 1602 with proposed, largely unexecuted, alterations by Carlo di Castellamonte in 1629 (Fig. 181).[80] A square building, with a central hall, octagonal dome and corner turrets, the palazzo followed designs for the suburban residences of the prince proposed by Serlio in his sixth book.[81] Dominating the composition is a giant Serlian entrance porch, similar to that of the Villa Medici in Rome. This was a building whose essence was imbued with the idea that architecture could symbolise sovereignty.[82]

Carlo Emanuele also used Serlianas to articulate the interior of the Grande Galleria of Castello, formed as a library and museum in 1595 and illustrated in *Theatrum Sabaudiae*, though these were not expressed as windows.[83] The driving force behind the Grande Galleria, and the Santuario of Vicoforto, was Alessandro Tesauro, an aristocrat who can be compared to Palladio's patron Daniele Barbaro as an intellectual and connoisseur of architecture. Tesauro developed the tradition of close associates of the ruler using a Serliana when he included one in the Villa Tesauro at Salmour, which he designed for himself in 1620 (see Fig. 25).[84]

The seventeenth century saw the continued pervasive use of the Serliana by the Savoyard family as they continued to struggle to achieve royal status. Carlo Emanuele's grandson Vittorio Amedeo, who succeeded as duke in 1630, proclaimed the royal status of the Savoyard family in 1632. His death in 1637 was followed by civil war that ended in 1642 with his widow Marie-Christine of France, sister of Louis XIII, emerging in control of the state. She ruled as dowager until her son Carlo Emanuele II came of age in 1648 but effectively maintained her hold on power until she died in 1663. Marie-Christine's continuation of the Savoyard quest for a royal crown received physical expression in the 1640s with the creation of a new royal square by Carlo di Castellamonte, the Piazza Reale, which re-oriented the city to the south. As in the forecourt of the Palazzo Ducale in Mantua a century earlier, this was articulated with a Serlian arcade. The piazza was terminated at the south end by a pair of churches, S. Carlo and Sta Christina, named after Carlo Emmanuele II and Marie-Christine, which, as the *Theatrum Sabaudiae* demonstrates, were originally to have Serlian windows in their façades and towers with Serlian openings, though when the facades were finally executed in the eighteenth and nineteenth centuries they were to different designs.[85]

The integration of the Serliana into the internal design of churches, seen earlier at SS Martiri and the

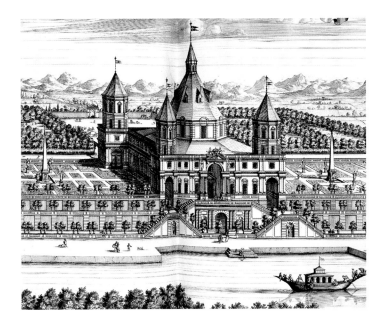

181 The royal hunting lodge at Viboccone, detail of an engraving from Jan Blaeu, *Theatrum Sabaudiae* (1682), showing the palace designed by Ascanio Vitozzi in 1602 with proposed, largely unexecuted, alterations by Carlo di Castellamonte in 1629 (British Library, London).

Madonna del Mondovì at Vico, was continued at three key architectural commissions by the House of Savoy in the second half of the seventeenth century: Guarino Guarini's rebuilding of the royal chapel of S. Lorenzo and creation of S. Sindone, the chapel of the Holy Shroud, both begun in 1668, and the creation of the chapel of Beato Amedeo of Savoy at Vercelli, built in 1682. At both S. Lorenzo and S. Sindone the treatment of the walls was generated by a repeated use of the Serliana. In S. Lorenzo a sequence of Serlianas was repeated at ground and first floor, while a Serliana arcade forms the lower level of S. Sidone, as Castellamonte had suggested in an earlier design for the chapel.[86] In the Chapel of Beato Amedeo at Vercelli the tombs of Carlo I, Yolande and Vittorio Amedeo I are placed in Serlian balconies similar to the tomb niches at the Madonna del Mondovì. For the Savoyards the repeated use of the Serliana was a clear statement of their asserted royal status, which finally became reality when Vittorio Amedeo II was crowned King of Sicily in 1713.

That the symbolic significance of the Serliana was also appreciated in northern Europe can be seen in the work of Hans Vredeman de Vries. Of all de Vries's architectural fantasies only one includes a Serliana. Appropriately, it is a depiction of the Palace of Solomon in a painting of 1596 showing Solomon greeting the Queen of Sheba.[87]

In the middle of the seventeenth century, Gerrit Houck-geest painted a *Judgement of Solomon*, now in Dessau, in which Solomon sits dispensing justice under a Serlian arch that bears a marked resemblance to Henri II's Tribunal in the Grande Salle of the Louvre.[88]

The Altes Schloss at Schleissheim, north of Munich, built by Heinrich Schön for Duke Maximilian of Bavaria, shows a similarly considered use of the Serliana.[89] Like the Medici and House of Savoy in Italy, Duke Maximilian was dynastically ambitious. His immediate goal was the acquisition of the electoral title formerly held by the Protestant branch of the family, the Electors Palatine. To achieve this he commissioned weighty works of antiquarian research, stressing the imperial rank of the family through the rehabilitation of his ancestor, Emperor Ludwig the Bavarian (1328–47). Maximilian achieved his goal when he was appointed elector provisionally in 1621 and permanently in 1648.[90] The Altes Schloss, a single-storey building of 1616 impressive for its correct use of rustic and alternating segmental and triangular pediments, is of particular interest for the central, covered staircase.[91] With its pediment, tripartite division and central arched opening, it clearly recalls the Serlian-like balconies of the Roman emperors, though the most direct comparison is with Count Hendrik III's Serliana balcony at Breda of 1536 (see Fig. 170).

Maximilian prospered at the expense of his distant cousin, Friedrich V of the Palatine. Exile was a perennial risk for ruling families in Europe in the sixteenth and seventeenth centuries, as Friedrich found to his cost when he was forced to flee his new Kingdom of Bohemia after the disastrous Battle of the White Mountains in 1620. As noted in chapter 5, the 'Winter King', as he came to be known, lived partly at The Hague and partly at Rhenen where the Koningshuis was built for him by Bartholomeus van Bassen. Van Bassen also painted at least two paintings showing Friedrich in idealised architectural settings. In one, dated 1634, the king and queen are shown dining in public in a magnificent chamber separated from the watching public by a large Serlian screen. Van Bassen's painting is clearly a fantasy, for the fenestration of the hall shows that it could not have been a real interior in the Koningshuis.[92] A second painting (now in a private collection in Denmark) depicts an imaginary palace, clearly identified as the Koningshuis by the handsome tower of S. Cunerakerk at Rhenen, dominated by a giant Serlian arch that recalls those of the Villa Medici in Rome and the palazzo of Viboccone outside Turin. There can be no

doubt that both paintings represent idealised versions of the Koningshuis, declarations of sovereignty by an exiled monarch who still hoped to return to his throne and wished to emphasise his royal status.

A close variant of van Bassen's painting by Houck-geest (who may have been van Bassen's pupil) of 1635, showing Charles I and Queen Henrietta Maria dining in public, survives in the British Royal Collection. The architectural setting, a large hall dominated by a giant Serlian arch, copies van Bassen's original closely though, intriguingly, the architectural detail has been tidied up. The columns supporting the Serlian arch are Ionic rather than Corinthian, the ornaments above the cornice have been replaced with plain panelling and the somewhat licentious door at the far end of the hall with its superimposed broken pediments has been replaced by a more correct doorcase. Perhaps one sees the influence of Inigo Jones at work but the key element survives: the king and queen dine in public in front of a giant Serlian screen, the symbol of their sovereignty.

There is thus a clear tradition dating from the first years of the sixteenth century and still strong in the middle of the seventeenth, a tradition to be found in Italy, Spain, France, Germany and the Netherlands, that associated the Serliana with royal authority, whether actual or sought. It is in this context that the absence of the Serliana in early seventeenth-century Dutch architecture and its careful use in contemporary English architecture needs to be examined.

In Venice the republic was solidly rooted. Power rested with the nobility and the office of Doge was severely constrained and held only for a year. Here the Serliana held no dangers and could be displayed as a badge of authority by leading nobles. There was no such certainty in the Dutch Republic, which had only just asserted its independence from the Habsburgs and where the House of Orange, descended from Charles V's deputy Count Hendrik III, were continually pushing to turn their post of Stadholder, or commander in time of war, into a hereditary, quasi-monarchical post. In this situation the royal symbolism of the Serliana was positively dangerous, whether used by the House of Orange or anyone else. It thus comes as no surprise that there are no Serlianas in Dutch seventeenth-century classicist architecture, despite their repeated appearance in Scamozzi's *L'idea della architettura*.

The situation was different in England where Charles I used architecture as a tool to emphasise his divine right to rule and the validity of his personal rule. Inigo Jones, who in 1613–14 was travelling with a prominent Roman

Catholic, the Earl of Arundel, would almost certainly have visited the Sala Regia in the Vatican, as well as the Palazzo Tè and the Uffizi.[93] He may also have passed through Turin at the end of his Italian tour. A drawing for the west façade of Charles V's palace at Granada, possibly from Jones's collection, was later in Lord Burlington's possession.[94] Jones certainly knew about the Escorial, which Charles, Prince of Wales visited on his trip to Spain and which had been published by Juan Battista de Herrera in his *Las estampas de la fabrica de San Lorenzo et Real de El Escorial* in 1589: the insertion of a royal pew into the chapel of his Whitehall designs seems to be modelled on that in the Escorial chapel.[95] He was also extremely familiar with Serlio's work. In this context his use of the Serliana is specifically imperial.

The tradition that England was an empire in its own right dated back to the Anglo-Saxon kings' claim of *imperium anglorum*.[96] English kings had worn the 'closed' crown, which symbolised the 'imperial' status of its monarch, since late in the fourteenth century. As Cuthbert Tunstall soothed Henry VIII in 1517, after advising him that he could not be a candidate for the Holy Roman Emperor: 'the Crown of England is an Empire of itself, much better than now the Empire of Rome: for which cause your Grace wears a close crown'.[97] This statement was made explicit in the preamble to the 1533 Act of Appeals which declared: 'this Realm of England is an Empire' (an assertion the Scots had already made sixty years earlier).[98] Contemporary theorists even went back as far as the Emperor Constantine to assert that status, pointing out that the symbols of the British empire remained as emblems of the English monarchy: the red cross, originally borne by Constantine, and 'a close crown Imperial in token that the land is an empire free in itself, and subject to no superior but God'.[99] It is in this context that Charles I declared Virginia, Somers Island and New England to be part of 'our Royal Empire descended upon us' in 1625.[100] Thus it was that Inigo Jones should have felt it appropriate to use the Serliana in his royal buildings.

The Serliana appears in two early, unbuilt designs made by Jones before his Italian trip of 1613–14. In his design for the New Exchange in the Strand of 1608 a single Serlian window is placed at the centre of the façade (see Fig. 7). The base of his proposed termination for the central tower of St Paul's cathedral, made the same year, is formed by a sequence of Serlianas (see Fig. 13). In both cases the designs were closely associated with the monarchy. The proposed restoration of St Paul's cathedral was ordered by James I, who promised to contribute liberally to the cost.[101] The New Exchange was established by his chief minister, the Earl of Salisbury, and was seen as a specifically British symbol. In both cases the Serliana could be seen as symbolising royal authority but it is noticeable that after the 1613–14 visit to Italy Jones's use of the Serliana was more closely tied to specifically royal projects.

The first of these is his third design for the Queen's House at Greenwich in 1616, which included a Serliana on the first floor of the side elevation (see Fig. 114).[102] Though this follows Scamozzi's Villa Molin, the model for this preliminary design, its use on the side elevation of the Queen's House would have been particularly appropriate, announcing the royal status of the building to those using the road below.

Jones's first executed Serliana was the east window of the Queen's Chapel at St James's Palace of 1623–6 (Fig. 182). It is also possible that a Serlian arch framed the altar of Jones's chapel at Somerset House, built in 1630–35 but possibly designed by Jones in 1623.[103] The Queen's Chapel was commissioned by James I as part of the architectural improvements made in anticipation of the marriage of the Prince of Wales to the Infanta of Spain, which was ratified on 20 July 1623.[104] The marriage never took place, but the chapel was completed for the prince's eventual bride, Henrietta Maria of France, whom he married in 1625. By then the prince had succeeded his father as Charles I. Like the Infanta, the new queen was a Roman Catholic and so required her own chapel.

In plan Jones's design follows the traditional form of royal chapels and differs little from Henry VIII's neighbouring chapel in St James's Palace. Nevertheless, its architectural language is overwhelmingly classical, its square-coffered, barrel-vaulted ceiling taken directly from Palladio's engraving of the roof of the 'Temple of the Sun and the Moon' in Rome.[105] The source of the great Serlian window over the altar is not so obvious.

There is no appropriate precedent for using a Serliana as the east window of a church or chapel in the work of Serlio, Palladio or Scamozzi. Serlio, who used the Serliana extensively in his designs for domestic buildings, used it only once in the body of a church over an altar. As that was for an octagonal building with a central altar it is an unlikely source for the Queen's Chapel.[106] Instead, Raphael's engraving *The Last Supper* was probably critical to Jones's decision (Fig. 183). In this the supper table takes the form of an altar, set below a large Serlian window, with Christ as the celebrant of this the first mass. The tripartite form of the Serliana, though

153

183   Mario Dente, engraving after Raphael, *The Last Supper*, c.1514 (British Museum, London).

presumably intended as a reference to the papacy, may also be seen to symbolise the Trinity.[107]

Jones's use of the Serliana was at its most extensive in his proposed plans for the Palace of Whitehall and for Somerset House. The repeated use of the Serliana nineteen times on the river front of Whitehall Palace has no precedent among the extensive uses of the Serliana discussed earlier, the closest parallel being the Palazzo Tè (see Fig. 169).[108] For Jones, the symbolism of the Serliana as a mark of sovereignty in a nation that had long stressed its imperial status as a sovereign country was clearly one of immense importance. This is made clear again at Somerset House, the queen's palace, where Serlianas are used over the entrance arch in the end pavilions and over the entrances in the wings (see Figs 92 and 93).[109] Jones also used a Serliana for what appears to have been the royal pews in the chapel of Whitehall Palace (see Fig. 190).[110]

Other uses of the Serliana before the Civil War show a comparable discretion. It can be found as the liturgical east window at the chapel of Castle Ashby, completed in 1630, the Church of St John the Evangelist at Stanmore, consecrated in 1632, and probably at the chapel at Wilton House, built after 1636.[111] Only three examples can be found on contemporary domestic buildings: on the principal elevation of Wilton House; in the Castle Ashby screen of about 1636; and in Webb's unexecuted design of 1648 for the Duke of Richmond at Cobham Hall.[112] The church at Stanmore, the first parish church built on a new site since the Reformation, was consecrated by Laud, then Bishop of London. Wilton House, where the Serlianas would have appeared in the middle of the royal apartments, was as discussed a quasi-royal palace.[113] Cobham Hall was designed for the king's cousin, the Duke of Richmond and Lennox, and is pointedly referred to as a 'palace' in Webb's drawing. Only Castle Ashby, one of the most ambitious private houses of the day, was not the work of an intimate member of the royal circle.

There was thus nothing 'Palladian' about Jones's use of the Serliana. It needs to be read instead as a powerful symbol of sovereignty, as indeed does the whole of the Palace of Whitehall, Jones's most important, though perhaps least appreciated, architectural project.

182 (*facing page*)   Inigo Jones, interior of the Queen's Chapel, St James's Palace, London, 1623–6.

Chapter 10

THE ARCHITECTURE OF SOVEREIGNTY III: WHITEHALL PALACE

INIGO JONES'S PALACE AT WHITEHALL HAS always presented something of a conundrum. Its scale and ambition sit uncomfortably with the fate of Charles I's monarchy: financial and political collapse, civil war and execution. It seems so implausible that Charles could really have hoped to build a palace on this scale that Jones's plans for Whitehall Palace have tended to be pushed into the architectural backwater reserved for 'might have beens' and have never been given the detailed examination they deserve.[1] However, though unbuilt, Whitehall Palace deserves to be seen as the summation of Jones's architectural career, as evidence of the wide-ranging variety of sources that came together to form his architectural language and as the clearest possible expression of architecture as political statement.

Jones's Whitehall Palace designs date from about 1638. In that year Richard Daye wrote in a letter that 'they say His Majesty hath a desire to build [Whitehall] new again in a more uniform sort'. This is confirmed by Sir William Sanderson's *Compleat History of the Life and Raigne of King Charles* (1658), which records how the livery companies made a payment towards a new palace instead of a fine after the Crown took legal action against them in the Star Chamber in 1635 for failing to establish enough English and Scottish tenants on their properties in Ulster. The companies were fined £70,000, though in 1637 a settlement was reached demanding only £12,000. According to Sanderson, those concerned were to have 'contributed a very ample Sum of Money by way of Composition towards the erecting of a Royal Palace for his Majesties Court in Saint James's Park, according to a Model drawn by Inigo Jones his excellent Architectour'.[2]

Such a palace might be thought impossible. The Civil War plays such a central part in English history that it is hard to set aside the knowledge of Charles I's catastrophic last years but in 1638 the king had been ruling without the interference of Parliament for nine years.[3] He was 38, in the prime of his life with every reason to believe he had decades more to live and with two male heirs to ensure the future of his line. The disastrous years of the 1620s, with their long and expensive wars with France and Spain (the unsuccessful naval expedition to Cadiz in 1625 alone had cost half a million pounds), were behind him.[4] The Bishops War with Scotland, which started the slide that led to the Civil War, was still a year away. The country had been at peace and increasingly prosperous since 1630, allowing the desperate state of government finances to be improved. Income was outstripping expenditure and accumulated debts were beginning to be paid off.[5] It was war that had a devastating impact on finances. The seven years of unfruitful wars with France and Spain had cost £2,560,000, at least equal to the ordinary revenues of England over that period.[6] If Charles could avoid entanglements abroad – and at home – then there would be the chance to build.

It is in this context and as only one, albeit the grandest, of a series of ambitious royal building projects during the 1630s, that Whitehall Palace has to be understood. This sequence of projects – the choirscreen at Winchester cathedral, the restoration of the White Tower at the Tower of London, the portico of St Paul's cathedral, Temple Bar, Somerset House and Whitehall Palace – was aimed at emphasising the monarch's authority during the height of the Personal Monarchy. The schemes should not be seen in isolation. They were part of a considered attempt to recover the impression of magnificence that was critical to a monarch's standing at home and abroad. After the failure of the French and Spanish

185 Charles Woodfield, engraving of 1714 showing the choir screen of Winchester cathedral by Inigo Jones, 1637.

186 Sebastiano Serlio, the Arco dei Gavi, Verona, from *Tutte l'opere d'architettura et prospetiva* (1619) III, fol. 112r.

wars Charles I's image desperately needed to be bolstered. At exactly the same time that Charles was planning a major architectural campaign, he was also striving to recover the nation's lost naval reputation by building a powerful and visually impressive new fleet funded by Ship Money. The finest of these new ships was the *Sovereign of the Seas* of 1637, the largest vessel of its age, which cost a staggering £65,586. It was not only immensely powerful, carrying a hundred guns, but was also decorated on the most lavish scale. As the well-travelled Peter Mundy described, 'Her head, waist, quarter and stern so largely enriched with carved work overlaid with gold that it appears most glorious even from afar, especially her spacious lofty stately stern, whereon is expressed all that art and cost can do in carving and guilding.' The carving and gilding alone cost £6,691, about half the expense of the Banqueting House at Whitehall, which came to £15,618, or a quarter that of acquiring the sumptuous art collection of the Gonzagas, which cost more than £30,000.[7] It was appropriate that having seen the wonders of many lands, Mundy thought

there were three things in which the English excelled every nation: the *Sovereign of the Seas*, St Paul's (recently adorned with its portico by Jones) and 'our sweet and artificial ringing of tuneable bells'.[8]

Charles I's intervention at Winchester cathedral is the only one of this sequence outside London but it is particularly telling. The monarchy's links with Winchester, home of the legendary Round Table of King Arthur, were close for it was here that the first Anglo-Saxon kings of England were crowned. If any city outside London could be considered royal it was Winchester and it is no coincidence that Charles II chose it as the site of his uncompleted palace in the 1680s. In 1636 Bishop Wren of Ely reported to Archbishop Laud that the king had expressed his disapproval of the state of the Norman choirscreen at Winchester on a progress the previous year. By April 1637 the decision had been taken to replace it with a new screen by Inigo Jones, which was built the following year (Fig. 185). This was a clear statement of royal authority, a royal, not a local project, initiated by the king, driven by his archbishop, designed by his surveyor and dominated by the twin statues of the king and his father.[9]

St Paul's cathedral had even stronger links with the monarchy and it was these that were celebrated in the great west portico – paid for by Charles I – the foundations of which were laid in 1635 (see Fig. 153). Its royal associations were boldly proclaimed in the inscription announcing Charles's responsibility and by the statues of kings that stood on the balustrade.[10] The restoration of the White Tower at the Tower of London was ordered in 1638 (Fig. 187).[11] Of all royal buildings, the White Tower had the most powerful royal associations. It was the oldest of the royal palaces, built, at least according to legend, by Julius Caesar – though the resonance of its real builder William the Conqueror was scarcely less. It was in the White Tower that monarchs had traditionally spent the night before their coronation (in fact, Elizabeth I was the last monarch to do so) and where Knights of the Bath were created. The tower was the home of the Crown Jewels, the royal records and, no less importantly, the great royal arsenal, a powerful symbol of royal might in the capital.

This restoration of the White Tower was no utilitarian affair. Instead of being left in the hands of the Board of Ordnance, as had been the case with the previous repairs in the 1620s, the project was given to Jones as the Surveyor of the King's Works. If simple practicality were all that was at issue repairs could have been carried out more cheaply in brick or some other ordinary building material, as had happened earlier. Instead, the existing ashlar was replaced with expensive, white Portland stone, which was used also for the extensive replacement of quoins, windows, doorways, buttresses and battlements. The respect shown for the historic significance of the structure is emphasised by the way Jones designed the windows to follow the basic language of the Romanesque architecture with round arches and the original double- or single-light arrangements. As Anna Keay and Roland Harris put it: 'The effect must have been dazzling: newly painted walls with their Romanesque features sharply edged with white Portland stone and all surmounted by the great weather vanes with their royal arms and imperial crowns freshly gilded . . . It is tempting to see the treatment of the White Tower in the 1630s, like the provision of the vast new British flag to be flown over it "upon all solemnities and triumphs", as in some way part of a tardy recognition of its potency as a symbol of the ancient English monarchy.'[12]

Two years earlier, in 1636, the Privy Council had directed the Recorder and certain aldermen of the City

187 Wenceslaus Hollar, detail of an engraving showing the White Tower, Tower of London, and the execution of the Earl of Strafford in 1641 (British Museum, London).

of London to confer with Jones about a gate at Temple Bar, the traditional entrance point into the City. The result was Jones's design for a grand structure modelled on a Roman triumphal arch, specifically on the Arch of Constantine in Rome. Two designs survive. One of them is dated 1638, showing that the project was no passing whim (Fig. 188).[13] Had it been built, the arch, placed where the monarch paused to be welcomed on entering the City, would have emphasised the authority of Charles I in the endlessly complex relationship between monarch and merchants. Nothing came of the project, presumably for reasons of cost.

If a line were drawn through the metropolis, the Tower of London would be at one end after which would come St Paul's cathedral and then Temple Bar. Just beyond Temple Bar, on the Strand, the principal street connecting the City and Whitehall, lay Somerset House, the London palace of Queen Henrietta Maria. Two schemes survive by Jones for rebuilding the street front of the palace, one of which, presumably the second because it appears to be a reduction of the first, is dated 1638 (see Figs 92 and 93). Nothing came of these plans, which have been discussed in chapter 6, again for reasons of cost, but they would have made a noble addition to the string of royal buildings that would have linked the Tower of London to the king's principal residence at Whitehall.

The existing Palace of Whitehall covered a large area but was of limited architectural distinction, despite the presence of Jones's Banqueting House.[14] For a man of Charles I's advanced aesthetic sensibility, deeply con-

188 Inigo Jones, design for Temple Bar, 1638 (RIBA Library Drawings Collection).

scious of how the arts helped shape the monarch's image, a new palace was an obvious project. Numerous mid-seventeenth-century designs survive for rebuilding Whitehall Palace.[15] Margaret Whinney broke these down into a series of different schemes: all except two, the 'C' and 'Z' schemes, which are not from Jones's office, are accepted as in the hand of Jones's assistant John Webb.

Of these two are believed to date from 1637–9, the 'P' and 'K' schemes. The 'P' scheme is generally accepted as representing Jones's own proposals for Whitehall Palace (Fig. 189). There is less certainty about the 'K' scheme, for which nine finished drawings–plans, elevations and sections–survive. Many of these take their ideas from the 'P' scheme but 'K' has the feel of an idealised exercise,

189 John Webb, after Inigo Jones, design for the river and park fronts of Whitehall Palace, *c.*1638, Whinney P8 (Worcester College, Oxford).

with symmetry a driving preoccupation. Moreover, as seen in chapter 7, the scheme fits more comfortably with Webb's aesthetic than that of Jones. Summerson described it as 'a recasting both in plan and detail by somebody else, presumably Webb, somebody who is moving away from Jonesian ideas', but John Bold, Webb's biographer, suggests that the scheme is by Jones and Webb working together, 'with the pupil drawing out and embellishing a series of given ideas, rather than working it all out for himself'.[16] It is possible that the drawings were intended for Webb's presumed architectural treatise.[17]

Twenty drawings survive for the 'P' scheme, varying from roughly worked out sketches to carefully annotated ground plans and elevations and detailed treatments of

elements such as staircases, sections of elevations, vestibules, halls and principal rooms such as the chapel. Many of the drawings have alterations sketched on them, showing that they remained working drawings. Some are incompatible in detail and there is no single definitive scheme but despite this they provide a clear impression of Jones's intentions for the palace.

The clearest understanding of Jones's proposed palace comes from the plan P4, a drawing that needs to be read with care because the right-hand side appears to be for the ground floor and the left-hand side for the first floor (Fig. 190). This shows that the palace was to be effectively square, with a square, colonnaded central court ringed by a sequence of ten lesser courts. The complex

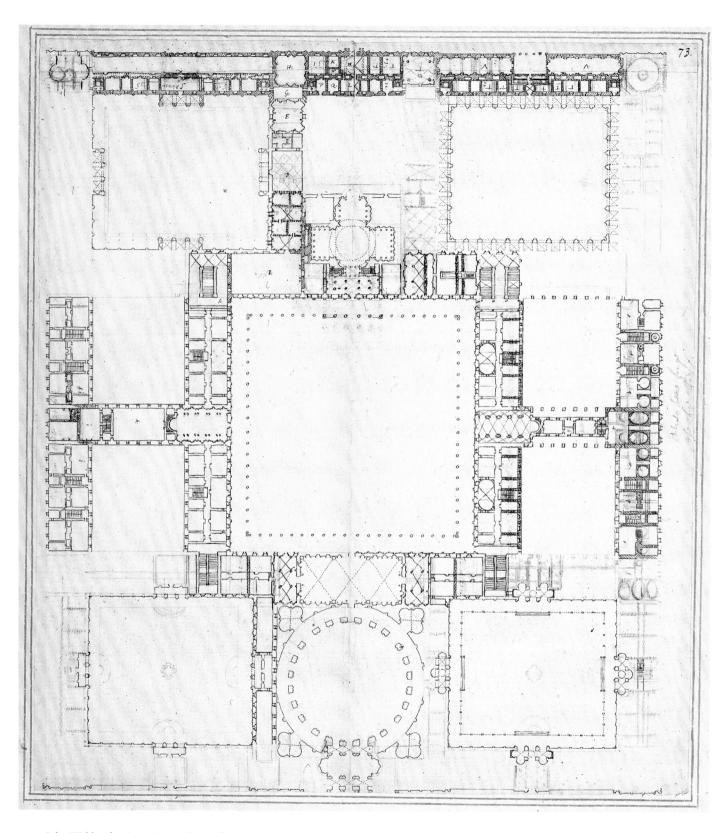

190   John Webb, after Inigo Jones, design for the ground plan of Whitehall Palace, *c.*1638, Whinney P4 (Devonshire Collection, Chatsworth, reproduced by kind permission of the Trustees of the Chatsworth Settlement).

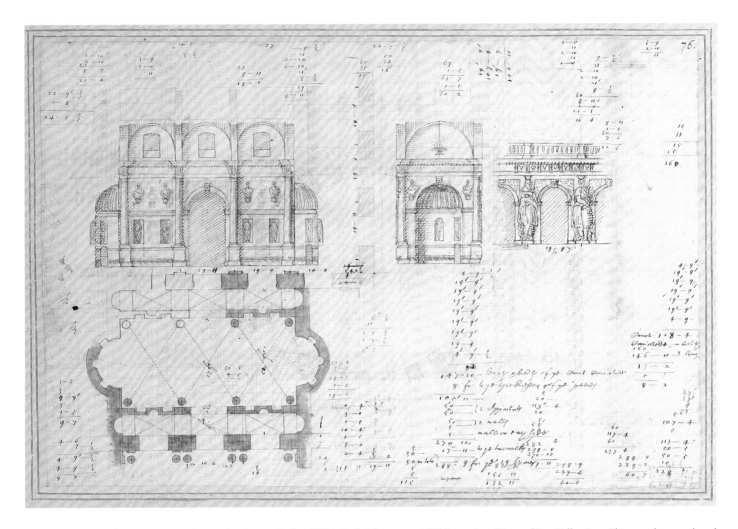

191   John Webb, after Inigo Jones, designs for the vestibule of Whitehall Palace, *c.*1638, Whinney P13 (Devonshire Collection, Chatsworth, reproduced by kind permission of the Trustees of the Chatsworth Settlement).

was approached from the river, through a circular court which led, via a vaulted vestibule inspired by the Roman Baths (Fig. 191), into the central courtyard. This would have been dominated by the massive six-columned portico of the royal chapel, the ceremonial heart of this palace (Fig. 192). Two apsed, basilican halls, one of them the Privy Council Chamber, the cornerstone of Stuart rule, were placed in the centre of the two side ranges (Fig. 193). Magisterial staircases in the two far corners of the courtyard would have led to the royal apartments on the first floor, arranged round two courtyards, one for the king, one for the queen. The plan shows that two of the lesser courts to the right were given over on the ground floor to kitchens, their function revealed by large ovens. Two to the left are filled with courtiers' lodgings, a sequence of small apartments opening off staircases like the sets of an Oxford college. The functions of the two

large courtyards flanking the circular court are not drawn in but would presumably have been more lodgings.

The two principal elevations were to the river and to the park. That on the river is dominated by a sequence of four tower-like pedimented pavilions, three storeys tall with a full sequence of pilasters and pairs of Serlian windows on the first and second floors (see Fig. 189). Three lesser pavilions of two storeys, each with a first-floor Serlian window, marked the entrances to the three courts. The park elevation had a thirteen-bay, three-storey central block with a pair of projecting towers with circular cupolas framing the boldly expressed royal arms and emphatic closed crown. Flanking ranges were punctuated by pavilions with three-storey pedimented pavilions at each end. In this elevation Serlian windows are restricted to the second floor of the central bay and the end pavilions.

163

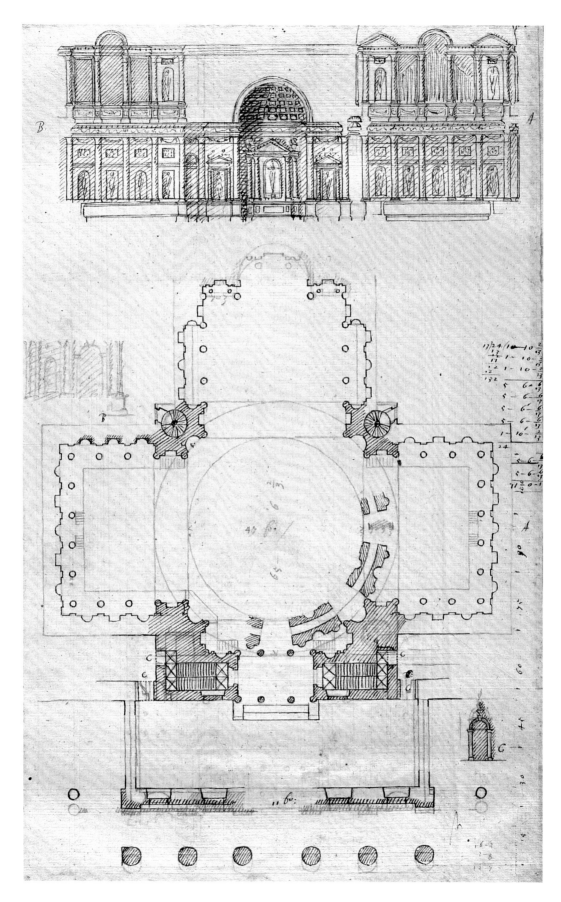

192   John Webb, after Inigo Jones, design for the chapel of Whitehall Palace, London, *c.*1638, Whinney P18 (Devonshire Collection, Chatsworth, reproduced by kind permission of the Trustees of the Chatsworth Settlement).

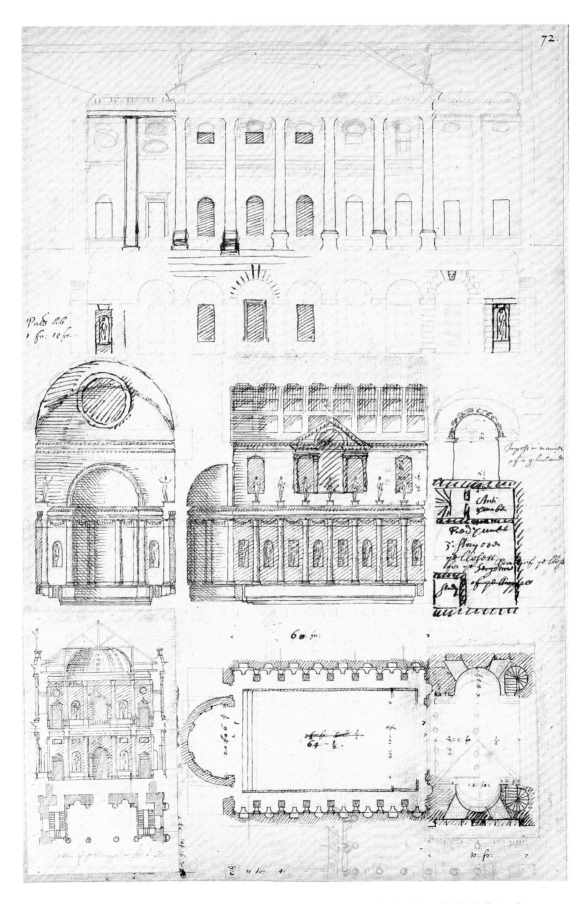

193   John Webb, after Inigo Jones, designs for the chapel and Privy Council Chamber of Whitehall, London, *c.*1638, Whinney P12 (Devonshire Collection, Chatsworth, reproduced by kind permission of the Trustees of the Chatsworth Settlement).

Jones's proposed palace was undeniably vast and Charles I had only to look across the Channel to the Louvre in Paris to see that such grand architectural visions were hard to realise, even by kings as rich and powerful as those of France. Yet analysis of Jones's drawings makes it clear that this was not a theoretical scheme. Though the drawings are fragmentary and incomplete it is clear that the Surveyor, always a busy man, devoted vast amounts of time to the design. The architectural language is carefully developed, with successive drawings showing how specific elements had been altered and refined. Detailed attention went into such mundane practicalities as where the kitchens were to go, the position of the buttery and spicery, where the pages' backstairs should be and how the courtiers' lodgings were to be arranged. Even details such as specific entablatures were considered. Despite its size this was a palace designed to be built.

The king had already shown that he was prepared to commit substantial sums to the architectural assertion of monarchical authority. Between 1634 and 1637 he had spent more than £8,000 on the great west portico of St Paul's cathedral. This was then close to completion and the king was no longer funding it from his own resources but with ecclesiastical fines from the Court of the High Commission.[18] Charles was not afraid of building if he had the opportunity. In 1638 he may well have thought he could afford to take a long view of architectural projects.

In reality the £12,000 extorted from the livery companies soon had to go to fund the disastrous Bishops War. Looking back with this knowledge, Jones's palace seems the final act of Stuart hubris, a symptom of a royal court so obsessed with Italianate culture that it was unable to see that a great palace was both financially impossible and politically foolhardy. Seen from 1638 a far different context emerges. Charles I's proposed palace has to be read as a deliberate political statement, a declaration in stone of his right to rule, made at a moment when such optimism seemed possible. In just the same way, thirty years later, Louis XIV marked his (successful) assertion of personal rule first with the new east front of the Louvre and then with the great palace at Versailles. By carefully analysing the messages explicit in the design it is clear that the proposed Whitehall Palace was as direct an allegory of monarchy as Rubens's paintings on the ceiling of the Banqueting House. It is self-consciously placed within the lineage of a great sequence of palace designs – the Temple of Solomon, the palace of Diocletian at Split, Hadrian's Villa at Tivoli, the palace of

Charles V at Granada, the Louvre and Philip II's Escorial in Spain – and is composed of a series of architectural elements that should be read as symbols of sovereignty. These include in particular the pediment and portico, the Serliana, the circular courtyard and the caryatid.

Jones's attitude towards the pediment, portico and Serliana, and their role as symbols of sovereignty, has been explored in the two previous chapters. It is sufficient to note here that it is in the Whitehall Palace designs that the pediment and the Serliana are used most extensively by Jones. The river elevation, the public front of the palace, was dominated by four three-storey pavilions, each with a pediment. Initially Jones also considered placing pediments over the three smaller intermediate pavilions but the drawing shows that he changed his mind and erased them. On the park front, Jones placed pediments over the corner pavilions and single-bay pediments over the lateral entrances. Pediments were no less important in Jones's 1638 design for the Strand front of Somerset House, which can be read as a condensed version of the Whitehall Palace designs. This would have had a pediment in the centre and over the end pavilions. Pediments were also used extensively in Webb's 'E' and 'K' schemes for Whitehall Palace. By contrast, Jones reserved the freestanding portico for a single use, the giant portico of the chapel.

To the pediments should be added the nineteen Serlianas on the river elevation and the three further Serlianas on the park elevation, a repetitive use of this symbol of sovereignty that clearly looks back to Diocletian's palace at Split. Split, on the Adriatic coast of what is now Croatia, may seem remote but in the sixteenth and seventeenth centuries it was a major port on the main trade route between Venice and the East and would have been familiar to generations of Venetians and others, including the distinguished Corner family, one of whose members was archbishop there early in the sixteenth century.[19] The palace at Split was certainly known to architects, its imperial mausoleum the probable source for the church Palladio's follower Francesco Zamberlan built at Rovigo. Three drawings of the palace, one in his hand (Fig. 194), survive among Palladio's drawings, one showing the overall plan, another the mausoleum in plan and the third a doorway. They were probably in Jones's collection.[20]

Strong parallels can be drawn between Diocletian's palace and the Escorial, reinforcing the argument that architects were aware of Split (Fig. 195). Both are rectangular complexes of almost identical dimensions designed to combine basilica and mausoleum that use variants of the Syrian Serliana. The parallels are particularly strong in the initial designs where the Escorial would have been marked by a sequence of towers, giving a castellated and defensive appearance like that of Diocletian's palace, and the forecourt approaching the basilica would have been lined with columns, as at Split.[21]

Jones would also have had access to a first-hand account from Marco Antonio de Dominis, Archbishop of Spalato (1566–1624). De Dominis sided with Venice in the row with Rome in 1605 and came to England in 1616 on the advice of Sir Henry Wotton when he fell out with Pope Paul V and was threatened with the Inquisition. He was lavishly received at the court of James I, given precedence after the Archbishops of Canterbury and York, and made Master of the Savoy and then Dean of Windsor, the latter a key post in the royal household. When his old friend was elected Gregory XV in 1621 de Dominis finally returned to Italy[22].

As Surveyor of the King's Works Jones would undoubtedly have had dealings with de Dominis as Dean of Windsor and one can imagine him quizzing him about Diocletian's palace. There are many parallels between Jones's palace design and Diocletian's palace. Both were isolated, regular, rectangular structures built round a series of courtyards, their external elevations punctuated by projecting towers that give the impression of a fortress. This similarity even goes as far as the arrangement of the towers, with Jones grouping the central pair of towers on the park front to form a symbolic gatehouse, placing a tower at each corner of the elevation and a further pair of towers in between, as at Split. De Dominis's information might explain an otherwise unprecedented feature of Jones's palace designs, the way he places Serlianas sequentially along the entrance elevation. There appears to be no precedent for this in post-Renaissance architecture and there is certainly no precedent in Palladio or Scamozzi but it resembles the way Serlianas were used sequentially along the entrance elevation at Diocletian's palace (see Fig. 163).

The other Roman imperial palace of which significant elements survive was more accessible, Hadrian's Villa at Tivoli near Rome. Tivoli attracted considerable interest from architects and antiquarians from the fifteenth century, including Francesco di Giorgio, Giuliano da Sangallo, Baldassare Peruzzi, Pirro Ligorio and Palladio.[23] It was undoubtedly the source for the circular court that is one of the most attractive features of Jones's Whitehall Palace design. The importance of this element in the proposed palace is evident from the way it was repeated by Webb in his 'K', 'E' and 'T' schemes. It was a feature

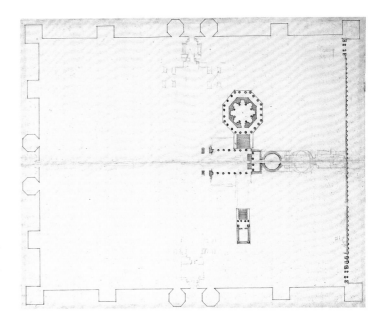

194 Andrea Palladio, plan of Diocletian's Palace at Split (Devonshire Collection, Chatsworth, reproduced by kind permission of the Trustees of the Chatsworth Settlement).

of the design that concerned Whinney who described it as 'very puzzling' and wondered whether it had some theatrical use, commenting that 'the exact function of the circular court is hard to explain, but it is so unusual in design that it must surely have had a special purpose'. She was in good company: Horace

195 Juan Bautista da Toledo and Juan de Herrera, the Escorial (from 1562), detail from a perspective view by Joan Blaeu after a drawing by Herrera or assistants (published as the Seventh Design of Herrera's *Las estampas de la fabrica de San Lorenzo et Real de El Escorial* (1589)), and published in *Atlas Maior sive Cosmographiae Blaviana* (1662).

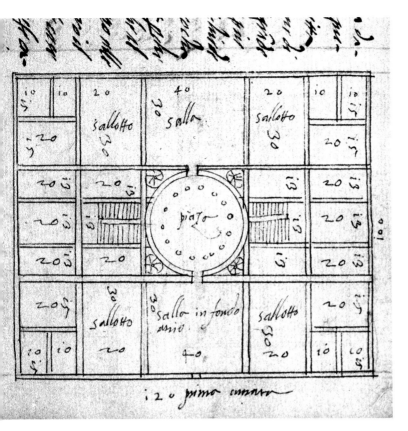

196 Francesco di Giorgio, design for a palace round a central circular courtyard, detail from a sixteenth-century copy of his manuscript treatise on architecture, c.1478–81, fol. 29r (Sir John Soane's Museum, London).

Walpole was similarly baffled by the circular court, describing it as 'a picturesque thought, but without meaning or utility'.[24] John Bold, following Orgel and Strong, suggests that the circular court was inspired by Scamozzi's reconstruction of Pliny's villa at Laurentium. He also wondered, following Whinney's suggestion of a theatrical use and Webb's reference to Jones's reconstruction of Stonehenge as a Roman temple (which Webb supported by reference to Vitruvius's description of the classical theatre), whether it was inspired also by Stonehenge.[25]

Jones's contemporaries, however, would have had little difficulty in appreciating the circular court in a royal palace as a symbol of sovereignty with firm precedents stretching back to the late fifteenth century.[26] The Island Enclosure at Hadrian's Villa provided a clear Roman imperial precedent. This was certainly the inspiration for the palace Francesco di Giorgio designed round a central circular courtyard in his manuscript treatise on architecture of about 1478–81, the first since Antiquity (Fig. 196).

Though never published, di Giorgio's treatise was highly influential, as the numerous manuscript copies in existence show. Fra Giovanni Giocondo, Leonardo da Vinci, Bramante and Raphael all knew di Giorgio, and Serlio; Barbaro, Palladio and Scamozzi all read his manuscript. His ideas form a crucial strand in the architecture of sovereignty.[27]

Imperial resonances, coupled with reference to Pliny's description of his villa at Laurentium, which was believed to be organised round a circular court, probably lie behind the circular court Raphael proposed in 1517 for the Villa Madama, built for Pope Leo X.[28] The circular court of Charles V's palace at Granada was undoubtedly inspired by Hadrian's Villa (Fig. 197). While the number of columns differed (32 against 40 at Hadrian's Villa), as did the order (Doric rather than Ionic), the dimensions were identical at 42 metres.[29] As a rare surviving fragment of a Roman emperor's palace the attraction of the circular court to Charles V and to subsequent monarchs was obvious.

Circular courts remained rare, a notable example being that of Vignola's Villa Farnese at Capraola of 1557, built for Alessandro Farnese, nephew of the previous pope, Paul III (1534–49).[30] They received their most direct association with sovereignty in Serlio's sixth book, which was almost certainly influenced by di Giorgio. Here circular courts were reserved for the residences of princes. The 'House in the Countryside of the exceedingly illustrious Prince' was a square villa-like structure with a central circular courtyard. The 'Royal Palace within the City' had a sequence of courtyards, one of the most important of which was circular (Fig. 198).[31] In France, Jacques I du Cerceau (about 1520–about 1585), who must have studied Serlio's sixth book, subsequently made a design for a palace laid out round a large circular court.[32] It is in this specifically royal context that Jones's proposed circular court must be understood.[33]

Two other architectural motifs long associated with sovereignty and used extensively by Jones in his designs for Whitehall are Persians and caryatids – male and female figures used in place of columns to support the entablature. A double order of Persians and caryatids was to be used for both the king's and queen's courts (Fig. 199). Jones also, or perhaps as an alternative, considered placing caryatids in the circular court. This idea was taken up in Webb's 'K' scheme where the circular court again proposed a double order of Persians and caryatids, though in the 'E' scheme the Persians and caryatids were reserved to two side courts, presumably the king's and queen's courts. Jones did not use Persians and caryatids on non-royal buildings.[34]

For the Greeks and the Romans, the use of Persians and caryatids had strong associations with the idea of imperial authority over conquered peoples. According to Vitruvius, the origin of the caryatid in Greek architecture can be found in the history of the town of Carya in the Peloponnese: the male inhabitants were killed by the Greeks in revenge for their alliance with the Persians and the women reduced to slavery. The women were represented by architects in public buildings in the form of pillars to perpetuate their shame.[35] The Greeks incorporated caryatids in the Erechtheion on the Acropolis at Athens as a symbol of their final triumph over the Persians.[36] In the Forum of Trajan 'Persians' represented the defeated Trojans.[37] Other examples could be found at Corinth.[38]

In 1510–14 Raphael had included grisaille caryatids in the lower part of the Stanza d'Eliodoro, which served as a small audience room for the pope in the Vatican. These specifically represented themes such as abundance, agriculture, peace, commerce and science, paying tribute to the benefits of good governance.[39] They were repeated in the fresco painted in one of the window embrasures of the Sala di Constantino in 1524–5 by Giulio Romano, in which Leo X appears at a Serliana balcony supported by a pair of giant caryatids.[40] Caryatids were also used to assert the sovereignty of the French monarchs at the Louvre. In Pierre Lescot's remodelling of the Louvre as an imperial palace for Henri II between 1547 and 1555 the entrance gallery of the Grande Salle (facing the Serliana-like Tribunal) was supported by four caryatids, contracted for by Jean Goujon in 1550 (Fig. 200). Hoffmann shows that these should not be read simply as generic imperial symbols but have a particular significance in the way they were carved without arms, as if they were somewhat battered antique statues. These recall a passage in Pliny the Elder's *Natural History* where the Emperor Augustus placed two of the four caryatids he had removed from the *tabernaculum* of Alexander the Great before the Temple of Mars Ultor and the other two before the Regia. In appropriating these symbols of the first universal monarch, Augustus was seeking to bolster his own claims to that position. By imitating the same gesture, Henri II was wrapping himself in the mantle of Alexander and Augustus.[41]

Interest revived in the use of caryatids at the Louvre early in the seventeenth century. A rare engraving by Jean Marot shows a proposed caryatid staircase for the Louvre.[42] This was not executed but Jacques Lemercier's

197   Pedro Machuca, courtyard of Charles V's palace at Granada, 1526.

design for the Pavillon de l'Horloge at the Louvre generated considerable interest when he installed four groups of two caryatids to replace the columns at the upper storey of the building and support the intricate pedestal at the base of the column. Built in 1639–42, these are directly contemporary with Jones's proposed caryatid court at Whitehall.[43] Slightly later, but an even

198   Sebastiano Serlio, design for the House in the Countryside of an exceedingly illustrious Prince, from *The Sixth Book of Architecture*, fol. 27r.

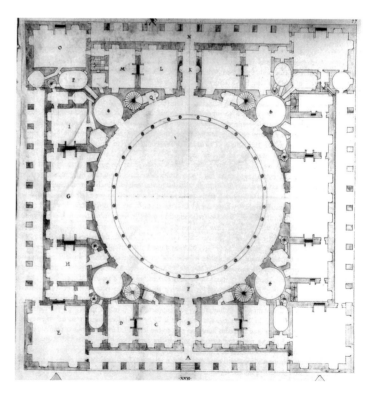

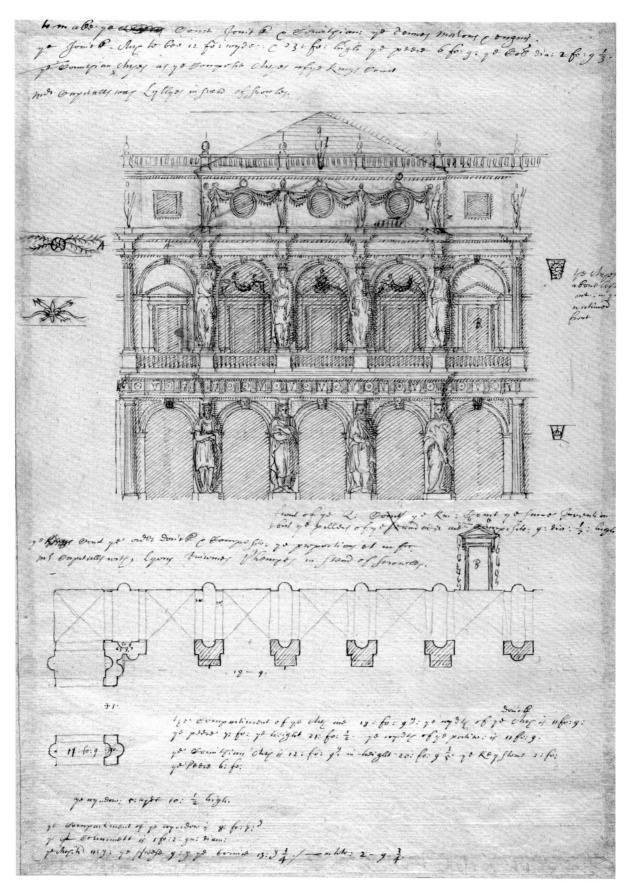

199 John Webb, after Inigo Jones, design for the elevations of the King's Court and the Queen's Court, Whitehall Palace, London, *c.*1638, Whinney P11 (Devonshire Collection, Chatsworth, reproduced by kind permission of the Trustees of the Chatsworth Settlement).

stronger assertion of the caryatid as a symbol of authority, is their use in the Room of Justice, where the sentence of death was pronounced, at Jacob van Campen's Amsterdam Town Hall of 1648.[44]

The Louvre even more than the palace at Granada and the Escorial must have been a constant source of comparison for Jones. As Serlio, who was probably commissioned to produce a scheme for the Louvre in 1541, commented: 'The house of a king must surpass all others in magnificence, size and richness of ornament, especially one that is to be at the service of the great king François.'[45] Sabine Frommel demonstrates that the scheme was designed for its site, if utopian in its belief that the necessary land could be easily acquired.[46] Though Serlio's proposal was rejected for Lescot's design it is probably the palace illustrated in his sixth book as the model for the city palace for the king.[47] Assuming that Serlio's plan was known to Jones, it would have reinforced his belief that the correct way to build a royal palace was to create an essentially square complex organised round a sequence of courtyards. Serlio may also have provided the precedent for the pair of basilican halls on either side of the principal courtyard of Jones's palace design.[48] The other Parisian palace of the French kings, the Tuileries, was also influential. Philibert de l'Orme's proposal for a grand rebuilding of the Tuileries was published by du Cerceau. Though it does not seem to have influenced Jones it is clearly the model for the plan of Webb's 'K' scheme, with its groups of three courts separated by a large rectangular court.[49]

Another symbol of imperial authorit was the basilica. Basilicas were covered halls which, Palladio explained, were 'those places in which judges presided under cover to administer justice and where, from time to time, very important business was conducted'.[50] The Stuart monarchs took the magisterial role of the monarchy seriously, as is clear from *His Majesties Speech at his first coming to the Starchamber*:

> Give thy Judgement to the King, O God, and thy righteousness to the King's son; the literal sense, upon the Prophet *David* and his Son *Solomon*, Godly and wise; the mystical sense, upon god and Christ his eternal Son, Just and Righteous; from which imitation all Governments, especially *Monarchies*, have been established. *Kings* are properly Judges, and sit in the Throne of God, and thence all Judgement is derived. . . . so all *Christian Kings govern*, whereby appears the near conjunction, *God* and the *King* upwards, the *King* and his *Judges* downward.[51]

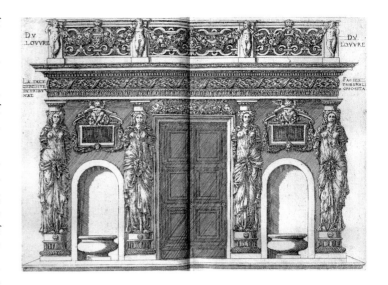

200 Pierre Lescot, Grande Salle of the Louvre (1550), from Androuet du Cerceau, *Les plus excellents bastiments de France* (1576), no plate numbers (British Library, London).

The association is emphasised by the name of the building, as Palladio pointed out: 'By definition the term basilica means "royal house".'[52]

Jones had turned to Palladio's reconstructions of the Roman basilica in his design of 1617 for the Star Chamber, where the committee of the Privy Council met to enact legislation presided over by the monarch. Per Palme notes that he adapted the model, which was intended for an ordinary judge, not a king, by enlarging the great niche in which the judge sat and reducing the number of columns in it from twelve to eight, adapting the niche in Palladio's reconstruction of the 'Temple of Jupiter the Thunderer' as more appropriate for the monarch.[53] In design the plan of the Star Chamber also recalls Palladio's plan of the 'Temple of the Sun and the Moon'. This led Palme to conjecture that Jones saw the building as a symbol of James I's divine authority, the gods of Sun and Jupiter being 'two deities which in the Stuart age were time and again cited as allegorical personifications of the sovereign, the crowned image of God, the very source of Justice'.[54] Jones included a similar apse, described as the 'great Neech' at the far end of the main floor of the Banqueting House to accommodate the throne on state occasions. This was removed at an early date, probably in 1625–6.[55]

Palladio's basilica was returned to by Jones for the two halls with apsed ends in the side ranges of the central court in Whitehall Palace. One of these was intended to be used as the Council Chamber. It is unclear what the

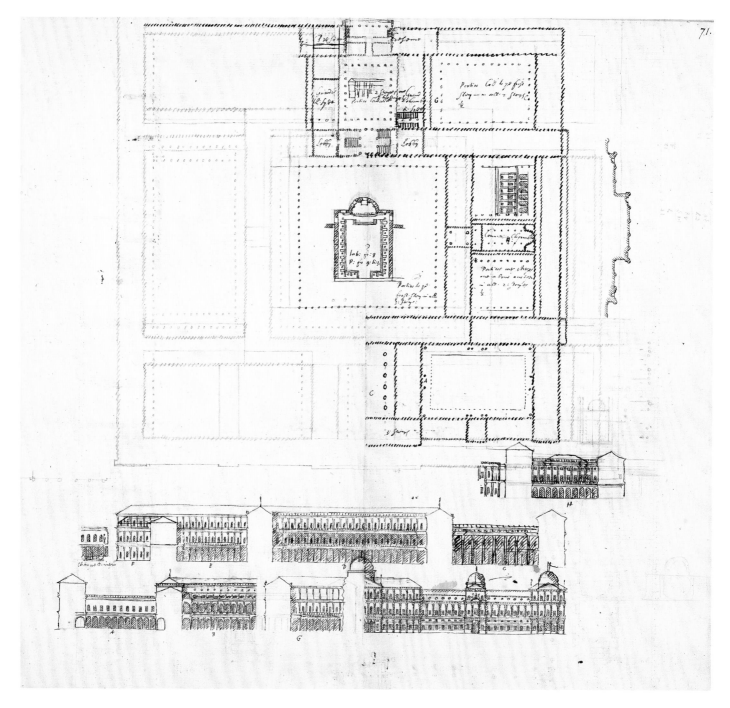

201   John Webb, after Inigo Jones, design for Whitehall Palace, London, *c*.1638, Whinney P1 (Devonshire Collection, Chatsworth, reproduced by kind permission of the Trustees of the Chatsworth Settlement).

other would have been. One possibility would have been the Star Chamber. Alternatively, it could perhaps have been intended for use as a Roman Catholic chapel for the queen.[56] In P1, which appears to be a preliminary design, Jones not only sketched the Council Chamber in place, annotating it as such, but drew it in greater detail in the space left by the central courtyard (Fig. 201). This drawing also shows that Jones intended the central colonnade to be double height, presumably inspired by those in Palladio's reconstructions of the Ancient Roman Town House, the Square of the Greeks and the Square of the Latins.[57] The parallel with the Ancient Roman

Town House is the closest and this should be seen as a major source for P1, with its atrium, colonnaded courtyard leading to a columned basilical hall and four-columned halls in the centre of the side range (Fig. 202).

The final specifically regal element in Jones's designs that needs to be noted is his use of a Palatine chapel, that is a two-level chapel in which the monarch would have sat at the upper level in a royal pew. This was the characteristic form of English royal chapels, as at Hampton Court and the Queen's Chapel at St James's Palace, but is of ancient origin, as can be seen by its use at Charlemagne's Palatine Chapel at Aachen.

Jones's Whitehall Palace design thus needs to be understood as the result of the careful assimilation of a wide range of symbols of sovereignty, some, like the portico, Serliana, caryatid and Persian being generic, others referring more specifically to earlier palaces, both antique and modern, others having a more general meaning. Perhaps the most important of these earlier buildings was the Temple of Solomon and in particular Juan Bautista Villalpando's elaborate reconstruction of it, *In Ezechielem Explanationes et Apparatus Urbis ac Templi Hierosolymitani, commentariis et imaginibus illustratus*, published in Rome in two volumes in 1596 and 1605 (see Fig. 39).

King Solomon was a crucial symbol for the early Stuarts. James I when presiding in the Star Chamber specifically compared his role to that of Solomon, a connection that was made explicit in Rubens's paintings for the ceiling of the Banqueting House, which included the subject of the Judgement of Solomon. 'I dare presume to say', declared Bishop Williams at the funeral of James I, 'you never read in your lives of two *Kings* more fully *paralleled* amongst themselves . . . Here the *Lawes* were justly administered, here all the *Tribes* were usually assembled, here the three *Kingdoms* were convened, here Edinburgh and Dublin were united like Jebus and Salem, in one *Jerusalem*. Whilst *Solomon reigned in this Jerusalem*.'[58]

Jones had shown an interest in reconstructions of the Temple of Solomon as early as the Cotton Memorial of about 1610–11, with its two columns inspired by those erected in the porch of the Temple of Solomon. His client, Sir Rowland Cotton, was a patron of Hebrew scholarship, first of the rabbinical scholar Hugh Broughton (1549–1612) and then of John Lightfoot (1602–75), later Vice-Chancellor of Cambridge University, who edited and published Broughton's work. In 1650 Lightfoot produced one of the most scholarly volumes on the physical appearance of the Herodian temple, *The Temple*

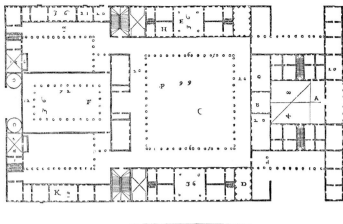

202 Andrea Palladio, reconstruction of the Ancient Roman Town House from *I quattro libri dell'architettura* (1570) II, p. 34.

Especially as it stood in the dayes of our Saviour, and he could well have been a source for Jones's ideas about the Temple in the late 1630s.[59]

Jones's Whitehall designs bear a strong resemblance to Villalpando's temple. It is nearly square, it is organised round a series of courtyards, the entrance elevation is long, relatively low and punctuated by four taller pavilions and, most significantly, the complex revolves round the chapel or Sanctuary.

Placing the chapel at the centre of a royal palace is highly unusual and was not suggested by Francesco di Giorgio or Serlio. It was the case at the Escorial, however, which Charles I saw on his trip to Spain in 1623, and which can also be read as a reconstruction of the Temple of Solomon (see Fig. 195).[60] Like Villalpando's temple this is essentially square, organised round a sequence of courtyards, with a relatively low façade punctuated by towers and a chapel in the centre. Jones's design emulates it in its domed chapel and in the way that the royal pew in the choir of the Escorial seems to be the source of the drawn-in royal pew in what appears to be a chapel at Whitehall (see Fig. 193).

It is not surprising that Charles I, with his strongly held views of the Divine Right of Kings, should have taken the Temple of Solomon, the ultimate symbol of divinely inspired authority, as a key model for his palace. In the late sixteenth and early seventeenth centuries the issue of royal authority and its divine origins was keenly debated. 'Rex est mixta persona cum sacerdote' (the

King is a combination of person and priest) was the traditional formula.[61] It was an issue that particularly concerned Charles I, not only within Britain but also internationally. The Church of England and the King of England, its Supreme Governor, were sensitive about their legitimacy in view of the break with the pope, the traditional fount of western European religious authority. Charles I's palace, had it been built, would have proclaimed his authority to his subjects and his divinely inspired legitimacy to his rival monarchs. As Parry has explained, 'Jones's designing of a New Jerusalem in St James's Park would have underlined the Solomonic connotations of Stuart kingship which had been reinforced by Bishop Williams . . . at the funeral of James I.'[62]

Philip II and Charles I were not alone in emulating the Temple of Jerusalem. As seen, in Germany the impressively large Augsburg Rathaus, begun by Elias Holl in 1615, and the Rathaus at Nuremberg, built in 1616–22 by Jakob Wolf, can also be read as evocations of the Temple of Solomon (see Figs 38, 35 and 39). The same is true of Jacob van Campen's town hall in Amsterdam, begun in 1648. Yet where the town councils of Augsburg and Nuremberg settled for emulating one element of the temple, the Sanctuary and the front range, Jones took the entire temple as his model. It is perhaps not surprising that the German schemes were both completed but the English was not even begun.

Chapter 11

JONES'S LEGACY

Inigo Jones died on 21 June 1652 at Somerset House in London, an appropriate setting for the great architect's deathbed. Though he had never managed to rebuild the palace on the grand scale he had once hoped, his work there had been substantial and ranged across the greater part of his career as Surveyor of the King's Works, from the lantern over the hall in 1617–18, to the Queen's Cabinet Room in 1626, the river stairs in 1628–31, the refitted Cross Gallery in 1635 and the new cabinet room in 1637, with the highpoint being the Queen's Chapel of 1630–35. Sadly, none of this survives, all having been destroyed when the original Somerset House was demolished over 1776–90.

It has been suggested that Jones died at Somerset House because of the high esteem in which he was held by the Commonwealth – many of the lodgings were occupied by senior Commonwealth figures and Oliver Cromwell later lay in state there – but the reality, as Michael Leapman has pointed out, is probably more mundane. Jones was not granted lodgings at Somerset House. On his return to London he lived in the Surveyor's lodging at Scotland Yard until 1651. He moved to Somerset House to stay with his kinswoman Elizabeth Jones, wife of Richard Gammon, who was the clerk of works there – probably when he was incapable of looking after himself.[1]

The fact, none the less, that Jones had continued to live in the Surveyor's lodgings is itself remarkable given that he had been dismissed from his post by Parliament in 1643 and replaced by Edward Carter, his former deputy in the repair of St Paul's cathedral. Jones's dismissal was hardly surprising since he had gone with Charles I to Yorkshire, presumably to assist in the siege of Hull in 1642, had lent him £500 that July and was subsequently captured in October 1645 at the siege of Basing Castle, where he had assisted with the fortifi-cations. As a royalist, Jones's estate was inevitably sequestrated but he reached an agreement to compound the sum of £1,000 and died relatively rich, leaving slightly more than £4,000 in his will. According to George Vertue he had successfully recovered the 'joint store of ready money' he and Nicholas Stone had hidden in Lambeth Marsh.[2] Equally importantly, at least for subsequent architectural history, he had managed to keep together his collection of architectural drawings and books, which he described as 'certain models and other like commodities which I only used and keep for my pleasure but of no profit, yet cost me £200 and upwards'.[3]

Jones's career never recovered from the collapse of the monarchy in 1642 but he continued working in a limited way after the end of the Civil War, playing a significant role in the rebuilding of Wilton House after the interior was gutted by fire in 1647, though with John Webb playing the principal role, Jones then being too old 'to be there in person'.[4] It is also possible, as seen in chapter 7, that he had some involvement in plans to rebuild Cobham Hall and in the rebuilding of Coleshill House. However, it is hard to believe that Jones's last years were happy, particularly after the shocking experience of the execution of his beloved monarch in 1649. According to Webb, he died 'through grief, as is well known, for the fatal calamity of his dread master'.[5] On 22 July 1650, aged 77, he made out his will, an act which suggests that he felt the end was near, dividing his estate between his pupil John Webb, who had married his kinswoman Anne Jones, and Richard Gammon. Jones was buried with his parents at St Benet's church, Paul's Wharf, where a monument was erected bearing reliefs of the Banqueting House and St Paul's cathedral. It was destroyed in the Great Fire of London of 1666 but fortunately recorded by John Aubrey (Fig. 203).[6]

203   John Aubrey, Inigo Jones's monument in St Benet's church, Paul's Wharf, London, destroyed
1666 (Bodleian Library, Oxford, MS Aubrey 8, fol. 19r).

The last years seem something of a damp squib after Jones's achievement before the Civil War and the great possibilities that seemed to loom in the late 1630s. The squib seems even damper in traditional accounts of Jones, where his Palladian manner is seen as too esoteric to have had much contemporary influence and to have fizzled out with his death, not to be revived for another sixty years. As Robert Tavernor puts it: 'The revolution in architecture he had initiated in England virtually died with him. His circle of influence was restricted to a few initiates in the Office of Works, such as John Webb and Nicholas Stone, but they had neither the authority nor the direct experience of Italy and Roman classicism to sustain the momentum Jones had created.'[7] The assumption is that Jones was of little importance in English architecture until early in the eighteenth century when his central role in what is commonly described as the Palladian Revival is undoubted. Yet this assessment of

Jones deserves to be amended because his influence was profound in his own time and helped dictate the course of English architecture over the next half-century.

Jones's mantle fell most immediately on his pupil Webb, to whom he left his architectural drawings and library. Webb had been thoroughly trained by Jones, the first English architect to receive that benefit. As he later wrote in 1660, when he was seventeen in 1628 'he was brought up by his Uncle Mr. Inigo Jones upon his late Majesty's command in the study of Architecture, as well that which relates to building as for masques triumphs and the like'.[8] Webb was of particular value to Jones as a draughtsman. His earliest datable drawings are for the Barber Surgeons' Hall in London of 1636–7. By 1638 he seems to have been developing an independent career as drawings survive for a lodge for John Penruddock at Hale in Hampshire and a stable for a Mr Fetherstone, probably at Hassenbrook in Essex, though both are small and neither is known to have been executed. More important are the extensive number of drawings Webb made for the Palace of Whitehall at the same time.[9]

More than two hundred drawings by Webb survive, divided among Worcester College, Oxford, the RIBA in London and Chatsworth House, Derbyshire. Unfortunately, without a careful study, such as that applied to Jones's drawings by Gordon Higgott, a proper appreciation of Webb's drawings, many of which are theoretical and not related to specific projects, is not easy and a chronology has yet to be firmly established. The most detailed investigation is Esther Eisenthal's study of his drawings reconstructing the Ancient House. From Webb's handwriting (and from the use of hatching, though others find this argument debatable) Eisenthal sees these as contemporary with the Somerset House and Hale Lodge drawings of 1638, that is when Webb was still in his late twenties and heavily involved with Jones.[10] Many of them are closely based on the engravings and text of Vitruvius's *I dieci libri dell'architettura*, Palladio's *I quattro libri dell'architettura* and Scamozzi's *L'idea della architettura universale*; others are Webb's own interpretation. They show Webb doing exactly what Jones had done before him, intensively studying these three canonical sources to equip himself to be an architect. Further evidence for this approach comes from Webb's own copy of Serlio's *Tutte l'opere d'architettura et prospetiva* (1619) and Palladio's *Quattro libri*, both of which he, like Jones, carefully examined and annotated. The Palladio includes a copy of instructions about the Queen's House dated 1639, which fits Eisenthal's dating. The Serlio notes, which include transcriptions of some

of the notes Jones had made in his own copy of Serlio, bear the date 16 January 1644, supporting the suggestion that Webb used the idleness of the Civil War years to further his architectural study.[11] Other drawings show Webb sticking close to the authors Jones had studied. Palladio and Serlio are repeatedly used, as are Philibert de l'Orme's *Le premier tome de l'architecture* (1569), Rubens's *Palazzi di Genova* (1622–6) and Gioseffe Viola Zanini's *Della architettura* (1629). This is hardly surprising given that Webb must have relied heavily on Jones's extensive library. All these books (except the Rubens) survive among Jones's books at Worcester College.[12]

Like Jones, Webb was not afraid to make his own judgements between the merits of the different authors, or indeed to vary from Jones's interpretation, but the projects need to be understood as self-education, presumably carried out under Jones's guidance. What is less clear is whether Webb's drawings can be taken as evidence that he planned to publish an architectural treatise, what architectural message that treatise would have put across and the degree to which it would have been imbued with a Jonesian message or, indeed, Jones's involvement in the project. Certainly some of the drawings, particularly those for the orders (Fig. 204), are neatly enough produced to be ready for engraving and two rambling texts 'of wyndowes' and 'of the Ionick Order' survive and could be rough draughts of parts of the text. On the one hand, a volume on the orders would have been the most attractive to potential readers, as is shown by the success of the publication of the sixth book, on the orders, of Scamozzi's *L'idea* in the Dutch Republic on its own in two editions in 1640 and in 1657 and Fréart's *Parallèle de l'architecture antique et de la moderne* in France in 1650. On the other hand, many of the drawings may simply have been the product of Webb's intensive self-education and others, particularly the small sketch plans, are probably best understood as office reference drawings.[13] Yet if Webb, perhaps working at Jones's behest, considered publishing a treatise, as Palladio and Scamozzi had done before, its failure to materialise severely restricted Jones's legacy as an architectural theorist. English architecture might have been far different had it been published.

The results of Webb's studies are evident in the 'E' and 'K' schemes for Whitehall Palace (assuming, as is generally believed, that these are essentially the work of Webb, not Webb's drawings of a Jonesian scheme) and particularly in the 'T' scheme, thought to date from 1647–8. The latter, in its extreme neo-classicism, with debts both to the Roman Baths and to his studies of the Ancient

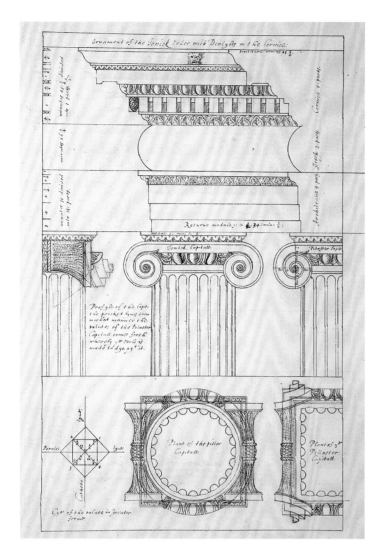

204 John Webb, the Ionic order (Worcester College, Oxford).

House, shows a fundamentalism in Webb's work found in Jones only at St Paul's, Covent Garden. Given that it was drawn up while Charles I was in captivity in Caris-brooke Castle it is hardly surprising that the result is an ideal rather than a practical proposal. Not that the Whitehall Palace designs were isolated in Webb's work. The plan of Durham House for the Earl of Pembroke in 1649 is clearly inspired by Scamozzi's House of the Roman Senators, one of the key sources in his study of the Ancient House, while his design for an Exchange, which Webb inscribed 'may serve for a Royal Exchange from a metropolis as London and ye like', is based on the Roman basilica.[14]

Webb's theoretical drawings show how the younger architect was educated firmly within the same canonical tradition as Jones but was confortable trying out his own

ideas. The same attitude can be seen in a sequence of designs based on earlier drawings by Jones. The best-known of these are for the Star Chamber, which Jones had designed in 1617 (Fig. 205).[15] No version of Jones's elevation for the Star Chamber survives but a plan does which, as Harris and Higgott point out, differs in many relatively minor but significant ways from Webb's version. It is clear that Webb reworked rather than copied Jones's drawings, much as he reworked Palladio and Scamozzi's versions of the Ancient House.

Another example of this approach can be seen in Webb's design for a five-bay villa with wings and towers (Fig. 206).[16] This is a variant on Jones's third Queen's House design, based in its turn on Scamozzi's Villa Molin (see Figs 114 and 115). Webb's drawing follows Scamozzi in the arrangement of the windows, attic and projecting clerestory, though the treatments of the doorcase, the choice of the order and the arrangement of the columns of the portico and the door and windows behind derive from Jones's drawing.[17] On top of this mix of Scamozzi and Jones Webb imposed his own elements. His version of the entablature is far more elaborate than Jones's and the rustic windows have been reduced in scale and take a form inspired by the ground-floor windows of Palladio's Palazzo Barbarano and Palazzo Valmarana.[18] The most important difference is Webb's use of rustication. Scamozzi and Jones restricted the rustication to the rustic, with both picking out the individual stones. By contrast, Webb continues the rustication into the piano nobile, but not the attic, and suggests smooth, continuous bands of rustication that is more emphatic in the rustic than the piano nobile.

This drawing highlights a particular characteristic of Webb's work and one that clearly distinguishes him from Jones. Though Jones used rustication, most notably at the Banqueting House and St Paul's cathedral (see Figs 107 and 153), it was never a dominant element in his aesthetic. For Webb, rustication and the manipulation of the texture of the wall surface through contrast with a smooth surface and the use of heavy keystones, quoining and stringcourses were central to his work. This is particularly evident at Amesbury Abbey, Wiltshire (about 1659; Fig. 207), which can be read as a development of the five-bay villa design (see Fig. 206). In this case Webb gave the first two storeys of windows emphatic keystones, heavily rusticated the rustic and piano nobile, but left a gap of plain stone between them and also left the attic smooth (as in the five-bay villa design).[19]

At the larger of the two Durham House designs of 1649 Webb gave the ground and first floors a background

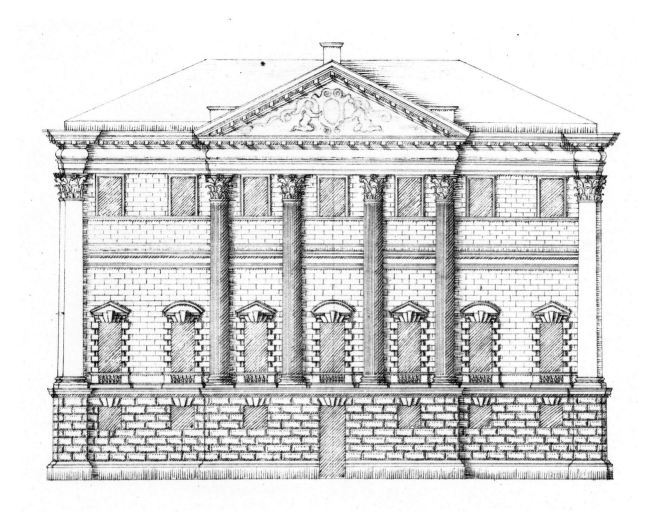

205   John Webb, after Inigo Jones, elevation of the Star Chamber, Whitehall, 1617 (Worcester College, Oxford).

206   John Webb, design for a five-bay villa with wings and towers (Worcester College, Oxford).

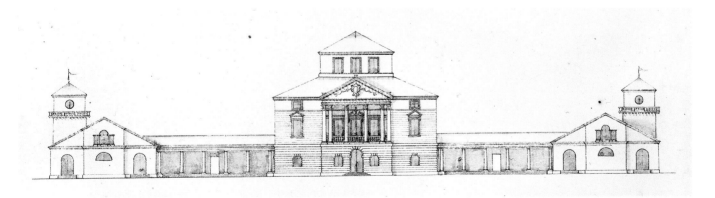

Ambresbury in Wiltshire the Seat of the Right Honourable the Lord Carlton president of Council.

207   John Webb, Amesbury Abbey, Wiltshire, *c*.1659, from Colen Campbell, *Vitruvius Britannicus* (1717) II, p. 8.

under the windows, and finally a smooth attic storey, separated by a thin stringcourse. This is a particularly interesting design because the overall design, though narrower (a three-bay rather than a five-bay frontispiece and flanking wings of three rather than four bays), is clearly derived from Scamozzi's Villa Verlato (see Fig. 117).[22] However, in its treatment of the rustic, the round-headed door and the emphatic keystones over the windows it follows Jones's preliminary Queen's House design (see Fig. 113), not Scamozzi. Given Webb's reworking of other earlier designs by Jones, this suggests that it might be based on a lost drawing by Jones for the long, thin villa design often associated with the Queen's House design, which was based on the Villa Verlato.

Evidence for the way Webb reworked Jones's designs, his love of complex textural effect and his regular use of emphatic keystones over windows suggests that the design for the elevation of the Star Chamber should be treated with caution (see Fig. 205). The extensive and varied use of rustication, the emphatic stringcourse and the rusticated window surrounds based on Palladio's Palazzo Thiene indicate that though the bones of the scheme may be Jones's, the detail is very much Webb's (see Fig. 106). A similar stylistic analysis suggests that both the 'K' (commonly dated to about 1638; Fig. 210) and the 'E' (which John Bold dates to the mid-1640s; Fig. 211) schemes for Whitehall Palace, which make extensive use of varied rustication, particularly channelled rustication, block rusticated columns and emphatic keystones, are the product of Webb's, not Jones's, aesthetic imagination.[23]

The elements that form this aesthetic can all be traced back to Palladio, Scamozzi and Jones. The emphatic stringcourses, the heavy keystones and rusticated win-

of channelled rustication but set this off with a plain plinth, a plain band running along the line of the rusticated quoins of the ground-floor windows and a plain attic (Fig. 208).[20] Webb's most complex elevation is the smaller design for Durham House (Fig. 209).[21] Here he suggested a channelled rusticated rustic with quoins and emphatic keystones over the windows and door, then a smooth mezzanine strip, a prominent stringcourse, then a smooth piano nobile with quoins and labels (or panels)

208   John Webb, larger design for Durham House, London, 1649 (Worcester College).

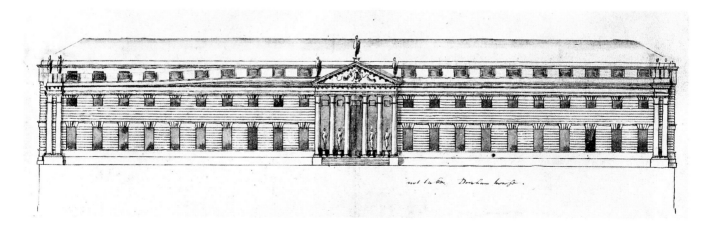

209 John Webb, smaller design for Durham House, London, 1649 (Worcester College, Oxford).

dow surrounds, the varied use of quoining and of plain bands within an otherwise rusticated surface linking keystones, can all be found in Palladio.[24] The continuously channelled rustication is derived from Scamozzi.[25] Nevertheless, it may be no coincidence that a similar interest in the use of rustication to create a richly articulated surface is also revealed in the contemporary work in France of Antoine le Pautre (as seen in his *Desseins de plusiers palais*, published in 1652; Fig. 213) and Louis le Vau, particularly at Vaux-le-Vicomte of 1657.[26]

Had it not been for the Civil War there can be little doubt that Webb would have succeeded Jones as Surveyor of the King's Works, with all the benefits of a full practical and theoretical training in architecture, which could be claimed by neither of the two Surveyors who supplanted him, Sir John Denham and Sir Christopher Wren. However, Webb's architectural skills were too valuable to be ignored. Having fitted up Whitehall Palace for Charles II's return he was paid for work at both Greenwich and Whitehall in 1661 and in that year was already contemplating the rebuilding of Whitehall Palace, as a sketch design dated 17 October 1661 shows.[27] He is generally credited with improvements to Somerset House for Queen Henrietta Maria, including the handsome, arcaded gallery, in 1661–4, produced further designs for Whitehall in about 1663–4 and in 1663 was given the responsibility for the new palace at

Greenwich (Fig. 212).[28] More than any of his competitors, Webb was the dominant architect of the first years of the Restoration.

At Greenwich Webb was able to put the idea of a richly articulated elevation he had developed in his drawings and domestic work into practice on a grander scale. In detail the design owes little to Jones or Scamozzi. It is a more 'Palladian' building than anything designed by Jones, relying in particular on the Palazzo Valmarana and Palazzo Barbarano (Fig. 214), which provided the model for the giant order, the pavilion attics, the channelled rustication of the walls and the form of the windows.[29] Yet it also shows awareness of what was going on across the Channel in France, the idea of two independent ranges facing each other across a courtyard probably being taken from le Vau's Château de Vincennes of 1658, which also anticipates Webb's use of the giant order and Palladian attics.[30]

Webb's architectural approach was not without stylistic progeny, specifically in the work of William Talman, who turned to Webb's Greenwich Palace as the inspiration for his revolutionary work at Chatsworth House, Derbyshire, in 1687 and, it can be argued, in what may be Talman's designs for Hampton Court.[31] Otherwise Webb's immediate architectural legacy is minimal, partly because, unlike Jones, he failed to train a successor, partly because the weakness of the Crown's finances

210 John Webb, 'K' design for Whitehall Palace, London, Whinney K6 (Worcester College, Oxford).

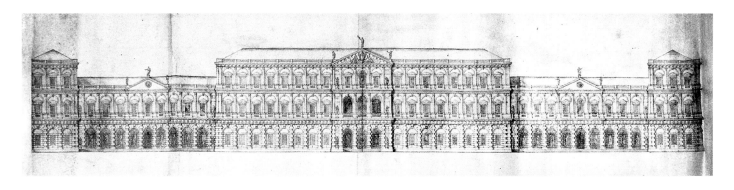

211 John Webb, 'E' design for Whitehall Palace, London, Whinney E9 (Worcester College, Oxford).

meant that work on Greenwich Palace was abandoned and schemes for Whitehall Palace proved abortive. Perhaps more importantly, though, Webb's fascination with richly articulated façades, seen not only in his grand public works but also in his smaller domestic work, was moving against the change in public taste. In England,

the Dutch Republic and France the trend was towards simpler elevations, with decoration increasingly reduced to the bare minimum.

In the Dutch Republic this is particularly evident in the work of Pieter Post and Philips Vingboons. Not surprisingly, given that he first acted as executant archi-

212 John Webb, King Charles Building, Greenwich Palace, 1663.

tect to Jacob van Campen, Post's early architecture reflects the ideals of the early Dutch classicists, with a strong reliance on the use of the pilaster. This is true of both his grander, public works for the House of Orange, such as his remodelling of Honselaarsdijk (1646), and of domestic work such as the country house at Vredenburg (1642; see Fig. 65). Yet the substantial town house he built at Rapenburg 8 in Leiden at the very end of his life in 1668 reveals a new sensibility (Fig. 215). This is dramat-

213 Antoine le Pautre, second design from *Desseins de plusiers palais* (1652).

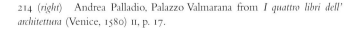

214 (*right*) Andrea Palladio, Palazzo Valmarana from *I quattro libri dell' architettura* (Venice, 1580) II, p. 17.

215   Pieter Post, Rapenburg 8, Leiden, Netherlands, 1668.

the norm. The first volume (with designs dating from 1635 to 1647) is fairly evenly split between pilastered and astylar designs, while in the second volume (with designs dating from 1649 to 1669) the ratio is more than two to one in favour of astylar elevations. For designs in the 1660s the ratio of astylar to pilastered elevations is ten to two. It is also noticeable that where most of the designs in the first book have some form of window surround, usually a simple cornice, most of those in the second volume have none.[33]

This growing interest in austerity was signalled by Vingboons in his first volume in a remarkable ideal design for a country house in which all ornament has been removed, including window surrounds so the window is cut straight into the wall, except for the pediment and the rusticated, pedimented doorcase.[34] It is a design clearly influenced by the austere buildings that appeared in the second volume of Rubens's *Palazzi di Genova*, published in 1626 (see Fig. 141).[35] None of Vingboons's executed designs achieved the same austerity, except Nittersum, built in 1669 for Joan Clent.[36] A similar tendency is evident in the work of the next generation of Dutch architects, as seen in such Amsterdam houses as Amstel 216 and Keizergracht 672–4 built by Adriaen Dortsman in the early 1670s, in Kasteel Amerongen, designed by Hendrik Schut in 1674, and in the careers of Jacob Roman and Steven Vennekool.[37]

Much the same was happening in England. The pilastered terraced houses in Great Queen Street, Lincoln's Inn Fields (about 1636–41; see Fig. 97) and Newington Green (1658), London, and individual houses such as Balmes Park, Middlesex (about 1635), Lees Court, Kent (about 1640), and Syndale House, Kent (about 1652), fit the contemporary Dutch tradition, particularly strong in bourgeois buildings, of the extensive use of pilasters, not for the carefully gradated representation of status but for simple ostentation. The use of pilasters began to fall out of fashion during the Commonwealth. It became exceptional after the Restoration, where town houses in the developments of the 1660s such as Bloomsbury Square (Fig. 216) and St James's Square (in contrast to Lincoln's Inn Fields before the Civil War) are universally astylar. The same is predominantly true of country houses, where Sir Roger Pratt's astylar Kingston Lacy, Dorset (1663; Fig. 217), proved far more influential than the pilasters of Hugh May's Eltham Lodge, Kent (1664).

In this growing move towards austerity Jones proved particularly prescient. At just the moment when van Campen and the Dutch classicists were promoting the pilastered elevation as the key to the new architectural

ically emphasised by the contemporary houses on either side of the building: these still carry the full panoply of pilasters common in Dutch town houses since the 1640s. By contrast, Post's design is a model of restraint, ornamented only by a simple pediment, restrained entablature and a great sweep of swags over an elaborate front door. The sophistication of the design makes it clear that this is not a case of a building being given minimal ornament because of its insignificance; relative austerity had been chosen for aesthetic reasons for what was clearly a prestigious project.[32]

A similar shift can be seen in the work of Vingboons, whose two volumes of works, *Afbeelsels der voornaemste gebouwen*, published in 1648 and 1674, reveal a distinct move from an architecture dominated by rich ornament and pilasters to one in which the astylar elevation became

216 Sutton Nichols, engraving of Bloomsbury Square, London, from John Stow, *Survey of London* (1754).

217 Sir Roger Pratt, design for Kingston Lacy, Dorset, 1663.

218　Peter Mills, Thorpe Hall, Northamptonshire, 1654–6.

movement, Jones, who had used it in his first designs for the Queen's House in 1616, eliminated it in the executed version begun in 1632 (see Fig. 136). Inspired by the austere message of Rubens's *Palazzi di Genova* Jones began to promote a greater austerity in domestic architecture – though not for royal palaces where propriety required lavish ornament. The Queen's House was not alone. A comparable austerity can be seen in Webb's drawing after Jones for what appears to be a small hunting lodge (see Fig. 149) and in the related drawing for what was probably Jones's last design, the buttery, perhaps for Cobham Hall, which dates from the late 1640s (see Fig. 150). Ornament, including rustication and entablatures, and in particular the windows, which are cut directly into the walls, has been reduced to a minimum. In this they represent an advance from Jones's designs of the early 1630s as both the Queen's House and what may be a preliminary design for the New Lodge at Hyde Park (1634–5; see Fig. 148) retain window surrounds.

Here the assumption that Webb is the heir to Jones's aesthetic proves a distraction. In achieving independence from Jones Webb turned his back on Jones's innovative austerity, experimenting instead with façades of real sculptural complexity. Focus on Webb has meant that Jones's achievement in the latter part of his career in anticipating the move to the greater austerity that is a marked feature of English and Dutch architecture in the second half of the seventeenth century has been overlooked.

Jones's greatest immediate legacy was at a simpler level, however, in the triumph of the simple, restrained manner for ordinary domestic architecture that he had advocated throughout his career. Jones's influence is apparent in the work of his circle of associates: John Webb; Nicholas Stone at Cornbury Park and the Goldsmiths' Hall; Edward Carter at Easthampstead Lodge and Bedford House; Isaac de Caus at Covent Garden and Wilton House; and Roger Pratt at Coleshill House. These were the elite of the building world and there is clear evidence in each case that Jones assisted them, clearly trying to impose his own aesthetic vision and, where necessary, using the Commission for Building to do so.

The spread of this manner outside Jones's immediate circle can be seen in the work of Peter Mills, who built the houses in Great Queen Street. The façade of Mills's Thorpe Hall, Northamptonshire (1654–6; Fig. 218), has much in common with Jones's thirteen-bay design apparently for Lord Maltravers at Lothbury (see Fig. 83). By the time domestic architecture picked up after the Restoration in 1660, it was this simple regularity, promoted by Jones as long before as 1618, that prevailed, most clearly in two prestigious new London housing developments, Bloomsbury Square and St James's Square.

His legacy is also evident in one of the most persistent of architectural motifs to be found in late seventeenth- and eighteenth-century British architecture, the use of the Serlian window over the altar in churches. Jones had introduced this at the Queen's Chapel at St James's Palace and it had been picked up at Great Stanmore church, Castle Ashby and Wilton House. After the Restoration, Christopher Wren placed a Serliana at the east end of the chapel at Pembroke College, Cambridge, designed in 1663 for his uncle Matthew, Bishop of Ely and former Dean of the Chapel Royal. Wren's action resonated across British architecture. It was the first of a sequence of Serlian windows in churches built under his aegis.[38] His example was picked up by the next generation of architects when they came to design the Fifty New Churches.[39] They were followed by a host of British, and American, church architects across the eighteenth century.[40]

Jones's legacy is apparent also in urban planning. Covent Garden provided the model for the Georgian town planning that dominated British architecture into the middle of the nineteenth century. This is not only because Jones introduced the idea of the regular London square but also because he created a miniature town, complete with public buildings, houses of varying degrees of affluence and above all the key practical requirement, the mews, which solved the problem of servicing the grand terraced house. It was the mews, developed at Covent Garden and taken up in the most prestigious pre-Civil War developments in Great Queen Street and Lincoln's Inn Fields, that made it possible for the English to abandon the idea of the urban courtyard house and build houses even for the grandest clients that opened straight onto the street. When large-scale urban development was revived in London at Hatton Garden, Bloomsbury Square and St James's Square, it was Jones's model of the miniature town, with mews, that prevailed.[41]

It is thus a mistake to believe that Jones's immediate architectural legacy was negligible and that it was not until the second decade of the eighteenth century that his ideas proved influential. Had the Civil War not intervened it would have been interesting to see how his growing interest in a radical austerity in architectural design would have developed. What is undoubted is that it anticipated similar developments in the Dutch Republic, though there is no evidence that the Queen's House influenced developments there. It is clear, however, that Jones's simpler, astylar architecture and his urban planning laid the foundation of what would come to be known as Georgian architecture. This, perhaps more than anything else, was his greatest legacy to English, and indeed British, architecture.

Notes

INTRODUCTION

1 Jones was 'one of the most independent architects in the Europe of his time, an artist of uncommon intellectual probity who declined to submit to the sway of any continental school and sought criteria which should have an absolute value independent of time and place. Such a quest can have been understood by only a handful of his contemporaries', declared Sir John Summerson of Jones in 'Inigo Jones: Covent Garden and the Restoration of St Paul's Cathedral', in John Summerson, *The Unromantic Castle and Other Essays* (London, 1990) p. 43.

2 See, for example, John Summerson, *Inigo Jones* (Harmondsworth, 1966) p. 36: 'If the architecture he [Jones] eventually built in England had been built in Italy it would have been against the tide.' Or Anthony Blunt, *Baroque and Rococo Architecture and Decoration* (London, 1978) p. 149: 'Thus in 1642, when the outbreak of the Civil War interrupted normal court life, the most modern architecture in the country was stylistically about a century behind central and northern Italy.' Or Howard Colvin, *A Biographical Dictionary of British Architects 1600–1840* (New Haven and London, 1995) p. 556: 'Nothing like these buildings had previously been seen in England, and in a baroque Europe they were an unexpected reaffirmation of High Renaissance principles which found no contemporary parallel in France or Italy.'

3 Surprisingly little attempt has been made to place Jones within his contemporary European context. An exception is John Peacock's study of Jones's masque designs, *The Stage Designs of Inigo Jones: The European Context* (Cambridge, 1995).

CHAPTER 1

1 John Harris, Stephen Orgel and Roy Strong, *The King's Arcadia: Inigo Jones and the Stuart Court* (London, 1973) pp. 52–5.

2 John Newman, 'Inigo Jones's Architectural Education before 1614', *Architectural History* XXXV (1992) pp. 18, 40.

3 *Historic Manuscripts Commission, Rutland* (London, 1905) IV, p. 446.

4 John Webb, *The most notable antiquity of Great Britain vulgarly called Stone-Heng on Salisbury Plain restored by Inigo Jones* (London, 1655) p. 1.

5 Andrea Palladio, *I quattro libri dell'architettura* (Venice, 1601), at Worcester College, Oxford. John Harris in the catalogue of the 'King's Arcadia' exhibition suggested that it is unlikely Jones bought the book in Venice in 1601 as there are no dated annotations before 1613. However, as John Newman subsequently demonstrated through his analysis of the dating of Jones's annotations, a significant number of annotations do pre-date 1613. Harris, Orgel and Strong, *King's Arcadia* pp. 64–5; Newman, 'Inigo Jones's Architectural Education' pp. 18–50.

6 J. A. Gotch, *Inigo Jones* (London, 1926) pp. 33, 38; John Peacock, *The Stage Designs of Inigo Jones: The European Context* (Cambridge, 1995) p. 7.

7 Michael Leapman, *Inigo: The Troubled Life of Inigo Jones, Architect of the English Renaissance* (London, 2003) p. 23.

8 Dudley Carleton, *Dudley Carleton to John Chamberlain, 1603–1624*, ed. with an introduction by M. Lee (New Brunswick, N.J., 1972) p. 145.

9 H. C. G. Matthew and Brian Harris (eds), *The Oxford Dictionary of National Biography* (Oxford, 2004) XXXVI, p. 461.

10 *Historic Manuscripts Commission, Rutland* IV, p. 446; James Lees-Milne, *The Age of Inigo Jones* (London, 1953) p. 21; John Harris and Gordon Higgott, *Inigo Jones: Complete Architectural Drawings* (London, 1989) p. 13.

11 Roy Strong, *Henry, Prince of Wales, and England's Lost Renaissance* (London, 1986) p. 110, citing information communicated to John Harris by G. B. Bredgade. The reference comes in the diary of Sivert Grabbe recording a dinner held on 10 July 1603 which lists the guests; Copenhagen, Royal Library MSS, Uldallske sams. 499, fol.147.

12 John Webb, *A Vindication of Stone-Heng Restored* (London, 1665) pp. 123–4.

13 Stephen Orgel and Roy Strong, *Inigo Jones: The Theatre of the Stuart Court* (London, 1973) p. 34; Howard Colvin,

14 Gotch argues that Jones's note in 1614, that he had again seen the fireworks celebrating the coronation of the pope, suggests he was in Rome at the time of the enthronement of Leo XI in May 1605. The previous papal coronations were in 1590 (Urban VII and Gregory XIV), 1591 (Innocent IX) and 1592 (Clement VIII), when Jones would still have been in his teens. Gotch, *Inigo Jones* p. 32.

15 Gordon Higgott, 'Inigo Jones in Provence', *Architectural History* XXVI (1983) pp. 24–34; Edward Chaney, review in *Burlington Magazine* CXXX (1988) pp. 633–4; *idem, The Evolution of the Grand Tour* (London, 1998) pp. 202 n. 68, 208.

16 Harris, Orgel and Strong, *King's Arcadia* p. 43.

17 John Newman, 'An Early Drawing by Inigo Jones and a Monument in Shropshire', *Burlington Magazine* CXV (1973) pp. 360–67.

18 Higgott, 'Inigo Jones in Provence' pp. 29–30, pls 14a–b.

19 Harris, Orgel and Strong, *King's Arcadia* pp. 28–33, fig. 32; Harris and Higgott, *Inigo Jones* p. 36.

20 Harris and Higgott, *Inigo Jones* pp. 36–7, cat. 3, fig. 5; Colvin, *Biographical Dictionary* p. 108.

21 Harris and Higgott, *Inigo Jones* p. 38, cat. 4.

22 *Ibid.*; James S. Ackerman, *The Architecture of Michelangelo* (London, 1961) figs 51c, 60.

23 Newman, 'Inigo Jones's Architectural Education p. 21.

24 Vaughan Hart and Peter Hicks, *Sebastiano Serlio: On Architecture* (New Haven and London, 1996) I, pp. 311, 422, 425.

25 See, for example, *ibid.*, (2001) II, p. 345.

26 Colvin, *Biographical Dictionary* pp. 607–8; Lawrence Stone, 'The Building of Hatfield House', *Archaeological Journal* CXII (1955) pp. 118–20.

27 Giles Worsley, 'Inigo Jones and the Hatfield Riding House', *Architectural History* XLV (2002) pp. 230–37.

28 Giles Worsley, *The British Stable* (New Haven and London, 2004) pp. 61–7.

29 Hatfield Papers, Hatfield House, SFP, I, 69; J. W. Stoye, *English Travellers Abroad* (London, 1952) p. 124.

30 Stoye, *English Travellers Abroad* p. 59; Hatfield Papers, SFP, I, 70, 123.

31 I owe this information to Paula Henderson. Harris and Higgott, *Inigo Jones* p. 48, cat. 9.

32 *Ibid.* p. 48, cat. 9, fig. 10.

33 Giles Worsley, 'Courtly Stables and their Implications for Seventeenth-Century English Architecture', *Georgian Group Journal* XIII (2004) pp. 114–15, fig. 1.

34 Parliamentary Survey, 1650, National Archive, Kew, E 351/3244–5.

35 Colvin, *Biographical Dictionary* p. 108.

36 *Ibid.*, pp. 607–8.

37 Peacock, *Stage Designs* pp. 72–3, fig. 21; Harris and Higgott, *Inigo Jones* pp. 31–2, fig. 4.

38 Harris and Higgott, *Inigo Jones* p. 30.

39 Newman, 'Inigo Jones's Architectural Education' pp. 18–50. The following account relies principally on Newman's analysis.

40 *Ibid.*, p. 22.

41 Inigo Jones quoted in *ibid.*, p. 29.

42 *Ibid.*, p. 49.

43 B. Alsopp (ed.), *Inigo Jones on Palladio* (1970) I, flyleaf; RIBA, London, Burlington/Devonshire Collection XIII/5.

44 Newman, 'Inigo Jones's Architectural Education' pp. 47–9.

CHAPTER 2

1 Mary F. S. Hervey, *The Life, Correspondence and Collections of Thomas Howard, Earl of Arundel* (Cambridge, 1921) p. 68.

2 D. Carleton, *Dudley Carleton to John Chamberlain, 1603–1624*, ed. with an introduction by M. Lee (New Brunswick, N.J., 1972) p. 145.

3 David Howarth, *Lord Arundel and his Circle* (New Haven and London, 1985) p. 39.

4 Allen B. Hinds (ed.), *Calendar of State Papers and Manuscripts: Venice* XIII, 1613–15 (London, 1907) p. 12.

5 Andrea Palladio, *I quattro libri dell'architettura* (Venice, 1570) I, pp. 19, 22; Vaughan Hart and Peter Hicks (eds), *Sebastiano Serlio: On Architecture* (New Haven and London, 1996) I, pp. 158, 162–5, 220–23, 224–31.

6 Hervey, *Life, Correspondence and Collections* p. 451.

7 I am grateful to Dr Gordon Higgott for pointing out to me that Arundel and Jones probably stayed in the Villa Molin and to Professor Konrad Ottenheym for the suggestion that the hall of the Queen's House was inspired by that of the Villa Molin. Edmund Sawyer, *Winwood Memorials* (London, 1725) III, p. 473. B. Alsopp (ed.), *Inigo Jones on Palladio, being the notes by Inigo Jones in the copy of I Quattro Libri dell'architettura di Andrea Palladio, 1601, in the Library of Worcester College, Oxford*, 2 vols (Newcastle upon Tyne, 1970) Bk IV, p. 105; Franco Barbieri and Guido Beltramini (eds), *Vincenzo Scamozzi 1548–1616* (Vicenza, 2003) pp. 369–74; Konrad [Koen] Ottenheym *et al., Vincenzo Scamozzi, Venetian Architect: The Idea of a Universal Architecture, Villas and Country Estates* (Amsterdam, 2003) p. 137.

8 Alsopp, *Inigo Jones on Palladio* I, p. 12.

9 Hervey, *Life, Correspondence and Collections* pp. 75–88; J. A. Gotch, 'Inigo Jones's Principal Visit to Italy in 1614: The Itinerary of his Journeys', *Royal Institute of British Architects Journal* XLVI, 3rd ser. (21 November 1938) pp. 85–6; Howarth, *Arundel and his Circle* pp. 30–51.

10 Aurora Scotti Tosini, 'Palladio e la Lombardia tra cinque e seicento: il ruolo della trattatistica', *Bolletino CISAP* 22, pt II (1980) pp. 63–78; Aurora Scotti Tosini (ed.), *Storia dell'architettura italiana: il seicento* 2 vols (Milan, 2003) II, pp. 453–4.

11 Vitruvius, *I dieci libri dell'architettura de M. Vitruvio tradotti e commendati da Daniel e Barbaro* (Venice, 1567; facsimile Rome, 1993) pp. 265–7, fig.; Palladio, *Quattro libri* III, 44–6.

12 Vitruvius, Bk V, ch. 1, v. 1; *I dieci libri* pp. 207–10, 277–82, figs; *The Ten Books of Architecture*, trans. Morris Hicky Morgan (New York, 1960) p. 131.

13 Palladio, *Quattro libri* III, pp. 32–7.

14 *Ibid.* II, p. 24–5, 33–4, figs; Vincenzo Scamozzi, *L'idea della architettura universale* (Venice, 1615) III, pp. 234–5.

15 Arnaldo Bruschi, *Storia dell'architettura italiana: il primo cinquecento* (Milan, 2002) pp. 425–6.

16 Tosini, *Storia dell'architettura italiana* II, p. 429.

17 *Ibid.* I, p. 118; II, pp. 341–3.

18 An MS copy of the *Trattato* survives in the British Museum. Alina Payne, 'Architectural Criticism, Science, and Visual Eloquence: Teofilo Gallaccini in Seventeenth-Century Siena', *Journal of the Society of Architectural Historians* LVIII (1999) pp. 146–54; James S. Ackerman, *Origins, Imitation, Conventions: Representation in the Visual Arts* (Cambridge, Mass., 2002) pp. 242–3; Tosini, *Storia dell'architettura italiana* pp. 619–20.

19 Edward Chaney, 'Inigo Jones in Naples', in John Bold and Edward Chaney (eds), *English Architecture Public and Private* (London, 1993) p. 42; Andrew Hopkins, *Italian Architecture from Michelangelo to Borromini* (London, 2002) p. 155, fig. 154.

20 Chaney, 'Inigo Jones in Naples', pp. 48–50, figs 21–2.

21 Hopkins, *Italian Architecture* p. 165, fig. 165.

22 Tosini, *Storia dell'architettura italiana* I, pp. 102–4.

23 *Ibid.* p. 115.

24 Hopkins, *Italian Architecture* p. 165, fig. 167.

25 Tosini, *Storia dell'architettura italiana* I, pp. 100–07, 113–19.

26 Henry B. Wheatley (ed.), *The Diary of John Evelyn* (London, 1906) I, p. 104. The foundations of the cathedral were laid by Bernardo Buontalenti in 1594. Amelio Fara, *Bernardo Buontalenti: l'architettura, la guerra e l'elemento geometrico* (Genoa, 1984) pp. 244–6, fig. 220.

27 Tosini, *Storia dell'architettura italiana* II, pp. 472–3.

28 Jones's annotations on Bk III, p. 50 of his *Quattro libri*. Alsopp, *Inigo Jones on Palladio*. For a more detailed discussion of Jones's criticisms see Gordon Higgott, 'Varying with Reason: Inigo Jones's Theory of Design', *Architectural History* XXXV (1992) pp. 51–77; Howard Burns, 'Note sull'inflesso di Scamozzi in Inghilterra: Inigo Jones, John Webb, Lord Burlington', in Barbieri and Beltramini, *Vincenzo Scamozzi* pp. 129–31.

29 Barbieri and Beltramini, *Vincenzo Scamozzi* pp. 288–96.

30 John Harris and Gordon Higgott, *Inigo Jones: Complete Architectural Drawings* (London, 1989) pp. 104–5.

31 Howarth, *Arundel and his Circle* p. 244 n. 52.

32 Konrad Ottenheym, 'Vincenzo Scamozzi's Legacy at the Borders of the North Sea: Exchange of Classical Architectural Ideas between Holland and England 1615–1665', paper given at the Georgian Group conference in London on 'Anglo-Netherlandish Architectural Connections in the Seventeenth Century', 17 January 2004.

33 Barbieri and Beltramini, *Vincenzo Scamozzi.*

34 Hart and Hicks, *Sebastiano Serlio* I p. 127.

35 *Ibid.* I, p. 251; Peter Murray, *Renaissance Architecture* (London, 1978) pp. 137–45.

36 Pierpaolo Brugnoli and Arturo Sandrini, *L'architettura di Verona nell'eta della Serenissima* (Verona, 1988) II, pp. 221; Tosini, *Storia dell'architettura italiana* II, p. 405.

37 Murray, *Renaissance Architecture* pp. 81–2, figs 143, 246.

38 Franco Borsi, *Bramante* (Paris, 1990) pp. 322–5.

39 Brugnoli and Sandrini, *L'architettura di Verona* I, pp. 220–21, II, p. 221. It says much for the High Renaissance

manner of Curtoni's work that it is uncertain whether the Corte Bricci is by Sanmicheli or by Curtoni. Stefania Ferrari (ed.), *Ville venete: la provincia di Verona* (Venice, 2003) p. 205.

40 Brugnoli and Sandrini, *L'architettura di Verona* II, pp. 220–22; Tosini, *Storia dell'architettura italiana* II, p. 415.

41 Claudia Conforti and Richard J. Tuttle, *Storia dell'architettura italiana: il secondo cinquecento* (Milan, 2001) pp. 202–16.

42 Aleotti may have known Scamozzi's tomb from the engraving in Giovanni Stringa, *Venetia città nobilissima* (Venice, 1604). Alternatively, he may have based his design on the frontispiece of Galasso Alghisi's *Delle fortificationi* (Venice, 1570), which like S. Carlo has superimposed round-headed aedicules between the outer columns, though the order here is Doric. Scamozzi also used the Arco dei Gavi for the tomb of Doge Pasquale Cicogna in 1595. Barbieri and Beltramini, *Vincenzo Scamozzi* pp. 88–91, 105; Conforti and Tuttle, *Storia dell'architettura italiana* pp. 209–10.

43 Conforti and Tuttle, *Storia dell'architettura italiana* pp. 202–16.

44 William Barnes, 'The Bentivoglios of Gualtieri', *Country Life* (23 April 1981).

45 Conforti and Tuttle, *Storia dell'architettura italiana* pp. 226–7.

46 Barbieri and Beltramini, *Vincenzo Scamozzi* pp. 121–5.

47 Elena Bassi, *Palazzi di Venezia* (Venice, 1987) pp. 104–9.

48 Barbieri and Beltramini, *Vincenzo Scamozzi* pp. 121–3.

CHAPTER 3

1 Leonardo Benevolo, *The Architecture of the Renaissance* (London, 1978) pp. 391–7.

2 Henry-Russell Hitchcock, *German Renaissance Architecture* (Princeton, 1981) esp. pp. 283–5, pl. 366; Norbert Nussbaum, *German Gothic Church Architecture* (New Haven and London, 2000) pp. 219–23.

3 Hitchcock, *German Renaissance Architecture* pp. 207–8, pl. 260.

4 The way the upper windows embrace the *oeil-de-boeuf* windows is particularly characteristic of Serlio (see esp. Bk VI, 53r, a MS of which is held in the Munich Staatsbibliothek). Hitchcock, *German Renaissance Architecture* p. 326, pl. 419.

5 Jane Turner (ed.), *The Dictionary of Art* (London, 1996) XXVII, pp. 660–61, 28, 361.

6 Konrad Ottenheym *et al.*, *Vincenzo Scamozzi, Venetian Architect: The Idea of a Universal Architecture, Villas and Country Estates* (Amsterdam, 2003) pp. 11, 15.

7 Turner, *Dictionary of Art* XXVIII, pp. 87–8; Wolfram Baer *et al.* (eds), *Elias Holl und das Augsburger Rathaus* (Regensburg, 1985) pp. 333–7.

8 Benevolo, *Architecture of the Renaissance* pp. 554–8, figs 633–4.

9 Hitchcock, *German Renaissance Architecture* p. 332, pl. 437.

10 Georg Skalecki, *Deutsche Architektur zur Zeit des Dreissigjahren Krieges* (Regensburg, 1989) p. 60, fig. 17.

11 Turner, *Dictionary of Art* XIV, pp. 678–80.

12 Elias Holl was also responsible for the similarly austere Schloss Schwarzenberg at Scheinfeld near Wurzburg 1607. Hitchcock, *German Renaissance Architecture* p. 314; Bernd Roeck, *Elias Holl: Architekt einer europäischen Stadt* (Regensburg, 1985) p. 119, pl. 17b.

13 Klaus Merten, *Schlosser in Baden-Württemberg* (Munich, 1987) pp. 251–4.

14 Hitchcock, *German Renaissance Architecture* pp. 325–6, pl. 421.

15 Baer, *Elias Holl* p. 34; Bassi, *Palazzi di Venezia* pp. 382–5.

16 The Gymnasium's three-storey projecting porch could be compared with Jones's 'Elevation for the entrance bay of an unidentified house'. John Harris and Gordon Higgott, *Inigo Jones: Complete Architectural Drawings* (London, 1989) p. 87.

17 Hitchcock, *German Renaissance Architecture* pls 398–400, 402, 404–5, 409, 413–16; Roeck, *Elias Holl* pp. 108, 177, fig.

18 The Bäckerzunfthaus (1602), the Stadtmetzg (1606), St Anna Gymnasium (1613). Roeck, *Elias Holl* p. 165, figs 8 and 15; Hitchcock, *German Renaissance Architecture* fig. 63. The engraving of the Englischer Bau in Hitchcock shows the north façade. It is probable that the two-bay attic projections of the south elevation, which resemble the Willibaldsburg, had similar gables. Hitchcock, *German Renaissance Architecture* pl. 410. Another example can be found on the Klericalseminat at Dillingen of 1619–22. Hitchcock, *German Renaissance Architecture* pl. 419.

19 In particular at the Kasteel at Buren, built by Alessandro Pasqualini in 1539–44, and the Moritzbau of the Residenzschloss at Dresden of *c.*1545–50. A possible source is Serlio's *Scena tragica* from his second book of 1545. Hitchcock, *German Renaissance Architecture* pp. 48, 105–6, 131–3, pls 43, 131–2.

20 Andrea Palladio, *I quattro libri dell'architettura* (Venice, 1570) II, XXXIII, XXXIV.

21 Serlio, Bk IV, 30, 42, 53; VII, 155, 177v. See also in Venice the Palazzo Valier, the Palazzo Ruzzini at Santa Maria Formosa, the Palazzo Pisani at Santo Stefano and the Palazzi Soaranzo. Bassi, *Palazzi di Venezia* pp. 98–103, figs 36–7, 92–6, 273–4, 494, 594–7.

22 Baer, *Elias Holl* pp. 73–92, fig.

23 Juan Bautista Villalpando, *In Ezechielem Explanationes et Apparatus Urbis ac Templi Hierosolymitani, commentariis et imaginibus illustratus* (Rome, 1596, 1605) II, lib. 2, cap. 13, 172, quoted in Catherine Wilkinson Zerner, *Juan de Herrera: Architect to Philip II of Spain* (New Haven and London, 1993) p. 50.

24 Harris and Higgott, *Inigo Jones* p. 89.

25 John Harris also sees parallels between the Augsburg Rathaus and the house believed to be Tart Hall illustrated in Wenceslaus Hollar's engraving of *Spring*. John Harris, Stephen Orgel and Roy Strong, *The King's Arcadia: Inigo Jones and the Stuart Court* (London, 1973) pp. 201–3.

26 Roeck, *Elias Holl* p. 210. Kilian also engraved the St Anna Gymnasium in 1623 but this is too late to have influenced Jones's 'Elevation for the entrance bay to an

unidentified house', which is dated 1616. *Ibid.*, p. 167; Harris and Higgott, *Inigo Jones* p. 87.

27 Greville's house as executed was three bays wide as against the five bays of the design associated with it, and it is possible that they are not related. However, Gordon Higgott dates this drawing to the 1616–19 period. Harris and Higgott, *Inigo Jones* p. 88.

28 Holl had been working on designs for remodelling the Rathaus since at least 1610. By 1614 these were coming to fruition. One, dated 27 March 1614, sees him considering what is described as a 'Römischer Palastfassadenentwurf'. Others, closer to the Rathaus as built, are dated 27 October and 13 November 1614. Baer, *Elias Holl* cat. 165, 260, 268, 271.

29 John Harris and A. A. Tait, *Catalogue of the Drawings by Inigo Jones, John Webb and Isaac de Caus at Worcester College, Oxford* (Oxford, 1979) p. 54.

30 Turner, *Dictionary of Art* II, p. 714.

31 *Ibid.*, XXVIII, p. 88.

CHAPTER 4

1 John Harris, 'Inigo Jones and his French Sources', *Metropolitan Museum Bulletin* (May 1961) pp. 253–64.

2 The authorship of the York House Watergate remains disputed between Jones, Sir Balthazar Gerbier and Nicholas Stone. Howard Colvin, *A Biographical Dictionary of British Architects 1600–1840* (New Haven and London, 1995) p. 397; John Harris, 'Who designed the York Water-Gate?', *Country Life* 83 (2 November 1989) pp. 150–51.

3 John Harris and Gordon Higgott, *Inigo Jones: Complete Architectural Drawings* (London, 1989) pp. 206–35.

4 Gordon Higgott, 'Inigo Jones in Provence', *Architectural History* XXVI (1983) pp. 24–34; Edward Chaney, review in *Burlington Magazine* CXXX (1988) pp. 633–4; *idem, The Evolution of the Grand Tour* (London, 1998) pp. 202 n. 68, 208.

5 National Archive, Kew, State Papers France, 78, vol. 62, fol. 184r and v, cited in *ibid.*, p. 32, n. 9.

6 Jean-Marie Pérouse de Montclos, *Philibert de l'Orme: architecte du roi (1514–1570)* (Paris, 2000) pp. 29–37.

7 *Ibid.*, p. 39.

8 Vaughan Hart and Peter Hicks (eds), *Sebastiano Serlio: On Architecture* (New Haven and London, 2001) II, p. 169.

9 *Ibid.*, pp. 230–31.

10 Ludwig H. Heydenreich, *Architecture in Italy 1400–1500*, rev. Paul Davies (New Haven and London, 1996) pp. 82–4, 140–41, figs 105 and 179.

11 Hart and Hicks, *Sebastiano Serlio* II, p. 309.

12 *Ibid. passim.*

13 Jean-Marie Pérouse de Montclos (ed.), *Le Guide du patrimoine: Isle de France* (Paris, 1992) pp. 442–8, 551–2; Anthony Blunt, *Art and Architecture in France 1500–1700* (London, 1953) pl. 78a.

14 Jacques Dupaquier, *Guide du vexin français* (Saint-Ouen-l'Aumone, 1993) p. 119.

15 Jean-Marie Pérouse de Montclos (ed.), *Le Guide du*

patrimoine: Paris (Paris, 1994) pp. 181–3; Blunt, *Art and Architecture in France* pls 71a, 72a; Hilary Ballon, *The Paris of Henri IV: Architecture and Urbanism* (New York and Cambridge, Mass., 1991).

16 Pérouse de Montclos, *Guide du patrimoine: Isle de France* p. 145.

17 Jean-Pierre Babelon, *Demeures parisiennes sous Henri IV et Louis XIII* (Paris, 1991) p. 152.

18 Blunt, *Art and Architecture in France* pl. 92b.

19 Babelon, *Demeures parisiennes* pp. 88, 93.

20 *Ibid.*, pp. 30–31, 155–7.

21 Jean-Pierre Babelon and Claude Mignot (eds), *François Mansart: le génie de l'architecture* (Paris, 1998) pp. 118–22, fig. 96; pp. 210–12, figs 186, 188, 189.

22 Pérouse de Montclos, *Guide du patrimoine: Paris* pp. 181–3; Blunt, *Art and Architecture in France* pls 71a, 72a; Ballon, *Paris of Henri IV*.

23 Leonardo Benevolo, *The Architecture of the Renaissance* (London, 1978) pp. 563–4, figs 641–3.

24 Rosalys Coope, *Salomon de Brosse and the Development of the Classical Style in French Architecture from 1565 to 1630* (London, 1972) pp. 44–6, pls 45–8; Jean-Marie Perouse de Montclos (ed.), *Guide de patrimoine: Centre Val de Loire* (Paris, 1995) pp. 384–6.

25 Louis Hautecoeur, *Histoire de l'architecture classique en France* (Paris, 1943) I, pp. 541, 577, fig. 411.

26 Coope, *Salomon de Brosse* p. 190.

27 John Harris, Stephen Orgel and Roy Strong, *The King's Arcadia: Inigo Jones and the Stuart Court* (London, 1973) p. 217.

28 Coope, *Salomon de Brosse* pp. 147–54, pls 189–95. It is interesting to compare de Brosse's use of bold Doric pilasters and entablature on the elevation of the Salle des Pas Perdus, built in 1619–24 (Coope pl. 191) with the Englischer Bau at Heidelberg, built in 1612–19.

29 *Ibid.*, pp. 183–7, pls 214–16.

30 Jane Turner (ed.), *The Dictionary of Art* (London, 1996) XIX, pp. 133–5; Michael Leapman, *Inigo: The Troubled Life of Inigo Jones, Architect of the English Renaissance* (London, 2003) p. 250.

31 Louis Battifol, *Autour de Richelieu* (Paris, 1937) pp. 121, 130. Lemercier's design is strikingly similar to a drawing, formerly in the collection of Sir Andrew Fountaine, of Michelangelo's planned west elevation of St Peter's in Rome. This shows a similar ten-columned portico under a dome on a wide flight of steps in the centre of what appears to be a side elevation. However, there is no evidence that Lemercier knew this drawing. Thomas Ashby, *Topographical Study in Rome in 1581* (London, 1916) fol. 4v.

32 Harris and Higgott, *Inigo Jones* p. 239.

33 Hilliard T. Goldfarb (ed.), *Richelieu: Art and Power* (Ghent, 2002) p. 166.

34 Coope, *Salomon de Brosse* p. 111. Dézallier d'Argenville translation mine; J. Summerson (ed.), *The Book of Architecture of John Thorpe*, Walpole Society (1966) p. 79 and pl. 58.

35 Gordon Higgott, 'The Revised Design for St Paul's Cathedral, 1685–90: Wren, Hawksmoor and Les Inva-lides', *Burlington Magazine* CXLVI (August 2004) p. 542; Simon Thurley, *Hampton Court: A Social and Architectural History* (New Haven and London, 2003) pp. 188–9.

36 Similar examples can be found on the Continent. In Vienna engravings made in 1701 of Fischer von Erlach's designs for the Schönbrunn Palace were sent out across Europe. Hans Aurenhammer, *J. B. Fischer von Erlach* (London, 1973) p. 108. Barbara Arciszewska's study of the Guelph family of Hanover shows that not only were there frequent visits between the courts of Hanover and Berlin but also that the correspondence between the two courts frequently referred to matters of architecture. Barbara Arciszewska, *The Hanoverian Court and the Triumph of Palladio: The Palladian Revival in Hanover and England c.1700* (Warsaw, 2002) p. 221.

CHAPTER 5

1 For Dutch seventeenth-century architectural drawings see Elske Gerritsen, 'De architectuurtekening in de 17de eeuw', in Jorgen Bracker *et al.*, *Soo vele heerlijcke gebouwen: van Palladio tot Vingboons* (Amsterdam, 1997) pp. 40–60.

2 Konrad [Koen] Ottenheym, 'The Amsterdam Ring of Canals: City Planning and Architecture', in P. van Kessl and E. Schulte (eds), *Rome–Amsterdam: Two Growing Cities in Seventeenth-Century Europe* (Amsterdam, 1997) pp. 33–49.

3 Konrad [Koen] Ottenheym, *Philips Vingboons (1607–1678) Architect* (Zutphen, 1989) pp. 16–20, fig. 3.

4 Konrad [Koen] Ottenheym, 'The Painters cum Architects of Dutch Classicism' in *Dutch Classicism in Seventeenth-Century Painting* (Rotterdam, 1999) pp. 34–53.

5 Jacobine Huisken *et al.*, *Jacob van Campen: het klassieke ideal in de Gouden Eeuw* (Amsterdam, 1995) p. 281.

6 *Ibid.* pp. 158–60, fig. 132.

7 I am grateful to Professor Konrad Ottenheym for this observation. Konrad [Koen] Ottenheym, 'Vincenzo Scamozzi's Legacy at the Borders of the North Sea: Exchange of Classical Architectural Ideas between Holland and England 1615–1665', paper given at the Georgian Group conference on 'Anglo-Netherlandish Architectural Connections in the Seventeenth Century', London, 17 January 2004; Ottenheym, *Philips Vingboons* p. 178.

8 John Fitzhugh Millar, *Classical Architecture in Renaissance Europe 1419–1585* (Williamsburg, Va., 1987) p. 130.

9 Howard Colvin, *A Biographical Dictionary of British Architects 1600–1840* (New Haven and London, 1995) pp. 299, 929–30.

10 Ottenheym, 'Painters cum Architects' pp. 42, 49, 53; Vanessa Bezemer Sellers, *Courtly Gardens in Holland 1600–1650: The House of Orange and the Hortus Batavus* (Amsterdam and Woodbridge, 2001) p. 294, n. 4.

11 Ottenheym, 'Painters cum Architects' pp. 43–4.

12 Ottenheym, *Philips Vingboons* pp. 32–3, fig. 21; Konrad Ottenheym, 'Painters cum Architects' pp. 42–3.

13 Hubertus Gunther, *Das Studium der Antiken Architektur in den Zeichnungen der Hochrenaissance* (Tubingen, 1988).

14 Erik Forssman *et al.*, *Palladio: la sua eredità nel mondo* (Milan, 1980) p. 79, fig.; J. J. Terwen and K. A. Ottenheym, *Pieter Post (1608–1669) Architect* (Zutphen, 1993) p. 17, fig.; Jorgen Bracker *et al.*, *Palladio: Bauen nach der Natur–Die Erben Palladios in Nordeuropa* (Hamburg, 1997) pp. 131–2, fig.

15 Photographs of these drawings are held by the Witt Library, Courtauld Institute of Art, London.

16 Ottenheym, 'Painters cum Architects' p. 36.

17 Vincenzo Scamozzi, *L'idea della architettura universale* (Venice, 1615) I, pp. 287, 317; Forssman, *Palladio* pp. 77, fig. 2.

18 Bezemer Sellers, *Courtly Gardens* pp. 12–13, 61–2, 82.

19 The Stadholder's court was much more influenced by French culture than the Dutch mercantile elite in the cities. For example, the court preferred the French tradition of closed chimneys while Dutch burghers preferred open chimneys with columns. French influence is also particularly evident in paintings commissioned by the court.

20 Bezemer Sellers, *Courtly Gardens* p. 295, n. 25.

21 *Ibid.* pp. 17, 20, fig. 12.

22 *Ibid.* pp. 35, 69, 70, 73.

23 *Ibid.* pp. 49–50, 72, 278, n. 143.

24 *Ibid.* pp. 68, 72, fig. 51. The model of the Luxembourg remained influential in the Dutch Republic. When René Descartes, who lived in Holland in 1639–49 and was a close friend of Huygens, much appreciated at the Dutch court for his architectural and mathematical expertise, was consulted by Anthonis van Zurck on his gardens at Bergen in 1641 he said the Luxembourg palace complex was the ideal to be followed. To assist van Zurck he ordered prints and drawings of both gardens and palace to be sent from Paris. *Ibid.* p. 72.

25 *Ibid.* figs 32–3, 64–5.

26 Andrea Palladio, *I quattro libri dell'architettura* (Venice, 1570) II, pp. 57, 63; Ottenheym, 'Peter Paul Rubens's *Palazzi di Genova* and its Influence on the Architecture in the Netherlands', in Piet Lombaerde (ed.), *The Reception of P. P. Rubens's* Palazzi di Genova *during the 17th century in Europe: Questions and Problems* (Turnhout, 2002) pp. 90–92.

27 Bezemer Sellers, *Courtly Gardens* pp. 61–2, 279, n. 2.

28 Though the central three bays of the Palazzo Cornaro project slightly they do not form a porch as they do at Ter Nieuburch. However, a similar porch to that at Ter Nieuburch forms part of the design for the Amsterdam Town Hall signed SGL, which is even more closely based on the Palazzo Cornaro, and another, also probably modelled on the Palazzo Cornaro, can be found on Pieter Post's Maastricht Town Hall. Ottenheym, *Philips Vingboons* p. 126, fig. 173; Terwen and Ottenheym, *Pieter Post* p. 168.

29 Bezemer Sellers, *Courtly Gardens* pp. 76, 301, n. 137.

30 This feature is also found at Honselaarsdijck.

31 *Ibid.* p. 155. For Huygens's library see *Catalogus van de bibiliotheek van Constantijn Huygens* (The Hague, 1903). For the Stadholder's library see A. D. Renting and J. T. C. Renting-Kuypers (eds), *The Seventeenth-Century Orange-Nassau Library: The Catalogue compiled by Anthonie Smets in 1686, the 1749 Auction Catalogue and Other Contemporary Sources* (Utrecht, 1993).

32 John Newman, 'Inigo Jones's Architectural Education before 1614', *Architectural History* XXXV (1992) p. 49.

33 A. G. H. Bachrach, *Sir Constantine Huygens and Britain, 1596–1687: A Pattern of Cultural Exchange I: 1596–1619* (Leiden and Oxford, 1961) pp. 64–70.

34 J. A. Worp, *De Briefwisseling van Constantijn Huygens* (The Hague, 1911–17) I, nr 122; R. L. Colie, '*Some Thankfulnesse to Constantine': A Study of English Influence upon the Early Works of Constantijn Huygens* (The Hague, 1956) pp. 11–34; cited by Ottenheym, 'Vincenzo Scamozzi's Legacy' n. 35.

35 Constantijn Huygens, note in his diary, 11 June 1620; cited in *ibid.*

36 Constantijn Huygens, 'De vita propria', ed. F. R. E. Blom (2002) verses 744–5; cited in *ibid.* n. 38.

37 Ottenheym, 'Vincenzo Scamozzi's Legacy'.

38 *L'Architettura di Leon Battista Alberti, tradotta in lingua fiorentina da Cosimo Bartoli* (Monte Regale, 1565) IX, p. 250, held at Worcester College, Oxford. Note datable to *c.*1615–19, transcription and reference courtesy of Dr Gordon Higgott.

39 In his text 'Domus' Huygens wrote: 'Pessime hoc tandem, si qui non veteris modo Architecturae modici periti, sed qui vel reliquias eius . . . strictim observassent, aedificia nostra contemplarentur, vix quidem a risu temperate, et illum scilicet nitorem nostrum, illam Belgicae ridentis elegantiam vel flocci facere . . .', 'Domus', fol. 742r and v, ed. F. R. E. Blom (1999) p. 18; cited by Ottenheym, 'Vincenzo Scamozzi's Legacy' n. 42.

40 Huygens, letter of 21 November 1637, The Hague, Koninklijke Bibliotheek, MS XLIX, 1, fol. 748; a summary in Worp, *Briefwisseling van Constantijn Huygens* II, nr 1765; cited by Ottenheym, 'Vincenzo Scamozzi's Legacy' n. 44; Bezemer Sellers, *Courtly Gardens* pp. 155–6, 295, nn. 29–30.

41 Worp, *Briefwisseling van Constantijn Huygens* II, RGP 19, letter 1301; cited by Bezemer Sellers, *Courtly Gardens* pp. 160, 297, n. 61.

42 Huisken, *Jacob van Campen* p. 163, fig. 136; Bezemer Sellers, *Courtly Gardens* p. 84, fig. 65.

43 Forssman, *Palladio* p. 82, figs; Huisken, *Jacob van Campen* pp. 163–5, figs 138–40; Guido Beltramini *et al.*, *Palladio and Northern Europe: Books, Travellers, Architects* (Milan, 1999) p. 157.

44 Worp, *Briefwisseling van Constantijn Huygens* II, RGP 19, letter 2149; cited by Bezemer Sellers, *Courtly Gardens* pp. 160, 297, n. 58.

45 Ottenheym, 'Peter Paul Rubens's *Palazzi di Genova*' p. 85.

46 K. A. Ottenheym, 'The Vitruvius Edition, 1649, of Johannes de Laet (1581–1649)', *Lias* XXV, 2 (1998) pp. 217–29.

47 Ottenheym, *Vincenzo Scamozzi, Venetian Architect: The Idea of a Universal Architecture, Villas and Country Estates* (Amsterdam, 2003) p. 24.

48 Ottenheym, 'Classicism in the Northern Netherlands in

49 Huisken, *Jacob van Campen* pp. 158–63.

50 *Ibid.* pp. 161–3, figs 134–6.

51 Jan Terwen, 'The Buildings of Johann Maurits', in E. van den Boogaart (ed.), *Johann Maurits van Nassau-Siegen 1604–1679: A Humanist Prince in Europe and Brasil* (The Hague, 1979) pp. 54–141.

52 Bezemer Sellers, *Courtly Gardens* pp. 161–3.

53 Huisken, *Jacob van Campen* p. 166, fig. 142; Bezemer Sellers, *Courtly Gardens* p. 84, fig. 65.

54 Huisken, *Jacob van Campen* pp. 168–72, 180–87, figs 145, 148–50, 163–73.

55 Ottenheym, *Vincenzo Scamozzi* p. 23.

56 *Ibid.* pp. 17–22.

57 Beltramini, *Palladio and Northern Europe* p. 156.

58 Ottenheym, *Philips Vingboons* pp. 121–7, figs 166a, 173–4; Ottenheym, *Vincenzo Scamozzi* pp. 25–31.

59 Ottenheym, 'Painters cum Architects' pp. 39, 42.

60 Guus Kemme (ed.), *Amsterdam Architecture: A Guide* (Bussum, 1996) pp. 63–4, 67.

61 Ottenheym, *Philips Vingboons* p. 23 and *passim*.

62 Ottenheym, 'Painters cum Architects' pp. 46–7.

63 Terwen and Ottenheym, *Pieter Post, passim*; Bezemer Sellers, *Courtly Gardens* pp. 27–8, figs 30–31, 40; Jean-Pierre Babelon and Claude Mignot, *François Mansart: le génie de l'architecture* (Paris, 1998) pp. 74, 160–67, figs 52, 134, 137–8.

64 Bezemer Sellers, *Courtly Gardens* pp. 49–50, 72, 278, n. 143.

65 Vaughan Hart and Peter Hicks, *Sebastiano Serlio: On Architecture* (New Haven and London, 2001) II, pp. 43, 75, 85.

66 Terwen and Ottenheym, *Pieter Post* p. 20, fig. 17.

67 Heimerick Tromp, *Private Country Houses in the Netherlands* (Zwolle, 1997) pp. 110, 172, 192, 260.

68 In England the building type is so commonplace that it passes largely without comment. In Yorkshire, for example, it was the overwhelmingly common model for new smaller country houses, as is shown by the eighteen examples in *Samuel Buck's Yorkshire Sketchbook* (Wakefield, 1979).

69 Terwen and Ottenheym, *Pieter Post* p. 164, fig. 193; Ottenheym, *Philips Vingboons* pp. 87, 258.

70 Giles Worsley, *The British Stable* (New Haven and London, 2004) pp. 106–10.

71 Philips Vingboons, *Afbeelsels der voornaemste gebouwen* 2 vols (Amsterdam, 1648 and 1674) I, p. 30; II, pp. 39, 44, 51–2.

72 Ottenheym, 'The Amsterdam Ring of Canals' p. 35, fig. 37.

73 Vingboons, *Afbeelsels* I, preface, quoted in Ottenheym, 'Painters cum Architects' pp. 34–53.

74 Katherine Fremantle, *The Baroque Town Hall of Amsterdam* (Utrecht, 1959); Eymert-Jan Goossens, *Treasure wrought by Chisel and Brush: The Town Hall of Amsterdam in the Golden Age* (Amsterdam, 1996).

75 Huisken, *Jacob van Campen* pp. 189–99, 284, figs 180–91.

76 *Ibid.* fig. 211.

77 At 1:10 these are what Scamozzi recommends for the Corinthian order, not the Composite.

78 Juan Bautista Villalpando, *In Ezechielem Explanationes et Apparatus Urbis ac Templi Hierosolymitani, commentariis et imaginibus illustratus* (Rome, 1596, 1605). I am grateful to Pieter Vlaardingerbroek for explaining to me the essence of his doctoral thesis on the Solomonic symbolism of the Amsterdam Town Hall.

79 Vatable's first designs were published in Robert Estienne's Paris Bible of 1540 and were subsequently re-used many times. Wolfgang Herrmann, 'Unknown Designs for the "Temple of Jerusalem" by Claude Perrault', in Douglas Fraser, Howard Hibbard and Milton J. Lewine (eds), *Essays in the History of Architecture presented to Rudolf Wittkower* (London, 1967) p. 155, pls 7–8. Herrmann's article includes an invaluable list of all the major works on the Temple of Solomon known and widely used in the seventeenth and eighteenth centuries, pp. 154–8.

80 Huisken, *Jacob van Campen* pp. 180–84, figs 166–9.

81 I am grateful to Professor Ottenheym for drawing these examples to my attention.

82 Ottenheym, 'Peter Paul Rubens's *Palazzi di Genova*' pp. 83–4, 88.

83 Krista De Jonge (ed.), *Bellissimi Ingegni, Grandissimo Splendore: Studies over de religieuze architectuur in de Zuidelijke Nederlanden tijdens de 17de eeuw*, Symbolae ser. B, XV (Leuven, 2000); Hans Vlieghe, *Flemish Art and Architecture 1585–1700* (New Haven and London, 1998) pp. 258–79.

84 Joris Snaet, 'Rubens's Palazzi de Genova and the Jesuit Churches of Antwerp and Brussels' in Lombaerde, *Reception of P. P. Rubens's* Palazzi di Genova, pp. 161–82.

85 Michael Jaffe, *Rubens in Italy* (Oxford, 1977) p. 7.

86 Marjon van der Meulen, *Rubens: Copies after the Antique*, (London, 1995) III.

87 Peter Paul Rubens, *Palazzi di Genova* 2 vols (Antwerp, 1622, 1626) I, foreword.

88 Rubens was responsible for a series of paintings in the church. Most were destroyed in a fire that destroyed the nave in 1718. Fortunately, the apse and two side chapels survived. The nave was rebuilt essentially as before.

89 Ottenheym, 'Peter Paul Rubens's *Palazzi di Genova*' p. 85; Krista De Jonge, 'Vitruvius, Alberti and Serlio: Architectural Treatises in the Low Countries, 1530–1620', in Vaughan Hart (ed.), *Paper Palaces: The Rise of the Renaissance Architectural Treatise* (New Haven and London, 1998) pp. 281–96; Ottenheym, 'Painters cum Architects' p. 36.

90 Ottenheym, 'Peter Paul Rubens's *Palazzi di Genova*' p. 85.

91 J. H. Plantenga, *L'architecture religieuse dans l'ancien duché de Brabant* (The Hague, 1926) pp. 75–110.

92 John Rupert Martin, *The Ceiling Paintings for the Jesuit Church in Antwerp* (London, 1968) p. 27.

93 Quoted in *ibid.* p. 25.

94 Vitruvius, *Dieci libri* I, vi, 4; Fra Giacondo, fol. 9v; Cesariano, fol. XXIv. It may be significant that Hawksmoor notes the Tower of the Winds as the source for the twin octagonal staircase turrets in his design for Worcester

College, Oxford, and that it is, therefore, presumably the source for octagonal turrets over the staircase towers of St George-in-the-East. Roger White, *Nicholas Hawksmoor and the Replanning of Oxford* (London, 1997) p. 76, fig. 77. The original design for S. Carlo Borromeo includes Serlian windows on the staircase towers, a highly unusual feature. Given the association of the Serliana with the pope this may have been intended to symbolise the particular loyalty the Jesuits felt they owed the church. These windows were omitted from the staircase towers as executed but others were introduced at a late date into a more prominent site at the top of the bell tower. Plantenga, *L'architecture religieuse* figs 119, 122.

95 This is noted by G. Morsch, 'Der Wechsel in den Planen zur Antwerpener Jesuitenkirche' in *Schülerfestgabe für Herbert von Einem* (Bonn, 1965) pp. 184–96.

96 Mary F. S. Hervey, *The Life, Correspondence and Collections of Thomas Howard, Earl of Arundel* (Cambridge, 1921) p. 172.

CHAPTER 6

1 The case for the Stoke Park pavilions will be put in chapter 7. The case for also attributing the stables at Burley-on-the-Hill, Rutland, to Jones will be made in this chapter.

2 Gordon Higgott, '"Varying with Reason": Inigo Jones's Theory of Design', *Architectural History* XXXV (1992) p. 56.

3 Inigo Jones, Roman Sketchbook, fol. 76r, Devonshire Collection, Chatsworth.

4 Henry Wotton, *The Elements of Architecture* (London, 1624) p. 119.

5 John Summerson, *Architecture in Britain 1530–1830* (Harmondsworth, 1977) pp. 155–70; Timothy Mowl and Brian Earnshaw, *Architecture without Kings: The Rise of Puritan Classicism under Cromwell* (Manchester, 1995); Andor Gomme, 'Chevening: The Big Issues', *Georgian Group Journal* XIV (2004) pp. 167–86. For an early analysis of the importance of Jones's astylar manner see Giles Worsley, *Classical Architecture in Britain: The Heroic Age* (New Haven and London, 1995) pp. 1–19.

6 Vaughan Hart and Peter Hicks (eds), *Sebastiano Serlio: On Architecture* (New Haven and London, 1996) I, p. 254.

7 John Harris, Stephen Orgel and Roy Strong, *The King's Arcadia: Inigo Jones and the Stuart Court* (London, 1973) pp. 64–7, 217–18; John Newman, 'Inigo Jones's Architectural Education before 1614', *Architectural History* XXXV (1992) pp. 18–50.

8 John Harris and Gordon Higgott, *Inigo Jones: Complete Architectural Drawings* (London, 1989) pp. 31, 33, 36, 76, 94, 96, 124, 131, 134, 136, 256, 270, 304, cat. 25, 26, 84; Hart and Hicks, *Sebastiano Serlio* (2001) II, p. 337.

9 Hart and Hicks, *Sebastiano Serlio* II, p. 3.

10 *Ibid*. II, pp. 4–155.

11 *Ibid*. II, p. 3.

12 Jane Turner (ed.), *The Dictionary of Art* (London, 1996) XIX, pp. 144–5.

13 Harris and Higgott, *Inigo Jones* p. 102, fig. 34.

14 Giles Worsley, *The British Stable* (New Haven and London, 2004) *passim*.

15 Howard Colvin, *A Biographical Dictionary of British Architects 1600–1840* (New Haven and London, 1995) pp. 558–9; Howard Colvin (ed), *The History of the King's Works*, IV (1982) p. 277.

16 Harris and Higgott, *Inigo Jones* pp. 180–81, cat. 50, fig. 47; Giles Worsley, 'Inigo Jones and the Hatfield Riding House', *Georgian Group Journal* XIV (2002) p. 236.

17 J. T. Smith, *Sixty-Two Additional Plates to Smith's Antiquities of Westminster* (London, 1809) p. 5.

18 Harris, Orgel and Strong, *The King's Arcadia* pp. 100–04; Harris and Higgott, *Inigo Jones* pp. 84, 126–8, 308–9, figs 41, 107. Harris and Higgott identify the building as probably being by Jones but do not note that it is a stable or discuss its significance as an early example of the astylar manner.

19 Colvin, *Biographical Dictionary* pp. 559–61.

20 *Ibid*. pp. 397, 561, 931.

21 Thomas Fuller, *The History of the Worthies of England* (London, 1662) p. 346.

22 Pearl Finch, *History of Burley-on-the-Hill* (London, 1901) pp. 101–2; Anne Blandamer, 'The Duke of Buckingham's House at Burley on the Hill', *Rutland Record* XVIII (1998) pp. 349–60.

23 Finch, *History of Burley-on-the-Hill* pp. 6–7; Blandamer, 'The Duke of Buckingham's House' pp. 355, fig. 2.

24 Jones also used similar gables on his design of *c*.1633–4 for the west front of St Paul's Cathedral and on his design for the elevation of a seven-window house with an iron pergola. Harris and Higgott, *Inigo Jones* pp. 88–9, 241–3, 260–61.

25 Linda Campbell, 'The Building of Raynham Hall, Norfolk', *Architectural History* XXXII (1989) pp. 52–67.

26 Lothbury House, as Maltravers House was known, lay on the north side of Lothbury, backing on to King's Arms Yard. No deeds survive, but a rental record for 1655 shows the property was substantial as the house and associated tenements, then apparently entirely let, brought in rents of £194 18s 3d. This compares, for example, to £120 19s 9d from the Dorking Manor copyholds in the same year. Harris and Higgott, *Inigo Jones* pp. 256–7, cat. 84–5; Arundel Castle MSS A 512. I am grateful to Dr John Martin Robinson, librarian at Arundel Castle, for this reference and for information about Lothbury House.

27 Colen Campbell, *Vitruvius Britannicus* 3 vols (London, 1717) II, pp. 4, 85.

28 Gomme, 'Chevening' pp. 170–71.

29 Newman, 'Inigo Jones's Architectural Education' p. 48..

30 Campbell, *Vitruvius Britannicus* II, p. 85.

31 Gomme, 'Chevening' fig. 1–3.

32 *Ibid*. pp. 172, 174–5.

33 Harris and Higgott, *Inigo Jones* pp. 312–13, figs 108–9.

34 Charles Cammell, *The Great Duke of Buckingham* (London, 1979) pp. 196–9.

35 John Britton, *The Natural History of Wiltshire* (London, 1847) pp. 83–4.

36 John Summerson, *Inigo Jones* (New Haven and London, 2000) p. 109.

37 Harris and Higgott, *Inigo Jones* pp. 88–9, cat. 22.

38 *Ibid.* p. 192, fig. 54.

39 Worsley, *Classical Architecture* p. 12, fig. 22; Bridget Cherry and Nikolaus Pevsner, *The Buildings of England: London 4, North* (London, 1998) pp. 442–5. The authenticity of the hipped roof was confirmed by Andor Gomme and Alison Maguire. Gomme, 'Chevening' p. 182, n. 12.

40 Similar pergolas or balconies can be found in Jones's design believed to be for Brooke House, in his pergola entrance to Sir Edward Cecil's house in the Strand, on the 1633 wing at Cornbury Park, Oxfordshire, at Wilton House, Wiltshire, on the Evidence House at Bedford House and on some of the houses on the Piazza at Covent Garden.

41 Felix Barker and Peter Jackson, *London: 2000 Years of a City and its People* (London, 1974) pp. 159–60, fig. 7; David Pearce, *London's Mansions: The Palatial Houses of the Nobility* (London, 1986) pp. 116–17, fig. 84; Harris and Higgott, *Inigo Jones* pp. 88–91, cat. 22, 23.

42 Mowl and Earnshaw, *Architecture without Kings* pp. 60–62, fig. 22.

43 Dianne Duggan, 'The Fourth Side of the Covent Garden Piazza: New Light on the History and Significance of Bedford House', *British Art Journal* III, 3 (Autumn 2002) pp. 60, 64, fig. 6b.

44 This was the date when a 'prayer landing' was consecrated in the house so construction work must have started a couple of years earlier. Hill and Cornforth, *English Country Houses* p. 239, fig. 405; John Newman, *The Buildings of England: West Kent and the Weald* (Harmondsworth, 1969) p. 336; Gomme, 'Chevening' p. 172.

45 Gervase Jackson-Stops, 'West Woodhay House, Berkshire', *Country Life* 181 (22 January 1987) pp. 44–8.

46 'A Description of Aldermaston House', *The Topographer* (1789) pp. 33–5; Mowl and Earnshaw, *Architecture without Kings* pp. 62–3, fig. 23.

47 Timothy Mowl, 'Welford Park: A New House for John Jackson', *Georgian Group Journal* IV (1994) pp. 51–4; Mowl and Earnshaw, *Architecture without Kings* pp. 70–71, fig. 27. The building contract in the Berkshire Record Office, Reading, is undated, but as Richard Jhones inherited Welford in 1652 and Jackson died in 1663, it must have been made at some point between those two dates.

48 Howard Colvin, 'The South Front of Wilton House', in *Essays in Architectural History* (New Haven and London, 1999) pp. 136–57. For the discussion of Wilton below I am indebted to this source. See also John Bold, *Wilton House and English Palladianism: Some Wiltshire Houses* (London, 1988) pp. 33–41, and Mowl and Earnshaw, *Architecture without Kings* pp. 31–47.

49 Colvin, *Biographical Dictionary* p. 298.

50 *Ibid.*, Giles Worsley, 'Courtly Stables and their Implications for Seventeenth-Century English Architecture', *Georgian Group Journal* XIII (2003) pp. 120–26; Malcolm Airs, 'Inigo Jones, Isaac de Caus and the Stables

at Holland House', *Georgian Group Journal* XIII (2003) pp. 141–60. No view of Stalbridge Park has come to light.

51 Colvin, 'South Front of Wilton House', figs 120–23.

52 Hill and Cornforth, *English Country Houses* pp. 90–96, fig. 135; John Bold, *John Webb: Architectural Theory and Practice in the Seventeenth Century* (Oxford, 1989) pp. 157–8; Mowl and Earnshaw, *Architecture without Kings* pp. 48–59 (further references are to be found on these pages).

53 Michael Leapman, *Inigo: The Troubled Life of Inigo Jones, Architect of the English Renaissance* (London, 2003) p. 337.

54 Colvin, 'South Front of Wilton House', p. 146.

55 Vaughan Hart and Peter Hicks, *Sebastiano Serlio: On Architecture* (New Haven and London, 2001) II, p. 301.

56 Priscilla Metcalf, 'Balmes House', *Architectural Review* (June 1957) pp. 445–6; Mowl and Earnshaw, *Architecture without Kings* pp. 134–5, fig. 62.

57 Barker and Jackson, *London* p. 118, fig. 2; Colvin, *Biographical Dictionary* pp. 656, 931.

58 Worsley, *Classical Architecture* pp. 12–13, fig. 24.

59 Harris and Higgott, *Inigo Jones* pp. 192, 298, figs 54, 91.

60 *Ibid.* p. 298, fig. 90.

61 Leapman, *Inigo* pp. 184–6, 219–20, 280–81.

62 Newman, 'Nicholas Stone's Goldsmiths' Hall' pp. 30–39, figs 26–9.

63 Howard Colvin, 'Inigo Jones and the Church of St Michael-le-Querne', *London Journal* XII, 1 (1986) pp. 36–9.

64 Ann Saunders (ed.), *The Royal Exchange*, London Topographical Society CLII (1997) p. 37, figs 9–10, 18.

65 John Fitzhugh Millar, *Classical Architecture in Renaissance Europe 1419–1585* (Williamsburg, Va., 1987) pp. 126–33, pls 71, 73, 74.

66 Hart and Hicks, *Sebastiano Serlio* II, pp. xiv–xvii.

767 *Ibid.* II, p. 309.

68 Hill and Cornforth, *English Country Houses* pls 21, 375; Summerson, *Architecture in Britain* pls 118–19; Hart and Hicks, *Sebastiano Serlio* II, p. 265.

769 Worsley, 'Courtly Stables' p. 119, figs 7–8.

70 Hart and Hicks, *Sebastiano Serlio* II, p. 209.

71 Worsley, 'Courtly Stables' p. 121, figs 10–11.

72 Worsley, *Classical Architecture* p. 9, figs 13–4.

73 Hart and Hicks, *Sebastiano Serlio* II, p. 231.

74 *Ibid.* II, pp. 263, 301.

75 *Ibid.* II, p. 372.

76 Harris and Higgott, *Inigo Jones* p. 87, cat. 21; Hart and Hicks, *Sebastiano Serlio* II, p. 233.

CHAPTER 7

1 Colen Campbell, *Vitruvius Britannicus* 3 vols (London, 1715) I, p. 2. Italics in original.

2 John Harris, *The Palladian Revival: Lord Burlington, his Villa and Garden at Chiswick* (New Haven and London, 1994) p. 57.

3 For example, Gordon Higgott's study of Inigo Jones's theory of design discussed below does not cover his annotations in Scamozzi. Gordon Higgott, 'Varying with

Reason': Inigo Jones's Theory of Design', *Architectural History* XXXV (1992) pp. 51–77. B. Alsopp (ed.), *Inigo Jones on Palladio, being the notes by Inigo Jones in the copy of I Quattro Libri dell'architettura di Andrea Palladio, 1601, in the Library of Worcester College, Oxford*, 2 vols (Newcastle upon Tyne, 1970).

4   An exception is Howard Burns, 'Palladio and the Foundations of a New Architecture in the North', in Guido Beltramini *et al.*, *Palladio and Northern Europe: Books, Travellers, Architects* (Milan, 1999) p. 35.

5   Andor Gomme, 'Chevening: The Big Issues', *Georgian Group Journal* XIV (2004) pp. 173–5; Timothy Mowl and Brian Earnshaw, *Architecture without Kings: The Rise of Puritan Classicism under Cromwell* (Manchester, 1995); Giles Worsley, *Classical Architecture in Britain: The Heroic Age* (New Haven and London, 1995) pp. 1–19.

6   The annotated copy of the *Quattro libri* is at Worcester College, Oxford. Most of Jones's Palladio drawings are held at the RIBA, London.

7   Gordon Higgott, 'Varying with Reason' pp. 51–77. The following account of Jones's design theory is indebted to Dr Higgott's work.

8   *Ibid.* pp. 52–3, 55–6, 62.

9   *Ibid.* pp. 62, 64.

10 *Ibid.* pp. 66–7.

11 *Ibid.* pp. 65, 72.

12 Jones's interest in the direct return to Antiquity can be paralleled in the arts in *The Painting of the Ancients, in three Bookes: Declaring by Historicall Observations and Examples, the Beginning, Progresse and Consummation of that most Noble Art*, published in 1638 by Franciscus Junius, secretary to the Earl of Arundel.

13 Andrea Palladio, *I quattro libri dell'architettura* (Venice, 1570) IV, pp. 38, 133; John Harris and Gordon Higgott, *Inigo Jones: Complete Architectural Drawings* (London, 1989) pp. 178–9, 182–3, cat. 49, 51.

14 Palladio, *Quattro libri* IV, 39; Margaret D. Whinney, 'John Webb's Drawings for Whitehall Palace', *Walpole Society* XXXI (1946) pls XIIb, XIIIc; Harris and Higgott, *Inigo Jones* p. 240, fig. 77.

15 Vaughan Hart and Peter Hicks, *Sebastiano Serlio: On Architecture* (New Haven and London, 1996, 2001) I, p. 221; II, pp. 249, 251; Harris and Higgott, *Inigo Jones: Complete Architectural Drawings* (London, 1989) pp. 248–50, cat. 81.

16 Harris and Higgott, *Inigo Jones* pp. 60–61, cat. 12.

17 A. Blunt, *Nicolas Poussin*, The A. W. Mellon Lectures in the Fine Arts, 1958 (New York, 1967), pp. 235–39; Beltramini, *Palladio and Northern Europe* pp. 187–9, figs 56f, 56g, 56h; Worsley, *Classical Architecture* pp. 95–106, 108–10.

18 A list of the books at Worcester College is published as Appendix III in John Harris, Stephen Orgel and Roy Strong, *The King's Arcadia: Inigo Jones and the Stuart Court* (London, 1973) pp. 217–18.

19 Harris and Higgott, *Inigo Jones* p. 328.

20 John Newman, 'Inigo Jones's Architectural Education before 1614', *Architectural History* XXXV (1992) p. 21.

21 Harris and Higgott, *Inigo Jones* pp. 126–8, cat. 40, fig. 43; Edward Chaney, 'Inigo Jones in Naples', in John Bold and Edward Chaney (eds), *English Architecture Public and Private* (London, 1993) pp. 48–50, figs 21–2. An engraving of the Porta Pia was published in an appendix to the 1607 edition of Vignola's *Regola delli cinque ordini d'architettura*, owned by Jones, who records Scamozzi's disapproval of two frontispieces being placed one above the other in the gate, which he notes is illustrated on pages 40 and 41 of Vignola. See Jones's annotated copy of Vincenzo Scamozzi, *L'idea della architettura universale* (Venice, 1615) II, p. 172.

22 I am grateful to Dr Higgott for this observation, which amends his comments in Harris and Higgott, *Inigo Jones* p. 134.

23 *Ibid.* pp. 90–91, 94–5, 198–9, 206–11, 216–34, 246–7; cat. 23, 25, 59, 63–5, 68–76, 80, figs 26, 46, 57, 66, 72, 73.

24 B. Alsopp, *Inigo Jones on Palladio* I, pp. 2, 6, 12, 13, 24, 31, 37; Burns, 'Palladio and the Foundations of a New Architecture' p. 33.

25 Higgott, 'Varying with Reason' p. 57.

26 Newman, 'Inigo Jones's Architectural Education' p. 21.

27 Harris, Orgel and Strong, *The King's Arcadia* p. 66; Konrad Ottenheym, 'Vincenzo Scamozzi's Legacy at the Borders of the North Sea: Exchange of Classical Architectural Ideas between Holland and England 1615–1665', paper given at the Georgian Group conference on 'Anglo-Netherlandish Architectural Connections in the Seventeenth Century', London, 17 January 2004.

28 I am grateful to Gordon Higgott for providing me with a transcript of Jones's annotations of his copy of *L'idea dell'architettura* now in the Worcester College Library, which is based on a transcription made by John Newman. I am also grateful to Dr Higgott for his observations on Jones's comments on Scamozzi, which substantially inform this section, and to Mr Newman for allowing me to use his transcription.

29 Inigo Jones's annotated copy of Palladio, *Quattro libri* I, p. 24.

30 Inigo Jones's annotated copy of Scamozzi, *L'idea* I, p. 235.

31 *Ibid.* I, pp. 196, 281; II, pp. 52, 109, 127.

32 *Ibid.* I, pp. 266, 314.

33 *Ibid.* I, pp. 46–8.

34 *Ibid.* I, p. 225.

35 *Ibid.*

36 *Ibid.* I, pp. 260–61, 311–17; II, pp. 62, 280, 296, 299, 308–9, 312.

37 *Ibid.* II, pp. 38, 135, 138.

38 *Ibid.* II, pp. 52, 58, 81, 84, 98, 101, 115, 118, 135.

39 *Ibid.* II, pp. 135, 138.

40 *Ibid.* I, pp. 266, 271–2.

41 *Ibid.* I, pp. 29–37, 246, 249; II, pp. 40–43.

42 I am grateful to Dr Gordon Higgott for his helpful observations on the three designs often called preliminary schemes for the Queen's House.

43 Harris and Higgott, *Inigo Jones* p. 66.

44 Jones was quicker to acquire his copy of Scamozzi than Rubens, who bought his on 28 June 1617 from Moretus's bookshop in Antwerp. Konrad Ottenheym *et al.* (eds), *Vincenzo Scamozzi, Venetian Architect: The Idea*

of a Universal Architecture, Villas and Country Estates (Amsterdam, 2003) p. 20.

45 See, for example, Inigo Jones's annotated copy of Palladio, *Quattro Libri*, II, p. 69.

46 William Grant Keith, 'Drawings by Vincenzo Scamozzi', *Journal of the Royal Institute of British Architects* (9 March 1935) pp. 525–35; Burns, 'Palladio and the Foundations of a New Architecture' p. 35; Franco Barbieri and Guido Beltramini (eds), *Vincenzo Scamozzi 1548–1616* (Vicenza, 2003) p. 180. It is possible that this group of drawings was more extensive and corresponded to the bulk of the preliminary drawings for *L'idea*. As Grant Keith noted in an earlier article, a significant number of the Palladio drawings owned by Jones have also subsequently disappeared. William Grant Keith, 'Inigo Jones as a Collector', *Journal of the Royal Institute of British Architects* (9 March 1925) p. 105.

47 I am grateful to Professor Sicca for this observation. The drawings contain cataloguing annotations that can also be found on other drawings related to Jones in the Burlington–Devonshire collection. Grant Keith believed these to be by John Webb, which would prove definitively that they were owned by Jones. Professor Sicca, in preliminary observations in Erik Forssman *et al.*, *Palladio: la sua eredità nel mondo* (Milan, 1980) p. 55, suggested they were by John Talman.

48 Internal evidence for dating the composition of *L'idea* is limited, though it had clearly been in preparation for many years. Apart from the design for the Palazzo Strozzi (I, pp. 248–9), dated 1602, the only dated engravings in the book are for stairs, inscribed 'Vinc Scam Arch. An. 1614' (I, p. 317; II, p. 314). The finishing touches to the book were made at the end of 1615 when Scamozzi dated the introductions to the various books between 6 August and 8 December.

49 Barbieri and Beltramini, *Vincenzo Scamozzi* pp. 144–6.

50 Harris, Orgel and Strong, *The King's Arcadia* p. 64.

51 L. Cust, 'Notes on the Collections formed by Thomas Howard, Earl of Arundel and Surrey', *Burlington Magazine* XIX (1911) p. 282; Howard Burns, 'Note sull' influesso di Scamozzi in Inghilterra: Inigo Jones, John Webb, Lord Burlington', in Barbieri and Beltramini, *Vincenzo Scamozzi* p. 129. The importance of Lord Arundel's collection of drawings as a source for Jones is impossible to gauge as they have been dispersed but it must have been profound. In 1632 Lord Maltravers writing to William Petty commented that 'my Lord chiefly affects them' [i.e. the drawings] and in 1637 the papal envoy Pangani saw a room with over 200 books of drawings by Leonardo, Michaelangelo, Raphael and others. David Howarth, 'Lord Arundel as an Entrepreneur of the Arts', *Burlington Magazine* CXXII (1980) pp. 690–92. Arundel's interest was not purely artistic. In 1632 he requested from Ferdinando, Duke of Mantua, 'a model of the courtyard of the Palazzo in Mantua that was built not long ago with a rustic order', probably the Cortile della Cavallerizza. John Bold, *Greenwich: An Architectural History of the Royal Hospital for Seamen and the Queen's House* (New Haven and London, 2000) p. 61.

52 Grant Keith, 'Drawings by Vincenzo Scamozzi' p. 528, fig. 5.

53 Scamozzi, *L'idea* I, p. 275; Harris and Higgott, *Inigo Jones* pp. 68–71, cat. 15, 16, fig. 19.

54 Alsopp, *Inigo Jones on Palladio* II, p. 62.

55 Palladio, *Quattro libri* II, pp. 47, 60; Scamozzi, *L'idea* I, p. 275; Harris and Higgott, *Inigo Jones* p. 68.

56 The two relevant exceptions, the Villa Pisani at Montagnana and the Villa Cornaro, give equal weight to the two floors but in each case there is a portico-in-antis on both floors, not a portico-in-antis on the first floor over a solid ground floor. Neither of Palladio's villas has full-height rusticated ground floors and plain first floors, as both the Villa Molin and the third preliminary design for the Queen's House do. Barbieri and Beltramini, *Vincenzo Scamozzi* pp. 369–74.

57 Burns, 'Palladio and the Foundations of a New Architecture' p. 57, cat. 2.

58 Harris and Higgott, *Inigo Jones* p. 70, fig. 19.

59 *Ibid.* pp. 66–7, cat. 13.

60 Scamozzi, *L'idea* I, p. 287. Another example of Scamozzi's unusual, long narrow villas is the Villa Ferretti Angeli at Dolo, on the banks of the Brenta, which Jones could have passed on his journey from Padua to Venice. However, this was not illustrated in the first edition of *L'idea*. Barbieri and Beltramini, *Vincenzo Scamozzi* pp. 356–7.

61 The staircase was never built and exists only in designs and drawings. I am grateful to Professor Ottenheym for pointing this out to me.

62 Palladio, *Quattro libri* II, p. 8.

63 *Ibid.* I, p. 62; II, pp. 6, 44, 53.

64 Scamozzi, *L'idea* I, pp. 126, 317; Konrad Ottenheym, *Vincenzo Scamozzi* pp. 195–9.

65 John Harris and A. A. Tait, *Catalogue of the Drawings by Inigo Jones, John Webb and Isaac de Caus at Worcester College, Oxford* (Oxford, 1979) fig. 68.

66 Harris and Higgott, *Inigo Jones* pp. 72–3, cat. 16.

67 I am grateful to Dr Higgott for pointing out the significance of the orientation. Barbieri and Beltramini, *Vincenzo Scamozzi* pp. 179–80.

68 Scamozzi, *L'idea* I, p. 277; Konrad Ottenheym, *Vincenzo Scamozzi* p. 142.

69 Harris and Higgott, *Inigo Jones* pp. 72–3, cat. 16; Scamozzi, *L'idea* I, pp. 273, 279.

70 Palladio, *Quattro libri* II, p. 60. Palladio shows ramped stairs at the Villa Trissino, similar to those on the second design for the Queen's House, but (unlike Scamozzi) he also shows stairs leading up to the portico, so this cannot be the source for Jones's projecting portico.

71 Bold, *Greenwich* pp. 46, 72–3.

72 I. R. Stevens, 'Byfleet House: "A Noble House of Brick"', *Surrey Archaeological Collections* L (1946–7) pp. 101–2, pl. xvi.

73 See Jones's annotated copy of Palladio, *Quattro libri* II, p. 64, Worcester College, Oxford. I am grateful to Dr Higgott for drawing my attention to this drawing and its possible link with Houghton Conquest.

74 Harris, Orgel and Strong, *The King's Arcadia* pp. 109–10,

figs 196–7; Harris and Higgott, *Inigo Jones* pp. 84–5, fig. 21.

75 It is probable that Jones only contributed the design of this portico and a similarly ambitious colonnaded portico on the west front rather than designed the whole of Houghton Conquest.

76 Harris and Higgott, *Inigo Jones* pp. 104–5, cat. 30, fig. 35.

77 This can be seen in Scamozzi's designs for the Palazzo Ravischiera, Genoa, for the Palazzo Cornaro in Venice and for the Palazzo Strozzi in Florence and on the Palazzo Trissino al Corso in Vicenza. Konrad Ottenheym, *Vincenzo Scamozzi* pp. 90–91, 113, 121.

78 Compare Palladio, *Quattro libri* I, pp. 45–8, with Scamozzi, *L'idea* II, pp. 113, 115 (by printer's error this latter page is numbered 91).

79 Scamozzi, *L'idea* II, pp. 113, 163.

80 H. C. G. Matthew and Brian Harris (eds), *The Oxford Dictionary of National Biography* (Oxford, 2004) XIII, pp. 988–90.

81 Campbell, *Vitruvius Britannicus* III, p. 7, pl. 9. It is possible that Jones added wings to an existing hunting lodge that was subsequently refaced by another architect. Photographs of the house before it was destroyed by fire in the possession of the current owner Mr Alexander Chancellor show that Campbell's plan was accurate in its essentials.

82 John Bridges, *The History and Antiquities of Northamptonshire*, ed. Peter Whalley (London, 1791) I, p. 328.

83 Oliver Hill and John Cornforth, *English Country Houses: Caroline* (London, 1966) pp. 61–4, figs 70–76.

84 John Summerson, *Architecture in Britain 1530–1830* (London, 1977) pp. 141–2; Howard Colvin, *A Biographical Dictionary of British Architects 1600–1840* (New Haven and London, 1995) p. 56.

85 The Villa Ferramosca was not illustrated in the first edition of *L'idea*, though preliminary drawings for it survive at Chatsworth. Scamozzi, *L'idea* I, p. 126. Barbieri and Beltramini, *Vincenzo Scamozzi* pp. 144–9, 288–92.

86 Palladio, *Quattro libri* II, p. 51; design for fortified palace for Count Sabras, p. 253; Palazzo Trissino al Corso, p. 260; design for Palazzo Fino, Bergamo, p. 263; Villa 'Il Paradiso', Castelfranco, p. 281; Villa Verlata, p. 287; Villa Cornaro at Pisuolo, pp. 296–7.

87 Harris and Higgott, *Inigo Jones* pp. 274–5, cat. 94.

88 Mowl and Earnshaw were the first to draw the visual comparison between the Stoke Park pavilions and the masque design. Mowl and Earnshaw, *Architecture without Kings* p. 83, figs 33–4.

89 Matthew and Harris, *Oxford Dictionary of National Biography* XIII, pp. 988–90. (Crane was not secretary to Prince Charles, as is sometimes stated.)

90 John Aubrey, *The Natural History of Wiltshire*, ed. John Britton (London, 1847) pp. 83–4.

91 Bold, *Greenwich* p. 53.

92 Dianne Duggan, '"London the Ring, Covent Garden the Jewel of that Ring": New Light on Covent Garden', *Architectural History* XLIII (2000) pp. 143–6.

93 Howard Colvin (ed.), *History of the King's Works* (London, 1982) IV, pp. 48–9; Derek Keene *et al.* (eds), *St Paul's: The Cathedral Church of London 604–2004* (New Haven and London, 2004) p. 175; Bold, *Greenwich* p. 53.

94 Harris, Orgel and Strong, *The King's Arcadia* p. 67.

95 Harris and Tait, *Catalogue of the Drawings* p. 18, fig. 16; Howard Burns, *Andrea Palladio 1508–1580* (London, 1975) p. 157, cat. 279.

96 Scamozzi, *L'idea* I, pp. 249, 287; Harris and Tait, *Catalogue of the Drawings* p. 18, fig. 16.

97 The influence of the Palazzo Strozzi on the first design for Somerset House is noted by Howard Colvin, 'The South Front of Wilton House' in *Essays in English Architectural History* (New Haven and London, 1999) pp. 151–2, figs 128–9.

98 Harris and Tait, *Catalogue of the Drawings* p. 18, fig. 17.

99 Scamozzi, *L'idea* I, p. 246; Jones's annotated copy of *L'idea* shows that he studied this design in considerable detail; Whinney, 'John Webb's Drawings' pl. IX.

100 For the 'ignudi', see the Palazzo Cornaro, the Palazzo Strozzi, the Palazzo Trissino al Duomo and the Palazzo Fino in Scamozzi, *L'idea* I, pp. 246, 249, 258, 263, and in Palladio's work the Palazzo Chiericati, Palazzo Iseppo Porto and Palazzo Barbarano in Palladio, *Quattro libri* II, pp. 7, 9, 23; for the constrast between a rusticated lower storey with mezzanine and plain upper storey see the palace for Count Sbaras and the Villa Verlata Fino in Scamozzi, *L'idea* I, pp. 253, 287; Whinney, 'John Webb's Drawings' pls XIIb, XIIIa. Neither element features in Palladio's *Quattro libri*.

101 Bold, *Greenwich* pp. 46, 53–4.

102 *Ibid.* p. 58.

103 Amelio Fara, *Bernardo Buontalenti: l'architettura, la guerra e l'elemento geometrico* (Genoa, 1988) pp. 141, 155, 161, 218, 226, figs 95, 112, 119, 180, 190.

104 James Lees-Milne, *The Age of Inigo Jones* (London, 1953) p. 84; John Summerson, *Inigo Jones* (New Haven and London, 2000) p. 7.

105 Fara, *Buontalenti* p. 141, fig. 95.

106 Bold, *Greenwich* pp. 55–6, figs 76–8.

107 See, for example, Fara, *Buontalenti* figs 120, 135, 222.

108 Claudia Conforti and Richard Tuttle, *Storia dell'architettura italiana: il secondo cinquecento* (Milan, 2001) p. 114.

109 *Ibid.* pp. 253–5.

110 *Ibid.* pp. 253–5, 374–5.

111 Peter Paul Rubens, *Palazzi di Genova*, 2 vols (Antwerp, 1622–6) I, figs 11, 23, 51, 52. Balustrades can be found on the Palazzi Parodi (1567–81), Cattaneo (1585–8), Durazzo-Pallavicini (*c.*1618), Podesta (1563–5), Campanella (1562– 5), dell'Acquedotto (1614), Spinola a Pellicceria (*c.*1580– 90), Negri (1602), Lomellini-Patrone (1565–8) and Bruzzo (after 1610). *Ibid.* I, fig. 64; II, figs 18, 19, 27, 33, 45, 48, 51, 54, 57.

112 Jones includes a reference to the Genoese use of loggias in his annotation to the *Quattro libri*. Alsopp, *Inigo Jones on Palladio* I, pp. 12–13.

113 John Harris suggests that Edward Carter's design for East Hampstead Lodge, made after 1628, is derived from the *Palazzi di Genova*, but the elevation fits comfortably into the astylar manner introduced by Jones and ultimately

derived from Serlio. The courtyard plan is compared with some plausibility by Mowl and Earnshaw to the Palazzo Doria in the *Palazzi di Genova* but the courtyard and loggia probably owe more to English Elizabethan and Jacobean traditions. Harris and Higgott, *Inigo Jones* p. 302; Mowl and Earnshaw, *Architecture without Kings* pp. 60–61, fig. 22; Rubens, *Palazzi di Genova* II, fig. 3. Mowl and Earnshaw suggest Rubens's engraving of S. Ciro as a source for Wren's Pembroke College Chapel, Cambridge, but this is derived from Serlio's reconstruction of the Temple at Tivoli. Mowl and Earnshaw, *Architecture without Kings* p. 202, figs 109–10; Worsley, *Classical Architecture* p. 52, figs 63–4. Hill and Cornforth suggest that the elevation of Thorpe Hall, Northamptonshire, was derived from Nicolo Spinola's palazzo, as illustrated by Rubens. It too is in the Jonesian/Serlian tradition. Hill and Cornforth, *English Country Houses* pp. 102–3, fig. 154; Worsley, *Classical Architecture* pp. 16–17, figs 26–7.

114 Harris and Higgott, *Inigo Jones* p. 328.

115 Konrad Ottenheym, 'Peter Paul Rubens's *Palazzi di Genova* and its Influence on Architecture in the Netherlands', in Piet Lombaerde (ed.), *The Reception of P. P. Rubens's* Palazzi di Genova *during the 17th century in Europe: Questions and Problems* (Turnhout, 2002) p. 81.

116 *Ibid.* pp. 83–4.

117 Rubens, *Palazzi di Genova*.

118 Konrad Ottenheym, 'Peter Paul Rubens's *Palazzi di Genova*' p. 85.

119 Pier Palme, *The Triumph of Peace: A Study of the Whitehall Banqueting House* (Stockholm, 1956) p. 79.

120 Rubens, *Palazzi di Genova* II, figs 3, 6, 9, 12, 15, 18, 19.

121 Konrad Ottenheym, 'Peter Paul Rubens's *Palazzi di Genova*' p. 97; L. B. Alberti, *De re aedificatoria* (Florence, 1485) VI, cap. 2.

122 John Bold, *John Webb: Architectural Theory and Practice in the Seventeenth Century* (Oxford, 1989) pp. 47–51, fig. 26.

123 David R. Coffin, *Pirro Ligorio: The Renaissance Artist, Architect, and* Antiquarian (Pennysylvania, Pa., 2004) pp. 62–3, fig. 51.

124 John Bold, *John Webb: Architectural Theory and Practice in the Seventeenth Century* (Oxford, 1989) p. 32. John Webb, no doubt influenced by Jones, specifically cited Ligorio along with Peruzzi, Labacco, Serlio and Palladio as authorities on porticoes. John Webb, *A Vindication of Stone-Heng Restored* (London, 1665) p. 36.

125 David R. Coffin, *Pirro Ligorio: The Renaissance Artist, Architect, and Antiquarian* (University Park, Pa., 2004) pp. 18–19.

126 Scamozzi, *L'idea* II, p. 58; Harris and Higgott, *Inigo Jones* pp. 264–5, cat. 90; Beltramini, *Palladio and Northern Europe* p. 134.

CHAPTER 8

1 Philips Vingboons, *Afbeelsels der voornaemste gebouwen* (Amsterdam, 1648) I, 29.

2 *Ibid.* 27.

3 J. J. Terwen, 'De ontwerpgeschiedenis van de Marekerk te Leiden', in H. van den Berg (ed.), *Opus Musium* (Assen, 1964) pp. 231–56; J. J. Terwen and K. A. Ottenheym, *Pieter Post (1608–1669) Architect* (Zutphen, 1993) pp. 206–7, figs 244–5.

4 Terwen and Ottenheym, *Pieter Post* pp. 48–53. Interestingly, Post considered placing a freestanding pedimented portico at the centre of the ranges linking the palace to the offices but this was never executed.

5 Oliver Hill and John Cornforth, *English Country Houses: Baroque* (London, 1966) figs 19, 205; John Summerson, *Architecture in Britain 1530–1830* (Harmonds-worth, 1977) pp. 162–4, fig. 119.

6 John Harris and Gordon Higgott, *Inigo Jones: Complete Architectural Drawings* (London, 1989) pp. 68–71, 100, 103–5, 110–13, cat. 14, 30–31, 33–4, figs 30–32; John Harris, Stephen Orgel and Roy Strong, *The King's Arcadia: Inigo Jones and the Stuart Court* (London, 1973) figs 261, 281.

7 Harris and Higgott, *Inigo Jones* pp. 70, 72–3, 191–2, 238–9, figs 19, 54, 78; Howard Colvin, 'The South Front of Wilton House', in *Essays in Architectural History* (New Haven and London, 1999) fig. 118.

8 Howard Colvin (ed.), *The History of the King's Works* (London, 1982) IV, pp. 48–9, 159–60; Harris and Higgott, *Inigo Jones* pp. 258–9, cat. 86. *The History of the King's Works* associates the drawing now believed to be for the third preliminary design for the Queen's House with the New Lodge.

9 John Harris and A. A. Tait, *Catalogue of the Drawings by Inigo Jones, John Webb and Isaac de Caus at Worcester College, Oxford* (Oxford, 1979) p. 41, fig. 83.

10 Hill and Cornforth, *English Country Houses: Baroque* p. 75, fig. 94.

11 John Bold, *John Webb: Architectural Theory and Practice in the Seventeenth Century* (Oxford, 1989) pp. 155–7, fig. 102.

12 I am grateful to Dr Gordon Higgott for this information. Vincenzo Scamozzi, *L'idea della architettura universale* (Venice, 1615) II, p. 58; Harris and Higgott, *Inigo Jones* pp. 264–5, cat. 90; Howard Burns in Guido Beltramini *et al., Palladio and Northern Europe: Books, Travellers, Architects* (Milan, 1999) p. 134.

13 Harris and Higgott, *Inigo Jones* p. 134–5, cat. 44, 45.

14 Harris and Tait, *Catalogue of the Drawings* p. 33, pl. 55.

15 I am grateful to Dr Higgott for sharing his views on the dating of the buttery drawing and its possible client. They will be published by him in due course.

16 Bold, *John Webb* pp. 155–7.

17 Raynham Hall is problematic. Timothy Mowl and Brian Earnshaw assert that the temple front was added in the 1650s. Timothy Mowl and Brian Earnshaw, *Architecture without Kings: The Rise of Puritan Classicism under Cromwell* (Manchester, 1995) pp. 159–62. They argue that the temple front is discordant with the rest of the elevation and that a later date is more appropriate for the plasterwork decoration in the Belisarius Room behind, part of the alterations made by Sir Horatio Townshend in 1659–62. Though a date in the 1650s would fit more comfortably other pedimented and porticoed elevations,

documentary proof is lacking. The fact that the interior decoration is later need mean no more than that the house had not been fitted up during Sir Roger Town-shend's lifetime. A dendrochronological test of the roof timbers might shed light.

18 See also, for example, Roger North's Rougham Hall, Norfolk, of the 1690s, the only seventeenth-century private house to be given a freestanding portico after the Restoration. Howard Colvin and John Newman (eds.), *Of Building: Roger North's Writings on Architecture* (Oxford, 1981) p. xv, fig. 1.

19 H. C. G. Matthew and Brian Harrison (eds), *The Oxford Dictionary of National Biography* (Oxford, 2004) XXVI, pp. 208–11.

20 Webb's design, probably unexecuted, for Colonel Ludlow's house at Maiden Bradley, Wiltshire (*c.*1646–50), had an implied portico with pilasters on the first floor. Bold, *John Webb* pp. 68–79, 90–102, 170–74.

21 C. L. Frommel, S. Ray and M. Tafuri, *Raffaelo Architetto* (Milan, 1984) pp. 241–85; Vaughan Hart and Peter Hicks, *Sebastiano Serlio: On Architecture* (New Haven and London, 1996) I, p. 127; Arnaldo Bruschi, *Storia dell'architettura italiana: il primo cinquecento* (Milan, 2002) pp. 122–3, 164, 176–7.

22 Claudia Conforti and Richard J. Tuttle, *Storia dell' architettura italiana: il secondo cinquecento* (Milan, 2001) pp. 74–7.

23 Stephano du Pérac, *Ichnographia templi divi Petri Romae in Vaticano ex esemplari Michaelis Angeli Bonaroti Florentini* (Rome, *c.*1607); James A. Ackerman, *The Architecture of Michelangelo* (London, 1961) pls 59b–61.

24 See n. 26 below.

25 James S. Ackerman, 'Palladio's Lost Portico Project for San Petronio in Bologna', in Douglas Fraser, Howard Hibbard and Milton J. Lewine (eds), *Essays in the History of Architecture presented to Rudolf Wittkower* (London, 1967) pp. 110–15; Lionello Puppi, *Andrea Palladio: The Complete Works* (London, 1975) pp. 245–8, 254, figs 395–6, 433–6.

26 Frommel, Ray and Tafuri, *Raffaelo* p. 224, fig. 2.10.4.

27 The drawing is in the Raccolta Bianconi, Biblioteca Trivulziana, Milan. Ennio Poleggi (ed.), *Galeazzo Alessi e l'architettura del cinquecento* (Genoa, 1975) fig. 314; *Galeazzo Alessi: Mostra di fotografie, rilievi, disegni, Genova, Palazzo Bianco 16 Aprile–12 Maggi 1974* (Genoa, 1974) fig. 98. The construction of S. Vittore is complicated. Vincenzo Seregni worked there from 1553 and Alessi was involved *c.*1564. The design of the upper portions was modified and completed by Pellegrino Tibaldi in 1568. Andrew Hopkins, *Italian Architecture from Michelangelo to Borromini* (London, 2002) pp. 70–74; Conforti and Tuttle, *Storia dell'architettura italiana* pp. 381, 384.

28 Isabella Balestreri, *La Raccolta Bianconi: disegni per milano dal manierismo al barocco* (Milan, 1995) pp. 92–3.

29 *Ibid.* pp. 38–45, figs; t. IV, p. 22.

30 Terwen, 'De ontwerpgeschiedenis' pp. 231–56; Terwen and Ottenheym, *Pieter Post* pp. 206–7, figs 244–5.

31 Ackerman, *Architecture of Michelangelo* pls 59b–62a; Ackerman, 'Palladio's Lost Portico Project' pp. 110–15. Louis

le Pautre also suggested a freestanding portico for the Chapelle de Port-Royal in Paris, begun in 1646, but this was rejected in execution. He published his unsuccessful design in his *Desseins des plusiers palais* in 1652. Robert W. Berger, *Antoine le Pautre: A French Architect of the Era of Louis XIV* (New York, 1969) pp. 7–15, figs 1–2.

32 Rudolf Wittkower, 'Carlo Rainaldi and the Architecture of the High Baroque in Rome', in *Studies in the Italian Baroque* (London, 1975) pp. 10–18, fig. 13; Jean-Marie Pérouse de Montclos (ed.), *Le guide du patrimoine: Paris* (Paris, 1994) p. 112, fig.

33 Foulke Robarts, *God's house and service according to the primitive and most Christian forme thereof* (London, 1639) p. 46.

34 Thomas Corns, 'Duke, Prince, King', in Thomas Corns (ed.), *The Royal Image: Representations of Charles I* (Cambridge, 1999) p. 14.

35 Gordon Higgott, 'The Fabric to 1670', in Derek Keene, Arthur Burns and Andrew Saint (eds), *St Paul's: The Cathedral Church of London 604–2004* (New Haven and London, 2004) p. 175.

36 Harris and Higgott, *Inigo Jones* pp. 241–3, fig. 79.

37 Higgott, 'The Fabric to 1670' p. 182.

38 John Webb, *A Vindication of Stone-Heng Restored* (London, 1665) p. 23.

39 Robert Tavernor, *Palladio and Palladianism* (London, 1991) p. 137.

40 Richard Krautheimer, *Rome: Profile of a City, 312–1308* (Princeton, 1980) pp. 24, 130, fig. 130. Fig. 259 shows S. Croce as Jones would have known it.

41 Thomas Ashby (ed.), *Topographical Study in Rome in 1581* (London, 1916) fig. 41.

42 Paul Letarouilly, *Edifices de Rome moderne* (Paris, 1860) p. 266; Andrew Hopkins, *Italian Architecture from Michelangelo to Borromini* (London, 2002) pp. 164–5.

43 Hopkins, *Italian Architecture* pp. 74–5.

44 See n. 27 above.

45 Balestreri, *La Raccolta Bianconi* pp. 38–45, figs; t. IV, p. 22.

46 Ackerman, 'Palladio's Lost Portico Project' pp. 110–15.

47 Conforti and Tuttle, *Storia dell'architettura italiana* pp. 193–7.

48 G. P. V. Akrigg, *Letters of King James* (Berkeley, Calif., 1984) letter 195, p. 397.

49 James I quoted in Per Palme, *Triumph of Peace* (Stockholm, 1956) p. 277.

50 John Newman, 'Laudian Literature and the Interpretation of Caroline Churches in London', in David Howarth (ed.), *Art and Patronage in the Caroline Courts* (Cambridge, 1993) pp. 168–88.

51 Higgott, 'The Fabric to 1670' pp. 176–8.

52 Foulke Robarts, *God's house and service* pp. 2, 41.

53 *Ibid.* p. 32.

54 R.T., *De Templis, A Treatise of Temples: wherein is discovered the ancient manner of building, consecrating and adorning of churches* (London, 1638) p. 17.

55 *Ibid.*, pp. 50–53.

56 Newman, 'Laudian Literature' pp. 172, 175, 181.

57 Dianne Duggan, '"London the Ring, Covent Garden

the Jewell of that Ring": New Light on Covent Garden', *Architectural History* XLIII (2000) p. 143.

58 R. T., *De Templis* pp. 4–5.

59 *Ibid.* p. 19.

60 *Ibid.* pp. 41, 43.

CHAPTER 9

1 For example, S. Wilinski, 'La Serliana', *Bollettino del centro internazionale di studi d'Andrea Palladio* VII (1965) p. 115; Peter Murray, *Renaissance Architecture* (London, 1986) p. 133; and John Belton Scott, *Architecture for the Shroud* (Chicago, 2003) p. 79. The use of the term Serliana is scarcely less problematic than that of Palladian or Venetian window. Though Serlio was the first to publish the Serliana, and thus to promote its use, he was not its inventor nor is he known to have used it in any executed buildings. However, the terms Palladian and Venetian window are even more deceptive and for that reason Serliana has come to be accepted as more appropriate.

2 Erik Forssman *et al.*, *Palladio: la sua eredità nel mondo* (Milan, 1980) p. 159.

3 Andrea Palladio, *I quattro libri dell'architettura* (Venice, 1570) II, pp. 58, 63; III, pp. 42–3. As well as the Villas Angarano and Poiana, Palladio also used Serlianas on the Villa Contarini-Camerini, the Villa Valmarana and the side elevation of the Loggia del Capitaniato in Vicenza and a number of villa designs. Lionello Puppi, *Andrea Palladio: Complete Works* (Milan, 1975) figs 106–15, 142–4, 345, 365. He also included a number of Serlianas on his design for the façade of the Church of S. Petronio in Bologna. *Ibid.* figs 392–4.

4 Rudolf Wittkower, 'Pseudo-Palladian Elements in English Neoclassicism' in *Palladio and English Palladianism* (London, 1974) pp. 155–63.

5 B. Patzak, *Die Villa Imperiale in Pesaro* (Leipzig, 1908) pp. 144ff.; 'Serliana', *Enciclopedia italiana* (Rome, 1936) XXXI, pp. 442f.; D. F. Brown, 'The Arcuated Lintel and its Symbolic Interpretation in Late Antique Art', *American Journal of Archaeology* XLVI (1942) pp. 389–94; Wilinski, 'La Serliana', (1965) pp. 115–24; S. Wilinski, 'La Serliana', *Bollettino del centro internazionale di studi d'Andrea Palladio* XI (1969) pp. 131–43; Fikret K. Yegül, 'A Study in Architectural Iconography: *Kaisersaal* and the Imperial Cult', *Art Bulletin* LXIV (1982) pp. 8–10, 22–3; Krista de Jonge, 'La Serliana di Sebastiano Serlio: appunti sulla finestra veneziana', in Christof Thoenes (ed.), *Sebastiano Serlio* (Milan, 1989) pp. 50–56.

6 E. E. Rosenthal, *The Palace of Charles V in Granada* (Princeton, 1985) pp. 208–9, 254–5; Roger J. Crum, 'The Iconography of the Uffizi Façade', *Art Bulletin* LXXI (1989) pp. 238–45; Leon Satkowski, *Georgio Vasari: Architect and Courtier* (Princeton, 1993) pp. 43–4.

7 For example, Raphael's unexecuted design for S. Lorenzo in Florence was probably responsible for a sequence of Serlianas placed in the west fronts of later churches starting with the façade of S. Bernadino in L'Aquila of 1525–7, designed by Cola dell'Amatrice, who

was closely connected with Rome. C. L. Frommel, S. Ray and M. Tafuri, *Raffaelo architetto* (Milan, 1984) p. 167; Arnaldo Bruschi, *Storia dell'architettura italiana: il primo cinquecento* (Milan, 2002) pp. 456–60, fig. These include Antonio da Sangallo's S. Bernardo, Piacenza (1525); G. Alessi's S. Barnaba, Milan (1558); M. T. Fiorio, *Le chiese di Milano* (Milan, 1985) p. 185; and Vignola's initial design for the Gesù in Rome as seen in G. Bonsegni's foundation medal of 1568; Rudolf Wittkower and Irma B. Jaffe (eds), *Baroque Art: The Jesuit Contribution* (New York, 1972) pp. 24–5, fig. 13b; Palladio's design for the west front of S. Petronio, Bologna (1578), Puppi, *Palladio* pp. 245–3, figs 392–4; G. A. Dosio and Niccolo Gaddi's proposed façade for Sta Maria del Fiore, Florence (1589); Claudia Conforti and Richard J. Tuttle, *Storia dell'architettura italiana: il secondo cinquecento* (Milan, 2001) p. 157, fig. Pattern books produced in eighteenth-century England, starting with James Gibbs's *A Book of Architecture* (1728), divorced the Serliana from all meaning so that builders and architects felt comfortable in using it on any building from a country house to a mill, by way of merchants' town houses and inns, for purely visual effect.

8 Other examples include the Corinthian Temple at Termessos; the fresco in the Cubiculum of the Villa of the Mysteries, Pompeii; the Temple of Hadrian at Ephesus; the Marble Court at Sardis; and the reconstructed Canopus or arcade at Hadrian's Villa, Tivoli. Margaret Lyttelton, *Baroque Architecture in Classical Antiquity* (London, 1974) pp. 28, 174, fig. 7; Yegül, 'Study in Architectural Iconography' pp. 8, 23, figs 1, 27, 28; John Ward-Perkins, *Roman Architecture* (London, 1988) pp. 95, 161, 173, figs 137, 250, 268, 265.

9 Earlier examples can be found, such as the façade of Brunelleschi's Pazzi Chapel, Florence (1420), but these appear to be isolated.

10 Fiorio, *Chiese di Milano* pp. 206–14.

11 Janice Shell, 'Amadeo, the Mantegazza and the Façade of the Certosa di Pavia', in J. Shell and L. Castelfranchi (eds), *Giovanni Antonio Amadeo* (Milan 1993) pp. 189–222.

12 Franco Borsi, *Bramante* (Milan and Paris, 1990) p. 204. Bramante designed the Canons Cloister in 1492, of which only one wing was built, and a further group of four cloisters in 1497, of which two were completed after 1576 to his plans.

13 Bruschi, *Storia dell'architettura* pp. 280–81.

14 *Ibid.* pp. 435–61; Borsi, *Bramante* pp. 287–90.

15 Puppi, *Palladio* fig. 326; Pier Luigi de Vecchi, *Raphael* (New York and London, 2002) p. 288, fig. 273. S. Eligio was completed by Baldassare Peruzzi who used similar high-level Serlianas in his design for remodelling S. Domenico in Siena *c.*1531. Bruschi, *Storia dell'architettura* p. 156.

16 Leopold D. and Helen S. Ettlinger, *Raphael* (Oxford, 1987) pp. 99–102, fig. 98. A screen of Serlianas usually attributed to Bramante can also be found at the Ninfeo at Genazzano, a structure clearly inspired by the Roman Baths. However, the date (some time within the first and second decades of the sixteenth century) and authorship

of the commission remain unclear. Borsi, *Bramante* pp. 326–9.

17   Berenice Davidson, 'The Decoration of the Sala Regia under Pope Paul III', *Art Bulletin* XLVIII (1976) pp. 395–420; Frommel, *Raffaelo in Vaticano* p. 124; Borsi, *Bramante* p. 296; Satkowski, *Giorgio Vasari* pl. 42.

18   David Armitage, *The Ideological Origins of the British Empire* (Cambridge, 2000) p. 33.

19   Another early example of the Serliana with papal connections is the choir of Sta Maria Maddalena at Capranica Prenestina: the cupola is encircled by Serlianas and the plan recalls Bramante's choir of Sta Maria del Popolo. The choir was built by Giuliano Capranica, nephew of the illustrious cardinal, and from 1502 in the service of Cesare Borgia. Uncertain chronology impedes a secure attribution to Bramante but the origin of the design suggests Bramante or one of his Roman followers. Bruschi, *Storia dell'architettura* pp. 55–6.

20   Ettlinger, *Raphael* pp. 176, fig. 167.

21   Frommel, Ray and Tafuri, *Raffaelo architetto* p. 167.

22   *Ibid.* pp. 343–7.

23   Borsi, *Bramante* p. 37; Manfredo Tafuri *et al.*, *Giulio Romano* (Cambridge, 1998) p. 329, fig; Henry A. Millon and Craig Hugh Smyth, *Michelangelo architetto: la facciata di San Lorenzo e la Cupola di San Pietro* (Milan, 1988); Martin Clayton, *Raphael and his Circle: Drawings from Windsor Castle* (London, 1999) pp. 114–15. A drawing also survives by Giulio Romano from his Mantuan period for a Serlian loggia with a rusticated portal. Tafuri, *Giulio Romano* p. 220, fig. 30.

24   Clayton, *Raphael and his Circle* p. 114, fig. 54.

25   Satkowski, *Georgio Vasari* p. 43.

26   R. Delbrueck, *Die Consulardiptychen und verwalte Denkmaler* (Berlin and Leipzig, 1929) pp. 235–42; cited in Crum, 'Iconography of the Uffizi Façade' p. 241.

27   Steven H. Wander, 'The Cyprus Plates: The Story of David and Goliath', *Metropolitan Museum Journal* VIII (1973) pp. 89–104, figs 1, 2, 4, 6.

28   Yegül, 'Study in Architectural Iconography', p. 23.

29   Rosenthal, *Palace of Charles V* pp. 208–10, 254–5. The early eighth-century palace of the exarchs at Ravenna has a large recess over its portal, which most scholars believe was a three-light loggia, and it was on this that the three-light window over the entry to Charlemagne's palatine chapel in Aachen is believed to have been based. Wilinski, 'La Serliana' (1965) pp. 115–23; Wilinski, 'La Serliana' (1969) pp. 131–43; H. Spielmann, *Andrea Palladio und die Antike* (Berlin, 1966) pp. 177, nos 247–8; Wittkower, 'Pseudo-Palladian Elements' pp. 155–9; R. Krautheimer, *Early Christian and Byzantine Architecture* (London, 1979) p. 40; Yegül, 'Study in Architectural Iconography' pp. 8–10, 23; Crum, 'Iconography of the Uffizi Façade' pp. 237–53; Satkowski, *Giorgio Vasari* p. 43.

30   Margaret Gibson, *The Liverpool Ivories* (London, 1994) pp. 17–18, pl. VIIb.

31   O. Panvinio, *De ludis circensibus* (Venice, 1600) p. 62, illustrated in Howard Colvin, *Essays in English Architectural History* (New Haven and London, 1999) p. 126, fig. 105.

32   Aurora Scotti Tosini (ed.), *Storia dell'architettura italiana: il seicento* 2 vols (Milan, 2003) I, pp. 102–4.

33   Murray, *Renaissance Architecture* p. 118, fig. 202; Paolo Portoghesi, *The Rome of Borromini: Architecture as Language* (New York, 1968) figs XCVI, CII, pls 123, 129.

34   Tosini, *Storia dell'architettura italiana* I, pp. 154–5, 184–5. Sta Maria in via Lata had particularly strong papal connections because it was built over the chapel said to incorporate the house where St Peter, the first pope, was imprisoned when he came to Rome. In the seventeenth century this became an object of such veneration that Alexander decided to restore it and make it accessible to the faithful, the work being carried out with unusual respect for Antiquity. In the eighteenth century prominent Serlianas were included in the remodelling of two papal basilicas: S. Giovanni in Laterano, remodelled by Alessandro Galilei in 1734 for Pope Clement XII, and Sta Maria Maggiore, remodelled by Ferdinando Fuga in c.1751 for Pope Benedict XIV. Bernini's scheme of 1653 for the Palazzo Ludovisi, designed for Niccolo Ludovisi, who married Costanza Pamphili, the niece of Innocent X, included a Serlian window over the entrance. A clear association is made with the pope through the positioning of the papal arms over the window. In the event, Bernini's design was not carried through, and when work was resumed by Carlo Fontana for the Hospite of S. Michele, the Serlian window was excluded. Franco Borsi, *Bernini* (New York, 1984) pp. 262, 315, figs 345–6.

35   F. A. Yates, 'Charles Quint et l'idée d'empire', in *Les fêtes de la renaissance* (Paris, 1960) II, pp. 67ff.

36   Anthony Pagden, *Lords of All the World: Ideologies of Empire in Spain, Britain and France c.1500–c.1800* (New Haven and London, 1995) pp. 40–41.

37   Rosenthal, *Palace of Charles V* pp. 208–9, 254–5.

38   The form of window chosen is known as the 'Syrian', in which the lintel of the arch runs into the lintels of the side openings, instead of springing from them, as in the 'Hellenistic' version of the Serliana. The Syrian arch was used at Diocletian's palace at Split, the Missorium of Theodosius and for the Serlian balcony in the Sala di Constantino. Despite its correct classical lineage, this was the less common form of Serliana. The arch of the Serliana in the window of the Sala Regia and the Benediction Window in the *Fire in the Borgo* are both 'Hellenistic' and this became the standard form in later centuries. Neither Serlio nor Palladio illustrates 'Syrian' Serlianas.

39   John Headley, 'The Demise of Universal Monarchy as a Meaningful Political Idea', in *Prince Albert Studies* XVI: *Imperium/Empire/Reich* (Munich, 1999) p. 42.

40   Conforti and Tuttle, *Storia di architettura* p. 241; de Jonge, 'La Serliana di Sebastiano Serlio' pp. 50–56.

41   Amedeo Belluzzi and Kurt W. Forster, 'Palazzo Tè', in Tafuri (ed.), *Giulio Romano* p. 176, fig. 215.

42   Conforti and Tuttle, *Storia di architettura* p. 192; *Felipe II: un principe del renacimento* (Madrid, 1998) p. 271.

43   Henry-Russell Hitchcock, *German Renaissance Architecture* (Princeton, 1981) pp. 47–8, pl. 141.

44 Pagden, *Lords of All the World* p. 14.

45 Armitage, *Ideological Origins* p. 31.

46 George Kubler, *Building the Escorial* (Princeton, 1982) p. 43.

47 Juan Battista de Herrera, *Las estampas de la fabrica de San Lorenzo et Real de El Escorial* (1589), seventh design. Jose Luis Sancho, *La arquitectura de los sitos reales* (Madrid, 1995) figs on pp. 410, 445.

48 Rutger Tijs, *Renaissance en Barock-Architectuur in Belgie* (Tielt, 1999) p. 63.

49 Though Volker Hoffmann identifies the imperial and Roman connotations of the tribunal he does not refer to the imperial connotations of the Serliana. It is perhaps significant that Solomon is seated in a similar Serlian 'tribunal' in Houckgeest's painting *The Judgement of Solomon*, now in the Schloss at Dessau. Volker Hoffmann, 'Le Louvre de Henri II: un palais impérial', *Bulletin de la société de l'histoire de l'art français*, année 1980 (1982) LI, pp. 44–51.

50 A less conventional contemporary use of the Serliana can be found at the château of the king's mistress, Diane de Poitiers, Anet, built by Philibert de l'Orme in 1548–53, where the main gateway takes the form of a Serliana.

51 Vaughan Hart and Peter Hicks, *Sebastiano Serlio: On Architecture* (New Haven and London, 2001) II, pp. xvi, xxi.

52 *Ibid.* p. xxvi.

53 *Ibid.* pp. 79, 140.

54 *Ibid.* pp. 79, 149.

55 *Ibid.* p. 129.

56 *Ibid.* pp. 106–10. Serlio also uses a Serlian arcade for the courtyard and garden front of his other 'noble Gentleman's House within the City' but not individual Serlianas. *Ibid.* p. 113.

57 Michael Kiene, *Bartolomeo Ammannati* (Milan, 1995) pp. 170–93.

58 Wittkower, 'Pseudo-Palladian Elements' p. 155; Wilinski, 'La Serliana' p. 115.

59 The origins of the Venetian Serliana tradition within a Veneto-Lombardan rather than a Roman tradition are explored by de Jonge in 'La Serliana di Sebastiano Serlio' pp. 50–56.

60 Hart and Hicks, *Sebastiano Serlio* I, p. 310.

61 *Ibid.* pp. 313, 315.

62 Deborah Howard, *Jacopo Sansovino: Architecture and Patronage in Renaissance Venice* (New Haven and London, 1987) p. 138; Elena Bassi, *Palazzi di Venezia* (Venice, 1987) pp. 334–7. Bassi's survey makes clear the extensive use of the Serliana in Venetian palaces.

63 Examples in Genoa include the anonymous Villa Spinola for Duke Spinola, of 1550, where a Serliana frames the stairs at the first floor; the Villa Grimaldi, Bisagno, of 1552–4, by G. Alessi for Giovanni Battista Grimaldi, humanist and banker to Charles V and the papacy, which had a Serlian arcade in the courtyard and first floor overlooking the courtyard; Conforti and Tuttle, *Storia dell'architettura* pp. 256–7; and the Villa Pallavicini delle Peschiere of 1558–62, by Galeazzo Alessi.

64 Tafuri, *Giulio Romano* pp. 266–75.

65 Hart and Hicks, *Sebastiano Serlio* I, pp. 274. Romano's use of the Serliana at Polirone may have inspired Peruzzi's study for a church interior with repeated Serlianas and the design of S. Agostino, Piacenza, c.1550, attributed to Cristoforo Lombardo, with its Serliana in the vault at the west end of the nave and further Serlianas forming the arcade separating nave and aisles. Tafuri, *Giulio Romano* figs 48–9. The monastery and church was built for the Lateran canons who had been evicted from their former monastery by Pier Luigi Farnese to build a fortress. Between 1547 and 1556 Piacenza was in imperial hands and either the emperor or Don Ferrante, governor of Milan, brother of Cardinal Ercole Gonzaga, the protector of the Lateran congregation, could have been behind the use of Serlianas, which could be read as an imperial or Gonzaga statement. Bruschi, *Storia dell'architettura* pp. 284–5.

66 Conforti and Tuttle, *Storia dell'architettura* p. 377; Guido Beltramini *et al.*, *Palladio and Northern Europe: Books, Travellers, Architects* (Milan, 1999) pp. 182–3, fig. 541.

67 Cosimo's use of the Serliana in the Palazzo della Signoria and on the Uffizi has been analysed by Crum and Satkowski, to whose analyses this account is indebted: Crum, 'Iconography of the Uffizi Façade' pp. 237–53; Satkowski, *Georgio Vasari* p. 43.

68 Kiene, *Bartolomeo Ammannati* pp. 99–101.

69 J. Hale, *Florence and the Medici: The Pattern of Control* (London, 1977) pp. 127–43.

70 Satkowski, *Georgio Vasari* p. 43.

71 Crum, 'Iconography of the Uffizi Façade' p. 248.

72 Amelio Fara, *Bernardo Buontalenti: l'architettura, la guerra e l'elemento geometrico* (Genoa, 1988) p. 271, fig. 241.

73 Conforti and Tuttle, *Storia dell'architettura* pp. 142–3.

74 Kiene, *Bartolomeo Ammannati* pp. 146–53; Conforti and Tuttle, *Storia dell'architettura* pp. 97, 99.

75 Kiene, *Bartolomeo Ammannati* (Milan, 1995) pp. 146–53, 159–69; Conforti and Tuttle, *Storia dell'architettura* pp. 41, 99, fig.

76 Robert Oresko, 'The House of Savoy in Search for a Royal Crown', in Robert Oresko, G. C. Gibbs and H. M. Scott (eds), *Royal and Republican Sovereignty in Early Modern Europe* (Cambridge, 1997) pp. 272–350.

77 Conforti and Tuttle, *Storia dell'architettura* p. 273; Nino Carboneri, *Ascanio Vitozzi: un architetto fra manierismo e barocco* (Rome, 1966) fig. 134.

78 Paola Cornaglia, 'A Mausoleum for Carlo Emanuele I: La Madonna del Mondovi a Vico' in Michaela Viglino Davico, *Ascanio Vitozzi: ingenere militare, urbanista, architetto (1539–1615)* (Perugia, 2003) pp. 190–209. Following the example of Sti Martiri, Serlian windows became a regular feature of the façades of churches associated with the House of Savoy, including that in the façade of the Church of Corpus Domine in Turin, attributed to both Carlo di Castellamonte and Antonio Vitozzi, begun in 1607 to fulfil a vow made during the plague by Carlo Emanuele. Tosini, *Storia dell'architettura italiana* pp. 483–4, fig.; Viglino Davico, *Ascanio Vitozzi* pp. 283–5. Other examples of Serlianas associated with the House of Savoy include the churches at Venaria Reale,

as illustrated in *Theatrum Sabaudiae*; Nostra Signora di Babilone, Caviglia, an oval chapel with Serliana portico, built probably 1609–15 apparently at the expense of Carlo Emanuele to the designs of Vitozzi; and the Santuario della Madonna Nera at Oropa, built with an arcade of Serlianas by the Duke of Savoy. *Ibid*. pp. 259–70, figs 235–7, 239.

79 Martha D. Pollak, *Turin 1564–1680* (Chicago and London, 1991) fig. 29. Other views of the façade at this date include an anonymous painting of 1608 and the fresco painting by Isidoro Bianchi in the main hall of the Valentino Castle in Turin. G. Romano, *Le collezioni di Carlo Emanuele I di Savoia* (Turin, 1995) p. 25; G. Romano, *Figure del barocco* (Turin, 1988) p. 49. I am grateful to Dottoressa Clelia Arnaldi and Dottoressa Enrica Pagella for assistance with information about the Castello and palazzo at Viboconne. I am also grateful to Dr Robert Oresko for discussions about Turin and the House of Savoy.

80 Nothing survives of the palazzo today, which was badly damaged during the Siege of Turin in 1706 and finally destroyed after the Second World War.

81 Hart and Hicks, *Sebastiano Serlio* II, pp. 54–7, 74–7, 84–7.

82 C. Roggero Bardelli, M. G. Vinardi and V. Defabiani, *Ville Sabaude* (Milan, 1990) pp. 122–39.

83 Pollak, *Turin 1564–1680* fig. 130.

84 Tosini, *Storia dell'architettura* II, p. 472, fig.

85 Pollak, *Turin 1564–1680* figs 69, 100.

86 John Belton Scott, *Architecture for the Shroud* (Chicago, 2003) p. 79, figs 54–5.

87 Heiner Borggrefe *et al.*, *Hans Vredeman de Vries und die Renaissance im Norden* (Munich, 2002) p. 143, fig. 10.

88 A photograph of the painting is held in the Witt Library of the Courtauld Institute of Art, London.

89 Hitchcock, *German Renaissance Architecture* p. 316, pl. 408.

90 Rainer Babel, 'The Courts of the Wittelsbachs c.1500–1750', in John Adamson (ed.), *The Princely Courts of Europe: Ritual, Politics and Culture under the* Ancien Regime *1500–1750* (London, 1999) p. 192.

91 Hitchcock, *German Renaissance Architecture* fig. 408.

92 The windows of the 'Koningshuis' are full length. In the painting there are square, attic windows over full-length windows.

93 A. W. Johnson, *Three Volumes annotated by Inigo Jones* (Abo Akademi University, Finland, 1997) p. xxix.

94 Rosenthal, *The Palace of Charles V* pl. 74.

95 Herrera, *Estampas de la fabrica de San Lorenzo*, Seventh Design; Margaret D. Whinney, 'John Webb's Drawings for Whitehall Palace', *Walpole Society* XXXI (1946) pl. XIIIc.

96 Armitage, *Ideological Origins of the British Empire* pp. 28–9.

97 Cuthbert Tunstall quoted in *ibid*. p. 34.

98 *Ibid*. pp. 35–6.

99 James Henrisoun, *An Exhortation to the Scottes to Conforme Themselves to the Honourable, Expedient, and Godly Union Betweene the Two Realmes of Englande and Scotland* (1547), cited in *ibid*. p. 39.

100 Charles I quoted in Pagden, *Lords of all the World* p. 15.

101 Gordon Higgott, 'The Fabric to 1670', in Derek Keene, Arthur Burns and Andrew Saint (eds), *St Paul's: The Cathedral Church of London 604–2004* (New Haven and London, 2004) pp. 173–5.

102 John Harris and Gordon Higgott, *Inigo Jones: Complete Architectural Drawings* (London, 1989) p. 71.

103 The sanctuary of the chapel was described by a Capuchin priest as 'a paradise of glory, about 40ft in height. There was a great arch, separated by two pillars, about five and a half feet from the two side walls of the chapel. The spaces between the two pillars and the wall served for passages between the sacristy and the altar.' Derek Wilson, *The King and the Gentleman* (London, 1999) p. 203; Simon Thurley, 'The Stuart Kings, Oliver Cromwell and the Chapel Royal 1618–1685', *Architectural History* XLV (2002) pp. 245–7.

104 Thurley, 'Stuart Kings' p. 240.

105 Palladio, *Quattro libri* IV, p. 38.

106 Hart and Hicks *Sebastiano Serlio* I, pp. 408–10.

107 It may be telling that a Serlian portal appears in the background of Perino del Vaga's *Raising of Lazarus* of 1538. Rosenthal, *Palace of Charles V* pl. 137. For a similar portal see John A. Gere, 'Two Late Fresco Cycles by Perino del Vaga', *Burlington Magazine* CII (1960) p. 8.

108 Whinney, 'John Webb's Drawings' pls IX, XIIIa.

109 *Ibid*. pl. XIIa.

110 *Ibid*. pl. XIIIc.

111 John Heward and Robert Taylor, *The Country Houses of Northamptonshire* (Swindon, 1996) pp. 132–4, fig. 165. John Newman, 'Laudian Literature and the Interpretation of Caroline Churches in London', in David Howarth (ed.), *Art and Patronage in the Caroline Courts* (Cambridge, 1993) pp. 172, 175, 181. A design for the side elevation of the proposed chapel at Wilton is illustrated in John Harris and A. A. Tait, *Catalogue of the Drawings by Inigo Jones, John Webb and Isaac de Caus at Worcester College, Oxford* (Oxford, 1979) fig. 92. The chapel was not built to this design but the plan in *Vitruvius Britannicus* (London, 1717) II, pl. 62, shows a wide west (liturgically east) window to the chapel that suggests it was a Serliana.

112 A Serliana form, though not actually a Serliana, was used by Jones to light the staircase of Sir Peter Killigrew's house. Harris and Higgott, *Inigo Jones* p. 312, cat. 118, fig. 110.

113 In the 'Grand Design' for Wilton House there would have been two Serlianas, one in the centre of each wing. In the reduced version that was built a single Serliana appears in the centre of the façade.

CHAPTER 10

1 Margaret Whinney's important article distinguishing between the different schemes for Whitehall Palace in the *Walpole Society* in 1946 remains the most considered examination of what Jones proposed. Other studies include those by John Summerson and John Bold. Simon Thurley's study of Whitehall Palace does not deal with Jones's proposed palace. Margaret D. Whinney, 'John Webb's Drawings for Whitehall Palace', *Walpole Society*

XXXI (1946) pp. 45–107; John Bold, *John Webb: Architectural Theory and Practice in the Seventeenth Century* (Oxford, 1989) pp. 107–25; John Summerson, *Inigo Jones* (New Haven and London, 2000) pp. 122–31; Simon Thurley, *Whitehall Palace: An Architectural History of the Royal Apartments, 1240–1690* (New Haven and London, 1999).

2 Richard Daye quoted in E. S. de Beer, 'Whitehall Palace: Inigo Jones and Wren', *Notes and Queries* (30 December 1939) pp. 471–3; William Sanderson quoted in Whinney, 'John Webb's Drawings' pp. 45–6; Bold, *John Webb* pp. 110; Michael Leapman, *Inigo: The Troubled Life of Inigo Jones, Architect of the English Renaissance* (London, 2003) pp. 324–5. Further confirmation of the date comes in a signed statement by William Emmett, whose family had a long association with the Office of Works, that Jones made designs for Whitehall in 1639. Whinney, 'John Webb's Drawings' p. 48.

3 The best account of these years is Kevin Sharpe, *The Personal Rule of Charles I* (New Haven and London, 1992).

4 N. A. M. Rodger, *The Safeguard of the Sea: A Naval History of Britain, 660–1649* (London, 1997) pp. 370–71.

5 Giles Worsley, *Classical Architecture in Britain: The Heroic Age* (New Haven and London, 1995) pp. 5–6.

6 Rodger, *Safeguard of the Sea* p. 371.

7 Howard Colvin (ed.), *The History of the King's Works* (London, 1982) IV, p. 329. (£712 of the Banqueting House cost was for a new pier for shipping stone at Portland.) John Bold, *Greenwich: An Architectural History of the Royal Hospital for Seamen and the Queen's House* (New Haven and London, 2000) p. 61. R. C. Temple (ed.), *The Travels of Peter Mundy*, Hakluyt Society, 2nd ser. LV, (1925) pp. 48–9.

8 Temple, *Travels of Peter Mundy* pp. 48–9; Rodger, *Safeguard of the Sea* pp. 388–9.

9 John Harris and Gordon Higgott, *Inigo Jones: Complete Architectural Drawings* (London, 1989) pp. 248–50, cat. 81, figs 80–81; Simon Thurley, 'Nearly our Greatest Palace', *Country Life* 199 (3 March 2005) pp. 92–4.

10 Gordon Higgott, 'The Fabric to 1670', in Derek Keene, Arthur Burns and Andrew Saint (eds), *St Paul's: The Cathedral Church of London 604–2004* (New Haven and London, 2004) p. 175. William Kent's engraving after a drawing by Jones shows ten kings; only two appear in Hollar's engraving. Harris and Higgott, *Inigo Jones* figs 75, 78.

11 I am grateful to Dr Anna Keay for allowing me to read a draft of the relevant chapter by her and Roland B. Harris in a forthcoming book on the White Tower (Edward Impey (ed.), *The White Tower*). This account of the White Tower is indebted to the information in that chapter.

12 Anna Keay and Roland B. Harris in Edward Impey (ed.), *The White Tower* (New Haven and London, forthcoming).

13 Harris and Higgott, *Inigo Jones* pp. 251–3, cat. 82–3.

14 Thurley, *Whitehall Palace*.

15 Whinney, 'John Webb's Drawings'.

16 Summerson, *Inigo Jones* p. 124; John Harris and A. A. Tait,

Catalogue of the Drawings by Inigo Jones, John Webb and Isaac de Caus at Worcester College, Oxford (Oxford, 1979) pp. 21–4; Bold, *John Webb* pp. 110–18. Bold suggests that the 'E' scheme is the work of Webb alone and datable to the mid-1640s, perhaps intended as presentation drawings to underline Webb's claim to the post of Surveyor in more propitious times. The 'T' scheme is believed to be that which Webb claimed to have been commissioned to design by Charles I while a prisoner at Carisbrooke Castle in 1648. Bold suggests the 'C' scheme may postdate the Restoration.

17 Webb's proposed treatise is discussed in Bold, *John Webb* pp. 21–35. According to Bold, Webb's theoretical drawings were made between c.1635 and 1650, which would encompass the assumed date of the 'K' scheme.

18 Higgott, 'The Fabric to 1670' pp. 181–2.

19 Deborah Howard, *Jacopo Sansovino: Architecture and Patronage in Renaissance Venice* (New Haven and London, 1987) p. 138.

20 Howard Burns, *Andrea Palladio 1508–1580* (London, 1975) p. 105, fig. 197.

21 George Kubler, *Building the Escorial* (Princeton, 1982) p. 43.

22 For de Dominis, see F. L. Cross and E. A. Livingstone (eds), *The Oxford Dictionary of the Christian Church* (Oxford, 2nd ed. 1974).

23 William L. Macdonald and John A. Pinto, *Hadrian's Villa and its Legacy* (New Haven and London, 1995).

24 Horace Walpole quoted in Whinney, 'John Webb's Drawings' pp. 62–3.

25 John Harris, Stephen Orgel and Roy Strong, *The King's Arcadia: Inigo Jones and the Stuart Court* (London, 1973) p. 147; Bold, *John Webb* p. 112.

26 It is possible that the idea that the circular courtyard was associated with monarchy was understood as early as the fourteenth century given the beautiful circular courtyard in the highly sophisticated palace castle of Bellver built for King Jaume II of Mallorca on the outskirts of Palma da Mallorca in 1309.

27 Lynda Fairbairn, *Italian Renaissance Drawings from the Collection of Sir John Soane's Museum* (London 1998) pp. 53, 86–7.

28 Pierre de la Ruffinière du Prey, *The Villas of Pliny from Antiquity to Posterity* (Chicago, 1994) pp. 62–8, 102–3, fig. 38.

29 Macdonald and Pinto, *Hadrian's Villa* p. 272.

30 The royal associations of the circular courtyard remained powerful into the eighteenth century. Nicodemus Tessin's plan for the Louvre in 1704 incorporates a large circular courtyard in the old Cour Carré. Robert de Cotte's first project for Joseph Clemens, elector of Cologne, for a *maison de campagne* in 1715 was a circle in a square. Marten Snickare, *Tessin: Nicodemus Tessin the Younger, Royal Architect and Visionary* (Stockholm, 2002) p. 122, fig. R. Neumann, *Robert de Cotte* (1994) pp. 80–87, fig 54.

31 Vaughan Hart and Peter Hicks (eds), *Sebastiano Serlio: On Architecture* (New Haven and London, 2001) II, pp. 52–7, 132–52.

32 Rosalys Coope, *Salomon de Brosse and the Development of the Classical Style in French Architecture from 1565 to 1630* (London, 1972) pp. 22, 34, figs 11, 36. Du Cerceau also designed a 'Bâtiment à Plaisir' laid out round a circular court which forms the grandest design in his third book, published in 1582.

33 Jones's circular court also pays homage to Bramante's proposed circular courtyard for his tempietto of S. Pietro in Montorio as illustrated by Serlio in his third book. Jones does not follow Bramante in the design of the courtyard itself, which is arcaded not colonnaded, has no niches and of course has no tempietto in the centre. Instead, he takes Bramante's suggestion that the solid corners left by inserting a circle in a square be hollowed out to produce three-apsed enclosures.

34 Whinney, 'John Webb's Drawings' pls XIII.a, XIV.a, XV.b, XVII.a, XXVIII.c.

35 Vitruvius, *The Ten Books of Architecture*, trans. Morris Hicky Morgan (New York, 1960) Bk I, ch. I, 5.

36 David Thomson (ed.), *Les plus excellents bastiments de France* (Paris, 1988) p. 30.

37 James Packer, 'Trajan's Forum in 1919', *American Journal of Archaeology* XCVI (1992) pp. 158–9.

38 American School of Classical Studies at Athens, *Corinth* I, ii (1941) figs 40, 50, 51; IX (1931) pp. 101–27.

39 Leopold D. and Helen S. Ettlinger, *Raphael* (Oxford, 1987) pp. 99–100, 173–4, figs 96, 165.

40 Franco Borsi, *Bramante* (Milan and Paris, 1990) p. 37, fig.

41 Volker Hoffmann, 'Donec totum impleat orbem: symbolisme impérial au temps du Henri II', *Bulletin de la société de l'art français*, année 1978 (1980) pp. 29–42; Volker Hoffmann, 'Le Louvre de Henri II: un palais impérial', *Bulletin de la société de l'histoire de l'art français*, année 1980 (1982) pp. 7–15; Thomson, *Les plus excellents bastiments* pp. 28, 43.

42 Coope, *Salomon de Brosse* p. 108, pl. 134.

43 Hilliard T. Goldfarb (ed.), *Richelieu: Art and Power* (Ghent, 2002) pp. 125–6, pls 36–7.

44 Jacobine Huisken *et al.*, *Jacob van Campen: het klassieke ideal in de gouden eeuw* (Amsterdam, 1995) p. 215, fig. 214; Sjoerd Faber, Jacobine Huisken and Friso Lammertse, *Of Lords, who seat nor cushion do ashame: The Government of Amsterdam in the 17th and 18th Centuries* (The Hague, 1987) pp. 16–17.

45 Frommel suggests that Serlio may have been influenced by a plan for a royal palace by Antonio da Sangallo dating from the 1530s. This was square, with a sequence of smaller courts arranged round a larger central court. Frommel further suggests that Sangallo was influenced by Alberti's advice that the multifarious functions of a royal palace should not be combined under the same roof but should be isolated and connected by roofs and corridors. It is possible that Jones was also aware of the implications of Alberti's advice and the way that it could be reconciled in a palace made up of courtyards. Sabine Frommel, *Sebastiano Serlio: Architect* (Milan, 2003) pp. 280–83, figs 285–6.

46 *Ibid.* pp. 267–71.

47 Hart and Hicks, *Sebastiano Serlio* II, pp. xvi, 142–3.

48 *Ibid.* pp. 142–3.

49 Thomson, *Les plus excellents bastiments* pp. 222–3.

50 Andrea Palladio, *The Four Books of Architecture*, trans. Robert Tavernor and Richard Schofield (Cambridge, Mass., 1997) Bk III, ch. XIX, p. 200.

51 *The Annals of King James and King Charles the First* (1681) fols 23ff., quoted in Per Palme, *Triumph of Peace: A Study of the Whitehall Banqueting House* (Stockholm, 1956) p. 190.

52 Palladio, *Four Books* Bk III, ch. XX, p. 203.

53 *Ibid.* Bk IV, ch. XIX, p. 283; Palme, *Triumph of Peace* pp. 187–8; Harris and Higgott, *Inigo Jones* pp. 98–100, cat. 29, figs 30–32.

54 Harris and Higgott, *Inigo Jones* pp. 98–9; Palme, *Triumph of Peace* pp. 183–91.

55 Summerson, *Inigo Jones* p. 42; Harris and Higgott, *Inigo Jones* pp. 110–11, 114–15.

56 The design P12 for a basilican hall is ambiguous. Though the form follows the Council Chamber in P1 it is not annotated as such. The idea that it might have been considered as a chapel is supported by a separate drawing inscribed 'Section of ye Chappell. 55 fo wide' that has been pasted on, by a later emendation to the principal elevation that inserts what appears to be a royal pew, set in a Serliana, and by a sketched layout of rooms that refers to the 'Sergeant of ye Chappell'.

57 Andrea Palladio, *I quattro libri dell'architettura* (Venice, 1570) II, p. 34; III, pp. 33–7.

58 Bishop Williams quoted in Palme, *Triumph of Peace* pp. 186, 235.

59 John Newman, 'An Early Drawing by Inigo Jones and a Monument in Shropshire', *Burlington Magazine* CXV (1973) pp. 360–67.

60 René Taylor, 'Architecture and Magic', in Douglas Fraser *et al.*, *Essays in the History of Architecture presented to Rudolf Wittkower* (London, 1967) pp. 81–109.

61 Palme, *Triumph of Peace* p. 277.

62 Graham Parry, *The Golden Age Restor'd* (Manchester, 1981) pp. 31–2.

CHAPTER 11

1 Timothy Mowl and Brian Earnshaw, *Architecture without Kings: The Rise of Puritan Classicism under Cromwell* (Manchester, 1995) pp. 31, 55, 72, 121; Michael Leapman, *Inigo: The Troubled Life of Inigo Jones, Architect of the English Renaissance* (London, 2003) pp. 341–2.

2 George Vertue quoted in Howard Colvin, *A Biographical Dictionary of British Architects 1600–1840* (New Haven and London, 1995) p. 557; Leapman, *Inigo* p. 342.

3 Leapman, *Inigo* p. 337.

4 Dr Gordon Higgott has confirmed in a personal communication that the annotations by Inigo Jones and John Webb on the drawings for the interiors at Wilton date from the 1640s. John Bold, *John Webb: Architectural Theory and Practice in the Seventeenth Century* (Oxford, 1989) p. 60, figs 35–7.

5   John Webb, *A Vindication of Stone-Heng Restored* (London, 1665) p. 123.

6   John Harris, Stephen Orgel, Roy Strong, *The King's Arcadia: Inigo Jones and the Stuart Court* (London, 1973) p. 209, cat. 405.

7   Robert Tavernor, *Palladio and Palladianism* (London, 1991) p. 145.

8   Colvin, *Biographical Dictionary* p. 1027.

9   Margaret D. Whinney, 'John Webb's Drawings for White-hall Palace', *Walpole Society* XXXI (1946) pp. 45–107; Bold, *John Webb* pp. 52–4, 161, pls 27, 105.

10 Esther Eisenthal, 'John Webb's Reconstruction of the Ancient House', *Architectural History* XXVIII (1985) pp. 7–31. However, Bold notes that Eisenthal's suggestion that hatching appears early in Webb's career and the use of wash later is problematic. Of the two early Somerset House drawings one is hatched and the other washed and Webb used both techniques towards the end of his career at Greenwich. Bold, *John Webb* p. 29. See also John Harris and A. A. Tait, *Catalogue of Drawings by Inigo Jones, John Webb and Isaac de Caus at Worcester College, Oxford* (Oxford, 1979) pp. 59–60.

11 Harris and Tait, *Catalogue of Drawings* pp. 60, 62; Bold, *John Webb* p. 29.

12 Harris, Orgel and Strong, *King's Arcadia* pp. 217–18.

13 Harris and Tait, *Catalogue of Drawings* pp. 59–93; Bold, *John Webb* pp. 23–35.

14 Giles Worsley, *Classical Architecture in Britain: The Heroic Age* (New Haven and London, 1995) pp. 47–50, figs 60–61.

15 John Harris and Gordon Higgott, *Inigo Jones: Complete Architectural Drawings* (London, 1989) pp. 98–100, cat. 29, 31–2.

16 Harris and Tait, *Catalogue of Drawings* p. 39, fig. 75.

17 Vincenzo Scamozzi, *L'idea dell'architettura universale* (Venice, 1615) p. 135; Harris and Higgott, *Inigo Jones* pp. 68–9, cat. 14.

18 Palladio, *I quattro libri dell'architettura* (Venice, 1570) II, pp. 17, 23.

19 Bold, *John Webb* pp. 94–101, fig. 63.

20 *Ibid.* p. 70, fig. 46.

21 Harris and Tait, *Catalogue of Drawings* p. 36, fig. 68.

22 Scamozzi, *L'idea dell'architettura* p. 158.

23 Whinney, 'John Webb's Drawings' pls XIV, XV, XXIII; Bold, *John Webb* p. 115.

24 See, for example, Palladio, *Quattro libri* II, pp. 5, 9, 14; IV, 17, 32–3.

25 Scamozzi, *L'idea dell'architettura* p. 118–19, 253.

26 Robert W. Berger, *Antoine le Pautre: A French Architect of the Era of Louis XIV* (New York, 1969) pls 18–20, 22, 30–32, 39.

27 Howard Colvin (ed.), *History of the King's Works* (London, 1976) V, pp. 140, 266; Bold, *John Webb* p. 122, fig. 83.

28 Bold, *John Webb* pp. 106–7, 121–7.

29 Palladio, *Quattro libri* II, pp. 17, 23.

30 Hilary Ballon, *Louis le Vau: Mazarin's College, Colbert's Revenge* (Princeton, 1999) pp. 23–31, figs 8, 11, 16.

31 Worsley, *Classical Architecture* pp. 86–7.

32 Vanessa Bezemer Sellers, *Courtly Gardens in Holland 1600–1650: The House of Orange and the Hortus Batavus* (Amsterdam and Woodbridge, 2001) p. 48, fig. 31; J. J. Terwen and K. A. Ottenheym, *Pieter Post (1608–1669): Architect* (Zutphen, 1993) pp. 93, 145, figs 102, 174.

33 Philips Vingboons, *Afbeelsels der voornaemste gebouwen* 2 vols (Amsterdam 1648 and 1674) repr. in Konrad [Koen] Ottenheym, *Philips Vingboons (1607–1678): Architect* (Zutphen, 1989) pp. 185–270.

34 Vingboons, *Afbeelsels* I, pls 54–5.

35 Konrad [Koen] Ottenheym, 'Peter Paul Rubens's *Palazzi di Genova* and its Influence on Architecture in the Netherlands', in Piet Lombaerde (ed.), *The Reception of P. P. Rubens's* Palazzi di Genova *during the 17th Century in Europe: Questions and Problems* (Turnhout, 2002) pp. 96–7.

36 Vingboons, *Afbeelsels* II, pls 57–9.

37 Guus Kemme (ed.), *Amsterdam Architecture: A Guide* (Bussum, 1996) p. 68; Jorgen Bracker *et al.*, *Soo vele heerlijcke gebouwen: van Palladio tot Vingboons* (Amsterdam, 1997) pp. 37–8, figs 29–30; Konrad Ottenheym, 'The Painters cum Architects of Dutch Classicism', in *Dutch Classicism in Seventeenth-Century Painting* (Rotterdam, 1999) pp. 34–53.

38 St Dionis, Backchurch (1670–84), St Mary-at-Hill (1670–95), St Olave, Old Jewry (1670–76), St Bride's, Fleet Street (1671–1703), St James, Piccadilly (1676–92), and St Andrew, Holborn (1684–92).

39 Thomas Archer included a Serlian east window at St Paul, Deptford (1712), as did Nicholas Hawksmoor at Christ Church, Spitalfields (1714), Colen Campbell in his design for a church in the Vitruvian style (1717), James Gibbs at St Martin's-in-the-Fields (1720), John James at St George's, Hanover Square (1721), and Hawksmoor and James at St Luke, Old Street (1727). Colen Campbell, *Vitruvius Britannicus* (London, 1717) II, p. 26; Kerry Downes, *English Baroque Architecture* (London, 1966) figs 399, 430, 433–4, 462.

40 For example,, James Gibbs's Marylebone Chapel, London (1721–2), All Saints, Derby (1723–6), St Mary's Patshull, Staffs (1742); Henry Flitcroft's St Giles-in-the-Fields, London (1731). Other provincial examples include William Etty's Holy Trinity, Leeds (1722–7), Francis Smith's All Saints, Gainsborough, Lincs (1734–44), Edward and Thomas Woodward's St Swithin, Worcester (1736), and John Carr's Kirkleatham church, Yorkshire (1759). Through Gibbs it spread to the British colonies, examples being Thomas McBean, St Paul's Chapel, New York City (1763–4), and Peter Harrison, King's Chapel, Boston (1749–54).

41 Giles Worsley, *The British Stable* (New Haven and London, 2004) pp. 106–10.

Select Bibliography

Malcolm Airs, 'Inigo Jones, Isaac de Caus and the Stables at Holland House', *Georgian Group Journal* XIII (2003) pp. 141–60.

B. Alsopp (ed.), *Inigo Jones on Palladio, being the notes by Inigo Jones in the copy of I Quattro Libri dell'architettura di Andrea Palladio, 1601, in the Library of Worcester College, Oxford*, 2 vols (Newcastle upon Tyne, 1970).

Christy Anderson, 'Masculine and Unaffected: Inigo Jones and the Classical Ideal', *Art Journal* LVI, no. 2 (Summer 1997) pp. 48–54.

Barbara Arciszewska and Elizabeth McKellar, *Articulating British Classicism: New Approaches to Eighteenth-Century Architecture* (Aldershot, 2004).

Jean-Pierre Babelon and Claude Mignot (eds), *François Mansart: le génie de l'architecture* (Paris, 1998).

Wolfram Baer *et al.*, *Elias Holl und das Ausburger Rathaus* (Regensburg, 1985).

Franco Barbieri and Guido Beltramini (eds), *Vincenzo Scamozzi 1548–1616* (Vicenza, 2003).

E. S. de Beer, 'Whitehall Palace: Inigo Jones and Wren', *Notes and Queries* (30 December 1939) pp. 471–3.

Guido Beltramini *et al.*, *Palladio and Northern Europe: Books, Travellers, Architects* (Milan, 1999).

Vanessa Bezemer Sellers, *Courtly Gardens in Holland 1600–1650: The House of Orange and the Hortus Batavus* (Amsterdam and Woodbridge, 2001).

John Bold, *Wilton House and English Palladianism: Some Wiltshire Houses* (London, 1988).

—, *John Webb: Architectural Theory and Practice in the Seventeenth Century* (Oxford, 1989).

—, *Greenwich: An Architectural History of the Royal Hospital for Seamen and the Queen's House* (New Haven and London, 2000).

Cyril Bordier, *Louis le Vau: architecte* (Paris, 1998).

Jorgen Bracker *et al.*, *Palladio: Bauen nach der Natur—Die Erben Palladios in Nordeuropa* (Hamburg, 1997).

—, *Soo vele heerlijcke gebouwen: van Palladio tot Vingboons* (Amsterdam, 1997).

Arnaldo Bruschi, *Storia dell'architettura italiana: il primo cinquecento* (Milan, 2002).

Howard Burns, *Andrea Palladio 1508–1580* (London, 1975).

—, 'Palladio and the Foundations of a New Architecture in the North', in Guido Beltramini *et al.*, *Palladio and North-*

ern Europe: Books, Travellers, Architects (Milan, 1999) pp. 17–55.

—, 'Note sull'influesso di Scamozzi in Inghilterra: Inigo Jones, John Webb, Lord Burlington', in Franco Barbieri and Guido Beltramini (eds), *Vincenzo Scamozzi 1548–1616* (Vicenza, 2003) pp. 129–32.

Colen Campbell, *Vitruvius Britannicus* 3 vols (London, 1715, 1717, 1725).

Edward Chaney, 'Inigo Jones in Naples', in John Bold and Edward Chaney (eds), *English Architecture Public and Private* (London, 1993) pp. 31–53.

Howard Colvin, 'Inigo Jones and the Church of St Michael-le-Querne', *London Journal* XII, no. 1 (1986) pp. 36–9.

—, *A Biographical Dictionary of British Architects 1600–1840* (New Haven and London, 1995).

—, 'The South Front of Wilton House' in *Essays in Architectural History* (New Haven and London, 1999) pp. 136–57.

Claudia Conforti and Richard J. Tuttle, *Storia dell'architettura italiana: il secondo cinquecento* (Milan, 2001).

Rosalys Coope, *Salomon de Brosse and the Development of the Classical Style in French Architecture from 1565 to 1630* (London, 1972).

Dianne Duggan, '"London the Ring, Covent Garden the Jewell of that Ring": New Light on Covent Garden', *Architectural History* XLIII (2000) pp. 140–61.

—, '"A rather fascinating hybrid": Tart Hall, Lady Arundel's Casino at Whitehall', *British Art Journal* IV, no. 3 (Autumn 2003) pp. 54–64.

Caroline van Eck, *British Architectural Theory 1540–1750* (Aldershot, 1988).

Erik Forssman *et al.*, *Palladio: la sua eredità nel mondo* (Milan, 1980).

Claire Gapper, 'The Impact of Inigo Jones on London Decorative Plasterwork', *Architectural History* XLIV (2001) pp. 82–7.

Lucy Gent (ed.), *Albion's Classicism: The Visual Arts in Britain 1550–1660* (New Haven and London, 1995).

Hilliard T. Goldfarb (ed.), *Richelieu: Art and Power* (Ghent, 2002).

Andor Gomme, 'Chevening: The Big Issues', *Georgian Group Journal* XIV (2004) pp. 167–86.

J. A. Gotch, *Inigo Jones* (London, 1926).

—, 'Inigo Jones's Principal Visit to Italy in 1614: The Itinerary of his Journeys', *Journal of the Royal Institute of British Architects* XLVI, 3rd ser. (21 November 1938), pp. 85–6.

William Grant Keith, 'Inigo Jones as a Collector', *Journal of the Royal Institute of British Architects* XXXIII (9 March 1925) pp. 95–108.

—, 'Drawings by Vincenzo Scamozzi', *Journal of the Royal Institute of British Architects* XLII (9 March 1935) pp. 525–35.

John Harris, 'Inigo Jones and his French Sources', *Metropolitan Museum Bulletin* (May 1961), pp. 253–64.

—, *Catalogue of the R.I.B.A. Drawings Collection: Inigo Jones and John Webb* (London, 1972).

—, *The Palladians* (London, 1981).

—and Gordon Higgott, *Inigo Jones: Complete Architectural Drawings* (London, 1989).

—and A. A. Tait, *Catalogue of the Drawings by Inigo Jones, John Webb and Isaac de Caus at Worcester College, Oxford* (Oxford, 1979).

—, Stephen Orgel and Roy Strong, *The King's Arcadia: Inigo Jones and the Stuart Court* (London, 1973).

Vaughan Hart and Peter Hicks (eds), *Sebastiano Serlio: On Architecture* 2 vols (New Haven and London, 1996, 2001).

Mary F. S. Hervey, *The Life, Correspondence and Collections of Thomas Howard, Earl of Arundel* (Cambridge, 1921).

Gordon Higgott, 'Inigo Jones in Provence', *Architectural History* XXVI (1983) pp. 24–34.

—, 'Varying with Reason: Inigo Jones's Theory of Design', *Architectural History* XXXV (1992) pp. 51–77.

—, 'The Fabric to 1670', in Derek Keene, Arthur Burns and Andrew Saint (eds), *St Paul's: The Cathedral Church of London 604–2004* (New Haven and London, 2004).

Oliver Hill and John Cornforth, *English Country Houses: Caroline* (London, 1966).

Henry-Russell Hitchcock, *German Renaissance Architecture* (Princeton, 1981).

Andrew Hopkins, *Italian Architecture from Michelangelo to Borromini* (London, 2002).

David Howarth, *Lord Arundel and his Circle* (New Haven and London, 1985).

Jacobine Huisken *et al.*, *Jacob van Campen: het klassieke ideal in de gouden eeuw* (Amsterdam, 1995).

A. W. Johnson, *Three Volumes annotated by Inigo Jones* (Abo Akademi University, Finland, 1997).

Michael Leapman, *Inigo: The Troubled Life of Inigo Jones, Architect of the English Renaissance* (London, 2003).

James Lees-Milne, *The Age of Inigo Jones* (London, 1953).

Jules Lubbock, *The Tyranny of Taste: The Politics of Architecture and Design in Britain 1550–1960* (New Haven and London, 1995).

Elizabeth McKellar, *The Birth of Modern London: The Development and Design of the City 1660–1720* (Manchester, 1999).

Timothy Mowl and Brian Earnshaw, *Architecture without Kings: The Rise of Puritan Classicism under Cromwell* (Manchester, 1995).

John Newman, 'Nicholas Stone's Goldsmiths' Hall: Design and Practice in the 1630s', *Architectural History* XIV (1971) pp. 30–39.

—, 'An Early Drawing by Inigo Jones and a Monument in Shropshire', *Burlington Magazine* CXV (1973) p. 360–67.

—, 'Laudian Literature and the Interpretation of Caroline Churches in London', in David Howarth (ed.), *Art and Patronage in the Caroline Courts* (Cambridge, 1993) pp. 168–88.

—, 'Inigo Jones's Architectural Education before 1614', *Architectural History* XXXV (1992) pp. 18–50.

—*et al.*, *Inigo Jones and the Spread of Classicism: Papers given at the Georgian Group Symposium 1986* (London, 1986).

Stephen Orgel and Roy Strong, *Inigo Jones: The Theatre of the Stuart Court* (London, 1973).

John Orrell, *The Theatres of Inigo Jones and John Webb* (Cambridge, 1985).

Konrad [Koen] Ottenheym, *Philips Vingboons (1607–1678): Architect* (Zutphen, 1989).

—, 'The Painters cum Architects of Dutch Classicism' in *Dutch Classicism in Seventeenth-Century Painting* (Rotterdam, 1999) pp. 34–53.

—, 'Peter Paul Rubens's *Palazzi di Genova* and its Influence on the Architecture in the Netherlands', in Piet Lombaerde (ed.), *The Reception of P. P. Rubens's* Palazzi di Genova *during the 17th Century in Europe: Questions and Problems* (Turnhout, 2002) pp. 81–98.

—*et al.* (eds), *Vincenzo Scamozzi, Venetian Architect: The Idea of a Universal Architecture, Villas and Country Estates* (Amsterdam, 2003).

Andrea Palladio, *I quattro libri dell'architettura* (Venice, 1570).

—, *The Four Books of Architecture*, trans. Robert Tavernor and Richard Schofield (Cambridge, Mass., 1997).

John Peacock, *The Stage Designs of Inigo Jones: The European Context* (Cambridge, 1995).

—and Christy Anderson, 'Inigo Jones, John Webb and Temple Bar', *Architectural History* XLIV (2001) pp. 29–38.

Lionello Puppi, *Andrea Palladio: The Complete Works* (London, 1975).

Bernd Roeck, *Elias Holl: Architekt einer europäischen Stadt* (Regensburg, 1985).

Herbert W. Rott, *Palazzi di Genova: Architectural Drawings and Engravings*, Corpus Rubenianum Ludwig Burchard XXII (London and Turnhout, 2002).

Peter Paul Rubens, *Palazzi di Genova* 2 vols (Antwerp, 1622, 1626).

Vincenzo Scamozzi, *L'idea della architettura universale* (Venice, 1615).

Sebastiano Serlio, *see* Vaughan Hart and Peter Hicks.

Kevin Sharpe, *The Personal Rule of Charles I* (New Haven and London, 1992).

Georg Skalecki, *Deutsche Architektur zur Zeit des Dreissigjahren Krieges* (Regensburg, 1989).

I. R. Stevens, 'Byfleet House: "A Noble House of Brick"', *Surrey Archaeological Collections* L (1946–7) pp. 101–2.

John Summerson, 'The Surveyorship of Inigo Jones', in Howard Colvin (ed.), *The History of the King's Works* (London, 1975) III, pp. 129–60.

—, *Architecture in Britain 1530–1830* (Harmondsworth, 1977).

—, 'Inigo Jones: Covent Garden and the Restoration of St Paul's Cathedral', in John Summerson, *The Unromantic Castle and Other Essays* (London, 1990) pp. 43–62.

—, *Inigo Jones* (Harmondsworth, 1966; New Haven and London, 2000).

Robert Tavernor, *Palladio and Palladianism* (London, 1991).

J. J. Terwen and K. A. Ottenheym, *Pieter Post (1608–1669): Architect* (Zutphen, 1993).

Simon Thurley, 'The Stuart Kings, Oliver Cromwell and the Chapel Royal 1618–1685', *Architectural History* XLV (2002) pp. 238–74.

Aurora Scotti Tosini (ed.), *Storia dell'architettura italiana: il seicento* 2 vols (Milan, 2003).

Jane Turner (ed.), *The Dictionary of Art* (London, 1996).

Richard Verdi, *Nicholas Poussin 1594–1664* (London, 1995).

Philips Vingboons, *Afbeelsels der voornaemste gebouwen* 2 vols (Amsterdam, 1648 and 1674).

Vitruvius, *I dieci libri dell'architettura di M. Vitruvio tradotti e commendati da Daniele Barbaro* (Venice, 1567; facsimile Rome, 1993).

—, *The Ten Books of Architecture*, trans. Morris Hicky Morgan (New York, 1960).

John Webb, *The most notable antiquity of Great Britain vulgarly called Stone-Heng on Salisbury Plain restored by Inigo Jones* (London, 1655).

—, *A Vindication of Stone-Heng Restored* (London, 1665).

Margaret D. Whinney, 'John Webb's Drawings for Whitehall Palace', *Walpole Society* XXXI (1946) pp. 45–107.

Rudolf Wittkower, *Palladio and English Palladianism* (London, 1974).

Jeremy Wood, 'Inigo Jones, Italian Art, and the Practice of Drawing', *Art Bulletin* LXXIV (June 1992).

Giles Worsley, *Classical Architecture in Britain: The Heroic Age* (New Haven and London, 1995).

—, 'Inigo Jones and the Origins of the London Mews', *Architectural History* XLIV (2001) pp. 88–95.

—, 'Inigo Jones and the Hatfield Riding House', *Architectural History* XLV (2002) pp. 230–37.

—, 'Courtly Stables and their Implications for Seventeenth-Century English Architecture', *Georgian Group Journal* XIII (2003) pp. 114–40.

Henry Wotton, *The Elements of Architecture* (London, 1624).

David Yeomans, 'Inigo Jones's Roof Structures', *Architectural History* XXIX (1986) pp. 85–101.

Photograph Credits

AKG Images, Berlin: 31
Alinari, Florence: 29, 177
Institut Amatler d'Art Hispanic, Barcelona: 168
Achim Bednorz: 32, 50
Berkshire Record Office: 88
Bibliothèque Nationale, Paris: 66
Biblioteca Reale, Turin: 180
Bildarchiv Foto Marburg: 30, 35
Bodleian Library, Oxford: 122, 203
British Library: 71, 97, 128, 163, 165, 181, 200, 213
British Museum: 80, 98, 156, 183, 187
Devonshire Collection, Chatsworth, reproduced by the kind permission of the Trustees of the Chatsworth Settlement: 3, 17, 78, 81, 120, 132, 133, 135, 147, 158, 190, 191, 192, 193, 194, 199, 201
Collage, City of London: 87, 216
Corbis: 23 (Mimmo Jodice), 24 (Vanni archive), 130 (Araldo de Luca), 179 (Massimo Listri)

Country Life Picture Library: 27, 28, 89, 94, 129, 217, 218
Courtauld Institute, Conway Library, London: 39, 44, 46, 108
Jan Derwig: 54, 59, 60, 61, 68, 70, 72
Photoservice Electa, Milan: 21
English Heritage NMR/James O. Davies: 6
Hachette Photos, Paris: 45, 48
A. F. Kersting: 8, 75, 90, 96, 107, 127, 157, 182
Koninklijk Huisarchief, The Hague: 56
Municipal Archives, The Hague: 67
Musées Royaux des Beaux-Arts de Belgique, Brussels: 73
National Maritime Museum, London: 2, 136, 137
Courtesy of Konrad Ottenheym: 53, 58, 60, 64, 69, 215
RIBA, London: 4, 5, 9, 14, 16, 40, 41, 49, 51, 74, 105, 110, 112, 113, 116, 118, 124, 125, 142, 150, 152, 185, 188

Rijksdienst voor de Monumentenzorg, Zeist (RDMZ): 64, 170
The John and Mabel Ringling Museum of Art, the State Museum of Florida: 62
© William C. Rolf 2000: 99
Royal Collection © 2006, Her Majesty Queen Elizabeth II: 76, 101
Scala, Florence: 42, 139, 155, 160, 162, 164, 167, 169, 174, 175, 176, 197
Vaclav Sedy: 18, 19, 131, 138
SLUB Dresden / Deutsche Fotothek: 37
Sir John Soane's Museum, London: 196
Collection of the Vatican Palace: 161
Collection of Woburn Abbey, The Duke and Trustees of the Bedford Estates: 123
Worcester College Library, Oxford: 1, 7, 13, 15, 20, 26, 38, 79, 82, 83, 85, 91, 92, 93, 102, 104, 114, 121, 148, 149, 189, 204, 205, 206, 208, 209, 210, 211
Emily Wraith: 144, 166
Zeeuws Museum, Middelburg: 52

Index